Commonsense
Handicapping

Commonsense Handicapping

The Logical, Left-Brained
Approach to Winning
at the Races

DICK MITCHELL

WILLIAM MORROW AND COMPANY, INC.
New York

Library of Congress Cataloging-in-Publication Data

Mitchell, Dick, 1939–
    Commonsense handicapping / by Dick Mitchell.
      p. cm.
    Includes bibliographical references
    ISBN 0-688-11362-1
    1. Horse race betting. I. Title.
SF331.M55   1993
798.401—dc20   92-38721

Printed in the United States of America

First Edition

1 2 3 4 5 6 7 8 9 10

BOOK DESIGN BY BERNARD SCHLEIFER

Dedications

To Sam Mitchell:
You're the greatest gift that I've ever received in this life. Words can't begin to express your magnificence. You're the cutest, most adorable, innocent, and beautiful human being on this planet. I can hardly believe the absolute profound joy that you bring into my life every day. I am so proud to be your father. You have given me so much, it's hard to even start to express my gratitude. Thank you, Sam—for being the wonderful son that you are.

To Cynthia Mitchell:
Thank you for Sam. Thank you for your courage to see things through to their final conclusion. Sam has a great mother. You have that knack to know exactly what Sam needs, and you give it to him. Sam is a happy child. You deserve all the credit.

To J. R. Mitchell:
Thank you for being our first child. You couldn't have been a better child. You were a star as an infant. We couldn't go anywhere without people coming up to us and wanting to hold and caress you. Though you have four legs and a tail and are an Australian shepherd, you're still "number one." You were a wonderful puppy, as you still are four-teen years later. You have given us so much joy and unconditional love, it's no wonder that we're crazy about you.

To Sue Ellen Mitchell:
Thank you for being our second child. You've given a new meaning to the word "mischievous." You're a holy terror. You can single-handedly wreak havoc and chaos on an unsuspecting world—and usually do! If it weren't for the fact that you're the most affectionate and enthusiastic puppy in the Western Hemisphere, who has nothing but kisses and love for everyone—you wouldn't get away with the stuff that you do. Your enthusiasm is contagious. It's no wonder that we enjoy you so much.

Acknowledgments

MANY THANKS TO Gordon Pine, director of research for Cynthia Publishing Company, for his great job of editing and proofreading the manuscript. His knowledge of the English language has saved readers from untold abuses of grammar and syntax. His knowledge of thoroughbred handicapping and his assiduous research have contributed many winning ideas to this volume.

My gratitude and thanks go to Kitts Anderson and Steve Unite. They are former students who give me the credit for making them winners. The reality is that they were both winners who happened to discover a computer program called FIVE-IN-ONE. They worked their butts off mastering this complicated piece of software. They deserve the credit for their achievements, not me. They are so good at using this software that they are now teaching others how to win using it and its successor ALL-IN-ONE. Kitts and Steve are responsible for the work done on the "Putting It All Together" workshop. Steve helped write the maiden, claiming, and non-claiming chapters. Steve is a good writer on the way to becoming a great writer. Kitts and Steve are fearless handicappers from the "swing for the fences" school of handicapping and betting strategy. Andy Beyer would be proud of them, as am I.

My gratitude and appreciation go to Ron Ambrose. He's one of the very best handicappers on this planet. His passion for teaching others how to win knows no limits. I can't count the number of times he has taken time out of his busy schedule to help fellow handicappers. An average workday for Ron is eighteen hours. I am proud of our association. We've been giving seminars together for the past three years. He's the author of many winning ideas contained in this text.

My sincerest thanks to all my students, past and present, for giving me the opportunity to do what gives me the greatest fulfillment: teaching.

My passion for teaching was learned from an absolute master teacher. His name was Brother Leo Quinn and he was a Franciscan brother who taught at St. Francis College in Brooklyn, New York. As you know, mathematics is not the easiest subject in the world to learn. Imagine the challenge it is to teach. Brother Leo made it look simple. To give you an idea of the power of his teaching, I didn't have to open a book for my first five courses in graduate school. I got straight A's. It's ironic, because I never managed to get a single A from Leo. He set high standards for me and higher standards for himself. My wish for the pedagogical health of this planet is that we could somehow clone Brother Leo so you and your progeny would have the good fortune to be one of his students. Bless you, Brother Leo—we miss you a lot.

My passion for life was learned from two master teachers: Helen and Olive Mitchell. They are my surrogate parents. Helen taught me how to achieve peace of mind. Olive taught me how to use humor when I ran out of patience and forbearance. They are the most loving and gentle people you'll ever meet. Bless them.

Contents

Introduction

HOWARD TOUSEY WAS ON the verge of death. He was a homeless indigent who haunted the slums on the south side of town. He hadn't changed his clothes in weeks. He hadn't bathed or shaved in months. He smelled like a sewer. He owned nothing but the tattered clothes on his gaunt frame. In order to just remain alive, he would collect aluminum cans, take them to the nearby recycling plant and exchange them for a few bucks.

Howard was alive, but not by much. He knew that his days were numbered. He bemoaned the fact that he never did very much with his life. He never educated himself. He never bettered himself. He was a victim of circumstance. Life had played a sadistic joke upon him. Everything was beyond his control. He wandered helplessly through this fast-moving and opulent world. Life was more than cruel to Howard. And now, his meaningless existence was coming to an end. He pondered these thoughts and they bothered him greatly. He was depressed and sad. All he knew how to do was pick up old cans. Not exactly the Yellow Brick Road.

Then an amazing thing happened. He met a fortune-teller. A psychic. They became friends. Howard came to trust his new friend over the course of the next few months. As his trust and friendship grew stronger, so did his interest in the occult. He was especially fascinated with reincarnation. He was enthralled by the fact that he could have been someone else in a former life. He came to believe strongly. He was obsessed. He had to find out about his previous lives. He scraped together the modest fee that his friend charged for a past life reading. Lo and behold, his new friend informed him that he had been none other than the great Abraham Lincoln in his last life. Howard was dumbstruck. How was this possible? How could such a great man devolve into such a derelict? The fortune-teller explained that we go through cycles, and that Lincoln toward the end of his life must have been quite depressed and thought of himself as an abject failure, hence this dominant thought would be manifested in his new incarnation.

Howard knew better. He knew that Lincoln was a giant. Howard was so excited he couldn't sleep a wink that night. At the crack of dawn he raced to the library, where he anxiously waited for the doors to open. It seemed like days before they would let him in. When they did, he voraciously attacked the card catalogue. He began. He meticulously noted every single reference to Lincoln. He read with the fervor and dedication of a zealot. His eyes were filled with wonder. He devoured the information with an intensity that he had never felt before. The more he read, the more excited he got. He was ready to burst. He read day after day with no sense of time whatsoever. The more he read, the better he felt about himself. He knew that he (Abraham Lincoln) was not destined to pick up aluminum cans, but he also knew that he was not above humble beginnings.

He secured employment as a laborer in a bottling plant. He worked hard and was task-oriented instead of time-oriented. He came in early and went home late. He never complained and always stayed to finish whatever he had started. It wasn't long before he was promoted. He used his natural leadership ability and was an excellent supervisor. It didn't take long for him to come to the attention of upper management. He made excellent business decisions that turned into profits for the company. It didn't take too long for management to realize that he was a natural leader. He, Abraham Lincoln, knew this from the moment he set foot in the door. He soon was elected to the board of directors of the company. He expected as much. When the company experienced a severe recession and things looked hopeless, Howard mortgaged everything he owned and purchased the company. He turned things around and became a multimillionaire. More important, he had a wonderful family, friends, good health—more than he could ever possibly wish for in ten lifetimes.

Then one day he learned of the death of his old friend, the fortune-teller. It was quite a shock when it came out that the fortune-teller hadn't been a spiritualist after all. He had been an impostor and a fraud. Howard was very distraught. How could this be? This meant that he wasn't the great Abraham Lincoln after all. But it was too late. Howard's achievements spoke for themselves. He had grown too much. Seen too much. Done too much. He couldn't possibly turn back. Howard Tousey now believed in Howard Tousey.

A similar story is repeated over and over in both fiction and real life. The key is expectation. The Law of Expectation assures that you get what you expect. If you expect failure, guess what you'll get? If you expect success, you'll get it. Henry Ford said, "Whatever you believe, you're right. If you believe you can—you can. If you believe you can't—you can't." Truer words were never spoken.

At this point you are probably saying, "Hey, wait a minute. I bought a book on the subject of handicapping. What the hell's going on? Who cares about Howard Tousey? Who cares about Henry Ford? He's dead. What's this gotta do with me?"

Everything. You're Pittsburgh Phil reincarnated. You've got the horses figured. You know what wins and you know what loses. You only bet on winning propositions and avoid losing ones. You're a winner. The only reason you bought this book is just to see what, if anything, is new.

Suspend your disbelief for a few moments and imagine that you visited a world-renowned psychic and she told you that you were the reincarnation of Pittsburgh Phil. Your mission in this life is to teach as many people as possible how to beat the races. How would you begin?

Here's how I would answer this question. It all begins with faith. Faith is another word for belief. You must believe that it's possible to win at the track. Next you must believe that *you* can do it. If you can't see yourself as a winner, forget it. Return this book for a refund. Regardless of how hard you study, how often you go to the races, and how much you know about thoroughbred handicapping—you're doomed.

If you can't believe in yourself, there's no point in continuing. Your destiny will always be in the hands of someone else. Rather than learn to win yourself, you'll invest in someone else's efforts. For instance, a stockbroker. Why understand the market when a broker can make all your decisions for you and just send you a check each month? Sorry, Charlie, it ain't gonna work. The number of people who are getting rich by taking their broker's advice can be counted on one finger or less. The same is true for handicappers. How many millionaires do you know who earned their fortunes by betting on the selections of other handicappers? About the population of unicorns: zero.

The bottom line is this—if you're gonna win, you're gonna hafta do it yourself! That's what this book is about. Doing it yourself. WINNING.

In my last book, *Winning Thoroughbred Strategies*, I spent three chapters detailing and describing winning players. Unfortunately, I chose three giants: Tom Brohamer, Mark Cramer, and James Quinn. They've each written epic books which I cannot recommend highly enough. Please read everything each has written. They're all winners who know their subject inside out. I consider each as one of my mentors. Without them, this book wouldn't have been possible. But I now realize that I should have chosen more down-to-earth models. I should have told you about the bus driver who paid his house off in cash. He sent his wife and kids to Cancun for a month on his winnings from one race. Or about the unemployable president of a multinational corporation who earned $80,000 at the races in his first year and considered himself a failure. Or about the student who paid cash for a new car from the proceeds from one exacta. Or about the writer who earned $96,000 in one race. Or about the surgeon who earns over $500,000 a year doing his thing and is thrilled to earn $10,000 a year at the races. Better yet, about the assistant district attorney who has resisted a number of attractive offers to go into private practice at a huge salary because she supplements her comparatively meager income by her winnings at the track. In fact, most offers don't approach her present combined income.

There are a lot of winners at the track. Probably more than ten thousand each year. That's the good news. The bad news is that there are a million or more regular racegoers. It's estimated that between one and two percent of regular racegoers are consistent winners. On any given day about five percent of the crowd has a winning day. Hence 95 percent lose or break even. Why should we even try to buck those odds?

Let's look at some dismal facts and then try to formulate an answer to the above question. According to the U.S. Census Bureau, 87 percent of workers of retirement age retire on annual incomes of $10,000 or less. That's barely above poverty level. According to the Internal Revenue Service, 85 percent of the people reaching age sixty-five don't even have $200 in the bank. Think about that. Seventeen out of twenty senior citizens can't write a $200 check that's not made of rubber. According to a study by the United States Department of Health and Human Services, 96 percent of Americans haven't achieved financial independence at the end of their working lives. They end up depending upon charity, family, or government social security checks.

The number-one reason, cited by the Internal Revenue Service, for financial failure among Americans is *the failure to make a plan to get more income—and failure to take action.* (If you don't have a plan—how can you take action?)

In America about four percent of the population is financially secure and about one-half percent have a net worth of over a million dollars.

The track is a microcosm of what goes on in real life. People behave at the track pretty much the same as they do elsewhere. A majority of citizens try to take shortcuts. They work just hard enough so they won't get fired. (What they don't realize is that their bosses are paying them just enough so they won't quit.) They come home from work, eat, watch some TV, and get to bed. They're usually a little behind on their bills and have to carefully watch what they spend. This lifestyle breeds a "poverty consciousness." When you're worried about the lack of money, this gives your subconscious a very powerful set of instructions. You are ordering it to find lack—and it will. Worry is your enemy. It's powerful. Many times it becomes a self-fulfilling prophecy. When you spend time watching TV, you are watching other people earn fabulous sums of money. Why not use this time to figure out a way to increase your income?

Thoroughbred handicapping offers you a very enjoyable way to increase your income. Unfortunately, it's not easy. But nothing of value is. If you do what everybody else is doing, you'll get the same results. The IRS gave us the answer. They suggested that the problem was the failure to make a plan to get more income, and failure to take action on that plan. We're going to set realistic goals, make a plan to achieve these goals, and carry out the actions necessary to realize our goals.

We're not going to do what everybody else does. In fact, in many cases we'll do the very opposite. We're going to enlist some very powerful allies. We're going to call upon the "laws of success." They are just as binding as the laws of gravity. We are going to enlist the services of a number of handicapping giants. We'll use the very best ideas of the top authors in the field who are winning players. The best of the best are William Quirin, James Quinn, Tom Brohamer, Andrew Beyer, Steve Davidowitz, Barry Meadow, and Mark Cramer. We'll shamelessly steal and use their finest and most profitable ideas. Remember the words of a great British author, "Talent borrows, genius steals."

Come with me on a fascinating journey. Its destination is the win window.

Commonsense
Handicapping

Chapter 1

Winners and Losers

WINNING IS AN ATTITUDE. It's about not being denied. Winners do what losers refuse to do. A loser refuses to keep records. A loser refuses to do original research or in fact read the research of others, never mind validate it. A loser doesn't read books on the subject of handicapping. A loser doesn't attend seminars or classes. A loser doesn't seek out a winner for advice. A loser views a losing day at the races as money irretrievably lost. A winner views the money left at the track as an interest-bearing loan that he will be back to collect, both principal and interest.

Losing is also an attitude. It usually involves greed in a subtle form. A loser wants something for nothing. He wants to win without doing the requisite work. A loser tends to have his ego invested in his selections. If his horse wins, he's a certified genius, and if it loses, he's a low life ignoramus. Hence the need for finding an excuse when he loses. A winner takes a more balanced view. He takes responsibility. He understands that there's only one real reason for losing a bet—he bought the wrong ticket. (Most of the time, this losing ticket is a good bet with a bad outcome.) He realizes that losing is part of winning. Most winners are former losers and understand that each losing race offers a handicapping lesson, not a lesson in creative excuse-making. A loser wants to forget the agony of defeat. A winner insists upon learning from defeat regardless of the pain and anguish.

It should be evident that it's possible to win at the races. Easy, no. Possible, yes. If you want to win you're going to have to do what winners do. Winners are willing to pay the price. The full price, no discounts, all up front. It's like being in a mountain cabin in the winter. If you want heat, you must first put wood in the fireplace. The winner gathers the wood, lights the fire, and gets the heat he seeks. The loser stands in front of the fireplace and asks for heat. He says, "First give me heat, then I'll give you wood." Needless to say, he refuses to pay the full price up front, hence he's denied. This metaphor may seem silly and farfetched, but that's exactly what the losing horse-race bettor is doing by refusing to pay the full price of time and effort to understand the mysteries of handicapping and money management.

The one characteristic that all losers and failures share is the inability to delay gratification. They want things now. They refuse to invest now for some future payoff. It's what I call the Polaroid Syndrome. Nature is abundant in its examples of investing now for a future payoff. The acorn doesn't become an oak tree overnight. The longer the gestation period, the longer a species will live. The brain surgeon doesn't learn his craft by mail order. You don't master a pastime as difficult as thoroughbred handicapping by purchasing a $50 system from some sleazebag who claims 70 percent winners at huge mutuels.

Successful people have a "long time-perspective." Take a doctor for example. He doesn't see any real income for at least twelve years, starting at age seventeen. Meanwhile, his fast friends quit school and get jobs. They can afford fancy cars with which to attract the girls. They get the girls and menial, unskilled jobs. Even though they have cash and fancy cars, they condemn themselves to a life of mediocrity by not paying the price. The future doctor has been investing his time wisely. He now earns in one year what his buddies earn in ten years, and he's going to continue to do so for the next forty or more years. (In addition, he may have to beat off the girls with a stick, given his economic prognosis.)

Same is true for winning handicappers. They endure the agony of defeat and learn from it. They don't demand to be winners overnight. They commit themselves to winning. They do whatever it takes to find the win window. Imagine a baby saying, "I'll try this walking thing a few times and if it doesn't work, the hell with it." Well, that's exactly what the loser does. The winner, just like the baby, persists until the desired result is achieved.

Human nature being what it is, we can be assured that 95 percent of our fellow citizens will not accept the challenge of winning at the races. Since we are playing a parimutuel game, this is a wonderful state of affairs for those of us who are willing to pay the price. The mutuels will actually pay us for our time and effort. Unfortunately, the time and effort must come before the pay. This isn't a very great price if we like to handicap and do research. In fact, many of us would rather handicap than do most other things. Whoever said that we can't be paid handsomely for doing something we enjoy?

Here's a lesson I learned late in life. It took a mid-life crisis and a very understanding wife for me to come to the following realization. When work is work, you're in the wrong business. Life is too short to trade a few bucks for your precious time. If your job is drudgery, quit. You'll be doing yourself and everybody who loves you a big favor. Yes, it will be tough at first, but when was the last time you saw a skeleton in the street? You'll find the way. You'll be forever grateful that you did. I know. It's better to do something that you really love and forget the money than to do something that makes you a rich prostitute. Prostitution may or may not be the world's oldest profession, but it's certainly one of the world's largest. Untold hundreds of thousands of people trudge off to work each day cursing the fact that they couldn't find a creative excuse to get out of it. A very small minority can't wait for the day to start. They curse the fact that the day only has twenty-four hours. They'd love to pass legislation requiring days and weeks to be much longer, and perhaps to abolish weekends altogether. They love what they do and they do what they love. That's the secret.

Scrully Blotnick, a professional writer and researcher, did a longitudinal study of ambitious college graduates. He tracked hundreds of NYU graduates for a period of twenty years. The vast majority of the successful ones labored at what they loved. They had no idea of their net worth. It didn't matter. One day their accountant mentioned to them that they had achieved millionaire status. Even more interesting, do you know what he found out about the best way for a millionaire to earn his second million? In real estate? In the stock market? At the track? No, absolutely not. The best way was the same way he earned his first million. By investing in himself. The bulk of those who didn't achieve the goal of $1 million chose their occupation or profession not because of love or intense interest, but only for the money.

Winners strive for excellence while losers strive to get by without doing too much work. Winners have goals, and plans to get them to their goals. Losers have daydreams. They dream about winning the lottery or about a long-lost relative dying and leaving them a fortune. Losers believe that winners are "lucky." They believe that external forces are responsible for their destiny. They never realize that each of us creates our own circumstances. We create our own destiny. "As ye sow, so shall ye reap." Sow thoughts of lack—reap failure. Sow thoughts of abundance—reap achievement.

Most people view wealthy people as successful. What they fail to realize is that successful people attract money and their wealth is merely a by-product of their success. The exception, of course, is inherited wealth. People are not successful because of wealth—they are wealthy because of their success.

By our behavior we choose to be a winner or a loser. We each have a success mechanism and failure mechanism built into us. Unfortunately, if we choose not to activate our success mechanism, our failure mechanism goes off automatically. People don't choose to fail, it happens automatically. If we choose success, then we must pay the price, the full price in advance. Most often the price for success is time and study. The price to be a successful musician is study with a qualified teacher and practice, practice, practice, and more practice. The price to be a successful handicapper is study with a qualified teacher and practice, practice, practice, and more practice.

The practice referred to is practice with positive feedback from a coach or teacher. Many of us still believe in the myth that "practice makes perfect." It ain't so. Practice makes permanent. If a music student practices the same mistake over and over, no progress takes place. He needs a coach or teacher to guide him and make sure he's doing things correctly. The same is true for the handicapper. This is the reason winners seek out other winners. They must learn to correct their mistakes. The toughest thing is to isolate the things that are causing you to make the same mistakes. Many a handicapper thinks he has twenty years' experience when in fact he has one year's experience repeated twenty times.

Losers can't appreciate that the world's best athletes, musicians, and artists all have coaches. The coach can't do what the athlete, musician, or artist can do, but he can give the achiever the necessary feedback that he needs to perfect his skill. We all need teachers. The maxim, "When the pupil is ready, the teacher will appear," is quite true. It's the natural order of things. "Seek and ye shall find." When you're looking for answers to your burning questions, a force within you radiates outward and contacts those resources that you need to get the answers. Once you make a commitment to winning, all the means that you need will appear.

The loser is involved, the winner is committed. To understand the difference between involvement and commitment, consider a breakfast of eggs and bacon. The chicken is involved, the pig is committed. If you say, "I will win or die," you're committed. If you say, "I'll try," you're involved. You're also right. You'll try and try and try. But you probably won't succeed. You'll be too busy trying. Trying is lying.

Most people confuse the desire to win with the "will to win." The desire to win is involvement; the will to win is commitment. The desire to win says, "I want to win." The will to win says, "I will do whatever it takes to win." See the difference? This same phenomenon is especially conspicuous among terminally ill patients. The ones who survive the longest have the strongest will to live. In fact, many outlive their doctors.

A team of mountain climbers who were making an assault on Mount Everest were studied by a team of physicians, one of whom was a psychiatrist. He asked each member of the team, "Will you make it to the summit?" The typical response was, "I'll give it my best shot." Only one climber, after some reflection, looked the questioner straight in the eye and said, "Yes, I will. I will make it to the top." He did. In fact, he was the only member of the team to do so.

My question to you is, "Will you make it to the top?" If you're willing to put the principles and information detailed in this book into practice, your answer will be a resounding "Yes." Let's get started.

Chapter 2

Ten Commandments
of Handicapping

WHEN THE GREAT HANDICAPPER FIRST tried to reveal himself to mortals, he blew it. He was carrying two very heavy and bulky stone tablets on which was written the truth of thoroughbred handicapping. On his way down from the mountaintop he stumbled. The stone tablets became tumbling projectiles and cascaded to the base of the mountain, breaking into hundreds of pieces. Embarrassed, the Great Handicapper retreated to higher ground, vowing that he wouldn't come down until racetracks eliminated the ugly and gruesome tax known as "breakage." If not for the assiduous archeological efforts of Justin Case, we would still be in the dark about handicapping revelation. Case solved the excruciating and arduous three-dimensional jigsaw puzzle. The tablets were re-created.

1. Thou shalt know thy track.
2. Thou shalt understand Ability.
3. Thou shalt understand Form and Condition.
4. Thou shalt understand Angles and Hot Stats.
5. Thou shalt understand "Wager Value."
6. Thou shalt make a Betting Line.
7. Thou shalt not bet against a legitimate favorite.
8. Thou shalt recognize false and vulnerable favorites.
9. Thou shalt keep detailed records.
10. Thou shalt never stop learning about handicapping.

If you follow and abide by all ten, you can't do anything else but win; you have no choice. These laws are as inviolable as the laws of gravity. If you're not winning or not winning as much as you should, the chances are you're violating one or more of these commandments.

The first commandment is very simple: know what's going on at your track. You must figure out what winners are doing at your track and only bet on horses that have the winning profile. This will be discussed in the next chapter. You must also know the trainers and their manipulations. You should be able to identify the jockeys they win with and the jockeys they rarely succeed with. You must be aware of any track bias. In general, you should be fully cognizant of what wins and what loses at your racetrack.

The next four commandments are the core of the handicapping process. Together they comprise an orderly and structured approach to handicapping. The first thing to do is assess the ability of each contender. Those horses found lacking in ability are eliminated. Second, determine the current form and condition of each of your contenders. Horses not meeting form and condition standards are discarded. Third, look for extenuating circumstances or angles. These include "hot stats" and other reasons out of the mainstream of speed, class, and form that say a horse should still be considered. Fourth, look for value. There will be a separate chapter devoted to each of these four commandments.

One of the biggest frauds that has ever been perpetrated on the handicapper is that the name of this game is picking winners. That's simply not true. Nobody picks winners better than the public. The public, year in, year out, gets approximately 33 percent right, betting every race, and still loses money. If you bet every public favorite, you would receive ninety cents for every dollar that you wagered. There is no handicapper on earth, Tom Brohamer, James Quinn, Andrew Beyer, Ron Ambrose, Mark Cramer, Gordon Pine, or anybody that you name that's going to get 33 percent right betting every race. It's just not going to happen. If you know anybody who feels that they want to take this up as a challenge, please send them to me. I'll book their action as long as they bet the same amount on every race. I'll pay track odds. We'll settle up at the end of a year.

There are handicappers who achieve rates higher than 33 percent, but they don't bet every race. They're very selective. That's their edge. The name of this game is not picking winners. It's picking winners that offer value. You can pick winners at the rate of 25 percent and make a very nice rate of return. If your average odds are 4-to-1 and you're picking winners at the rate of 25 percent, you're making a 25 percent rate of return. Picking one winner in four and getting paid an average of 4-to-1 means that you're losing three out of four bets. When you win, you win four units, and when you lose, you lose one unit. Hence, in four bets you gain one unit profit. That's a 25-percent return on investment (ROI). There are investment fund managers who would give one of their organs to get this kind of return; in some cases, a vital organ. We'll spend a lot of time on the issue of value.

The sixth commandment is the key to winning at the track. The question most often asked at a racetrack is, "Who da ya like?" It's typically answered, "I like the five horse but I'm afraid of the nine." This answer is vague at best. A much better answer would be, "I'll take the five at 5-to-2 or the nine at 4-to-1." Most handicappers refuse to bet on any horse other than their top pick. This is what keeps many of them from the win window. How often have you heard a handicapper complain after a juicy long shot wins, "I circled that horse—I had him"? When you ask if he bet the horse, he answers in the negative. The reason that he didn't bet the horse was because it wasn't his top pick. I'll spend a good deal of time trying to convince you that you should often bet on horses that aren't your top pick. You should always bet on horses that offer value, and avoid the low-priced underlays. An underlay is a horse that is offering less odds than its probability of winning demands. If a horse has a 33 percent chance to win the race and is going off at even money, it's no bet. An overlay is just the opposite. Consider the same horse with a 33-percent chance to win going off at 3-to-1. What a bargain. This will all be explained in the betting strategy portion of this book.

The seventh and eighth commandments remind us that races divide themselves into two groups: races that have a legitimate favorite, and races that don't. A legitimate favorite is the class of the field, the speed of the field, and is in form and condition to deliver his ability. Anything less and you have a vulnerable favorite. We will spend a good deal of time learning how to distinguish among favorites. We will learn about three classes of favorites: legitimate, vulnerable, and false.

The ninth commandment is probably the most violated commandment of all. The vast majority of handicappers haven't the foggiest clue about their performance. Not one in a hundred could answer the following questions: "What is your overall win percentage for the past 200 races?" "What's your average mutuel for the past 200 races?" "What's your ROI in turf races?" "What's your ROI in dirt sprints?" If someone were to wake you up in the middle of the night and ask you these questions and you could answer them correctly, the chances are practically certain that you are a winning handicapper.

The last commandment should be self-evident. This game is dynamic. It's forever changing. In the seventies you could win a lot of money using speed figures to predict adjusted final times. Today, you'll be lucky to break even using these methods. Please notice that the tenth commandment didn't say to never stop learning about money management. This is because money management is finite and mathematical. The truth of mathematics is absolute. What was true fifty years ago will be true a thousand years from now. Once you learn the principles of money management, they are yours for life. My best advice on the subject is to read and digest Barry Meadow's excellent book, *Money Secrets at the Racetrack*. It's by far the best book ever written on the subject of money management. Once you digest its contents, you'll have solved a huge part of the thoroughbred handicapping-investment puzzle.

Chapter 3

Know Thy Track

SUPPOSE YOU'VE OBSERVED THAT in the last 75 dirt sprint races at your track, post position number one (the one post) recorded only one winner. In addition, the last twelve favorites coming from the one post failed to win. Your top figure horse is coming out of the "one-hole." Do you bet it?

A particular jockey is on a cold streak. He has zero wins in his last seventy races. He's riding the horse with the best figures in the race. Do you bet on this horse?

The horse with the best figures has never won on this track. He is zero for seven at today's distance. Another horse figures within two lengths of him and is three for five on this track. Which one should we bet?

Unless you have taken vows of poverty or the odds are astronomical, you wouldn't bet the top figure horse in the above examples. Situations such as these come up every day, and the betting public usually makes the top figure horse the favorite. By tuning in to what is winning and losing at your track, wise investment decisions are relatively easy to make.

It's critical that you plug yourself into what's happening at your track. Track bias, pace bias, hot trainer and jockey stats are wonderful opportunities for profit. On the other side, it's vital to know what is **not** winning at your track and bet against it.

The very first thing that you need is an accurate set of par times for your track. Next, you need the par times for all the tracks from which horses ship in to your track. I recommend that you get a set of pars for all the tracks in North America. (The very best, in my opinion, is Gordon Pine's *Par Times*, available from

Gambler's Book Club, *American Turf Monthly*, Cynthia Publishing et al. See Appendix A for selected information services.) Par times are the expected times that a race will run for a given distance, surface, and class. For example, let's look at the six-furlong dirt pars for Hollywood Park for 1991. (They were compiled from the races in 1990.)

Hollywood Park—6 furlongs dirt			
Class Level	First Call	Second Call	Final Time
Stakes	21^2	44^1	$1:08^2$
Classified	21^2	44^1	$1:08^4$
NW3	21^3	44^2	1:09
Clm 100,000	21^3	44^2	1:09
Clm 80,000	21^3	44^3	1:09
Clm 62,500	21^3	44^2	$1:09^1$
NW2	21^4	44^3	$1:09^2$
Clm 50,000	21^4	44^4	$1:09^2$
Clm 40,000	21^4	44^4	$1:09^2$
Clm 32,000	21^4	44^4	$1:09^3$
NW1	22	45	$1:09^3$
Clm 25,000	22	45	$1:09^4$
MSW	22	45	1:10
Clm 20,000	22	45	1:10
Clm 16,000	22^1	45^1	$1:10^1$
Clm 12,500	22^1	45^1	$1:10^2$
MCl	22^1	45^1	$1:10^3$
Clm 10,000	22^1	45^2	$1:10^4$

We notice that the bottom-of-the-barrel horses are the $10,000 claimers. A four-year-old $10,000 claiming horse is expected to run six furlongs on a fast track in $1:10^4$. It's interesting to note that maiden claimers (MCl) are expected to run a tick faster at the second call and final time than the $10,000 claimer. Notice also that maiden special weights (MSW) are expected to run the same as $20,000 claimers. NW1 stands for non-winners once, NW2 is for non-winners twice, and NW3 means non-winners three times. Classified includes classified allowance; non-graded stakes, both restricted and open; and non-graded handicap races. Stakes includes all graded stakes regardless of Grade 1, Grade 2, or Grade 3 designation.

This information is crucial. It makes the handicapping process simple. We only consider those horses who have demonstrated the ability to run close to the par as contenders. Unless no horse in the field can run to the pars, we use this information as an objective standard to separate contenders from pretenders. When no horse can run to the par, we then analyze the probable pace. More on this in the next chapter.

You must realize that these par times don't necessarily represent the times that the winner actually ran. Unless the race was won in a wire-to-wire fashion, the winner of the race ran times that were different than the pars. Suppose a $20,000 claiming six-furlong race ran exactly to the par times of 22 45 1:10 and the winner was two lengths behind at the first call and one length behind at the second call. Using the approximation of one-fifth of a second equal to one length, we see that the winner didn't run 22 45 1:10. He ran 22^2 45^1 1:10. This distinction between race pars and the winner's actual time becomes quite important. We will create a set of "win pars." This is the best way to plug into what's winning at your track.

Before we look more closely at win pars, let's first consider the running styles of horses. There are four basic styles: front runners, pressers, stalkers, and closers. The front runner is the horse that can be found on or very close to the lead. The presser is the horse that puts pressure on the leader to continue at the current pace. The stalker is the horse that is content to not let the pace get away from him. He's usually found from one to three lengths back, stalking the leaders. Many times he's the leader of the second group of horses. The closer is the late pace horse who comes from behind by virtue of conserving his energy until the final part of the race. It's very wise to try to identify the probable pace of a race and to label the running styles of the contenders. Each distance and surface on your racetrack usually favors one of the above running styles. In other words, different distances and surfaces develop "running-style biases."

The idea of profiling winners is simple. We want to know what's winning at our track. By cataloguing the performance of winners, we are hoping to find recurring patterns that we can recognize. It's a fancy way to observe the "running style" that is dominating on that surface for a given distance. This will let us zero in on contenders that match our profile, and eliminate those horses that are at a disadvantage. Hopefully we will find different profiles at the different distances. In 1990 I made a lot of money at Del Mar by observing that the six-furlong races demanded front-running, early-speed horses and that 6½ furlongs favored stalkers who remained about three lengths off the pace. Since most handicappers believe that a sprint is a sprint, they tended to back front runners at 6½ furlongs. I was very generously rewarded with prices that I almost didn't deserve. For a brief period, it seemed too easy.

A "win profile" is made from the race charts. A profile doesn't include the graded stakes races and bottom-of-the-barrel claiming races. It's a good idea to keep separate male and female profiles. It's also a very good idea to keep separate maiden profiles. You'll have a separate profile for each different distance, surface, and track condition.

A typical profile looks like this:

6 furlong dirt			WIN PROFILE						HOL
			----- Pace Times ----			Winners' Times		1st C	2nd C
Date	Race	Class	1st C	2nd C	Fin C	1st C	2nd C	B.L.	B.L.
26MAY91	1	C25,000	22.00	45.00	110.20	22.00	45.00	0.00	0.00 F
30MAY91	7	C62,500	22.00	44.60	109.80	23.08	45.58	6.20	5.70 C
31MAY91	9	*C10,000	22.00	44.60	109.60	22.00	44.60	0.00	0.00 F
1JUN91	10	C12,500	22.00	44.80	110.40	22.00	44.80	0.00	0.00 F
2JUN91	4	C20,000	21.80	44.80	110.20	21.80	44.80	0.00	0.00 F
7JUN91	4	C16,000	22.00	45.00	111.20	22.00	45.00	0.00	0.00 F
8JUN91	7	NW1	21.60	44.60	109.40	22.54	45.13	5.50	3.10 S
12JUN91	2	C25,000	22.00	45.20	110.40	23.82	46.18	10.10	5.60 C
12JUN91	5	C50,000	22.00	44.40	109.20	22.00	44.40	0.00	0.00 F
13JUN91	8	NW3	22.00	44.00	108.20	22.02	44.00	0.10	0.00 F
Averages:		NW1	21.93	44.71	109.89	22.36	44.99	2.43	1.60

A glance at the 1st C B.L. (first call beaten lengths) column tells us that no winner was more than 10.1 lengths out at the first call. The 2nd C B.L. (second call beaten lengths) column tells us that no winner came from more than 5.6 lengths off the pace. This race was quite atypical. We see that 70 percent of the six-furlong dirt sprints were won by front runners, and 60 percent in a wire-to-wire fashion. Doesn't bode well for closers. We see that front runners were dominating. Therefore we look for horses that will either set the pace or press the pace. Please note the asterisk (*) before the class of the May 31, 1991, race. It indicates that this race doesn't contribute to the averages on the bottom. This is because it's a bottom-of-the-barrel race, hence the computer throws it out of its calculations.

The best way to interpret a profile is to look at the last ten races. See if a recognizable pattern is present. If the data seem to be all over the place, it may be because you are experiencing an unbiased track or a track on which the bias is changing. If you can detect a changing track and correctly determine the new bias, you'll reap huge rewards. It usually takes a while for the public to catch on to the change.

If you average the beaten lengths at each call, you'll get a characterization for that distance. In the above case, the first-call average beaten lengths is approximately 2½ and the second call average is approximately 1½. This strongly suggests that a horse must not lose touch with the pace. If the average second-call beaten lengths was four or more, then you have a closer's profile. Horses who figured to take the lead at the second call would be at huge disadvantage.

The more you work with profiles, the more in touch with your track you become. In order to win consistently **you must know what is winning at your track**. You then bet on horses that have the correct profile and avoid ones that don't. Please remember to only look at the last ten races in your profile to characterize your track. If the last three or four races are a radical departure from what happened previously, it may be that the track is changing. The sooner we can recognize a changing track, the better. It usually takes the public a long while to catch on.

Compare this profile with the seven-furlong profile for the same time period.

```
7 furlong dirt                    WIN PROFILE                              HOL

                     ----- Pace Times ----    Winners' Times   1st C  2nd C
Date   Race  Class   1st C   2nd C   Fin C    1st C   2nd C     B.L.   B.L.
-----------------------------------------------------------------------------
24APR91  8  CLF      21.40   44.00   121.20   21.73   44.35     2.00   2.10  S
27APR91  1  *C10,000 22.80   46.80   124.60   23.53   47.27     4.10   2.60  S
27APR91  2  *C10,000 23.00   46.80   125.40   23.94   47.54     5.20   4.10  C
28APR91  1  C50,000  22.00   45.00   123.40   22.27   45.02     1.60   0.10  F
12MAY91 10  C12,500  21.80   44.60   123.00   22.78   45.29     5.70   4.00  C
26MAY91 10  *C10,000 22.20   45.00   123.00   22.56   45.26     2.10   1.50  P
29MAY91  4  C20,000  22.00   44.80   123.40   22.81   46.15     4.70   7.70  C
29MAY91  5  C40,000  22.20   45.00   121.80   22.20   45.00     0.00   0.00  F
2JUN91   2  C40,000  21.80   44.40   124.20   22.24   44.67     2.60   1.60  P
5JUN91   3  C25,000  22.20   44.80   122.60   22.20   44.80     0.00   0.00  F
-----------------------------------------------------------------------------
Averages:   C32,000  21.91   44.66   122.80   22.32   45.04     2.37   2.21
```

We see quite a different situation. The six-furlong profile had 70 percent of the races won by front-running horses. The situation is now reversed. Only 30 percent of these races were won by the front-running style. The pressers, stalkers, and closers were dominating.

The more you work with profiles, the more you will realize that each distance on each surface must be treated differently. In this case it's dead wrong to lump sprints together and handicap them the same way.

I'd like to share two dramatic examples to illustrate the power of profiles. The first compares maidens to winners at 1¹⁄₁₆ miles at Hollywood Park.

```
8.5 furlong dirt                    WIN PROFILE                              HOL

                     ----- Pace Times ----      Winners' Times    1st C  2nd C
Date      Race  Class    1st C   2nd C  Fin C    1st C    2nd C    B.L.   B.L.
-------------------------------------------------------------------------------
27MAY91    7   CLF       46.20  109.60 141.20    46.20   109.60   0.00   0.00 F
31MAY91    3   C25,000   47.00  111.60 144.00    47.00   111.60   0.00   0.00 F
31MAY91    7   C40,000   46.80  111.00 142.80    46.80   111.00   0.00   0.00 F
2JUN91    10  *C10,000   46.40  111.60 144.20    47.22   112.02   4.60   2.30 S
6JUN91     1  *C10,000   46.60  111.40 144.00    46.60   111.40   0.00   0.00 F
7JUN91     6   C25,000   46.20  110.80 142.80    46.39   110.80   1.10   0.00 F
9JUN91     7   NW1       45.80  110.20 143.60    48.19   111.76  13.10   8.60 C
12JUN91    3   NW3       45.60  109.60 141.60    45.60   109.60   0.00   0.00 F
13JUN91    1   C16,000   46.20  110.80 143.40    46.73   111.09   3.00   1.60 P
13JUN91    3   C32,000   46.80  111.60 144.40    48.11   112.26   7.20   3.60 C
-------------------------------------------------------------------------------
Averages:      C40,000   46.33  110.65 142.98    46.88   110.96   3.05   1.73
```

```
8.5 furlong dirt                    WIN PROFILE   MAIDENS                     HOL

                     ----- Pace Times ----      Winners' Times    1st C  2nd C
Date      Race  Class    1st C   2nd C  Fin C    1st C    2nd C    B.L.   B.L.
-------------------------------------------------------------------------------
11MAY91    2   C20,000   47.00  112.20 145.60    47.00   112.20   0.00   0.00 F
15MAY91    4   MSW       46.00  111.20 143.00    47.07   111.38   6.00   1.00 P
17MAY91    9   C20,000   47.40  112.20 144.20    47.69   112.20   1.60   0.00 F
19MAY91    3   MSW       47.00  111.40 142.60    47.00   111.40   0.00   0.00 F
22MAY91    6   C25,000   47.60  111.80 143.40    47.62   111.80   0.10   0.00 F
26MAY91    4   NW2       46.60  111.80 145.20    46.87   112.07   1.50   1.50 P
31MAY91    2   C20,000   46.20  111.40 145.00    46.20   111.40   0.00   0.00 F
31MAY91    6   C20,000   46.20  111.20 145.40    46.20   111.20   0.00   0.00 F
5JUN91     9   MSW       46.20  111.40 144.40    46.29   111.49   0.50   0.50 P
12JUN91    9   C20,000   45.80  110.60 143.20    45.80   110.60   0.00   0.00 F
-------------------------------------------------------------------------------
Averages:      MSW       46.60  111.52 144.20    46.77   111.57   0.97   0.30
```

As we would expect, the final times are slower for maidens, but look at the difference in running styles. Maidens had to be on or near the lead at the second call or they were history. If a maiden was two lengths behind at the second call, he had no chance whatsoever.

The next example is equally dramatic. It compares dirt routes to turf routes. Unfortunately, I couldn't compare the one-mile dirt to the one-mile turf because Hollywood Park no longer runs one-mile dirt races.

```
8.5 furlong dirt                    WIN PROFILE                              HOL

                     ----- Pace Times ----      Winners' Times    1st C  2nd C
Date      Race  Class    1st C   2nd C  Fin C    1st C    2nd C    B.L.   B.L.
-------------------------------------------------------------------------------
27MAY91    7   CLF       46.20  109.60 141.20    46.20   109.60   0.00   0.00 F
31MAY91    3   C25,000   47.00  111.60 144.00    47.00   111.60   0.00   0.00 F
31MAY91    7   C40,000   46.80  111.00 142.80    46.80   111.00   0.00   0.00 F
2JUN91    10  *C10,000   46.40  111.60 144.20    47.22   112.02   4.60   2.30 S
6JUN91     1  *C10,000   46.60  111.40 144.00    46.60   111.40   0.00   0.00 F
7JUN91     6   C25,000   46.20  110.80 142.80    46.39   110.80   1.10   0.00 F
9JUN91     7   NW1       45.80  110.20 143.60    48.19   111.76  13.10   8.60 C
12JUN91    3   NW3       45.60  109.60 141.60    45.60   109.60   0.00   0.00 F
13JUN91    1   C16,000   46.20  110.80 143.40    46.73   111.09   3.00   1.60 P
13JUN91    3   C32,000   46.80  111.60 144.40    48.11   112.26   7.20   3.60 S/c
-------------------------------------------------------------------------------
Averages:      C40,000   46.33  110.65 142.98    46.88   110.96   3.05   1.73
```

```
8 furlong turf                  WIN PROFILE                         HOL

                    ----- Pace Times ----    Winners' Times   1st C  2nd C
Date    Race Class  1st C   2nd C   Fin C    1st C   2nd C     B.L.   B.L.
-------------------------------------------------------------------------
28APR91  8 *STAKES I 46.20  109.60  133.40   46.50  109.90     1.70   1.70 P
4MAY91   5 *STAKES I 47.00  110.60  134.40   47.67  110.81     3.70   1.20 P
9MAY91   8  NW3      47.00  110.80  134.20   47.74  110.82     4.10   0.10 P
11MAY91  9  C62,500  45.40  109.00  134.00   46.15  109.63     4.30   3.60 S
26MAY91  5  NW2      47.00  110.40  134.20   48.58  111.36     8.60   5.30 C
2JUN91   5  NW3      48.00  111.20  134.20   48.95  112.31     5.10   6.10 C
2JUN91   9  C80,000  47.60  110.60  133.80   47.98  111.16     2.10   3.10 S
7JUN91   8  CLF      45.60  109.60  133.40   46.21  109.78     3.50   1.00 P
-------------------------------------------------------------------------
Averages:   C100,000 46.77  110.27  133.97   47.60  110.84     4.62   3.20
```

We see that 60 percent of the dirt races were won by horses on the lead at the second call, while on the turf no races were won by front runners. Pressers, stalkers, and closers dominated the turf. You'll learn later that late speed is king on the turf and early speed dominates maiden races. These profiles confirm these assertions.

All the profiles were generated by Cynthia Publishing's FIVE-IN-ONE Version 2 computer program. You can accomplish the same thing manually. It takes about twenty minutes a day to update your profiles, and this investment will pay dividends beyond all proportion to the time invested. You'll put yourself into the top two percent of all handicappers by simply knowing the par times and running styles that are dominating at your track.

Win profiles are derived from the racing charts. Please use the following table for your approximations of time and distance.

Time & Distance Equivalents for Beaten Lengths		
1 length	10 feet	.20 seconds
½ length	5 feet	.10 seconds
¼ length	2½ feet	.05 seconds
Neck (nk)	2 feet	.04 seconds
Head (hd)	1 foot	.02 seconds
Nose (no)	½ foot	.01 seconds

From the above table we can see that three-fourths of a length is equivalent to 7½ feet in distance and .15 seconds in time. A neck is .2 lengths, a head is .1 lengths, and a nose is .05 lengths. Please don't be too concerned about the accuracy of these approximations. Our intention isn't to be exact but simply to build an approximate profile of what's winning at our track. We are going to record the win pace-call times and beaten lengths for all distances between five furlongs and 9½ furlongs. (Class laughs at pace at 1¼ miles or longer distances.) In a sprint race (less than one mile), we'll record the quarter-mile, the half-mile, and the final time of the winner, plus the beaten lengths at these calls. In a route race (one mile or longer), we'll record the half-mile, six-furlong, and final time of the winner plus the beaten lengths at these calls. We are taking data from the results charts and converting them to reflect past performance data. In a past performance line, the beaten-length data tells you how far **behind** this horse was from the front runner at that particular call. The result chart, on the other hand, tells you the number of lengths a horse was **ahead** of the next horse. Let's look at the charts of a sprint race and a route race and derive the numbers that would be entered into a win profile.

SECOND RACE **Hollywood** JUNE 16, 1991

6 FURLONGS. (1.08) MAIDEN CLAIMING. Purse $17,000. 3-year-olds and upward. Weights, 3-year-olds, 116 lbs.; older, 122 lbs. Claiming price $32,000; if for $28,000 allowed 2 lbs.

Value of race $17,000; value to winner $9,350; second $3,400; third $2,550; fourth $1,275; fifth $425. Mutuel pool $378,300. Exacta pool $373,765.

Last Raced	Horse	M/Eqt.	A.	Wt	PP	St	¼	½	Str	Fin	Jockey	Cl'g Pr	Odds $1
29May91 ^{9}Hol^{2}	Dusty Sassafras	B	3	116	10	8	8^{2}	$6^{\frac{1}{2}}$	$4^{1\frac{1}{2}}$	1^{2}	ValenzuelPA	32000	1.90
	Bob's Bearcat	B	3	116	6	7	$5^{2\frac{1}{2}}$	$3^{2\frac{1}{2}}$	$1^{1\frac{1}{2}}$	$2^{3\frac{1}{2}}$	DesormuxKJ	32000	17.40
24May91 ^{2}Hol^{4}	Keelung	B	3	109	3	6	$6^{1\frac{1}{2}}$	$7^{1\frac{1}{2}}$	$5^{\frac{1}{2}}$	3^{1}	Lovato A J^{5}	28000	4.80
17May91 ^{2}Hol^{7}	Crystal Nat	LBb	3	116	8	5	$7^{\frac{1}{2}}$	8^{3}	$6^{1\frac{1}{2}}$	$4^{2\frac{3}{4}}$	Stevens G L	32000	4.70
22May91 ^{2}Hol^{6}	Russian Winter	B	4	122	9	1	2^{1}	2^{hd}	2^{hd}	$5^{\frac{1}{2}}$	Santos J A	32000	17.60
24May91 ^{2}Hol^{6}	Tank's Ruler	LB	3	116	7	3	10	$9^{1\frac{1}{2}}$	9^{5}	$6^{\frac{3}{4}}$	Garcia J A	32000	24.10
22May91 ^{2}Hol^{2}	Barry McGuigan	LBb	5	121	5	2	$1^{\frac{1}{2}}$	1^{hd}	$3^{\frac{1}{2}}$	$7^{\frac{3}{4}}$	DelhoussyeE	28000	4.30
24May91 ^{2}Hol^{11}	Thal Val Echo	LBb	4	120	1	9	3^{hd}	5^{1}	$8^{1\frac{1}{2}}$	$8^{\frac{1}{2}}$	Flores D R	28000	52.70
14Nov90 ^{4}Hol^{3}	Lodi Tune	LB	3	116	4	4	4^{1}	4^{hd}	7^{hd}	9^{7}	Pincay L Jr	32000	6.80
	Foolish Flame	b	5	122	2	10	$9^{\frac{1}{2}}$	10	10	10	Patton D B	32000	72.70

OFF AT 1:35. Start good. Won driving. Time, :22 , :45^{1}, :58^{2}, 1:11^{2} Track fast.

$2 Mutuel Prices:			
12–DUSTY SASSAFRAS	5.80	4.00	2.80
8–BOB'S BEARCAT		13.40	6.40
5–KEELUNG			3.60

$2 EXACTA 12–8 PAID $105.00.

(Please note the convention that we are using regarding times. When times are represented in fifths of seconds, we'll use a superscript: 22^2 means 22 and two-fifths. When times are represented in tenths of seconds, we'll use a decimal point: 22.2 means 22 and two-tenths.)

We see that the times we are interested in were 22 45^1 $1:11^2$. It's best to convert these times into tenths of seconds. The converted times are 22 45.2 1:11.4. Since Dusty Sassafras was eighth at the first call and sixth at the second call, we must concern ourselves with seven horses and five horses respectively. At the first call, we must add the beaten lengths for the seven horses in front of Dusty Sassafras and their time equivalents:

Horse's Position	Lengths Ahead	Time Equivalent (seconds)
First	½	.10
Second	1	.20
Third	hd (.1)	.02
Fourth	1	.20
Fifth	2½	.50
Sixth	1½	.30
Seventh	½	.10
	7.1	1.42

The time equivalent is calculated by multiplying the beaten lengths by .2.

The first horse was Barry McGuigan, the second was Russian Winter, and so forth. The check that you are correct is to multiply the beaten lengths by .2 and see if the answer is the same as the total of the time-equivalent column. We now note that the winner ran the first call in 23.42 seconds (22 plus 1.42) and was 7.1 lengths behind. (This is atypical of maiden races.)

We now look at the second call (half-mile in sprints) column:

Horse's Position	Lengths Ahead	Time Equivalent (seconds)
First	hd	.02
Second	hd	.02
Third	2½	.50
Fourth	hd	.02
Fifth	1	.20
	3.8	.76

We see that the winner ran the second call in 45.96 seconds (45.2 plus .76) and was 3.8 lengths behind at the second call. Our profile entry looks as follows:

Pace Times			Win Times		B.L.1	B.L.2	Style
22.00	45.20	1:11.40	23.42	45.96	7.1	3.8	Closer

EIGHTH RACE
Hollywood
JUNE 16, 1991

1 ¼ MILES. (1.46⁴) 13th Running of THE SILVER SCREEN HANDICAP (Grade III). $150,000 added. 3-year-olds. By subscription of $100 each, which shall accompany the nomination, $1,500 additional to start, with $150,000 added, of which $30,000 to second, $22,500 to third, $11,250 to fourth and $3,750 to fifth. Weights, Tuesday, June 11. SHOULD THE WINNER OF EITHER THE KENTUCKY DERBY, THE PREAKNESS OR THE BELMONT BE A STARTER, THE ADDED MONEY WILL BE INCREASED TO $300,000. Starters to be named through the entry box by closing time of entries. Hollywood Park reserves the right not to divide this race. Should this race not be divided and the number of entries exceed the starting gate capacity, high weights on the scale will be preferred and an also eligible list will be drawn. Total earnings in 1991 will be used in determining the order of preference of horses assigned equal weight on the scale. Failure to draw into this race at scratch time cancels all fees. Trophies will be presented to the winning owner, trainer and jockey. Closed Wednesday, June 5, 1991 with 13 nominations.
Value of race $158,800; value to winner $91,300; second $30,000; third $22,500; fourth $11,250; fifth $3,750. Mutuel pool $397,039. Exacta pool $414,745.

Last Raced	Horse	M/Eqt.A.Wt	PP St	¼	½	¾	Str	Fin	Jockey	Odds $1
18May91 5Hol1	Compelling Sound	b 3 118	2 5	4²	3½	3⁴	3⁶	1nk	Stevens G L	1.80
18May91 10Pim5	Best Pal	LB 3 123	1 2	22½	22½	22½	11½	23½	Valenzuela P A	.90
18May91 8GG1	Caliche's Secret	LBb 3 117	4 1	12½	11½	1½	21½	35	Pincay L Jr	5.30
18May91 8GG4	Pillaring	LB 3 115	5 3	3¹	41½	4hd	4hd	4½	Solis A	24.20
27May91 1GG2	Key Recognition	LB 3 116	3 4	5	5	5	5	5	Delahoussaye E	8.40

OFF AT 5:12. Start good. Won driving. Time, :23⁴, :47 , 1:10³, 1:34⁴, 1:47⁴ Track fast.

$2 Mutuel Prices:

2-COMPELLING SOUND	5.60	2.40	2.20
1-BEST PAL		2.40	2.10
4-CALICHE'S SECRET			2.40

$2 EXACTA 2-1 PAID $11.20.

A route race is a little tricky because the charts give five points of call and we use only three of them. The times we're interested in were 47 1:10³ 1:47⁴. It's best to convert these times into tenths of seconds. The converted times are 47 1:10.6 1:47.8. Since Compelling Sound was third at the first call and third at the second call, we must concern ourselves with two horses at each call. For the first call we must add the beaten lengths for the two horses in front of Compelling Sound and their time equivalents.

Horse's Position	Lengths Ahead	Time Equivalent (seconds)
First	1½	.30
Second	2½	.50
	4	.80

The first horse was Caliche's Secret and the second was Best Pal. The check of multiplying the beaten lengths by .2 to see if the answer is the same as the total of the time-equivalent column works in this case. We now note that the winner ran the first call in 47.80 seconds (47 plus .80) and was four lengths behind.

We now look at the second call (six furlongs in routes) column:

Horse's Position	Lengths Ahead	Time Equivalent (seconds)
First	½	.10
Second	2½	.50
	3	.60

We now see that the winner ran the second call in 1:11.2 seconds (1:10.6 plus .60) and was three lengths behind at the second call. Our profile entry looks as follows:

Pace Times			Win Times		B.L.1	B.L.2	Style
47.00	1:10.60	1:47.80	47.80	1:11.2	4	3	Stalk

If you religiously keep a win profile for each distance and surface for older males, older females, maiden special weight, and maiden claimers, the track will be yours. You'll put yourself into the upper two percent of handicappers at your track. Is it worth twenty minutes a day to leap over 98 percent of your competition?

In addition to the win profile, you should catalogue the "horses for courses" at your track. This can be done manually with a file box of three-by-five cards. Simply write down each winner's name, distance, class, trainer, and jockey on a blank card. File these cards alphabetically. Use a paper clip to keep the cards together for multiple winners. This technique is especially powerful for short meetings such as Saratoga and Del Mar. A horse who has won at today's distance on today's surface, especially a multiple winner, is always dangerous. Many favorites have never won on today's track and have had many opportunities to do so. These favorites are vulnerable.

You must get to know the trainers at your track. Some are specialists. They are particularly good with some types of races and not so good with others. In the mid-eighties D. Wayne Lukas was always a leading trainer. His forte was young dirt horses. Many of his "child prodigies" such as Capote, Success Express, and Tejano were has-beens by the ripe old age of three. His record on turf was poor. In spite of his huge success, a handicapper was wise to eliminate his turf entries. Not until 1988 did he begin to show any skill with turf horses.

In 1983 New York trainer Oscar Barrera won 21 percent of his starts. In spite of this outstanding record, only 3 percent (1 for 29) of his victories were on the turf.

At the 1987 Saratoga meeting, Mack Miller sent 36 horses to post. He won 14 of these starts for a win rate of 38.8 percent. His average winner paid $8.44. For every dollar invested in a Mack Miller start, the investor received $1.64. If you followed up by investing in all of Miller's starts in 1988, you would have been rewarded with a 35.7 percent win rate at an average mutuel of $8.40, for an ROI of 50 percent. At the same Saratoga meeting, Bob Klesaris sent 15 horses to post with 5 victories at an average mutuel of $11.44, for a 90 percent ROI.

Charlie Whittingham is one of the finest trainers who ever drew a breath, yet it's not wise to back maiden first-timers coming from his barn. On the other hand, Richard Matlow is an obscure trainer with a very small stable. It's very unwise not to back first-time starters from his barn. The more you know about the trainers on your circuit, the larger the edge you'll have on your competition.

One could make the spurious argument that the horse runs the race, and the trainer and jockey are supplemental. If this were true, how do you account for the fact that twenty percent of the trainers win over eighty percent of the races? Same is true for jockeys. It's real important to be plugged into every aspect of what's winning at your track. In southern California the jockey factor isn't that important because we have the finest jockey colony ever assembled. If your top horse is being ridden by any of the top ten riders, there's no need to be terribly concerned. But there are exceptions. Martin Pedroza is a wonderful jockey when it comes to sprint races. In route races his ROI is abysmal. It's not terribly wise to back his horses in routes unless poverty is a high priority on your agenda.

This isn't true for other racing circuits. There are jockeys who are absolutely awesome. They seem to win far more than their fair share of races, and you have to take this into consideration. Imagine yourself at Oaklawn Park. You are watching the post parade. The first seven contenders look okay. The eighth contender is a lot shorter than all the other horses. In fact it looks very much like an alligator. Pat Day is riding this reptilian-looking creature. You can bet that this creature won't go off at odds greater than 4-to-1. Reason: Pat Day.

Keeping a win profile and noting the post position bias stats published in the track program and sometimes in the *Racing Form* will go a long way toward keeping you informed as to what's winning at your track. Add to this trainer and jockey information, hot stats, and horses for courses—you'll have the beginnings of an arsenal that will keep you commuting to the win window.

Let's now turn our attention to the question of a horse's ability.

Chapter 4

Ability

WE ARE GOING TO DEFINE ability in terms of speed, pace, and class. Most handicappers don't have a consistent method of dealing with these factors. These are by far the most significant factors in thoroughbred handicapping. I call them "the big three." Most of your winners will come from horses that have an edge on at least one of these factors.

THE CLASS FACTOR

Let's begin with the class factor. It's by far the simplest of the big three. To determine the class of a horse, you need only ask two questions:

1. Has this horse won at today's level or higher?
2. Can it run to the pars and profile needed to win at today's level?

If the answer to either question is affirmative, there's no need to consider the class factor any longer. This horse has the class to win. It now becomes a question of form and condition. All the class in the world means nothing if a contender isn't in form and condition. Ask Mike Tyson after he fought Buster Douglas.

Many very competent handicappers are faked out by the class factor. Consider the following past performances of a horse named Eluding.

Eluding — Ch. f. 3(Mar), by Kris S—Lewzier, by George Lewis — Lifetime 1991 6 1 1 1 $15,000
SOLIS A — $16,000 — Br.—Meadowbrook Farms Inc (Cal) — 115 — 10 1 2 2 1990 4 M 1 1 $9,940
Own.—La Croix Barbara — Tr.—La Croix David — $25,090

9Jun91- 1Hol	fst	6f	:22²	:45²	1:11²	ⓕClm 32000	5	5	5³	5³½	5⁷½	7¹¹½	Solis A	LB	119	13.40	71–11	PssonForPokr116¹½TBDzzlng116¹FrntrNrsng116¹½	Jostled 1/2	9
29May91- 3Hol	fst	6½f	:22¹	:45¹	1:17²	ⓕClm 40000	6	1	2hd	1hd	3¹½	5⁴½	Delahoussaye E	LB	116	6.00	81–12	FhdiBy114½StchsMistress116noSvntyBlowZro116hd	Weakened	6
11May91- 7Hol	fst	6f	:22¹	:45	1:10³	ⓕClm 37500	4	4	5²	4⁴½	4⁶½	4⁷	Solis A	LB	114	19.80	89–13	WelcomeMssngr119⁴DonctlTwo116²Quitr107¹	4-wide stretch	8
26Apr91- 9Hol	fst	6f	:21³	:44³	1:11³	3+ⓕMd 32000	6	8	5³½	4⁴½	3²½	1¹½	Solis A	LB	115	3.90	82–14	Eluding115¹½LibertedBelle117¹½ProperProphecy115hd	Driving	12
8Feb91- 5OP	fst	6f	:22	:46²	1:10⁴	3+ⓕMd Sp Wt	5	4	2½	2½	2¹½	3⁹½	Kutz D		112	2.30	75–18	Danzig Queen120⁷ Maid O Gold120²½ Eluding112nk	Tired	9
27Jan91- 4OP	fst	6f	:22¹	:46³	1:12	3+ⓕMd Sp Wt	8	2	2¹	2hd	2¹½	2½	Kutz D		114	6.90	78–16	Hy Vanity114½ Eluding114³ Motel Rendeavous114¹½	Gamely	10
31Dec90- 6SA	fst	6½f	:22	:45¹	1:17¹	ⓕMd 50000	6	5	5²	4¹½	3⁴	4⁶½	Solis A	LB	117	4.00	77–15	DollCollction117²MrktingMix117⁴½Pondrous115hd	No mishap	12
22Dec90- 4Hol	fst	6f	:21⁴	:45³	1:11¹	ⓕⓈMd Sp Wt	1	4	2hd	1hd	5²½	5⁷½	Solis A	LB	118	6.50	75–06	SymphonyAtSe118²½LibertdBll118nkMadyMck118¹½	Gave way	8
22Jun90- 3GG	fst	5f	:21¹	:44³	:57	ⓕMd Sp Wt	8	1	3¹½	2²	2⁴	2⁸	Steiner J J		117	4.30	92–10	Mi Lucia117⁸ Eluding117¹ Miami Vacation117½	2nd best	8
13Jun90- 3GG	fst	5f	:21	:44³	:57³	ⓕMd Sp Wt	5	3	3¹½	3²	3¹½	3³	Gonzalez R M		117	4.10	94–11	WomanOfMystery117¹Awestmind117²Eluding117³½	Hung late	8

Speed Index: Last Race: –18.0 3–Race Avg.: –10.6 10–Race Avg.: –6.8 Overall Avg.: –6.8
LATEST WORKOUTS Jly 2 Hol 4f fst :48³ H

This was a claiming $16,000 race for fillies who were non-winners of two races. One of the best public handicappers in the country made the following comment: "Faltered after encountering trouble and now *takes a big class drop. . .*" What class drop? Look at the par chart for this distance at Hollywood Park. This horse is making a huge class rise. She won a maiden claimer at five ticks slower than par and now faces winners capable of running $1{:}10^3$ or better. There is absolutely no evidence that she can run any faster than 1:11 and change. A mere glance eliminates her on the class factor.

Track: HOL	6 Furlongs dirt		
Class level	1st C	2nd C	Fin C
STAKES I	21.2	44.1	108.2
CLF	21.2	44.1	108.4
NW3	21.3	44.2	109.0
C100,000	21.3	44.2	109.0
C80,000	21.3	44.3	109.0
C62,500	21.3	44.3	109.1
NW2	21.4	44.3	109.2
C50,000	21.4	44.4	109.2
C40,000	21.4	44.4	109.2
C32,000	21.4	44.4	109.3
NW1	22.0	45.0	109.3
C25,000	22.0	45.0	109.4
MSW	22.0	45.0	110.0
C20,000	22.0	45.0	110.0
C16,000	22.1	45.1	110.1
C12,500	22.1	45.1	110.2
MCL	22.1	45.1	110.3
C10,000	22.1	45.2	110.4

Please don't be confused by where the horse was entered. It doesn't matter. What matters is the level at which the horse succeeds. The way to deal with the class factor is to simply scan all the contenders in a race and ask the above two questions. If the answers are negative, you can draw an X through that horse's name. It's a non-contender. One affirmative answer is enough to qualify this horse on the class factor. In the workshop section, where we handicap a day's card, this concept will be repeated ad nauseam.

I realize that this approaches a world's record for brevity on the subject of class. But that's all there is to it if you define it in terms of speed. Let's now take a look at speed and pace.

THE SPEED FACTOR

Most handicappers really don't understand the concept of speed. Try to answer this devilishly simple question: A man travels one mile at an average speed of 30 miles per hour and a second mile at an average speed of 90 miles per hour. What's his average speed for the entire trip? Ninety-nine out of one hundred handicappers would respond with the incorrect answer of 60 mph. The reason for this error is a lack of understanding of the relationships among speed (velocity), distance, and time.

There's a pace handicapping methodology that defines average pace for a six-furlong distance as the sum of the velocities for each of three quarter-mile fractions divided by three. Most practitioners don't realize that this made-up construct has nothing to do with the correct physical interpretation of average speed. Average speed is correctly defined as total distance divided by total time. Hence in the above question, the correct answer is figured by dividing 2 miles by 160 seconds. One mile at 30 mph takes 120 seconds (two minutes) to complete. One mile at 90 mph takes 40 seconds or two-thirds of a minute to complete. Therefore the average speed was 2/160 miles per second. To convert to miles per hour, simply multiply this number by 3600 (the number of seconds in an hour) to get the correct answer of 45 miles per hour. The obvious reason why 60 mph couldn't be correct is because to average 60 mph for 2 miles would take two minutes. This is impossible because the driver used up his two minutes in the first mile.

While we're on the subject of speed conundrums, please consider the following: Two horses win their respective six-furlong races in a wire-to-wire fashion with the fractional time 22 45 1:10. Because of the imprecision of the clock, which only measures to one-fifth of a second accuracy, their actual times were 22.19 45.00 1:10, and 22.00 45.19 1:10. Now consider their times for the second fraction. The first horse traveled the second quarter-mile (1320 feet) in 22.81 seconds, and the second horse covered the same distance in 23.19 seconds. The average speed for the first horse was 57.87 feet per second, and the average speed for the second horse was 56.92 fps. The differential between the two speeds is .95 fps. If we apply this differential over the 23 seconds that the fractional times suggest the second quarter to be, we see that this represents 21.85 feet. *That's over two lengths!* In other words, there could have been a difference of two lengths and we wouldn't know it from the data in the *Racing Form*. This is why I have always resisted methods that purported to be very precise. How could any method be reliable when the "error factor" due to clocking is so gross?

In the first quarter-mile of a sprint race, there is a one-length uncertainty. In the first half-mile there are two lengths of uncertainty. That is, you can't be sure that a horse didn't run a length faster or slower at the quarter and two lengths faster or slower at the half. Hence any speed method should take this into consideration. I have yet to read about or hear about this concept discussed in the literature of horse racing except in *Winning Thoroughbred Strategies*. This same error factor is present in route races. Any speed method must compensate for this by allowing for a one-length variance at the first call and a two-length variance at the second call. Statistically these errors have a tendency to cancel each other by the time the final time arrives, hence it's most improbable to have experienced the maximum error, which would be close to three lengths. Therefore we will only insist upon a two-length leeway in the final time.

Please don't be too concerned about the timing "error factor." Larger errors can be generated by a horse's trip. For example, consider the difference between running in the "one-path" versus running in the "six-path" over a distance of a mile. The usual approximation is to add at least one length per path per half-mile, hence we have at minimum a twelve-length difference if the horses finish together at the wire. My main point is that you shouldn't insist upon too much precision when discussing speed.

The point that I will be making over and over is that *it's not how fast a horse runs, it's how it runs fast that's important*. Any speed method that doesn't consider pace is bound to fail. There are many California horses that can run six furlongs in less than 1:10. There are damn few that can accomplish this when they are asked to do the first quarter in less than 22 and the first half in less than 45.

Whenever you hear prerace commentary, it's always focused upon the probable pace of the race. That's for a very good reason. Any race, whether for horses or humans, can be lost by misapplying too much early speed. Consider a mile race for humans. If a sprint pace is set by one of the contestants, you can be sure he won't be around at the finish. If a number of contestants decide to chase this blistering pace, then not only isn't the first contestant a factor in winning the race, he also compromises the chances of the others who decide to follow. This same thing happens, all the time, in horse races. Horses who aren't serious contenders themselves can and do compromise the chances of horses who vie for the lead with them.

We must be able to judge the various pace scenarios that could develop in a race. The very best book written on the subject of pace analysis is Tom Brohamer's *Modern Pace Handicapping*. I strongly recommend that you pick up a copy and digest its contents. Brohamer is a consistent winner. In fact, he's one of the most consistent handicappers that I have the good fortune to know. If you can marry the concepts discussed in this book with Brohamer's material, you'll never look back. Winning will become the natural order of things.

Traditional speed handicapping uses par times and track variants. The goal of speed handicapping is to predict the final time that a horse will run. It's fairly obvious that the horse with the best final time will be the winner. What could possibly be wrong with this? Only the fact that final times are usually a function of the pace of the race, and that daily variants are a function of the class of the race. Using traditional methods, the handicapper must be able to adjust for each circumstance. Unfortunately, this means that he or she would have to forego any semblance of normal family life and spend a few hours every day just resolving all the class, pace, and projected time versus actual time conflicts. Even if this were accomplished, the handicapper would still have to deal with distance switches, shippers, and all the familiar handicapping challenges.

Ideally, we want a method that is quick and uses the information found in the *Daily Racing Form*. This method must consider the pace, class, and running style of the contenders. It must be able to handle distance switches and horses shipping in from other tracks. It must be straightforward and easy to apply, and at the same time give us insight into the race we are handicapping. After numerous computer studies and playing with this for eight years, I am now satisfied that the method suggested in this book will accomplish all the above and more.

It all starts with accurate par times. We must know what to expect in a given race. Also, because "pace biases" develop and last anywhere from a few days to an entire meeting, we must have a mechanism to observe them and to cash in on them. Therefore, the first thing we must do is catalogue what winners are doing at our track. This is accomplished by making a "win profile." We simply write down the winners' times versus the race times and record the beaten lengths at the first two calls. A glance at this table will give us a profile for this distance on this surface. What's most revealing about this profile is the fact that you can establish a maximum requirement for beaten lengths at each call and eliminate all horses who don't figure to meet this requirement. Please review the last chapter if you're unclear about win profiles.

Once we have made our profiles, we now have a standard that we can use to separate contenders from non-contenders. Next we must be able to pick a race out of a horse's past performances to represent what he'll do today. (This skill is easily mastered once you understand the form factor, which is discussed in the next chapter.) If necessary, we'll adjust the representative race to the distance and surface of today's race, taking the DRF variant into consideration. We'll note the running style of the horse. We'll then examine the probable pace scenarios and decide if we have a betting opportunity or not.

At first this method will seem difficult. Hang in there. After a while it'll become second nature, and you'll have a big advantage in that you'll have a perspective on handicapping that very few handicappers are even aware of. That's your edge. If you see things like everybody else, you'll be on the favorite most of the time. We're looking for false and vulnerable favorites. This method finds them. Best of all, you'll understand exactly why a favorite can be beat, or perhaps why it's not too smart to bet against it. Please read the Workshop Section a number of times. The race comments and analyses contain a good number of handicapping principles that you must be aware of. This method wins. I know. I have the profits to prove it. Yes, it's not easy. Nothing of value is. It'll take some time and effort to understand. Pay the price. Do the work. You'll be thrilled with the results.

THE PACE FACTOR

What part of a race determines whether a competitor is in form and condition? A number of authors have suggested that it's the third fraction. They argue that this is the most demanding part of the race because it's a test of determination, since the horse is knocking on the door of exhaustion. Sounds plausible, but like many plausible-sounding things, it withers under the light of scrutiny. Some authors have gone so far as to define "ability time" as the time it takes to run the last fraction. My computer studies say the very opposite. In fact, *the last fraction is the least predictive*, except in the case of turf racing. Hence, so-called "ability time" becomes "inability time." We have demonstrated in over tens of thousands of races that stretch gain or stretch loss is statistically insignificant and that the last fraction is the least predictive of the three.

The most predictive fraction is the second fraction. Tom Brohamer refers to this fraction as "turn-time," because at most distances the second fraction of a race involves running around some part of the final turn. He correctly points out that "within this fraction, the race becomes most intense and pretenders are exposed." Many times the horses with the best last fractions have already lost touch with the pace and lost the race, and are only picking up the pieces by passing tiring horses in the stretch. In races for cheaper horses, and especially maiden claiming races, the turn-time factor can almost stand by itself as a method for finding the eventual winner. When Ron Ambrose and I were at Louisiana Downs last year for a seminar, all the sprint races that weekend were won by horses that had the first, second, or third best turn-times.

Bill Quirin correctly pointed out that the universal bias is early speed. Horses that have the lead at the quarter pole (a quarter-mile from the finish line) are dangerous. They don't have to worry about getting around a "wall of horses." They don't have to worry about horses lugging and impeding their path. One of the best bets in all thoroughbred racing is the lone speed horse. If a contender figures to have a three length or longer lead at the quarter pole, regardless of time, it's usually the winner. Lee Rousso, a very gifted handicapper, loves to find the lone speed in cheap races. Regardless of how bad the horses look, he figures the probable pace of the race, and if he finds a "Lone F," he sends it in. He has cashed many long-shot winners using this technique.

Consider the following running line: 22 45 1:10 5^2 4^1 5^4 7^8.
Is this a good race or a poor race? Most handicappers would say
that it's a poor race because the horse lost ground in the stretch
and failed to beat half the field. They would be wrong. This is
actually a good race. This horse stayed on or near the pace for
two-thirds of the race. In fact, it actually gained on the pace
between the first call and the second call. The position calls and
beaten lengths as written in the *Daily Racing Form* are very
deceptive. Most handicappers think that the 4^1 represents what
happened for the first half of the race. They don't realize that the
second call in a six-furlong race means that the race is two-thirds
complete. It's even more extreme at the mile distance. The second
call occurs when 75 percent of the race is complete.

The above horse, if he's not a known quitter (affectionately
known as a "quitting rat"), is one of the best opportunities in
thoroughbred handicapping if he runs against a softer pace next
time out.

Let's look at the second fraction of the above running line.
This horse gained one length on a second fraction time of 23
seconds (45 minus 22), hence he ran the second quarter in 22^4.
That's a very good turn-time in southern California. Horses that
exceed the turn-time par win more than their fair share of races.
In a study involving over 300 sprint races, we simply made a
two-dollar bet on the top adjusted turn-time horse in each race.
We got back $2.19 for every two dollars bet. Not bad. A 9½
percent return using nothing except the factor of turn-time. If we
threw out the "quitting rats," the return soared to over 20 percent.

It's never very wise to use a single factor unless the stats are
overwhelming. It might be wise to check out the cheap sprint
races at your track to see if the single factor of adjusted turn-time
throws a big profit rate. If it does, you've cracked the code. If not,
read on.

Adjusted turn-time is ability time. This factor, more than any
other, has proven to be representative of a horse's form and condition. Just as new early speed is a sign of form improvement,
improving turn-time is also a positive indication of a horse coming into form. When a horse runs its fastest adjusted turn-time,
it's usually at the top of its form cycle.

Consider the following two wire-to-wire running lines:

1. 22 45 1:10
2. 23 46 1:10

Which is better? It depends. I usually prefer the former. Even though they both have the same 23 second turn-time, the first horse figures to be five lengths in front of the second at the quarter pole. Unless the track is heavily biased toward closers, I'll take the first horse. The above example points out the need to consider turn-time in conjunction with the second call. I call this factor "adjusted turn-time." To compute adjusted turn-time, we first calculate the horse's actual turn-time and then add this number to the horse's actual second call time. The smaller, the better.

Just to make sure that you understand these concepts, let's do a few examples.

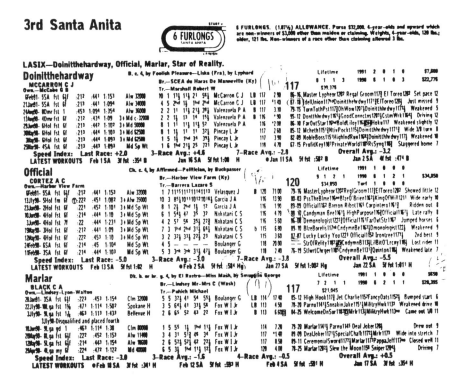

The 6½ dirt pars for NW1 at Santa Anita were: 21^4 44^3 $1:16^2$ (in fifths), or 21.8 44.6 1:16.4 (in tenths). (The reason we use tenths is to allow for beaten half-lengths. It's always best to convert everything to tenths. To convert to tenths, simply multiply the number of fifths by two.) Using the February 6 race, Doinitthehardway had a raw turn-time of 22.8, hence an adjusted turn-time of 67.0 (22.8 plus 44.2).

Using the same February 6 race for Official, his first fraction time was 24.4 and his second fraction was 47.6. His turn-time was 23.2 and his adjusted turn-time was 70.8.

Using the January 20 race for Marlar, his first fraction time was 23.1 and his second fraction was 45.8. His turn-time was 22.7 and his adjusted turn-time was 68.5.

The adjusted turn-time par is at least 67.4 (in tenths). The reason that I say "at least" is because the win profile may allow eventual winners to be a few lengths behind the race par times.

It's easy to see that Doinitthehardway has a definite pace advantage within this group. His above par adjusted turn-time makes him a threat. If they run similar fractions today, he'll have an eight-length lead after a half-mile. It's real tough to overhaul this kind of lead. Needless to say, Doinitthehardway won this race easily.

ABILITY STANDARDS

It's not a bad idea to develop an "ability time" par. This can easily be accomplished from observing the win profile. Simply adjust the fractional par times by the average beaten lengths of the winner for each of the last ten races at today's distance and surface, and then calculate the ability time par. Then add this number to the second call par. Suppose our win profile demanded that horses must be within approximately two lengths at the first call and one length at the second call. Therefore, we would take the race pars for six furlongs and adjust them by two lengths at the first call and one length at the second call.

Example: The Santa Anita 6F $20,000 claiming pars are 21^4 45 1:10^1. To develop the turn-time par, we adjust these times by beaten lengths from our profile. Hence the adjusted times (in fifths), are 22^1 45^1 1:10^1. We now observe that the "turn-time par" is 23 seconds (45^1 minus 22^1) and the adjusted turn-time is 68.2 (23 plus 45^1). We now have an "ability time par." We look for horses who have demonstrated an ability time of 68.2 or less. (Please note that we used fifths because things came out evenly. As mentioned before, it's best to convert to tenths.)

We now have an ability standard. If horses are to win a $20,000 claiming race at Santa Anita, they should have an ability time that's close to 68.2. Please remember that we always allow a two-length leeway, so don't start eliminating contenders unless their ability times are greater than 68.4.

Thus far we have examined class, pace, and ability standards. We must now consider the problem of distance changes and shippers. We want to develop a set of standards that we can use to compare apples to apples. Unfortunately, we must make some questionable assumptions. The first assumption is that horses will run consistently across all distances, and run comparative performances on different tracks. This of course denies the horses-for-courses phenomenon and the distance preferences that horses usually display. Handicapping isn't an exact science. We have to settle for the truth of percentages instead of precise truth. We have the same problem that meteorologists have; namely, that our truth is a percentage truth while the result is absolute. The weatherman says that there's a thirty percent chance of showers tomorrow. He really can't be correct. It either rains the next day or not. We're doing the same thing. We say that a horse has a thirty percent chance to win a race. It either wins or not. With this in mind, let's fearlessly attack the problem of distance switches.

DISTANCE-TO-DISTANCE ADJUSTMENTS

All adjustments are made by comparing the par times and noting the differentials. These differentials are the adjustments. You first adjust the race for beaten lengths and then you apply the differentials. (If you first applied the differentials and then applied the beaten lengths, the result would be the same.)

The handicapper chooses a representative race for a contender. It's usually best to choose a race at the same distance as today's race. Many times this isn't possible, hence the need for distance adjustments.

Suppose that today's race is a six-furlong sprint for allowance non-winners of two races at Santa Anita. The par times for this level of race are: 21^3 44^2 $1:09^2$. The horse that we are considering only shows a recent 6½-furlong race at Santa Anita. This horse shows a running line of 22^3 45^3 1.15^4 $3^{2½}$ 4^1 5^4 $5^{5½}$. The way we accomplish the adjustment is to line up the pars for six furlongs and for 6½ furlongs and note the differentials.

6F pars (today's race)	21^3	44^2	$1:09^2$
6½F pars (paceline)	21^2	44^2	$1:16$
differential	0^1	0	-6^3

The differentials become the adjustments. The above says that the 6½F runs one tick (.2 seconds) faster at the quarter, runs the same to the half, and the final half-furlong is run in 6.6 seconds. In order to bring these performances together, we must add a tick (one-fifth second) to the 6½F first call, leave the second call alone, and deduct 6.6 seconds from the final time.

We first look at the horse's 6½F times adjusted by beaten lengths. It's best to work in tenths of seconds to allow for half-lengths: 22^3 is the same as 22.6; 45^3 can be written as 45.6; and $1:15^4$ is the same as 1:15.8. We see that this horse was 2½ lengths behind a 22.6 pace at the first call. This means that his adjusted first call time becomes 22.6 plus .5 (which is 2½ × .2) seconds, for a total of 23.1. He was one length behind a 45.6 at the second call. This means that his time was 45.8. He was 5½ lengths behind 1:15.8 at the wire. His final time was 1:16.9. We now apply the differentials to get his 6F adjusted times. They are 23.3 45.8 1:10.3.

Let's do a more extreme example. Suppose we had to use a route race of 1¹⁄₁₆ miles with the following paceline: 47 $1:12^2$ $1:44^1$ $4^{1½}$ 2^1 2^{nk} 1no in the same Santa Anita NW2 race. The Santa Anita NW2 1¹⁄₁₆ mile pars are: 45^4 1:10 $1:42^1$. Let's first convert all times to tenths of seconds.

6F pars (today's race)	21.6	44.4	1:09.4
1¹⁄₁₆ pars (paceline)	45.8	1:10.0	1:42.2
differential	−24.2	−25.6	−32.8

For this example, let's apply the differentials before we apply the beaten lengths, and then do it the other way just to prove that we get the same result. We'll take the raw 1¹⁄₁₆ mile time in tenths and apply the above differentials. The raw times of 47 1:12.4 1:44.2 adjusted to 6F become 22.8 46.8 1:11.4. We now apply the beaten lengths for adjusted final times of 23.1 47 1:11.4.

Doing it the other way, we see that 1½ lengths behind a 47 is 47.3, and one length behind a 1:12.4 is 1:12.6, and the final time is unchanged. Subtracting 24.2 from 47.3, we get 23.1. Subtracting 25.6 from 1:12.6 (which is 72.6), we get 47, and subtracting 32.8 from 1:44.2, we get 1:11.4.

In the workshop section (Chapter 13) we'll review this adjustment procedure and take it one step further. For the moment, just realize that you must first line up the pars and figure the differentials. Apply the differentials to the raw times, then adjust for beaten lengths, or adjust for beaten lengths first and then apply the differentials. I usually do it the second way. It doesn't matter—the results are the same either way. This is an example of an operation which is "commutative." It means that the order doesn't matter. A non-commutative operation is putting on your shoes and socks. Please try to avoid route-to-sprint adjustments and vice versa when possible. Let's now look at track-to-track adjustments.

TRACK-TO-TRACK ADJUSTMENTS

The principle is the same. You line up the pars for a representative distance with the pars for the distance of today's race. (You can actually do a distance adjustment at the same time.) This allows you to bring together races at distances that are not even offered at your track with today's distance. Once this is done, you can apply the beaten lengths and then the differentials or vice versa. We now have the wherewithal to bring races from all over the country onto your track. This is especially important when dealing with graded stakes races. Please note that you always compare the pars at the class of today's race with the same class at the foreign track. It may be that the horse in question is moving up in class for today's race. One of our underlying assumptions is that class is speed. If a horse can run with the pars of a higher class, then it has been running with competition below its level of ability. This also eliminates the need for class adjustments.

Suppose today's race is a one-mile claiming $12,500 race at Santa Anita whose par times are 47.4 1:12.6 1:38.8. A contender shows a $10,000 claiming race run at 1 mile 40 yards at Penn National. The running line is as follows: 46^1 1:12 $1:43^1$ 2^1 1^1 1^2 1^2.

We must compare the $12,500 one-mile pars at Santa Anita to the $12,500 1 mile 40 yards at Penn National. It's vital that you use the class of today's race.

Santa Anita $12,500	1 mile	47.4	1:12.6	1:38.8
Penn National $12,500	1 mile 40	46.4	1:12.0	1:43.4
differential		+1	+.6	−4.6

To bring these tracks and distances together, we must add a second to the Penn National first call, we must add .6 seconds to the second Penn National call, and finally we must subtract 4.6 seconds from the Penn National final time.

The Penn National running line in tenths was 46.2 1:12 1:43.2. Applying the differentials, we get 47.2 1:12.6 1:38.6. Applying the beaten lengths, the final adjusted times are 47.4 1:12.6 1:38.6. These times are quite competitive.

Our method is now almost complete. We know how to recognize contenders. We have class, pace, and ability standards. We know how to handle distance switches and track switches. Our method assumes zero track variance. (Usually not the worst assumption in the world, as you'll see.) The only thing left is how to handle daily track variants. Since we don't want to spend our lives computing variants, we must find a way to deal with the *Daily Racing Form* (DRF) variants.

THE DRF VARIANT

The DRF variant comes under heavy fire from experienced speed handicappers. Some of the criticisms most mentioned are that it's based on too few races, it fluctuates by day of the week because of class, and it's not based upon class pars. All of the above and more notwithstanding, a way must be found to be able to deal with this most inaccurate way of doing things. After reams of computer paper and many computer algorithms, I think that there's a reasonable way to deal with this issue.

Fortunately, the DRF in recent years has separated the sprint and route variant for a given day. Instead of using class par times, they use the fastest race run at the distance over the past three years as their standard. All speed ratings are based upon these unusually very fast times. Average variations from these times is what constitutes the DRF daily sprint and route variant. When you look at the columns labeled SR and TV, you'll see numbers such as 84 10. The 84 means that this race was 16 ticks slower than the fastest time recorded for this distance. The 10 means that all the races of the same type (sprint or route) averaged out to 90 for that day. The variant is the average deviation from your standard. A quick check to see if a race ran fast or slow is to add the speed rating to the track variant. In this case 84 plus 10 is 94. This indicates a slow race for the track conditions. Numbers below 100 indicate slow, and numbers above 100 indicate fast, considering the prevailing conditions. Actually we want to see the SR number being large. Don't get too excited by a 56 44. You would much rather see a 90 10.

The DRF variant must be composed of two parts. The first part is the difference between today's class-level par and the fastest race run in the past three years. The balance is due to unexplained conditions.

Consider the following Santa Anita $25,000 claiming 6F running line:

$$22^1 \ \ 45 \ \ 1{:}11^3 \ \ \ 3^1 \ \ 3^{1\frac{1}{2}} \ \ 3^1 \ \ 1\frac{1}{4} \ \ \ 78 \ \ 17$$

How do we interpret this 17 variant? The 78 speed rating indicates that this race was run 22 ticks slower than the fastest race in the past three years. Hence it must have been $4\frac{2}{5}$ faster than the $1{:}11^3$, which means that it had to be $1{:}07^1$. This also happens to be the track record. Our class pars for $25,000 claiming show that 1:10 is to be expected. Therefore $2\frac{4}{5}$ seconds (14 ticks) can be explained by class. This is the difference between $1{:}07^1$ and 1:10. Therefore, 14 points of the 17 can be explained. Hence the 17 DRF variant means that we can't explain 3 ticks. We therefore attribute them to track conditions. The trick is how to apply the three ticks. The track caused the race to be three ticks slow. The standard approach is to apply the variant proportionally to the distance of the fractions. In this case the fractions are equal, so we would apply 1 tick per fraction. What's tricky is that we have to apply 1 tick to the first fraction, two ticks to the second fraction, and three ticks to the final time.

The reason for this is that variance is cumulative, if we assume that it occurs uniformly throughout the entire track. (As we shall see, this assumption is generally false and gets us into deep trouble.) Again, using the standard approach, we end up upgrading the first call by 1 tick, the second call by 2 ticks, and the final time by 3 ticks. Hence the pace-adjusted times of 22.4 45.3 1:11.6 must be variant-adjusted to 22.2 44.9 1:11.

To illustrate the effect of a variant adjustment, suppose the above pace line read:

22^1 45 $1:11^3$ 3^1 $3^{1\frac{1}{2}}$ 3^1 $1^{\frac{1}{4}}$ 78 22

This suggests that 8 ticks are unexplainable by class. This means that the track was real slow that particular day. We must therefore adjust the first call by ⅔ ticks or 2.67 lengths, the second call by 5.34 lengths, and the final time by 8 ticks. The 22.4 45.3 1:11.3 times must be variant-adjusted to 21.86 44.23 1:10. We now see that this represents a near-par performance. That's as it should be, considering that the DRF speed rating plus track variant adds up to 100, which suggests a par performance.

This adjustment can also be negative, as in the following case.

22^1 45 $1:11^3$ 3^1 $3^{1\frac{1}{2}}$ 3^1 $1^{\frac{1}{4}}$ 78 10

This suggests that −4 lengths are unexplainable by class. This means that the track was fast that particular day. We must therefore adjust the first call by −4/3 ticks (−.27 seconds) or minus 1.33 lengths, the second call by − 2.66 lengths (−.53 seconds), and the final time by −4 ticks (−.8 seconds). The 22.4 45.3 1:11.3 times must be variant-adjusted to 22.67 45.83 1:12.4. We now see that this represents a sub-par performance. That's as it should be, considering the DRF speed rating plus track variant adds to 88, which suggests a sub-par performance.

This variant adjustment gets even trickier at different distances. Below is a table showing how to allocate the unexplained part of the DRF track variant to the first two calls using the standard approach. All of it is applied to the final time.

Furlongs	1st Call	2nd Call	Final Time
6	.33	.66	1.00
6½	.31	.62	1.00
7	.29	.57	1.00
7½	.27	.53	1.00
8	.50	.75	1.00
8½	.47	.70	1.00
9	.44	.67	1.00
9½	.42	.63	1.00

You must be very careful in using this adjustment. It can actually project a horse faster than his ability at the second call. Always do a reality check on your adjusted figures. Go back to the past performances and verify that the horse has actually run to the projected times. If he hasn't, you must dampen the adjustment.

Gordon Pine, a very gifted handicapper, squares the fractional contributions from the above table. So, for example, in a six-furlong race, he doesn't use the .33 .66 fractional adjustments. He uses .11 and .44 as his multipliers for the first and second call contributions respectively. He argues that the DRF variant is a bad number. He has done extensive studies that prove you can disregard the DRF variant altogether and not suffer a significant loss of ROI. He Has Found a Compromise Solution. You simply square the first call and second call adjustment. The new variant allocation table looks as follows:

Furlongs	1st Call	2nd Call	Final Time
6	.11	.44	1.00
6½	.10	.38	1.00
7	.08	.32	1.00
7½	.07	.28	1.00
8	.25	.56	1.00
8½	.22	.49	1.00
9	.19	.45	1.00
9½	.18	.40	1.00

The best way to deal with the DRF variant is to dampen it. This is a case where the theory and the reality are in disagreement. The theory sounds plausible, but it doesn't stand up to a harsh reality check. When theory and reality disagree, reality prevails. I suggest that you use Gordon Pine's adjustments.

If the variants for your contenders are all within four points of each other, skip the variant adjustment.

Please note that I don't recommend speed methods at classic distances (1¼ miles and above), because class laughs at pace at 1¼ miles and longer distances. The only exception is the Kentucky Derby. Since none of the contenders have gone the 1¼-mile distance, they can be rated from their 8½-furlong races.

There's one final idea that you must abide by, or forever be the victim of slow horses. It's the concept of chaos. Whenever you have a race in which no horse can run to the pars or profiles— you have chaos. Chaos means random disorder or lack of order. That's exactly what happens in these kinds of races. You can take your figures and throw them out the window. Your fourth choice is just as likely to win as your first choice. It's best to pass these races or take a very aggressive stand and "swing for the fences."

Ron Ambrose discovered this powerful concept when he did a study of why favorites fail. I confirmed this principle from the results of a study that investigated winning horses that paid huge mutuels. One of my specialties is to find exacta combinations that will pay over 50-to-1 and have a 5 percent or more chance of winning. Needless to say, these opportunities only arise in races where chaos prevails.

The principle of chaos is so powerful that it can be used to determine if a race is playable or not. If you're like Ron Ambrose, you'll define a playable race as a race that contains no more than three contenders. (Ambrose's definition of a contender is a horse that can run to the final-time win pars and has the proper pace profile.) In other words, Ambrose detests chaos. Ambrose can afford to be picky. He lives in Las Vegas and has over a hundred races per day to choose from. He averages about eight or nine plays per day.

If you're like me, you'll get excited about races where chaos prevails. You usually can take the top three public favorites and throw them out. Normally, the way I play these races is to take the top five ability-time horses (regardless of win odds) and look at the matrix of the twenty possible exacta combinations. I bet all exactas that are paying over $100.

Please tune in to the concept of chaos. Every race that you handicap can be labeled "predictable" or "chaotic." There are strategies for each type of race.

We now have the wherewithal to compare any performance on any track to any other performance on the same or different track and take the DRF variant into consideration. Please read each example in the workshop section very carefully (Chapter

13). It's meant to elaborate on the fundamental concepts presented thus far.

All the ability in the world will do an athlete absolutely no good unless that athlete is in form and condition to deliver it. Let's now turn our attention to the form factor.

Chapter 5

Form and Condition

LET'S MAKE THE FORM FACTOR dramatic. Suppose that you can eliminate a typical everyday plain vanilla favorite because of your knowledge of the form factor. A 2-to-1 favorite. If you can do this, it doesn't matter what other horse you bet on, because you have an edge. The 2-to-1 favorite takes more than 33 percent of the pool. If you can eliminate one-third of the pool and you're playing where the track take is less than 20 percent, you have a nice edge. In most states the track take is anywhere from 15 to 19 percent. In the worst case, you have a 14 percent edge. It doesn't matter which other horse you bet on, it's most likely an overlay. With a little handicapping, you'll be able to make a very judicious investment. Please believe me when I tell you that 4-to-5 favorites can be eliminated almost as easily as 2-to-1 or 5-to-2 lukewarm favorites. The average handicapper really doesn't have a good knowledge of the form factor, and therefore can't make these eliminations. Please study this chapter carefully. If you learn its lessons, you'll be able to eliminate many false and vulnerable favorites—a skill that you'll be able to turn into cash.

When we look at the form factor, there are five considerations that we have to keep in mind. They are: recency, workout pattern, form cycle, form angles, and form eliminations. What we're trying to accomplish is a correct prediction of whether a horse will improve, decline, or remain about the same. If we can find a race favorite who is going south, and at the same time find an undervalued horse who is going north, we'll have the best of it. Let's get started with recency.

RECENCY

In days of old, handicappers were urged to never bet on a horse that had been away from the racetrack for a specific number of days. Usually 30 days. Fred Davis pointed out that 14 days was magic. In other words, horses coming back in less than 14 days won far more than their fair share of races. One handicapping author took this to the extreme and advised his readers never to bet a horse that had been away for more than 14 days. That wasn't good advice. As a matter of fact, it was bad advice. The concept of recency, because of the proliferation of racing dates, must be redefined. Horses are asked to perform more than they would under ordinary circumstances. They are pushed to the limits of their physical abilities and need time after a hard campaign to rest and recuperate. Periodic layoffs allow them to avoid serious injury and begin a new training cycle that'll bring them to the peak of their ability. The recency factor is a function of class. The higher the class, the longer a horse can lay off without serious form deterioration. If a graded stakes winner is off for 45 days, it's not going to bother us too much. However, if a $10,000 claimer's off for 45 days without any workouts, we're going to be rather suspicious. Our computer studies have generated some magic numbers. The number for maidens is about 17. In other words, if a maiden is coming back in less than 17 days, we won't require a workout. We'll accept its current form. For claiming horses, the magic number is in the low twenties. Again, if a claiming horse has run within the last three weeks, we won't require a workout. Allowance horses are up in the mid-twenties; maximum is 28 days. Beyond that we'll insist on at least one workout. I'll give you the workout criteria in the next section. The main idea is, recency standards need not be too strict. The guidelines are simple. As we descend the class ladder, we'll insist upon more recent races. Horses not meeting our standards have form clouds over their heads. You should draw a squiggly line around the horse's name in the *Racing Form* to denote a form cloud. This horse becomes suspicious because it should be either training or racing into form.

There's a very logical and profitable way to deal with the layoff factor. You look for evidence that this horse can successfully come back from a layoff. You scan its past performances and find what it did after a layoff. If it won or ran an excellent race after a previous layoff, you'll accept its current form. If it failed, you'll reject its current form. The idea is simple. If a horse has demonstrated that it can succeed after a layoff, you have no reason to be suspicious of its form. If, on the other hand, it has demonstrated that it needs a race or two to get into shape, you now conclude that it probably won't succeed today.

What do you do when you don't see a previous layoff? Mark Cramer gave us the answer if it's a young horse with less than ten races. You look at his first-time start. If it was a win or an excellent race, you accept its current form. If it was a poor to mediocre race, you reject its current form. Mark Cramer is a very clever and creative handicapper. Please read everything that he has ever written, especially his last book, *Thoroughbred Cycles*. It's a wonderful book and contains lots of form factor information. He's been a winning player for over twenty years and is the person most responsible for my success at thoroughbred handicapping. He taught me how to win.

Here's a very valuable piece of research, compliments of Ron Ambrose. Prevailing handicapping wisdom says that it's easier for a laid-off horse to succeed in a route than a sprint. The usual explanation is that a sprint demands grueling fractions, and most sprinters need to race into condition. Whereas, a route race doesn't demand too much because it's a more tactical race. Sounds plausible. Yes, it does—but the data say otherwise. Ambrose's study concludes that it's much more likely that a sprinter will succeed after a layoff than a router. If a router has never won (or run to the pars) after a layoff, he's an automatic throw-out for me.

If you don't see a previous layoff and the horse has more than ten races, you must apply the workout standards.

WORKOUTS

Have you ever gone to a racetrack and watched the morning workouts? I don't know about you, but to me it's organized chaos. I can't figure out what's going on. There's no way you can tell who the horses are. There's only one or two clockers, with five or six horses running at the same time. It's just a mess. Then you watch a workout and you don't know if a 110-pound jockey is working the horse or if a 140-pound exercise rider is riding the horse. You don't know the starting point of their workout. The only time that you can be sure is when it's a gate work. To add to the confusion, some trainers work their horses fast and others insist upon not exerting them in the morning.

Given this chaos, my feelings on the subject are that I'm not terribly concerned about the time of a workout. I'm only concerned with the frequency. I'm not impressed by things like bullet works. There are horses who are morning glories. Workout time is only significant when it's faster than race time. In other words, if a horse works four furlongs in 47^3 and the winner's par is 47^4, this horse is actually working out faster than race time, and that should get your attention. That's significant. Again, the only time that workout time is significant is when it's faster than race time. Please don't worry about whether a horse had a bullet workout or not.

Our computer studies have proven that frequency of workouts is far more important than time. Workouts are hand-timed and subject to huge errors. Many workouts go unpublished. In general, these data are suspect. Ron Ambrose discovered that the workout factor that's most statistically significant is "furlongs per day." Very similar to the recency criteria, workout criteria are a function of class. The higher the class, the more lenient the standards become.

Here's how you determine furlongs per day: Consider only workouts since the horse's last race. If it's a first-time starter or a horse off a long layoff, we'll use all of the horse's visible works. Next, add up the number of furlongs and then divide this by the number of days since the earliest of these works. Let's do a few examples to make sure that we understand this concept.

This was the fourth race at Hollywood Park on July 10, 1991. Miss Radar last ran on September 5, 1990. She has been off for ten months. Her earliest visible work was on June 22. That was 18 days ago. She has worked a total of 17 furlongs in 18 days. This is quite acceptable.

Miss Sundial is a first-time starter. She has worked only 17 furlongs since June 6. This isn't acceptable. She only averaged one-half furlong per day. We require almost a full furlong per day for maidens.

Wendy's Star is also coming off a layoff. She has worked 19 furlongs since June 12. This is marginal at best. She averaged .68 fpd. This number should be closer to 1.

Nordic Valentine is a first-time starter. She has worked 26 furlongs in 28 days. This is acceptable.

Zaida has worked 18 furlongs in the last 20 days. This is acceptable.

Again, for maidens, you want to see close to an average of one furlong per day. You can cheat a little. You can add 5 furlongs to the total of 4 workouts or 3 furlongs to the total of 3 workouts. To illustrate, consider Zaida's workout performance. You would add 5 furlongs to her 4 works' total of 18 to get an average of 1.28 fpd. You also could have added 3 furlongs to her three works' total of 14 to get an average of 1.21 fpd. The reason for this "cheat factor" is the conclusions of Ron Ambrose's longitudinal study of maiden winners. He found by adding these respective numbers of furlongs to the totals, he included 80 percent of all maiden winners.

For claiming horses, you want to see close to an average of .67 furlongs per day with no cheat factor. For allowance and stakes horses, you want to see an average of at least .6 fpd.

Remember to only apply these standards when a horse lacks recency. Next we'll tackle the question of how to predict whether a horse will improve, decline, or run about the same as previously.

FORM CYCLES

Most handicappers aren't tuned in to form cycles. The interesting thing about form cycles are that they not only apply to horses, they apply to human athletes as well. The idea is to train up to a peak performance knowing full well that the price is form regression. Athletes are willing to train up to a point where they're at a physical peak. Then they push themselves beyond it. They'll then achieve a personal best. They understand that when they expend this energy, it will actually cause a form decline. The goal of Olympic training is to get to a peak just before your event and then expend maximum energy. Mary Lou Retton, the gold medal gymnast, freely admits that she'll never get back to her 1988 form.

A similar phenomenon happens with horses. When a horse reaches its peak condition, it's ready for a personal best. If that personal best is too much better than its previous best, this usually results in a temporary form regression known as the "bounce."

Most of the literature talks about a personal best being achieved after a layoff as a good predictor of a bounce. This is true. However, the bounce is a more generic concept. When older horses achieve a personal best (or "top") that's significantly above their previous best, you should be looking for the bounce. You must be very careful with two-year-olds and young three-year-olds. They can improve and decline dramatically. It's very difficult to establish a top for young horses. However, it's rather easy to deal with older horses. In fact, you can't go too far wrong by assuming that an older horse has already shown you its top. It's very wise not to try to predict a dramatic form improvement for older horses. That's not to say that it doesn't happen. It does. But it's damn hard to predict.

It's nice to be able to predict a bounce because the public usually solidly backs a recent victory. When a recent victor bounces, the public usually doesn't back the horse the next time out, and many times it "bounces back." The public tends to zig when they should zag, and vice versa. If we are tuned in, we'll be zigging when we should zig and zagging when we should zag. We predict the bounce and get off the recent victor—then we predict a bounce back and usually get generous odds.

Form cycle analysis is not an exact science. The idea is to scan a horse's past performances near the distance of today's race and see if we can determine a pattern. We know that horses are athletes, hence subject to form cycles. The more we practice, the more accurate our predictions will become. A little trick is to look for a horse's personal best and see if its recent races are approaching it or tailing away from it. Please remember that classy horses have longer form cycles. A graded stakes winner can run practically the same numbers for all ten of its past performances. The bottom of the barrel horses at your track may have one- or two-race form cycles. Some can never put two good races back to back. It's interesting to study repeat winners at the lower levels. In southern California, where the bottom is $10,000 claimers, winners fail to repeat over 88 percent of the time. A recent $10,000 claiming winner coming back into a $10,000 race is an automatic throw-out.

The very best way to observe form cycles is to watch the pattern of adjusted final times for a given distance on a fast track. This means that you must have good speed figures. If you don't, the next best thing is to add the DRF speed rating to the DRF variant and note the pattern in the totals. If you use the Beyer numbers, you have fairly good speed numbers.

If you use the *Daily Racing Form* speed rating plus the variant, consider ratings within 4 points as equal. For example, a horse has run 88, 85, and 89 in its last three races. Your conclusion would be that he ran basically the same race three times in a row. It's only when the range is 5 points or more that we attach any significance to the numbers. Same for the Beyer numbers. Suppose that you saw, in chronological order, 93, 95, and 104 ratings. What would your conclusion be? This is an improving pattern. Would you predict improvement or decline the next race? The correct answer is that it depends. If the horse was a three-year-old, you could predict improvement. If the horse was a four-year-old and its personal best was 104, you could predict a decline. If the horse's personal best was above 104, you would predict a number near 104. The best way to practice is to take out a *Racing Form* and look at all the races below the last one. What do they predict? Was the prediction correct? After a little practice, you'll get the correct answer most of the time. What's really important about doing this exercise is that you are tuned in to the form factor. Would you like to see what a typical false favorite looks like? Consider the past performances of Irontree. He was entered into a six-furlong claiming $25,000 race at Hollywood Park on June 21, 1991. He was the lukewarm 5-to-2 favorite.

Look at the numbers for his last five races: 102, 96, 103, 102, and 95. We see a big race after a layoff, followed by a regression, followed by two good races, then followed by a slight regression.

Irontree Ch. g. 4, by Blade—Baby Doon, by Matsadoon
VALENZUELA P A $25,000 Br.—McMillin Bros (Ky) 118 Lifetime 13 4 2 1 $84,828 | 1991 5 1 1 0 $27,350 | 1990 8 3 1 1 $57,470
Own.—Burke G W Tr.—Mitchell Mike

12Jun91- 5Hol	fst	6f	:22	:442	1:091	Clm 45000	2	7	31½	42	55	67½	Solis A	LBb	114	7.40	86-09	OnForNn1182¾DnwProspctr116½LrnsQst1162¾	Stumbled start	7
30May91- 7Hol	fst	6f	:22	:443	1:094	Clm 62500	7	2	32½	32	42¾	41¾	Valenzuela P A	LBb	117	5.00	89-13	OneForNn114noCoveWy1171DnweProspctor114¾	Bumped late	8
18May91- 7Hol	fst	6f	:212	:441	1:093	Clm 50000	6	1	31½	31	2½	1½	Valenzuela P A	LBb	116	*2.40	92-11	Irontree116½ Happy In Space116nk Snow Perch1163¾	Driving	7
5May91- 4Hol	fst	6f	:22	:443	1:091	3↑Alw 36000	4	5	76¼	76	58½	48¾	Pincay L Jr	LBb	118	5.00	85-11	DblRoug1144½MstrLyphor1183½ShnngPrnc112¾	5-wide stretch	7
22Apr91- 3SA	fst	6½f	:213	:443	1:161	Clm c-40000	6	3	42	3½	1hd	2nk	Stevens G L	LBb	115	4.00	89-13	Doncreer115nkIrontree1153Movinglikewinner1156	Bumped 1/16	6
30Sep90-10Fpx	fst	6½f	:212	:451	1:161	3↑Alw 36000	4	2	31	21	21	43¼	Flores D R	LBb	115	*1.50	93-07	Petrolero-Ar1181½ Kipper Kelly115nkComical1141½	No excuse	5
16Sep90-10Fpx	fst	6½f	:214	:444	1:161	3↑Alw 34000	8	2	31	2hd	11	14	Flores D R	LBb	114	3.60	95-09	Irontree1144 Ideal Union1121½ Its Unbelievable1123	Driving	8
31Aug90- 5Dmr	fst	6f	:214	:443	1:093	Clm 32000	3	3	1½	11½	13	12¾	Stevens G L	LBb	117	12.90	92-13	Irontree1172¾ One For Nana1161½ Hoku117¾	Ridden out	9
6Aug90- 3Dmr	fst	6½f	:214	:44	1:153	Clm 50000	5	4	41¼	31½	33	711¾	Desormeaux KJ	Lb	117	16.00	78-08	Gundaghia1164 Devine Force1102¾ Stan's Boy1151½	Faltered	9
28Jly90- 6Hol	fst	6f	:214	:45	1:094	3↑Md 50000	9	2	1hd	1½	12	1nk	Desormeaux KJ	Lb	116	2.20	91-11	Irontree116nk Jawan1172¾ Marfa's Boy1162¾	Driving	12

Speed Index: Last Race: −5.0 3–Race Avg.: 0.0 10–Race Avg.: −0.4 Overall Avg.: −0.4
LATEST WORKOUTS May 27 Hol 3f fst :36 H May 1 Hol 3f fst :352 H

He's dropping fifty percent in class, even though he had an excuse in his last race—he stumbled at the start. This doesn't make any economic sense whatsoever. Why would the horse's connections sell it for half its value after it posted a decent number while having an excuse? There are only two reasons. They have taken vows of poverty and are liquidating their present assets or they are trying to sell distressed merchandise. As a handicapper, you must be suspicious of either reason. Please take every opportunity to bet against these kinds of favorites.

Here's an example of a pattern that you like to see:

Surprise Ambush Ro. h. 5, by Relaunch—A Surprise, by Bold Bidder
PEDROZA M A Br.—Hilary Jr–Hilary III–Boone–Huger (Ky) 121 Lifetime 24 2 5 3 $75,680 | 1991 2 1 0 0 $11,000 | 1990 5 0 1 0 $10,150 | Turf 3 0 0 1 $5,475
Own.—Siegel M–Jan–Samantha Tr.—Mayberry Brian A

26May91- 1Hol	fst	6f	:22	:45	1:101	Clm 25000	4	2	1½	11½	12½	15	Pedroza M A	LB	116	5.10	89-12	SrprsAmbsh1165Lyphrd'sFn1142ArYoMyCsy116nk	Ridden out	7
10May91- 9Hol	fst	6½f	:214	:442	1:161	Clm 25000	8	5	11	1hd	31½	76¾	Pedroza M A	LB	116	14.00	84-13	One For Nana1162 Ruff Hombre1181½ Edict116½	Gave way	12
17May90- 3Hol	fst	6f	:22	:444	1:091	Clm 40000	6	3	43	32	42	46	Pedroza M A		117	12.20	88-11	High Hook1172¾ Happy Idiot117¾ Pinecutter1172¼	Weakened	7
18Apr90- 6GG	fst	6f	:212	:434	1:10	Alw 20000	5	3	32½	32	43½	42½	Doocy T T		119	3.20	85-13	HeftyFee119hdToughSwabbie1191FairwayBrgin1191½	No rally	7
25Mar90- 7SA	fst	6½f	:214	:451	1:161	Clm 40000	4	1	3½	1½	2hd	23½	Pedroza M A		116	6.20	85-15	ChprrlMotl1163½SurprsAmbush1163½Wtch'nWn1201	Gave way	8
25Jan90- 5SA	fm	*6½f	ⓣ:212	:433	1:134	Alw 34000	6	5	53	64	64½	76½	Pedroza M A		120	4.00	86-06	SomForst1202SwngShft1201ShdwySml117¾	Broke awkwardly	10
10Jan90- 7SA	fst	1	:45	1:094	1:352	Alw 37000	7	3	32	2½	3½	55¾	Stevens G L		118	7.50	84-15	Stphn'sSoonr120½RollingDont1201½MntnStrm1161¾	Weakened	8
26Dec89- 4SA	fst	1	:461	1:102	1:353	Alw 37000	1	2	21	21½	32½	35¾	Pedroza M A		117	8.30	85-13	Mythical Being1174 Rolling Donut1201¾ SurpriseAmbush117¾		10
12Nov89- 7SA	fst	1	:452	1:094	1:361	Alw 34000	1	3	32½	33	31½	42	Pedroza M A		118	14.00	86-14	ExplodingProspect1181½CollegeCredit111½RecordBoom118hd		8
30Sep89-10Fpx	fst	6½f	:213	:45	1:17	3↑Alw 33000	2	1	42½	65½	72½	78¾	Sibille R		116	8.20	82-13	Charlatan1144½ Ask The Man111¾ Clever Return115½		7

Speed Index: Last Race: +1.0 3–Race Avg.: −1.0 6–Race Avg.: −1.6 Overall Avg.: −1.9
LATEST WORKOUTS Jun 12 Hol 4f fst :463 H May 23 Hol 3f fst :361 H Apr 26 Hol 5f fst :594 H

Today's race is a 6½-furlong allowance $32,000 for non-winners of $3000 other than maiden, claiming, or starter. Look at his last three sprints at Hollywood Park: 99, 97, 101. He won his last race convincingly, even though he ran basically the same race three times in a row. He is now moving up into a very soft allowance condition. This makes economic sense. He's quite acceptable on form.

Mid-range claiming horses are the bread and butter of most racing cards. Horses that tend to maintain a three- or four-race form cycle are the ones you want to back. You look for consistent horses that have the ability to run back to the same number three or four times in succession. Those are the ones you can have a reasonable degree of confidence in. The ones that don't have cycles that long should make you reluctant to bet with both hands. It's a very good idea to bet against horses that can't maintain at least three good races in a row.

Another excellent method of determining a form cycle is to look at the horse's ability times. If they are improving, the horse is coming to the top of his game. If they are declining, so is the horse's form. If they are fairly constant, the horse is a steady performer.

Also, look for newfound early speed—it's a sign of form improvement. It's a wake-up sign. The key to performance improvement is the ability to sustain speed for longer distances. Look for horses who ran against a brisk pace last time, ran close to the ability par, and figure to have the lead today. Most of the time these horses are able to sustain their speed.

Before we move on to the subject of form angles, let me share with you some of the more blatant myths regarding the form factor. The first is to look for horses that beat at least half of the field in their last race. The truth is, position is meaningless at any point in a previous race. Position is not a predictor of today's outcome. This is even true for the first call. Consider the following running lines:

1. 22^4 45^4 $1{:}11$ 1^2 1^1 2^3 3^5
2. 22 45 $1{:}10$ 3^2 4^2 5^3 7^4

The first horse never had a position worse than third, beat half its field, and was on the lead for two-thirds of the race. The second horse never had a position *better* than third, and failed to beat half its field. If these two matched up today, I would unequivocally bet on the second horse. It figures to have a two-length lead at the second call and be six lengths better at the wire. I hope this demonstrates the futility of position handicapping. Position isn't important, time is. Three lengths behind a 45-second half-mile is still two lengths faster than the leader who ran a 46-second half.

The next pervasive myth that I'd like to debunk is that stretch gain is important. Handicappers are advised not to bet on horses that lost lengths in the stretch of their last race. We have computer studies of tens of thousands of races that clearly conclude that stretch gain or stretch loss is statistically insignificant. That is, they have no predictive value whatsoever.

Another great myth is that a horse's "come home time" (the time it takes to run the last fraction) in its last race is an indicator of ability. Nothing could be further from the truth, except in turf races. Come home time is usually a function of the pace of the race. Horses who let the pace get away from them can and do have faster come home times than the winner of the race. As discussed earlier, the second fraction time is the best predictor of ability.

FORM ANGLES

A form angle is a circumstance where a horse will improve its form dramatically. The very first one that comes to mind is a concept called "horses for courses." It's simply the observation that some horses run better at particular tracks than at others. You must be really careful not to back horses that have demonstrated they don't like today's track. Mark Cramer showed me a neat way to keep track of horses for courses. He kept a small file of three-by-five cards. He would record the winner's distance, time, class level, track condition, and surface for every race on a day's card. He would file these cards alphabetically. Whenever a horse won more than once on a track, he would paper-clip the cards together for that horse. He recorded every race for the meeting, whether he went to the track or not. He would then put away this file until the next meeting at that track. He showed consistent profits simply by betting all multiple winners coming back at near the same distance (within one-half furlong) and near the same class (within one class level) regardless of any other factor. He found three particularly lucrative situations. The first was Del Mar, the second Fairplex, and his most profitable was Saratoga in the rain (sloppy or muddy track condition).

Normally I'm not in favor of single-factor handicapping, but

Cramer proved to me that you could make consistent profits by observing this phenomenon. He also proved that this works with European racing, where the meetings are very short. It's not easy to observe this angle by reading the *Racing Form* because you only see the horse's last ten races. In some areas you can buy this information. If you can't for your area, it would be a very wise idea to invest in a few small card files and religiously record this information. It's well worth the time and effort. Ask Mark Cramer.

The next form angle was also discovered by Mark Cramer. It's called the "class drop—jockey switch" angle. It happens when a horse is dropping in class and making a positive jockey change. When a horse is dropping in class, it's generally negative, so why would a leading jockey take the mount? (Please note two things: a positive jockey switch is a switch to a better rider or to a rider who has won with the horse before; a class drop is when a horse has won at above this level, not simply been entered at above today's level. If a horse has had a victory above today's level, then it's a class drop. If it hasn't, then it's not a class drop.) Top jockeys pretty much get their pick of mounts. Why would a top jockey choose to ride a horse that's not in form and condition? It must be assumed that the horse's connections had a good story to tell the jockey's agent. This angle has shown consistent profits since the early eighties, when Cramer first wrote about it. Please watch for it, it's powerful.

The next form angle is also from Mark Cramer. It's the "class drop—track switch" angle. Why would the horse's connections go through the expense of shipping a horse unless they had intentions of collecting purse money? This angle becomes especially strong when the horse has won on today's track and/or gets a positive jockey switch.

The next three form angles are "LBG." Lasix, blinkers, and gelded. Always watch for these, they are known form improvers. Lasix has been said to be a performance enhancer, diuretic effects and bleeder-prevention aspects notwithstanding. A number of credible studies have shown that a horse will improve its adjusted final time when given this medication. These studies are controversial. Whether they are true or not, I can tell you as a handicapper that Lasix allows some horses to sustain their speed longer. I look for horses who have bid and hung. That is, run a good race until the top of the stretch and then faded. Those horses coming back on Lasix the first and second times are dangerous.

Our studies of West Coast racing conclude that the second time on Lasix after running a race near the pace shows close to a 50 percent flat-bet profit. When a horse gets Lasix for the first time, it indicates positive trainer intention.

Blinkers on or off are also a sign of positive trainer intention. When a horse adds blinkers, the intention is to improve early speed by reducing distractions. When blinkers come off a horse, the intention is to slow his early speed by adding distractions. Generally speaking, it's wise to use the above criteria to determine if we can accept a horse's current form or expect some improvement. If a horse that got off slowly or failed to show early speed in its last race is getting blinkers today, we should expect improvement from its last race. If a horse blistered the early fractions and faded in its last race while wearing blinkers and they are coming off today, we can expect some improvement. Please remember that we are looking for a change in equipment. If a horse ran with blinkers last time and he's running with blinkers today, we accept his current form. Same for not wearing blinkers both times.

Recent gelding is considered as the ultimate equipment change. Many times this has a dramatic effect on a horse's performance. On the West Coast we found that recent geldings win over 20 percent of their first or second starts after being gelded. Watch this one. It's powerful.

Breeding becomes a form angle in the mud and on turf. Certain sires produce an inordinate percentage of winners on the turf. Watch for mud marks in the *Daily Racing Form*. The *Racing Form* also gives a list of the current best mud sires. Please cut this out and save it for a rainy day.

FORM ELIMINATIONS

Form eliminations are automatic throw-outs. Some of them that I'll suggest will make your hair stand up on end. The first one is a graded stakes winner running under allowance conditions. He's an automatic throw-out. Yes, he's the class of the field. Yes, he's probably the fastest horse in the field. But, is he well-intended? The answer is no. I don't care what the circumstances are, I throw him out. But wait. What about a horse who's shipping in and prepping for a major race within a week or two? Throw him out. He's not well-intended. You can bet that the jockey's instructions will be to take it easy with the horse. Why risk a horse's condition for a small purse? There is a general principle operating when discussing form eliminations. *If it doesn't make economic sense, it doesn't make handicapping sense.* Why would a graded stakes winner who's used to winning hundreds of thousands of dollars in purse money run in an allowance race for $30,000? It doesn't make sense.

It's pretty obvious that the horse's connections are asking a form question when they enter a graded stakes winner under allowance conditions. You, as a handicapper, shouldn't be betting on questionable propositions. Will these horses beat you from time to time? Sure. But when they do, they do at ridiculously low odds. I have made sinful profits by betting against these horses. I suggest that you do the same. This doesn't apply to horses who have run in graded stakes races and lost. It only applies to winners.

The next automatic throw-outs are recent claiming winners not moving up. If a horse has just won a $10,000 claiming race and comes back at the same level, he's an automatic throw-out. We studied repeat winners at the same level and found that less than 12 percent go on to repeat. The natural odds against repeating are about 7-to-1 against.

Same is true for recent claims coming back at the same level or lower. They seldom win and they usually go off at low odds. Again, these situations don't make economic sense. Would you buy a car for $16,000, put it in your garage for a month, and then offer it for sale for $12,500? Not unless you have taken vows of poverty. Why would a horse's connections claim a horse for $16,000, sit out the jail period, and then enter him for $12,500? It makes no economic sense, unless they plan on taking the purse, the claiming price, and the proceeds of some large bets as part of it. In general, it's wise to bet against these suspicious class drops unless you know that the trainer gets away with these maneuvers. (It pays to "Know Thy Track.")

The last automatic throw-out is a closer stretching from a sprint to a route. Many handicappers believe that closers are well-suited to stretch out because they just need the extra distance. This false belief will lead to poverty and despair. A closer in a sprint has misappropriated his energy and figures to do the same in a route. The best candidate for a stretch-out is the even-paced sprinter—the horse who was four or five lengths back and never lost touch of the pace. The slower route fractions will be very much to his liking.

Please study the form factor. I urge you to read Mark Cramer's *Thoroughbred Cycles*. The ability to eliminate horses on the form factor, especially when they're favorites, will put you ahead of 95 percent of the handicappers at your track.

Chapter 6

Angles

ANGLES ARE EXTENUATING circumstances. Some are so strong they can override the fundamental handicapping factors of class, speed, pace, and form. Most are not. They should be used to complement your basic handicapping. They give you evidence to help you further evaluate a particular contender. Angles can both be positive or negative. Negative angles are especially fascinating because they can become automatic eliminations. For example, consider a maiden first-time starter in a route race. Probability studies show that for every dollar you invest in first-time starters in maiden routes, you can expect to get back forty cents. Therefore it's very safe to automatically eliminate them from further consideration. It's very wise to start cataloguing negative angles. The more of these we have in our bag of handicapping tricks, the easier our elimination process will become.

Please don't consider this discussion of angles to be comprehensive. It's not. New angles are discovered every day. You must be constantly searching for them. I will share my favorite ones with you.

First and foremost, please understand that ability and current form always take precedence over angles. We first look at fundamentals—then we consider extenuating circumstances. If, and only if, a positive angle is strong enough to show a flat-bet profit by itself, do we ever choose it over fundamentals. In the case of a negative angle, we must be sure that it's strong enough to be an automatic elimination.

Suppose one horse has the top trainer, a top jockey, loves to win on this course, has a favored post position, and is running against another horse with an inferior jockey, inferior trainer, no victories on this course, but has superior figures with no form knocks. They are both going off at 5-to-1. Which one should you choose? It depends. I tend to favor the figure horse. It's our job to weigh the evidence. Positives should outweigh negatives. If, however, the second horse was running against a strong bias, I would prefer the first. Since we knew there was a very strong bias against the second horse, this became an automatic elimination. In this case, we chose the very strong angle over fundamentals.

Many players make the mistake of choosing a horse on the basis of an angle and never consider the fundamentals. This is a blunder. Angles should simply aid you in making fine distinctions. It's when two horses are very close on the figures that you separate them by angles. It's only when an angle is powerful enough to make a flat-bet profit that it can take precedence over the fundamentals. In the case of negative angles, they must be so overwhelming as to cause automatic elimination.

Most handicappers have trouble with class rises and class drops. They are actually very simple. The trick is to view them in context. A class drop is a negative sign. It's an admission on the part of a horse's connections that it can no longer succeed at its previous level of competition. A class rise is a positive sign. It's a statement of optimism on the part of a horse's connections. They think it can succeed at a higher level of competition. Class drops are confusing to many handicappers. Bill Quirin, in his landmark book *Winning at the Races*, pointed out that a 30 percent class drop is the strongest impact statistic in racing. Some might believe that such a class drop is a positive factor. It's not. Mark Cramer didn't help clear the confusion when he published his "class drop—jockey switch" method. He revealed that betting all horses that showed a drop from previous levels of competition accompanied by a positive jockey change yielded around 30 percent winners at average odds of 4-to-1. Here again we're led to believe that a class drop is a positive factor. The truth is, it's never a positive factor by itself. It becomes positive only when put in the context of positive trainer intention.

Our job as handicappers is to determine when a horse will benefit from a class drop and when it won't. Again, the solution lies in considering trainer intention. Is it the trainer's intention to offer this horse for sale at a bargain price in order to rid himself of a hay-gobbling monster, or is he really trying to find the proper level of competition for his equine athlete? How can we tell the difference? The answer is that we must find strong evidence that the trainer is trying to win the race. If we can't, we must conclude that we're witnessing a distressed merchandise sale. Please remember that a class drop is a drop below the horse's last win level, as discussed previously.

When a horse is dropping in class, he must be accompanied by at least one positive sign that the trainer is trying to win. Here's a list of positive signs:

- Positive Jockey Change
- Early Speed in Last Race (especially if new)
- Improving Ability Times
- Distance Change (with proper profile)
- Surface Change (with proper profile)
- Equipment Change
- Medication Change
- Track Change

Whenever we consider a horse who's dropping in class, we'll require at least one of the above positive indicators. Let's look at each of these positive signs in a little more detail.

POSITIVE JOCKEY CHANGE

This is a switch to a higher-rated rider or to a rider that has won with this horse before. Jockey standings can be found in the racing newspapers or in the track program. Don't be too excited by a change from the fifth-leading rider to the fourth. Do get excited by a switch to a jockey that has won with the horse before. Mark Cramer points out an interesting positive jockey change in *Thoroughbred Cycles*. It's the switch from Gary Stevens, the country's leading jockey, to Joy Scott. At the time, Joy Scott was winning less than one race in fifty, but had won with this particular horse, while Stevens managed to lose whenever he rode the horse.

EARLY SPEED IN LAST RACE

Most handicappers confuse early speed with early position. Consider the following running lines:

22 44^3 1:09^4 5^4 4^5 4^5 4^5
23 46^1 1:11   1^1 1^2 1^3 1^4

The second horse is perceived by many as the early speed horse. He's not. The first horse ran 22^4 45^3 1:10^4. The second horse ran 23 46^1 1:11. The first horse is the early speed horse. He ran faster to both the first and second calls. Newfound early speed to the first call is significant. It's even more significant if the horse showed improvement in the first two calls. The most important improvement is the time to the second call. We are looking for "wake-up" horses. New early speed is a traditional positive form sign. Horses coming into form often show improving early speed.

IMPROVING ABILITY TIMES

The eventual winner of a race comes from the top five "ability time" horses over 80 percent of the time. Needless to say, this factor is quite important. In some cases, extreme. A conscientious student of mine pointed out that in Maryland, for the entire 1991 race season at both Laurel and Pimlico, the winner was found among the top three ability-time horses 83 percent of the time! Ability time for dirt races is computed by adding the turn-time to the second call. These times are adjusted for beaten lengths. A class dropper who can run to today's ability par is a very dangerous horse.

DISTANCE CHANGE

It's much more likely that a sprinter stretching out into a route will succeed than a router going short into a sprint. If you understand pace handicapping, you'll immediately understand the reason for this. The pace is much more demanding in a sprint race, and horses that lack early speed are at a very big disadvantage. The easiest way to see this is to compare par times for a sprint race to the par times for a route race on the same track. Consider the 1991 Hollywood Park par times for six furlongs vs. 1 1/16 miles for $20,000 claimers.

| 6 furlongs | 22 | 45 | 1:10 |
| 1 1/16 miles | 47 | 1:11^3 | 1:43^3 |

A sprinter who can run within nine lengths of the second-call par in a sprint is running a faster-than-par route first fraction. A sprinter who can run within seven lengths of the final-time sprint par is running to the second call of the route faster than par. Quirin has pointed out that early speed is the universal bias. A mediocre sprinter looks like a champion. He gets an easy early lead and just keeps going. The router is at a very big disadvantage. He's expected to improve his half-mile time by ten ticks just to stay competitive.

The proper stretch-out pattern is even pace. Consider the following running lines:

$$22 \ 45 \ 1{:}10 \qquad 5^4 \ 4^4 \ 4^4 \ 4^4$$
$$22 \ 45 \ 1{:}10 \qquad 7^8 \ 6^7 \ 3^5 \ 2^4$$

Most handicappers reason that the second horse is a better bet because he should improve his position as the distance increases. This is absolutely false. The proper analysis is that this closer lost touch with the pace and misspent his energy, and will probably do so again in a route. The reason that we prefer the top horse is because he won't lose touch with the route pace and will most probably maintain his early speed advantage. The closer isn't a good profile for stretch-out. It's the even-pace horse that we prefer.

The proper stretch-in pattern is superior internal route fractions. Within every route race is a sprint race. In order for a router to succeed, he must have demonstrated that he can run near the sprint pars. Simply check his adjusted second call time and compare it to the final-time pars at six furlongs for today's class level. If he's on or near it (within two ticks), we can accept him as a contender. Most of the time these horses don't come anywhere near the sprint par, which explains why so few succeed.

SURFACE CHANGE

I want you to consider turf racing as happening on another planet. That about summarizes the relationship between turf and dirt. A horse's dirt ability doesn't mean anything on turf, unless we have evidence to suggest that he can transfer this ability to grass. Same for turf horses coming onto dirt for the first time. The proper dirt-to-turf profile is to have a productive turf sire. In other words, heredity is the key. I use Bill Quirin's list of turf sires along with Sports Institute's Sire Book. The first two times on turf, I simply look at the horse's daddy. If he's a productive sire (ROI greater than 50 percent) then it's an automatic win bet on his progeny. If there's more than one first- or second-time-on-turf horse in the race, I usually bet the one with the most productive sire. In the absence of a turf sire, I look for ability to handle a high-variant non-fast track.

The proper turf to dirt profile is early speed on turf. While early speed on turf is easy to see for American past performances, it's sometimes very difficult to establish with foreign horses because we don't get pace calls, we only get final times. We are dependent upon the comments of racing writers. Mark Cramer has just come back from a year in Europe and really understands European racing. He loves early speed turf horses that ship to North America and are put on the dirt. Before Cramer taught me this, I used to simply watch their first dirt race. My incorrect assumption had been that they didn't have current dirt form, hence they were form eliminations. Now I know better.

EQUIPMENT CHANGE

Blinkers-on is an indication that a trainer wants to improve the early speed of a horse, while blinkers-off seeks to do the opposite. What's really important is the fact that the trainer is making a change. It's up to us to determine if the change will be beneficial. It could be that a trainer is taking blinkers off a horse on a speed-favoring track. This might not be to the horse's advantage. We must have evidence that the change will improve the horse's chances—otherwise we discount it.

Gelding is the "ultimate equipment change." Recent (first and second races) geldings win 20 percent of their races on the West Coast. This should get our attention. It's not easy to keep track of recent geldings. Unless we make a scrupulous effort, this factor will elude us. Please pay attention to announcements made at the track that such-and-such horse is now a gelding. When you hear this announcement, take the time to investigate the horse's past performances. He may be a monster longshot that has a look at this race. It's worth the few seconds it takes to check this out.

MEDICATION CHANGE

We suspect that Lasix is a performance enhancer. It's most effective on horses that bid and hung. The second time on Lasix is especially powerful when preceded by at least one race that was run within two ticks of the second call par. It's interesting to see horses that fail the first time on Lasix after a bid-and-hung performance. The next time—the horse's second time on Lasix— it scores big at huge prices, because the public is unable to forgive its previous, seemingly poor performance.

TRACK CHANGE

This is a positive indication by virtue of the fact that the horse's connections would bear the shipping expenses. This becomes especially interesting if the horse has won at this track before and is getting the rider that won with him.

Please note that the last four positive indicators were already mentioned in the form factor chapter. They were called form angles. In fact, the class drop—jockey change was also mentioned.

The main point of this chapter is that ability and form take precedence over angles unless the angles are strong enough to show a flat-bet profit by themselves. Angles are best used in conjunction with your class, speed, pace, and form assessments. Most often the numbers themselves tell the story. This is especially true in the case of a class rise. You need only answer the question: Can the horse run to the pars of today's competition level? If he can run within a few ticks of par and we have evidence to predict improvement, we can accept this horse as a contender. We then look at the probable pace scenario and compare it to our track profile. We always give the edge to horses that best fit the win profile.

Let's now take a look at one of the most interesting and misapplied concepts in thoroughbred handicapping.

Chapter 7

Wager Value

ONE OF THE biggest frauds ever perpetrated on the racing public is that the way to win at thoroughbred handicapping is to pick lots of winners. You'll hear the voice of ignorance bleating, "Every winner is an overlay." Picking winners is immensely overrated. Nobody picks winners better than the public—yet for every dollar you invest in its selections, you get back only ninety cents. This isn't too bad when you consider that the track take exceeds ten percent. In other words, the public would be a winning player if it weren't for the track take.

I have the good fortune to know a good number of winning handicappers. There isn't one whom I know that can pick more winners than the public. That is, bet every race for a long period of time and achieve a 32 percent win rate. In fact, most can't achieve this win rate even by being selective. Tom Brohamer, James Quinn, and Ron Ambrose can boast win rates over 32 percent. The reason they're able to achieve this is because they're highly selective about which races they choose to invest in. Normally they get between one and three plays per day at a single track, averaging about two plays per day. Mark Cramer has a 25 percent hit rate, as does your author. We get an average of three plays per day. The difference is average mutuel. Mark and I average over $12, while Quinn, Brohamer, and Ambrose average around $8. The key to this discussion is a concept called "edge."

Your edge on any bet is the success rate multiplied by the average payoff (expressed as "odds-to-1") minus the failure rate.

$$\text{Edge} = P(W) \times O - P(L)$$

P(W) represents the probability of winning the bet. O is the "odds-to-1" and P(L) is the probability of losing the bet. [P(W) + P(L) = 1).]

James Quinn's personal goal for the 1991 race season was to achieve a 37 percent win rate at average odds of 5-to-2. I am happy to report that he exceeded this goal and had a most profitable year, one of the best he can remember. Let's calculate the edge on his avowed goal.

$$Edge = .37 \times 2.5 - .63 = .295$$

Please note that 5-to-2 is the same as 2.5-to-1 (our formula requires the odds to one dollar instead of two). It was Quinn's goal to achieve an edge of 29.5 percent. In other words, for every dollar he put through the mutuels, he expected to get back close to $1.30. Not a bad way to invest his money.

Mark Cramer has a 25 percent win rate at an average mutuel over $12. His minimum edge is:

$$Edge = .25 \times 5 - .75 = .50$$

Does this mean that Cramer is better than Quinn? Absolutely not. Cramer suffers much longer losing streaks than Quinn. Also, Quinn invests a lot more money than Cramer, hence his annual profits are much higher than Cramer's.

My dear friend and colleague Ron Ambrose has a combined edge of 15 percent on all his bets. He makes a lot of place and show bets. His 1992 goal is to put $1 million through the mutuel windows. If he achieves this goal, he will earn at least $150,000 in 1992.

We now see that it's not win percent that's most important, nor is it average mutuel. What really counts is your overall edge multiplied by the amount of money that you'll put through the mutuels.

Please indulge me by doing the following exercise. Write down your daily goal for profits at the track. This figure represents the average amount of money you want to earn per day. Typical responses are $100, $200, and more. You must realize that this number is an average—it doesn't mean that you'll win every day. A good way to arrive at this number is to calculate how much your time is worth per hour. If you make $20 per hour at your regular job and you go to the track on weekends, then you probably spend ten to fifteen hours a week on handicapping. Say ten. Then you want to average $200 per weekend or $100 per day. So you would fill in the earnings per day blank with the number $100.

Next write down the largest win bet that you're capable of making without having a heart attack—the largest win bet within your comfort zone. Then write down the largest place or show bet that you're capable of making comfortably.

Average earnings per day _____

Largest win bet   _____

Largest place/show bet   _____

If your largest win bet didn't exceed your average earnings per day, your expectations are totally unrealistic. If you answered $100 per day earnings and your largest win bet was $20, you were being quixotic. You were dreaming. Let me explain.

The very best professional players earn between 20 and 40 percent on their win bets. Most average around two prime bets per day. This means that if you're in the middle of this group of superior handicappers, your ROI will be around 30 percent. How much do you have to put through the mutuels, at a 30 percent profit rate, to earn $100 per day? That's right—$333. This means you must bet an average of $167 per race!

The very best professional players earn between 10 and 20 percent on their place and show bets with the same number of prime plays per day—namely two. Because place and show betting is much safer, they can bet much more and maintain their safety margin. If you wish to earn $100 per day on place and show bets, you must put between $500 and $1000 through the mutuels per day. That's a unit bet between $250 and $500.

It's a pretty good rule of thumb to say that your maximum bet should be almost double your daily earnings goal. How's that for a dose of reality? Not too pleasant, eh? Unfortunately, truth is sometimes painful. The truth of winning a lot of money at the track is that you're going to have to bet a lot of money. When some sleazebag tells you that you can make your living on $20 bets, plunge a dagger into his heart before he finishes his next sentence. Then go to his house and burn it down. Then go to the Hall of Records and erase any trace of his existence. He's a contagion that you must stop from spreading. You'll be doing your fellow handicappers a big favor. Or, if you're more benevolently inclined, just consider him a bulltickey artist and forget him.

Does this sound familiar? "I have uncovered a major flaw in horse racing that allowed me to win over $1000 per day, for the last three years!" This is the headline from a direct mail piece that I received last week. It gets better. One of the subheads inside goes on to claim, "I have been pulling down over $1000 per day on $20 win and place bets for the past three years! This is playing just one track at a time. Profits from playing multiple tracks at race books have amounted to $2000 to $3000 a day!!!" If you believe this, I have a bridge to sell you. It spans the East River in New York City and it's yours for a pittance. The above profit claim is so outrageous that it's humorous. This scumbag is pushing your greed button. He's promising you that you can win a whole bunch of money without doing any work whatsoever. There are more than 50,000 systems that have been sold to horseplayers over the past twenty five years. Have you ever heard documented proof of one single millionaire as the result of purchasing one of these systems? Please don't send for any mechanical mail order system regardless of the claims and guarantees. They're garbage. (Both the product and the seller.)

There are no shortcuts to winning. You'll have to pay the price, which is time and effort. More on that later.

Let's now address ourselves to the question of determining "wager value." Is there a way for us to assure ourselves that we are making good bets? Absolutely. The ability to judge whether the odds offered represent an overlay or not, in my opinion, is the fundamental difference between the winning player and the average player. Winning players have this skill. According to Dr. James Quinn, "A mark of the expert is the ability to make substantial profits on relatively low-priced horses. Handicappers as a group may be spinning wheels on straight bets below 3-to-1, as the research has indicated, but experts should be prepared to distinguish the attractive overlays at low odds from the hundreds of relatively poor risks." The way to achieve this expertise is to learn how to create a betting line. A reasonably accurate betting line solves most of the selection and money management dilemmas.

Making an accurate betting line is the quintessential skill required for success in thoroughbred wagering. Most professionals are very precise about describing a horse's chances to win a race. They make distinctions between a 20 percent chance and a 22 percent chance. It's the difference between a 4-to-1 horse and a 7-to-2 horse. Can you tell the difference? In order to be a winning player you're going to have to learn to perform this feat. The only way you can learn to make these distinctions is to practice, practice, and practice some more. After you've made lines on at least one hundred races, it's wise to review your results. Did your 2-to-1 shots win 33 percent of the time? Did your 3-to-1 horses win 25 percent of the time? The more lines that you make and get positive feedback on, the sharper these skills will become.

You'll learn by making a lot of mistakes. You must understand the importance of failure in your quest for success. Each mistake is a learning experience. You should not fear mistakes, you should only fear not learning from them. They're inevitable.

Let's begin with some basic ideas on probability, odds, and betting lines. Mathematical probability can range from zero to one. A probability of zero means impossibility, and a probability of one means certainty. The closer to zero—the more uncertain, the closer to one—the more probable. It's reasonably certain that some horse will win a given race. Which one? That's the trick to handicapping. In a race, every horse has some chance of winning. The great Secretariat could lose to a $10,000 claimer if his jockey fell off or if he impeded another horse and was disqualified. It's true then that the sum of the probabilities of all the horses must add up to 1. The way we apportion these probabilities among the horses is what makes us skillful handicappers.

There's a relationship between odds and probabilities. In fact, they're really the same thing expressed in different ways. Even money and 50 percent probability are synonymous. A 2-to-1 horse has a 33⅓ percent chance of winning the race. A 3-to-1 shot has a 25 percent chance of winning. The relationship between probability and odds can be stated as follows:

$$\text{Probability} = \frac{1}{\text{"odds-to-1"} + 1}$$

If you know the "odds-to-1," you can calculate the probability by adding 1 and taking the reciprocal; 4-to-1 can be expressed as $1/(4+1)$ or ⅕, which is 20 percent. Whether you refer to a horse as a 4-to-1 shot or as a horse having a win probability of 20 percent, you're saying the same thing. To convert any odds to "odds-to-1," you simply divide the second number into the first.

For example, 7-to-2 is 3½-to-1. You divide the 2 into 7 to arrive at the result; 8-to-5 is 1.6-to-1; 4-to-5 is .8-to-1.

If you know the probability and want to convert to odds, the relationship is as follows:

$$\text{``Odds-to-1''} = \frac{1}{\text{Probability}} - 1$$

If a horse has a 25 percent chance to win, its fair odds are 3-to-1 because 25 percent = .25, and 1/.25 = 4, and 4 − 1 = 3. If a horse has a 10 percent chance to win, its fair odds are 9-to-1.

The following odds percentage table should help in converting probability to odds and vice versa.

Odds Percentage Table			
1–10	90.91	4–1	20.00
1–5	83.33	9–2	18.19
2–5	71.42	5–1	16.67
1–2	66.67	6–1	14.29
3–5	62.50	7–1	12.50
4–5	55.56	8–1	11.11
1–1	50.00	9–1	10.00
6–5	45.45	10–1	9.09
7–5	41.67	11–1	8.33
3–2	40.00	12–1	7.69
8–5	38.46	15–1	6.25
9–5	35.71	20–1	4.76
2–1	33.33	25–1	3.85
5–2	28.57	30–1	3.23
3–1	25.00	50–1	1.96
7–2	22.22	99–1	1.00

Understanding the relationship between odds-to-1 and probabilities, we are now ready to explore the concepts of the betting line. Even though every horse in a race has some chance to win, we don't try to make distinctions among our non-contenders. We simply give them a group probability. Who cares whether a horse has a 5 percent chance or a 6 percent chance? We only consider horses that have at least a 15 percent chance of winning the race. The trick to making a betting line is to first separate the contenders from the non-contenders. Typically we give the group of non-contenders a 20 percent probability of winning. In other words, we'll accept the notion that "stuff happens" at a racetrack. That is, twenty percent of the time we can't explain the results of a thoroughbred race. The size of the field determines the size of the S.H. pile. For typical races with eight to twelve competitors, the pile will be 20 percent. As the size of the field gets smaller, we'll reduce the size of the S.H. pile. We'll reduce it by 4 percent for each horse less than eight. So for seven-horse fields, the contenders get 84 percent of the betting line and the non-contenders get 16 percent. In six-horse fields, the contenders get 88 percent of the line. In five-horse fields, the contenders get 92 percent of the line, and so on.

Let's begin with a simple example of how to make a line on a race. Suppose that we're handicapping a contentious race that contains nine entries, five of which have very little chance to win the race. However, the other four are inseparable. Their adjusted second call times and final times are all within two ticks of each other. How do we make a line on such a race? It's actually very straightforward. We give each of our contenders a line of 4-to-1 and the entire S.H. pile containing the other five horses also gets a 4-to-1 line. We had to divide 80 percent equally among the contenders. Since there were four of them, they each get a 20 percent probability, which is the same as 4-to-1 odds.

Most races don't come up as simple as this example. Usually one or two horses have an advantage over the others. Let's suppose you liked your top horse a little more than your second pick. Your third and fourth picks were scare horses that you figured had about an equal chance. Your line would look something like this.

Horse A	5–2	29%
Horse B	3–1	25%
Horse C	6–1	14%
Horse D	6–1	14%
		82%

If your line doesn't come out exact, it's okay. You want to get as close to 80 percent as you reasonably can. If you miss by two or three points, don't be too concerned. This isn't a precise science. Because our lines are subject to error, we must offset this by demanding a premium over our estimates. Barry Meadow suggests that 50 percent over our estimate will compensate us for possible errors. I tend to be a little more formal and insist upon a minimum 20 percent ROI on any win bet. In the above case Barry Meadow's overlay line would look as follows:

	Line	Bet
Horse A	5–2	4–1
Horse B	3–1	9–2
Horse C	6–1	9–2
Horse D	6–1	9–2

My overlay line would look as follows:

	Line	Bet
Horse A	5–2	7–2
Horse B	3–1	4–1
Horse C	6–1	8–1
Horse D	6–1	8–1

Barry's way is a lot simpler. My way involves a lot of calculation. The advantage to my way is that you tend to accept more horses as possible bets. The disadvantage is that you must be more precise because there's less room for error. Having made lines on thousands and thousands of races, I am quite comfortable in not insisting on such a large premium.

My way to compute the permissible odds to accept in order to guarantee a 20 percent edge is to simply divide the estimated probability into .2 plus P (L). Our estimated probability on Horse A was 29 percent. We divide .29 into .2 plus .71. The quotient becomes 3.14, therefore we round up to the nearest odds level, which is 7-to-2. We estimated Horse B's probability of winning at 25 percent, therefore his losing probability is 75 percent. We add the 75 percent to 20 percent and divide by 25 percent. The quotient becomes 3.8, which means we round up to 4-to-1. For Horses C and D, our win estimate was 14 percent, hence our lose estimate was 86 percent. We add 20 percent to our lose estimate and divide by 14 percent. This becomes 106 percent divided by 14 percent. The result is 7.57, which we round up to 8-to-1.

There are three types of favorites: legitimate, vulnerable, and false. When you have a legitimate favorite, only one horse gets a line. The balance of the field goes into the S.H. pile. Therefore, this is the exception to the 80–20 rule of line making. The only time that you bet against a legitimate favorite is when you've taken vows of poverty and have decided to divest yourself of your worldly goods. You don't go shopping for overlays against a legitimate favorite. A legitimate favorite is the speed of the field by three ticks or better, with the proper pace profile and running style, and fits the class demands of today's race. You never bet against such horses. You either find a way to bet on them or skip the race.

You only make betting lines that contain multiple contenders when there is either a false or vulnerable favorite. In the case of a false favorite, this horse gets no line whatsoever. He goes into the S.H. pile. Vulnerable favorites always get a line.

A good rule of thumb is to start your line at 5-to-2 or higher when you have a vulnerable favorite. A legitimate favorite starts at 2-to-1 or less. James Quinn was absolutely correct when he said that the mark of the expert is to be able to make money on relatively low-priced horses. You'll know you have arrived when you can make a large bet on a 6-to-5 shot because he's 4-to-5 on your line.

The line-making process begins with your contenders. First you decide if your top pick is a legitimate favorite. If he is, you estimate his chances of winning. The balance of the horses collectively are assigned the difference between your estimate and 100. Remember, if you give him an even-money line, you're saying that his chances equal the chances of all the horses in the field combined. It happens, but not too frequently. If your top pick isn't a legitimate favorite or is a horse other than the public favorite, then his line should probably be 5-to-2 or more. You apportion 80 percent or more, depending on the size of the field, to your contenders. The balance of the horses are put into the S.H. pile and are assigned the balance of the percentages so that your line adds up to near 100 percent. If you get to the track and see that the public favorite isn't among your contenders at all, beware. Take another look at the race. You may have missed something. If you're sure that you didn't, you've got yourself a false favorite. It's a good idea to take a big swing at this race because you're sure to be getting good value on at least one of your contenders. You'll get a much better flavor for this process in the workshop section.

Please begin the procedure immediately. For every race that

you handicap, write down your contenders and assign each an estimate of what you think its win chances are. Compare them to the public's estimates and exploit the difference.

Now that you have been exposed to the correct way of ascertaining wager value for win bets, let me share with you an incorrect method that can work. For the past few years, I have been envious of Ron Ambrose's success. We go to the track together and damn if he doesn't win just about every time. He drives me crazy. He goes over and over the upcoming race, looking for new clues. He makes his wager at the last possible moment. He checks everything. Place and show prices, exacta prices, betting action, and proportional odds from double or exacta pools are a few of his favorite indicators. He has a sixth sense for when "things don't quite feel right." He winds up passing most races. When he does make a bet, it's a substantial one. His win bets start at $200 and go as high as $5000. His place and show bets can go to $10,000 depending upon the size of the pools. His exacta bets are usually in the $200 to $500 range. You would think that a handicapper who bets this much money would have a very sophisticated way to make a betting line, wouldn't you? You're gonna love it. Ambrose's method is simplicity itself.

The way Ambrose makes a line is easy. His number of contenders is his odds line. That is, if he has three contenders—they're each 3-to-1. If he has four contenders, they're each 4-to-1 and the balance of the field is also 4-to-1. When I asked him how he derived this unorthodox approach, he responded, "It's all in my records." He observed that when what he considered to be a playable race had two contenders, one of them won about 66 percent of the time. When he had three contenders in a playable race, one of them won about 75 percent of the time. Most races fell into these groups. When he encounters races with four or more contenders, he usually passes unless the odds are irresistible.

As I said earlier, he drives me crazy. He's selection-oriented and has an urgent need to cash every bet that he makes. He hates uncertainty. As he says, "Often wrong, but never in doubt." He wants to understand every race in its minutest detail. He handicaps the whole card but usually only finds one or two races that deserve a bet. Maiden races are his specialty. He loves them. He's the best maiden race handicapper that I have the good fortune to know.

My advice is to practice constructing a betting line the correct way unless you're a very high percentage handicapper. If you can get 66 percent with two horses in those races you consider playable, then by all means use the Ambrose technique. You may want to review your records to see how this technique would have worked for you. If it works, use it.

Before we leave this topic, I'd like to recommend a method that will help you to master the subject of "wager value." Finding wager value is employing good betting strategy. You must know how to choose the very best bet that a handicapping situation allows. The way to accomplish this is to master each type of parimutuel bet, one at a time. The very best reference that I can give you is Barry Meadow's *Money Secrets at the Racetrack.* Just about everything you need to know about betting is contained in this one book. Start with win betting. Once you've achieved a 20 percent ROI for a significant number of win bets, you can then take on serial betting such as the daily double and daily serial triple. Once you've achieved a 20 percent ROI for a significant number of daily double bets, you can then tackle the daily serial triple. Once you've mastered all the win bets, both single and serial, you then tackle place and show betting. Once you've achieved a 10 percent ROI for a significant number of place and show bets, you're ready to take on exacta and quinella wagering. You then simply progress up the ladder until you get to the Pick-6. You should demand at least a 20 percent profit on all wagers except place and show. It's probably easiest and best to follow the sequence of bets discussed in *Money Secrets.*

There are four categories of thoroughbred races that require separate handicapping methods. They are: maidens, claimers, non-claimers (allowance and stakes), and turf races. The next four chapters will detail each category.

Chapter 8

Maidens

CONTRARY TO POPULAR OPINION, maiden races are the most predictable kind of races offered to the thoroughbred investor. Consider that the public favorite, on average, wins around 33 percent of all races. Then consider that the public favorite wins about 37 percent of all maiden races. The reality of maiden races is that they are easier to predict than the races in general.

It's amazing to me that so many handicappers consider these races to be difficult. Maybe it's because maiden races provide us with much less handicapping information than we're used to seeing; hence it's much more difficult to make an intelligent choice because we simply don't have enough solid information. The reality is that the reverse is actually true: the less information, the less confusion. It's actually easier, not harder, to make handicapping decisions.

The bulk of this commonsense material on maidens comes from the research and work of Ron Ambrose, who in my opinion is the best maiden handicapper in the country. His study of maidens isn't based on opinions. It's based solely on the cold, hard evidence provided by data from thousands of maiden races. Although Ambrose's study focused primarily on maidens on the southern California circuit of Santa Anita, Hollywood Park, and Del Mar, his fundamental analysis of form and speed in maiden races generalizes well to all racetracks. Ron Ambrose is a professional player who lives in Las Vegas and specializes in maiden races.

The commonsense approach to maiden races starts with the premise that they're very predictable. Additionally, they're usually comprised of full fields. Full fields attract widely-scattered betting; hence the winner will pay more than it would if it were entered in a smaller field. We're offered an irresistible combination: very predictable races and generous mutuels. What's even better is that 20 percent of all races carded are maiden races. How lovely. I hope this is sufficient to motivate you to pay close attention to this chapter. If you're going to win big money at the races, it's imperative that you master maiden races, which are an essential ingredient of serial bets such as the daily double, the daily triple, the Pick-6, and even more common exotics, including the trifecta. Maidens are critical to your racetrack financial health.

Gordon Pine, director of research for Cynthia Publishing, made an amazing discovery. He found that the "bet-down" factor can be crucial. In southern California more than 70 percent of all maiden allowance winners (MSW) are bet down from their morning-line odds, and 60 percent of maiden-claiming winners are similarly bet down. Let's define what we mean by a "bet down." It's best to do this by a couple of simple examples. For instance, a maiden-race entrant that's 5-to-2 on the morning line is a bet down if its actual track odds are 2-to-1 or lower. These kinds of horses deserve our attention. Lest you think that bet-downs are limited to low-priced horses, here's another example of a bet-down. A maiden's morning line is 20-to-1; its track odds are 10-to-1. That's a bet-down as well.

In southern California we must be apprehensive about maidens that aren't bet down from their morning-line odds. These principles generalize to the rest of the country. While the statistics may not be as dramatic, you must be wary of horses that aren't bet down from their morning line; maidens who aren't, win less often than they should. By sticking with the percentages, you'll be right most of the time. The only time you should even remotely consider a maiden that isn't bet down from its morning-line odds is when there's some really compelling piece of handicapping information that the public has overlooked and that's potentially decisive.

Before discussing how to handicap and wager on maidens, it's important first to distinguish between the two types of maiden races: maiden special weights and maiden claiming. Maiden special weights are really allowance races. The entrants are protected from being claimed and aren't for sale. On the other hand, maiden-claiming races subject their entrants to possible claim, just as in open claiming races. Maiden-claiming runners are up for sale. This is an important dichotomy. Consider yourself as the owner of a horse. You have an unproven, untested, unknown quantity in your possession. Until the animal has actually run, you really don't know where the horse fits classwise. If you think your horse has even a sliver of potential, it would be in your best interest to protect him until you were proven wrong. You wouldn't subject him to a claim prematurely. Now you should see why distinguishing between the two types of maiden races is important. In theory, entrants of maiden special weight races will progress to the non-winners allowances, restricted and open stakes, and graded stakes on their way to becoming champions. If the owner debuts his horse in a maiden-claiming race, he's admitting that his horse probably isn't going to be the next Secretariat.

Our operational definition of class must change for maidens. (It was simply defined as the level at which the horse has succeeded in the past.) Since maidens have never won even one race, our previous definition becomes somewhat problematic. To begin, let's remember the owner's intentions in entering his horse in either of the two kinds of maiden races. We'll accept the owner's initial judgment on where his horse is first entered. In other words, until the horse actually shows us through racing competition where he can be competitive, it's reasonable to consider the horse as fitting the particular kind of maiden race in which it's initially entered. So a maiden in a maiden special weight race belongs there until he proves that he doesn't. Likewise, a first-time starter that's entered in a maiden-claiming race should be viewed as fitting that kind of race and a cut below the maiden special weight horses. Now in light of this assumption, we are presented with one of the largest drops in all of racing: the descent from maiden special weight to maiden-claiming races. The owner at first will not want to risk losing his horse via claim, so the horse is entered in the maiden special weight races. As the horse clearly and successively proves that it just cannot be competitive in maiden special weight races, the owner will be less protective of his horse and drop it into a maiden claimer. Yet how do you know that this is really a precipitous drop? A glance at the *Gordon Pine Par Times* for your track answers this question. In most cases, it's a three- or four-level drop. The table shows the class levels for the major southern California tracks. Note the difference between MSW and MCL.

6 Furlongs dirt

Class level	SA			HOL			DMR		
	1st C	2nd C	Fin C	1st C	2nd C	Fin C	1st C	2nd C	Fin C
STAKES	21.2	43.4	108.1	21.4	44.0	108.2	21.4	44.1	108.1
CLF	21.3	44.0	108.3	21.4	44.0	108.4	21.4	44.1	108.3
NW3	21.3	44.0	108.4	21.4	44.0	109.0	21.4	44.1	108.4
C100,000	21.3	44.0	108.4	21.4	44.1	109.0	21.4	44.2	108.4
C80,000	21.3	44.1	108.4	21.4	44.1	109.0	21.4	44.2	108.4
C62,500	21.3	44.1	109.0	21.4	44.1	109.1	21.4	44.2	109.0
NW2	21.3	44.1	109.0	21.4	44.1	109.1	21.4	44.3	109.0
C50,000	21.3	44.2	109.0	21.4	44.2	109.1	21.4	44.3	109.1
C40,000	21.3	44.2	109.1	21.4	44.2	109.2	21.4	44.3	109.2
NW1	21.3	44.2	109.1	21.4	44.2	109.2	21.4	44.4	109.2
C32,000	21.3	44.2	109.2	22.0	44.3	109.3	22.0	44.4	109.3
C25,000	21.3	44.3	109.3	22.0	44.3	109.4	22.0	44.4	109.3
MSW	21.3	44.3	109.3	22.0	44.3	109.4	22.0	44.4	109.4
C20,000	21.3	44.3	109.4	22.0	44.4	110.0	22.0	45.0	110.0
C16,000	21.3	44.4	110.0	22.0	44.4	110.1	22.0	45.0	110.0
C12,500	21.4	44.4	110.1	22.0	44.4	110.2	22.0	45.0	110.1
MCL	21.4	44.4	110.2	22.0	44.4	110.3	22.0	45.1	110.3
C10,000	21.4	45.0	110.2	22.0	45.0	110.3	22.0	45.1	110.3

Keying on the significance of this huge class drop from maiden special weight to maiden-claiming races, James Quinn in his outstanding *The Handicapper's Condition Book* advises a ruthless approach to handicapping maiden-claiming races: first, throw out first-time starters; second, throw out horses that have previously lost even one maiden-claiming race. Quinn then writes that the handicapper should exclusively favor horses that are dropping from maiden special weight races into maiden claimers. This approach, while very restrictive, managed to show a profit in southern California in the mid-eighties.

The research of Fred Davis indicated that a second-place finish in a horse's most recent maiden race has a high impact value in predicting a maiden win the next time out. The mechanical approach of favoring last-out second-place finishers in maiden races was also profitable in the 1980s.

Sadly, those days have passed. The Quinn and Davis guidelines, while still helpful, aren't enough. To keep on top and in the black when playing maiden races, the contemporary handicapper must adopt a new approach that'll allow him to take advantage of the very generous and lucrative opportunities that maidens offer. Ambrose discovered such an approach. His most recent study was born of genius. He asked the question, "For all the maiden races that don't conform to either the Quinn or Davis guidelines, what kind of patterns emerge most often?" In other words, how do winners of maiden races appear in the past performances? From his painstaking research, Ambrose uncovered a simple truth: the answers lie in fundamental handicapping. The secret is, "there is no secret." You simply apply the principles taught thus far, and maidens are yours. You'll own them. You'll wish that every race on the card was a maiden race. Ambrose does. So do I.

In evaluating both the speed and form criteria of maidens, ability time is the key. Among experienced maidens, the horses with the top five ability times in a given race will win over 80 percent of the time. This technique serves us well in determining the speed of true contenders, as well as providing a barometer with which we can gauge a horse's current form. Successively faster ability times imply improving current form. Successively slower ability times predict form decline. Consistent ability times suggest form consistency.

But before we can accept ability time as the overriding factor in maiden races, we must consider it in light of another potentially decisive factor: the prevailing track bias. Much has been written in the literature about the importance of biases: Beyer and Davidowitz provided us with subjective contour and speed biases; Brohamer and Sartin with objective numerical standards of pace biases. The commonsense conclusion that we can draw from the work of each of these writers is that classier horses can overcome even the severest of biases. Conversely, when we transfer this conclusion to the much lower-grade stock in maiden races, track bias becomes a crucial handicapping consideration. We're going to measure the bias or lack thereof for each combination of distance, surface, and sex of maiden runners. The essential tool for this measurement is the win profile.

Ambrose's maintenance of win profiles for the last several years has uncovered several critical points concerning the running styles of maidens. Maidens race greenly. They run as fast as they can for as far as they can. Forget about jockeys trying to rate maidens or conserve their speed for tactical reasons. Rarely do deep closers win maiden races. When a horse passes several others in the late stages of a maiden race, you can be almost certain that it's just overtaking tired horses, not demonstrating any true late-running ability on its own.

A profile par should be maintained for each combination of surface, distance, and maiden class level at your racetrack. Separate profiles should be kept for females. When we evaluate the chances of experienced maidens, the ability par and win profile are indispensable. We will demand that the experienced maidens be able to run to the ability par and fit the win profile snugly. These objective standards will enable us to determine which experienced maidens are contenders today. What often happens, especially in maiden-claiming races, is that the experienced runners fail to meet either objective standard presented by the ability par or win profile. In other words, we have chaos. This is when we should focus our attention on the first-time starters.

What information are we given about a first-time starter? We are given its sire, dam, broodmare sire, trainer, owner, breeder, jockey, and workouts. This information is helpful, but the one piece of information about a first-time starter that matters most isn't found in the *Daily Racing Form*. It's in the track program. A first-time starter that's the morning-line favorite should get your attention. Ambrose's massive study showed that when a maiden first-time starter is the morning-line favorite and is a bet-down, that horse wins over 40 percent of the time. When the track handicapper makes this first-timer his top pick, he must have some added information that's unknown to us. Unfortunately, automatic profits in the win pool proved to be absent from these high-probability horses. A commonsense approach dictates that we respect these first-timers to win, but derive profits from them in the other pools, especially the place and show pools.

When we look at other first-time starters in maiden races open to three-year-olds and up, we should prefer the three-year-olds to their older counterparts, because there is usually a question of fitness and condition clouding older first-timers. Why else would they have been kept from racing for such a long time? Now, there are several trainers on each circuit—on the West Coast, Charlie Whittingham, in the East, Shug McGaughey, for example—who take great care not to rush their charges to the races prematurely. Watch out for them.

A look at the Dosage Index and the average winning distance of the sire's other progeny gives us more clues. As mentioned earlier, maiden races are won on or near the lead; hence we would like to see a Dosage profile tilted toward the brilliance wing. In the absence of Dosage profiles, the average winning distance of the sire's other progeny tells us which first-timers will sprint well in their debuts and which should stretch out successfully in subsequent starts. Sports Institute in Las Vegas publishes these sire statistics. (See Appendix A.)

The Ambrose study revealed that longshot (odds of 9-to-2 and higher) maiden winners predominantly have leading jockeys for riders. The Paretto Principle rules again: 20 percent of the jockeys ride 80 percent of the winners.

How do we cash monster mutuels in maiden races? Obviously, the worse a horse looks in the past performances, the higher its price on the tote board. A giant step toward this goal is for us to know when a maiden starter is a false or vulnerable favorite. The win profiles point out the low-priced underlays unlikely to win because their running styles go against the winning flow. Another approach we can use is to eliminate a first-time starting favorite that's trained by a leading trainer who isn't adept with first-time starters. There is a lovely example here in California. Charlie Whittingham is terrible with first-time starters. His stables are filled with the best horseflesh in the country, animals who usually go on to the top of their divisions. It makes very little economic sense for Charlie to go all-out for a relatively small maiden purse with a first-time starter when there are some six-figure jackpots to be won down the road. A punishing initial effort may jeopardize the horse's ability to capture those bigger prizes. So Charlie schools his horses their first time out, and usually the education lasts for several more maiden attempts. When the foundation has been laid, the horse will finally break its maiden. Returning to the earlier point, many bettors who don't know any better will bet Charlie's first-timers blindly, basing their wagers solely on the Whittingham reputation, even though that reputation was not built on success first time out. This provides us with the wonderful situation of correctly betting against a suspicious favorite.

First-time starters confront us with an immediate problem: How do we determine their current form and condition? As you can probably guess, the only way we can gauge a first-time starter's fitness is through its printed workouts in the past performances. Again, Ambrose provides the commonsense guideline. Rather than concentrate on the speed of the workouts, we should be more concerned with the frequency of the workouts. The key here is the ratio of furlongs to days. Typically, the past performances will show a horse's last four workouts. Note the number of days between today (the date of the race) and the date of the fourth, or least recent, workout. Then sum the number of furlongs worked in the listed workouts. The ratio of the number of days to the number of furlongs worked out should be at least 1.00. A figure of .90 is acceptable; .70 isn't. A little trick that Ambrose uses is to add three furlongs to the total of three workouts, or five furlongs to the total of four workouts, and insist upon an average of one furlong per day.

Evening Rain

Dt. b. or br. f. 3(May), by Expressman—Early Night Rain, by Night Invader

NAKATANI C S (236 32 43 42 $1,113,175)
Own.—Kerr James R & William

$32,000 Br.—Kerr James R & William (Cal)

Tr.—State Warren (25 5 3 1 $104,659)

Lifetime 1991 0 M 0 0
0 0 0 0

117

Speed Index: Last Race: (—)   3–Race Avg.: (—)   12–Race Avg.: (—)   Overall Avg.: (—)

LATEST WORKOUTS   Mar 21 SA 5f sly 1:04¹ H (d)   Mar 15 SA 3f fst :36² H   Mar 9 SA 6f fst 1:16 Hg   Mar 4 SA 5f fst 1:02² Hg

Evening Rain was entered in the second race at Santa Anita on March 25. Her least recent workout was on March 4, 21 days ago. She worked five, six, three, and five furlongs, or 19 furlongs total. Her furlongs-to-days ratio is 19-to-21 (19/21), or .90. She passes the current-form and condition test. Using the Ambrose method, her furlong total of 19 is augmented by 5, so she has a 24/21 ratio. This is equal to or greater than 1.00, hence acceptable.

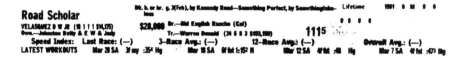

Road Scholar ran in the ninth race at Santa Anita on April 1. His least recent workout was on March 7, 25 days ago. He worked four, four, six, and three furlongs, or 17 furlongs in all. His furlongs-to-days ratio is 17-to-25 (17/25), or .68. If it weren't for the correction factor, he's a throwout. Ambrose would have a 22/25 ratio, which is marginally acceptable.

The speed of a first-time starter's workout becomes important when it's faster than the par for the class of the maiden race in which it's entered. Par can represent not only final-time par, which most players notice, but also pace or second call par, which most players don't notice. If the second-call winner's par was 47^4 and the horse worked in 47^3, this would be significant.

Extenuating circumstances or angles take on more significance in maiden races because we lack other more fundamental information in these events. A very strong influence is exerted by trainers, especially those who are proven magicians with first-time starters. By the way, the statistic to look out for here isn't win percentage, but a positive ROI. Trainer intent with a first-timer can often be determined with the conditioner's choice of jockey. Such combinations, already proven successful, will team up again on the basis of repeating that success. This information doesn't appear in the past performances. In the West you can obtain it from Cynthia Publishing Company in California; in the East and Midwest, from Bloodstock Research in Kentucky. And if it's not available for your local circuit or track, you shouldn't curse the fates. In fact, you probably should throw a party, get down on your knees, look to the heavens and thank the Great Handicapper. You can rest assured that if this vital information isn't available for sale to your competitors, 99 percent of them won't do the necessary research to uncover these priceless nuggets of invaluable handicapping gold. As a winner, you will. And you'll be generously rewarded with a source of recurring overlays that your fellow "handicappers" will overlook.

Mark Cramer uncovered a profitable subset of overlay mutuels. When a drop in class is accompanied by a positive rider change to a leading jockey, head to the windows. It's truly a dynamite sign of excellent trainer intent, and a hot angle on its own. Look for it in the maiden-claiming ranks and even the open claiming divisions. The class drop—jockey switch angle, especially in combination with improving form as measured by ability times, signals a horse on the verge of breaking its maiden.

A final positive maiden angle I'm going to share with you is really powerful because it's widely ignored. Everything else being equal, in sprint races, maidens breaking from the inside posts (gates 1, 2, 3) are less likely to win than their rivals breaking outside of them. Horses on the outside aren't subjected to the myriad opportunities for troubled trips as are their interior counterparts. On the inside, a horse may be pinched back by two other horses sandwiching him as they veer in and out at the same time. The outside horse can't be veered in. When I mentioned the results of Ambrose's research on this angle to Jim Quinn, he nearly had a stroke. Upon recovering from his apparent apoplexy, Quinn gave me the old business about the tons of evidence that said post position was meaningless as a handicapping factor. I told him that, yes, this is true 80 percent of the time; the other 20 percent, or in all maiden races, it's an issue that must be reckoned with. The evidence that I presented Quinn was simply the fact that of all the maiden race favorites that failed at Santa Anita, it was twice as likely that the failed maiden favorite had an inside post versus an outside post. Also, the maiden race favorites that did manage to win were twice as likely to have an outside post.

There are two negative angles concerning maidens that you should always bet against. The first is the first-time starter that shows three or more gate works in its listed workouts. You can bet the ranch and the dog that such a horse is having problems getting out of the gate. And since speed is king in these maiden races, the tardy gate horse usually won't be able to reach a favorable striking position at the crucial first and second calls.

The second negative angle you should be aware of is the first-time starter in a maiden-claiming route race. Ambrose's research shows that these win less than 5 percent of maiden-claiming routes—a definite horse to bet against.

To convince you of the profit potential from maidens, let me share Ron Ambrose's results with you. Ambrose makes big money at the track, mainly on the strength of his profits from maidens. He generally bets $500 to $2000 on them to place and show. His win bets vary from $200 to $1000. He has an absolutely astounding hit rate with maidens. His top pick wins close to 40 percent, it runs second 72 percent, and is in the money 89 percent. He has managed to average over $7 in the win hole, $3.20 in place and $2.70 in the show. He never bets to win unless he can get 5-to-2, at least $3 to place and $2.60 to show. It doesn't take a rocket scientist to figure out that he has a huge edge on these bets. This year he intends to make over $150,000 at the track. His goal is to put at least $1 million through the mutuel windows. I can promise you that a large bulk of this will be on maiden races. Pleased be advised that he lives in Las Vegas and has over one hundred opportunities per day. He couldn't accomplish this betting at a single track. Ambrose is super selective. He exudes a confidence seldom seen on this side of Mount Olympus. He's a professional in every sense of the word. If you ever get a chance to attend one of his seminars, seize it. You'll learn more in a few hours with him than by reading all the handicapping books ever written. I am proud to be his associate. He has taught me more than I have taught him, yet he considers me as one of his teachers.

If you take a commonsense approach to handicapping maiden races, your top horse should win around 30 percent of the maiden races. This is a conservative estimate. If you're a budding Ron Ambrose, you can improve this figure to upward of 40 percent. So the next time someone tells you that maiden races can't be beaten, just smile and say thanks to the poor sucker. You were probably talking to a living brain donor.

Try this sample race for yourself. Simply apply the speed, pace, and ability time techniques discussed thus far. The race pars are 22.00 45.40 1:17.60. The ability time par is 68.80.

As always, the pace profile was early. The approximate closing odds were:

Stalvoy	6–1
Triton	50–1
True Pride	13–1
Turn To Trial	99–1
Final Slice	50–1
Crystaltransmitter	9–2
Prospector's Ridge	5–2
Wine Master	50–1
Desse Zenny	5–1
Mean Eye	99–1
Terrific Trip	9–5

6th Santa Anita

6½ FURLONGS. (1.14) MAIDEN CLAIMING. Purse $13,000. 3-year-olds and upward. Weights, 3-year-olds, 118 lbs.; older, 120 lbs. Claiming price $50,000, if for $45,000 allowed 2 lbs.

Coupled—Final Slice and Wine Master.

LASIX—Stalvoy, Prospector's Ridge, Mean Eye, Terrific Trip.

Stalvoy
DESORMEAUX K J
Own.—Saron Stable
$50,000
B. c. 3(Jan), by Stalwart—Queen Savoy, by Nashua
Br.—Robertson C J (Ky)
Tr.—Jones Gary
118

Lifetime	1991	4	M	0	1	$5,480
5 0 0 1	1990	1	M	0	0	$1,580
$5,480

Speed Index: Last Race: −14.0   3-Race Avg.: −7.3   4-Race Avg.: −7.2   Overall Avg.: −8.4
LATEST WORKOUTS   Nov 5 SA   3f fst :35¹ H   Oct 26 SA   5f fst 1:12⁰ H

Triton
SORENSON D
Own.—Morrison D
$45,000
B. g. 4, by Gallant Best—Salty Sonia, by Dupars
Br.—Westworth Farms (BC-C)
Tr.—Anderson Robert B
118

Lifetime	1991	5	M	0	1	$3,134
9 0 0 1	1990	4	M	0	0	$1,700
$4,834

Speed Index: Last Race: +5.0   3-Race Avg.: +2.6   8-Race Avg.: −0.6   Overall Avg.: −1.7
LATEST WORKOUTS   Nov 5 Fpx   4f fst :49² H   Oct 30 Fpx   5f fst 1:01⁴ H   Oct 8 EP   5f fst 1:02³ H   Sep 27 EP   5f fst 1:02¹ H

True Pride
BAZAN J
Own.—Anthony—Herbert & Hoyt
Entered 5Nov91– 2 SA
$45,000
Gr. g. 3(Apr), by Truly Lucky—Her Pride, by Gin Tour
Br.—Frauzman R & Dolores (Cal)
Tr.—Craigmyle Scott J
116

Lifetime	1991	2	M	0	1	$3,820
2 0 0 1	1990	0	M	0	0	
$3,820

90ct91-Disqualified and placed third
Speed Index: Last Race: −4.0   2-Race Avg.: −6.5   2-Race Avg.: −6.5   Overall Avg.: −6.5
LATEST WORKOUTS   Nov 3 Fpx   4f fst :47 Hg   Oct 12 Fpx   5f fst 1:00 H   Sep 25 Fpx   3f fst :35 H   Sep 19 Fpx   5f fst :59¹ Hg

Turn To Trial
ATKINSON P
Own.—Rancho Jonnla
$50,000
Blk. b. or g. 3(Jan), by Turn to Mars—Tribulation, by Tembour
Br.—Rancho Jonnla (Cal)
Tr.—Sutton Jerry
118

Lifetime	1990	0	M	0	0	

Speed Index: Last Race: (—)   3-Race Avg.: (—)   12-Race Avg.: (—)   Overall Avg.: (—)
LATEST WORKOUTS   Nov 2 SA   3f fst :36³ H   Oct 27 SA   4f my :49² H   Oct 21 SA   5f fst 1:17² Hg   Oct 15 SA   6f fst 1:15¹ H

Final Slice
CASTANON A L
Own.—Golden Green Farm & Manning
$45,000
Blk. b. or br. 3, by Ruffinal—Slice Off, by Off
Br.—Vlne 6 (Cal)
Tr.—Manning Dennis R
118

Lifetime	1991	1	M	0	0	

Speed Index: Last Race: (—)   3-Race Avg.: (—)   12-Race Avg.: (—)   Overall Avg.: (—)
LATEST WORKOUTS   Nov 4 Fpx   3f fst :38² H   Oct 30 Fpx   4f fst 1:15 Hg   Oct 24 Fpx   5f fst 1:04 Hg   Oct 19 Fpx   4f fst :49² H

Crystaltransmitter
PEDROZA M A
Own.—Siegel M–Jan–Samantha
$50,000
Ch. c. 3(Mar), by Lines of Power—Crystal Stone, by Pappa Fourway
Br.—Aspiration Stud (Ky)
Tr.—Mayberry Brian A
118

Lifetime	1990	0	M	0	0	

Speed Index: Last Race: (—)   3-Race Avg.: (—)   12-Race Avg.: (—)   Overall Avg.: (—)
LATEST WORKOUTS   Oct 27 Hol   5f fst 1:01² H   Oct 18 Hol   5f fst 1:00¹ H   Oct 13 Hol   5f fst 1:13⁴ Hg

Prospector's Ridge
TORRES H
Own.—Dahlberg Farms
$50,000
Ch. c. 3(Feb), by Marco—LP† Orphan Julie, by Cox's Ridge
Br.—Sturgis J R (Cal)
Tr.—Grossman Dean
115

Lifetime	1991	11	M	5	1	$48,840
11 0 5 1	1990	0	M	0	0	
$48,840

Speed Index: Last Race: +1.0   3-Race Avg.: +1.0   5-Race Avg.: −2.4   Overall Avg.: −2.3
LATEST WORKOUTS   Nov 1 SA   5f fst 1:00¹ H   Oct 13 SA   3f fst :36³ H   Oct 8 SA   4f fst :47 H   Oct 2 SA   6f fst 1:13⁴ H

Wine Master
SOLIS A
Own.—Golden Green Farm & VanDenBroeck
$50,000
Blk. b. or br. 3(Mar), by Desert Wine—Set Aside, by Buffalo Lark
Br.—Cardiff Stud Farm (Cal)
Tr.—Headley Robert
118

Lifetime	1991	2	M	0	1	$2,170
2 0 0 1	1990	0	M	0	0	
$2,170

Speed Index: Last Race: −15.0   2-Race Avg.: −10.5   2-Race Avg.: −10.5
LATEST WORKOUTS   Oct 18 Fpx   6f fst 1:13⁵ H   Sep 14 Fpx   5f fst 1:02³ H   Sep 7 Fpx   4f fst :49 Hg

Desse Zenny
VALENZUELA P A
Own.—Whittingham C
$50,000
B. h. 5, by Papplone—Ecstacism, by What a Pleasure
Br.—Bobins & Sons (Fla)
Tr.—Whittingham Charles
120

Lifetime	1991	9	M	1	3	$6,575
9 0 1 3	1990	4	M	1	2	$14,680
$20,625

Speed Index: Last Race: 0.0   3-Race Avg.: −5.0   3-Race Avg.: −5.0   Overall Avg.: −7.0
LATEST WORKOUTS   Nov 1 SA   4f fst :47¹ H   Oct 19 SA   4f fst :47⁰ H   Oct 13 SA   5f fst 1:14 H   Oct 7 SA   6f fst 1:14⁰ H

Stalvoy This horse should benefit from one of the most powerful class drops in racing, that from maiden special weight to maiden claiming. Don't be fooled by this one's seemingly lackluster Oct. 3 race. In that race, he no doubt "bounced" off his overexertion in his August 31 race, in which he threw a personal best in his first start back from a seven-month layoff. Expect him to "bounce back" today and run a much improved race over his last one, perhaps even as good as the August 31 race. Any doubts about current form are removed when you consider his impressive workout pattern of 15 furlongs in 12 days, and the fact that Desormeaux stays on. Strong contender on class and form. On the numbers, he ran the August 31 race slightly slower than today's par. But in his first two career races, he ran to the pars demanded today.

Triton This one lacks a true running style. He has no early speed, doesn't force the pace, and really doesn't close. A deadly combination, even in a maiden-claiming race. Today's par to the second call is 45.40. He's never broken 46. A no-win jockey and an unknown trainer close the argument. Out.

True Pride This guy was all-out and even had to cheat to finish in front of softer maiden claimers. Another one with a no-win rider, and the class rise is really curious, since, as Ambrose puts it, the class elevator only goes one way in maiden races: down. Rarely do maidens win going up. Throw him out.

Turn To Trial First-timer with trainer who's been shut out with maiden claimers. Low-percentage rider doesn't help. Form is acceptable, as horse has been working out an average of a furlong per day. But the experienced runners can run to the pars and throw above-average ability times, so this one's chances diminish. Elimination.

Final Slice Makes debut with unknown trainer and jockey behind him. Sire rating is uncompetitive. No problems with form; this guy's worked 18 furlongs in 19 days. Faces same dilemma as Turn To Trial in that the experienced maidens have shown some ability. Non-contender.

Crystaltransmitter Mayberry-Pedroza combination is always dangerous, and horse does have highest sire rating of the first-timers in this field. However, there is a form cloud over this one since he's worked just 19 furlongs in 31 days. Experienced maidens hold the edge. Toss out.

Prospector's Ridge A classic sucker horse. All those second-place finishes fooled the public into believing that a win was imminent, but he's disappointed the crowd every time. The crowd caught on in his last race, and dismissed him at 5.80-to-1, but not before he burned their money as the favorite four straight times, followed by a short-priced loss at 2.20-to-1. Even though this one is finally descending into the maiden-claiming ranks, he's unlikely to be helped by the class drop. Though he's run to today's pars in every one of his races, he's the kind you should avoid like the plague. It's obvious he just doesn't want to win. The **# Races** box automatically steers you away from them. Elimination.

Wine Master His form actually declined, despite the drop from maiden special weight company into maiden claiming. He's never run faster than 47 to the second call. Eliminate.

Desse Zenny Two starts at this level, including one as a beaten favorite. His prolific futility shown in **# Races** box. Elimination.

Mean Eye Two starts at this level, two with higher. No betting action in any of them. Can't run to today's pars. Toss out.

Terrific Trip Improved effort in last after finally being dropped to maiden-claiming level, and has shown he can run to the pars. Likely to be very tough again. Contender.

Below is the actual worksheet used by Steve Unite to handicap this race. This is what we affectionately call a "maidenform." It lets the user view all the pertinent handicapping factors at a glance. The top part of the form contains the speed and pace data. The date, race number, distance, and class information are self-explanatory. The win pars information is crucial. If you don't have win pars for maidens at your track, you should use the next best thing, which is the Gordon Pine par times. The ability-time par is vital. The balance of the form is dedicated to information specific to each horse.

PP stands for post position. Remember, in maiden sprints we give the edge to outside horses. That is, if inside and outside horses have basically the same numbers, the edge goes to the outside horse. It was the case in this race.

Name is self-explanatory.

 # Races refers to the lifetime total. We prefer lightly raced horses to horses with ten or more races. A straight maiden (MSW) begins to be demoted, in our opinion, if it takes more than three starts to become a winner. A maiden-claiming horse begins to be demoted, in our opinion, if it takes more than five starts to become a winner.

Class Last Race points out class drops. Especially significant is the drop from straight maiden to maiden claiming.

Days Since Last Race is concerned with recency. The magic number is 17. Over 17 days since last race requires at least one workout.

Ability Time is especially predictive in maiden sprints. This is the time it takes to run the second fraction (turn-time) added to the second call time.

Fur. Per Day is the ratio of total furlongs worked to the days since most distant workout. We want this ratio to be close to

MAIDENFORM

Date 11/7/91 Distance 6.5 f dirt Win Pars This Type Race:
Race # 6 Class ncl 50 22.00 45.40 17.60

Ability Time Par 68.80

PP	Name	# Races	Class Last Race	Days Since Last	Ability Time	Fur Per Day	6F Works	Tr.	Jock	Sire FTS Index	L	B	G
1	STALVOY	5	MSW	35	68.00	1.25	2	+	+				
2	TRITON	9	c40 (open cl)	26	68.25	1.11	0	−	‾ (no w/h jock)				
3	TRUE PRIDE	2	M32	20	68.20	1.00	0	−	‾ (no w/h jock)				
4	TURN TO TRIAL	0	N/A	N/A	N/A	.91	2	−	−	28			
5	FINAL SLICE	0	N/A	N/A	N/A	.95	1	−	−	24			
6	CRYSTAL TRANSMIT	0	N/A	N/A	N/A	.61	1	+	+	33			
7	PROSPECTOR'S RIDGE	11	MSW	21	67.50	.83	1	−	=				
8	WINE MASTER	2	M50	22	68.20	0 no works s.l.r.	2	⌣	=	'			
9	DESSE ZENNY	9	M50	14	67.40	.67	2	+	=				
10	MEAN EYE	4	M50	22	68.15	.75	0	⌣	−				
11	TERRIFIC TRIP	7	M50 (cal-bred)	22	67.70	1.50	3	+	=				
12													
13													
14													
15													
16													

1.00. We'll use the Ambrose trick of adding three furlongs to the total if we use three works, and adding five furlongs to the total if we use four works.

6F Works is looking for long workouts. Just as Bill Scott pointed out the importance of the five-furlong work back East, Ambrose found that six-furlong works are a positive factor out West. Remember that length of workout is usually a trainer preference. Brian Mayberry, an especially productive trainer with maidens, usually uses four-furlong works. So please don't interpret the lack of six-furlong works as a negative.

Tr. stands for trainer. We look at the trainer's ROI for today's distance under today's class conditions. This information can be purchased in major racing areas. If it can't, that's reason for celebration. Keep it yourself and get a huge edge. You may also consider starting a small business providing this information for a fee.

Jock stands for Jockey. We are looking for positive jockey changes. A positive jockey change is a change to a leading rider or a switch to a rider who wins frequently for the horse's trainer.

Sire FTS Index is an index number that measures the productivity of a particular sire in producing first-time starters that win. This information is rather tough to get. Sports Institute in Las Vegas has published this type of data, but I'm not sure if they still do.

LBG stands for Lasix, blinkers, and gelding. We are looking for first- and second-time Lasix horses. We are looking for equipment changes. We don't care that a horse is wearing blinkers if he wore them in his last race. Gelding, the ultimate equipment change, is very powerful the first and second races back. This is a tough statistic to keep. It's very worthwhile to keep or buy this information. On the West Coast, recent geldings win 20 percent of their first or second races after being gelded, and show a flat-bet profit.

This race was an uninspiring maiden-claiming field made up of blah first-timers, proven losers at today's level, a classic sucker horse, and two legitimate contenders. Stalvoy and Terrific Trip each have a strong look at this race, and not much separates them on cold handicapping dope. Their turn-times are equal, while Terrific Trip has a little edge in ability time (67.7 to 68). They both show strong workout patterns and competent trainers. We must give a slight edge to Terrific Trip. Stalvoy has one of the strongest maiden handicapping factors going for him, the class drop from straight maiden to maiden claiming. But the numbers favor Terrific Trip. My line on this race was:

Terrific Trip	5–2
Stalvoy	7–2

If our competence is equal to the public's, our top two contenders should win this race about half the time.

The public has spoken. They make Terrific Trip the favorite at 9-to-5, way under our win-bet odds of 5-to-2. But they dismissed Stalvoy at 6.20-to-1. Our decision is simple. We have clear "wager value" on Stalvoy, who's paying almost twice what he should. A very nice overlay. He won straight and returned a generous $14.40.

SIXTH RACE

Santa Anita

NOVEMBER 7, 1991

6 ½ FURLONGS. (1.14) MAIDEN CLAIMING. Purse $19,000. 3-year-olds and upward. Weights, 3-year-olds, 118 lbs.; older, 120 lbs. Claiming price $50,000; if for $45,000 allowed 2 lbs.

Value of race $19,000; value to winner $10,450; second $3,800; third $2,850; fourth $1,425; fifth $475. Mutuel pool $356,327.

Last Raced	Horse	M/Eqt.A.Wt	PP St	¼	½	Str	Fin	Jockey	Cl'g Pr	Odds $1
30ct91 6SA4	Stalvoy	LBb 3 118	1 5	3 1½	3 2	1½	1 1½	DesormuxKJ	50000	6.20
16Oct91 4SA2	Terrific Trip	LBb 3 118	11 3	5 2	4½	4 2	2 1½	Flores D R	50000	1.90
17Oct91 6SA3	Prospector's Ridge	LB 3 113	7 2	2hd	2hd	2½	3 1½	Torres H5	50000	2.80
24Oct91 4SA3	Desse Zenny	Bb 5 120	9 1	6 4	6 6	5 1	4 1	ValenzuelPA	50000	5.20
	Crystaltransmitter	B 3 118	6 4	1½	1hd	3 1	5¼	Pedroza M A	50000	4.90
18Oct91 4SA3	True Pride	B 3 116	3 6	4½	5 1½	6 2½	6 3	Bazan J	45000	13.00
16Oct91 4SA7	Wine Master	Bb 3 118	8 10	9 1	8 2	7 2	7 1½	Solis A	50000	a-52.70
12Oct91 7EP5	Triton	B 4 118	2 7	7hd	7hd	8 6	8 13	Sorenson D	45000	57.60
	Final Slice	B 4 118	5 8	8 1½	9 4	9 2	9 1½	Steiner J J	45000	a-52.70
	Turn To Trial	B 3 118	4 11	10 10	10	10	10	Atkinson P	50000	146.00
16Oct91 4SA5	Mean Eye	LB 4 118	10 9	11	—	—	—	Patton D B	45000	107.80

Mean Eye, Pulled up.
a-Coupled: Wine Master and Final Slice.

OFF AT 3:11. Start good. Won driving. Time, :22 , :44⁴, 1:10², 1:17¹ Track fast.

$2 Mutuel Prices:			
2-STALVOY	14.40	5.80	3.80
10-TERRIFIC TRIP		3.90	2.80
7-PROSPECTOR'S RIDGE			2.80

It pays to master maiden races. The challenges are first-time starters, class drops, distance switches, and shippers. We prefer first-time starters in chaos races or when they're the morning-line favorite bet below their morning line. Class drops must qualify under ability time. Distance switches and shippers are handled the same way as we discussed in chapter 4, Ability. Maidens will become a very strong profit center for you if you'll master the lessons of this chapter. Let's now take a look at claiming races.

Chapter 9

Claiming Races

THE FUNDAMENTAL PRINCIPLE OF handicapping that applies to claiming races is: *If it doesn't make economic sense, it doesn't make handicapping sense.* This is the approach that will guide every aspect of our analysis of claiming races. The sport's headlines may focus on champions and Grade 1 races, but for most horsemen—owners, trainers, jockeys—it's a faraway dream. Reality dictates that success in the claiming game is of vital financial importance to the majority of human connections of equine athletes. Similarly, for us as winning players, we cannot hope to survive parimutuelly without netting consistent profits from these bread-and-butter contests, the most common kind of race carded.

Here's an example of a violation of the laws of economics, and therefore a violation of the laws of handicapping. A trainer claims a horse for $25,000. Rather than entering it within thirty days at the mandatory higher level, he sits the horse out for a month. He then enters it for $16,000. This makes no economic sense whatsoever. It's equivalent to your buying a car for $25,000, letting it sit in your garage for a month, and then offering the car for sale for $16,000. Why would you sell a $25,000 commodity for $16,000? Perhaps if you've bought a lemon that isn't worth $25,000, you'd want to cut your losses by recovering part of your investment. Now, why would a trainer sell a $25,000 horse for $16,000? Trainers are not philanthropists giving away the store. The trainer's obviously got damaged goods which he's trying to unload on some other poor, unsuspecting horseman. Beware of these fire sales. Thankfully, the public usually overlooks the suspicious drop off the claim and instead sees it as a sign of total class domination, and they hammer these shaky droppers like there's no tomorrow. This is just terrific; it gives us the wonderful situation in which we can crush a race by betting against a completely false favorite. As winners, we'll pray for and take full advantage of these lovely opportunities.

As to every broad guideline or rule, there is at least one exception. Not all these drops off claims are completely negative. The notable exclusion is when a horse is "foldered." This usually occurs at the lowest and next-to-lowest rungs of the claiming ladder. An illustration is in order. In southern California the two cheapest claiming levels are $12,500 and $10,000. A trainer will claim a horse for $12,500. Instead of entering it at the mandatory higher level within thirty days, the trainer sits the horse out and enters it for $10,000. Consider that the horse will most likely win at the $10,000 level. Consider that this horse will also most likely get claimed. The purse for this level is $10,000. The winner's share is 55 percent, or $5,500. The claim enriches the owner another $10,000. The original claim is for $12,500. The cost of caring for the horse for one month is approximately $1,500. Total investment: $14,000. Total return: $15,500. Profit in one month: $1500. A 12 percent ROI in thirty days. That's not bad investing; the annualized return is over 140 percent! You must know about the trainers on your circuit who get away with this move. That's one of the rare exceptions in which a drop off a claim makes economic sense.

Maiden claimers are usually not worth the open price of their maiden-claiming price. A horse that wins for a maiden-claiming price of $32,000 will most often be overvalued. The par times indicate such a maiden-claiming winner is more accurately valued at the open price of approximately $16,000.

Ninety-five percent of the time, the laws of economics will dictate how we'll handicap claiming races. A claimer should race for a higher claiming price after it wins. The reason is clear: If a horse wins for a certain price, it's worth roughly that price. To lessen the likelihood of having the horse claimed from him, the trainer will run it at a higher price after the win. However, there are certain trainers on each circuit for whom the laws of economics are suspended. These guys will win again on the drop after the win, so be on the lookout for them. You'll need to purchase trainer data or do your own research to identify these maneuverers. In the absence of this information, by adhering to the laws of economics, you'll be correct more often than you'll be wrong in your claiming-race analysis.

As always, we apply our four major criteria: ability, form, angles, and value.

Ability is a horse's class and speed capabilities. In claiming races, class refers to the horse's selling price, not to the race's purse value. A horse's "real class" is defined as the selling price at which it has previously won or come close (within two lengths of par). Just because a horse is entered for a particular claiming price doesn't mean it's that class of horse. A horse can be entered for a $50,000 tag today, yet it may really have only exhibited its class successfully at the $20,000 level. He's not a genuine $50,000 claiming horse; he's a $20,000 horse.

Much has been written about the claiming-class, selling-price drop; specifically, that a 30 percent reduction in claiming price represents the most positive impact value in racing (Quirin, 1979). True, drops tend to result in an improved effort, but only for horses that have shown evidence that the drop is truly necessary. A horse that has been getting trounced at a certain claiming price probably requires a class drop to become competitive. But as Tom Brohamer warns in *Modern Pace Handicapping*, a horse that's in contention at the stretch call of its race and then drops back really doesn't require a drop in class; the horse has shown he belongs and can compete at that level. Hence this kind of drop is suspicious. After all, by being competitive, the horse has demonstrated he's worth roughly that price. If so, why would the trainer offer it at a cheaper price? Most likely, something is amiss physically. The trainer suggests this by trying to unload the horse at a reduced price. So, as for these huge drops being sharp class edges with positive impact values, please be wary. Excellent corroborating evidence can be found in information concerning trainer patterns; examination of the statistics will help you determine the intent, positive or negative, behind the class drop.

In claiming races open to three-year-olds and up, you should favor the older horses early in the year. After July or August this edge goes away. In addition to the older horses being more physically mature and experienced through seasoning, the younger horses, especially three-year-old claimers, are overvalued in comparison to their elders. In spring and summer prefer the older horses to their still-developing younger counterparts.

By the end of the calendar year, three-year-olds race at no statistical disadvantage to older horses, especially in sprints. The opposite is true for maiden-claiming races open to three-year-olds and up. A four-year-old or older horse still trying to break its maiden in a maiden claimer is a decided failure. In these dismal events, youth will be served.

The jockey factor itself is relatively unimportant. However, a jockey switch is significant if it's to a leading rider or to one who has ridden the horse to victory previously. Again, the laws of economics prevail. Remember, the top jockeys on the grounds can pick and choose among virtually all the horses. The jockey's agent determines which mounts his client will ride. The jockey's agent works on a commission basis, so it's in his best interest to secure "live" mounts for his rider. A change to the leading rider isn't a coincidence; it's a sure sign of positive trainer intent.

The speed and pace capabilities of the claiming horse will become apparent through the already-mentioned components of ability times, win pars, and pace profiles. It's essential that we measure ability against the horse's current form and condition. The form factor is critical in claiming races. Most claimers, especially the cheaper stock, have very short form cycles. They rarely put together good races back-to-back. Non-claimers are more reliable. They're taken better care of, and race less frequently, because of the larger purses in non-claiming races. For claimers, this ain't so. Most have physical problems. Yet these bread-and-butter horses need to race more regularly in order to keep their connections solvent. Unlike their non-claiming counterparts, most claimers aren't given the luxury of regular time off to recuperate from their various ailments. In this sense, determining the form cycles of horses becomes indispensable in our quest for profits in claiming races.

The claiming horse's current form cycle can be gauged by its performance since its most recent layoff. When evaluating a claiming horse returning from a layoff, don't expect too much in its first race back, unless the horse has shown that it can be a factor when fresh from a similar layoff. The question to ask is: How has he performed off a layoff in the past? If the past performances don't show a previous layoff and the horse has less than ten career starts, Mark Cramer has our answer. As noted before, in his beautifully written *Thoroughbred Cycles* he contends that the horse's first career start gives us an indication of the horse's capabilities off a layoff. Cramer's studies have shown a correlation between success in the horse's debut and subsequent success off layoffs.

If the first race after a layoff is lackluster, expect some improvement in the next one. The third race after a layoff is magical, as Quirin has proven. However, the prices on third-race-back horses can be miserly, especially if there has been improvement in the second race back. You must anticipate improvement well in advance of the public; in other words, in the second race back. Typically, these returning horses round into winning form by showing speed to the second call in their first race back, equal to or greater than the previous best ability time prior to the layoff. Don't worry about final time. Consider only ability time. You'll cash some monster prices before the public realizes this horse is back to the top of its prelayoff form cycle.

Among the positive angles in handicapping claimers is the horse-for-course phenomenon. Consider the plight of a claimer imprisoned at a track for which he has no affinity. Six, seven or even as many as ten races show in this guy's past performances— all of them dismal, all of them at the track that he hates. When the next meet opens at the track at which the horse has won (often more than once), the horse-for-course subtleties will escape the understanding of the crowd. The public will see poor recent form. If you're tuned in to the horse-for-course angle, you'll go beyond the static history of the ten races in the past performances and watch with glee as this horse balloons up to 20-to-1 on the tote board. Your edge is in knowing that this particular horse is partial to today's track. Most of your fellow handicappers won't know this. Take full advantage of this lovely situation.

Distance is not promoted as an essential yardstick. However, you should demand at least a competitive performance at today's specialty distance. Devil's Bag was the perfect horse. His Dosage Index was 1.00 and his center of distribution was zero. This suggests the perfect complement of speed and stamina. Yet Devil's Bag never won a race around two turns. If a Grade 1 horse such as Devil's Bag had this defect, you can bet that ordinary claiming horses are subject to even odder idiosyncracies about distance and layout. More than the distance itself, concentrate on the peculiarities of layout at this distance and racetrack. Some horses can't win the standard two-turn routes at mile or longer tracks. Yet when they ship to bullrings at which routes are run around three or more turns, they become world beaters. For example, Hollywood Park has begun carding one-turn 7½-furlong races. The two-turn milers from Santa Anita don't always adapt successfully to the Hollywood race. Prefer the claimers who've shown a liking to the unusual Hollywood layout. Another textbook example can be found in the 6½-furlong sprints down the unique hillside turf course at Santa Anita. How weird is this trip? It features the only right-handed turn in American racing. Then, while running down a hill, the horses encounter a patch of the main dirt track at the top of the homestretch, where the course finally levels out. Classier horses adapt athletically to these gonzo races; claimers usually don't. Course and distance specialties are the rule in claiming races. It pays to know the finicky course and distance preferences of ordinary claimers.

As mentioned earlier, few claiming horses have reliable form cycles. They're hard-pressed to win consecutive races. Records of one win in 18 or so starts are not atypical. The horse that has won 4 out of 18 starts deserves extra credit, especially if it's been able to show a form cycle that lasts for more than two or three races. In-and-outers fill typical claiming fields. Consistent horses stick out. They merit an edge.

On the recency factor, 21 is the magic number. We'll accept a horse that has raced within the last 21 days. No workouts are necessary during that period, in light of the grueling racing schedules most claimers endure. If the horse last raced within 22 to 30 days, demand at least one workout, and preferably two, as a sign of acceptable readiness. The line must be drawn at 30 days. Here, examine previous performance patterns after layoffs of similar length. (Most of the time, you'll insist upon two-thirds of a furlong per day as a reliable workout rate.) Also evaluate the workout schedule during comparable periods of inactivity. The major question you should ask is: What does this horse's workout pattern look like when the animal is in top form?

Form cycle is easily determined. Simply add the *Daily Racing Form*'s speed rating and track variant for each of the most recent races. At this writing, the *Form* is in the process of supplementing its speed rating and track variant numbers with the superior Beyer speed figures. Five is the magic number. Where fluctuations of up to 4 points up or down in these numbers suggest steadiness in the form cycle, dramatic improvement or decline is signaled when these numbers vary 5 or greater points between races. Make sure that an abnormally fast or slow pace didn't take its toll on the final figure. The great advantage of evaluating form cycle with the Beyer numbers is that distance-to-distance variations affect the Beyer number less drastically than they do the S.R. plus T.V. *Form* numbers. Using the sum of the speed rating and the track variant makes comparing apples to apples a much more difficult task. The Beyer numbers make comparisons between various unrelated distances more tenable. Nonetheless, it's still a wise idea to determine the tendency—improving, declining, or consistent—of the form cycle exclusively among races at similar distances and surfaces. Once you start looking at the numbers for dirt routes on fast tracks, it's best to stay with dry dirt-route numbers for form-cycle evaluation purposes. Try to remain consistent in your comparisons.

Class in claiming races is a fleeting concept. Meteoric rises and equally rapid descents can attend the same horse in the span of a single race meeting. Complicating these quick ups and downs is their unpredictability: improvement and decline can often happen without warning or explanation. All we can say for sure is that if a horse was victorious or competitive at a certain level in the (hopefully) not-too-distant past, it has the basic ability to win at that level again. The question to ask is: Has the horse won at today's level or at a higher level at some time, anytime, in the past? If the answer is yes, then the horse is a definite contender on class alone. Considering the mercurial nature of claiming animals, the horse may pop up and win again. After all, he's done it before. If the answer is no, then several subsequent questions must be asked: Has this horse won recently at a lower level, in good enough time to be competitive at today's higher level? Beyer's dictum, "Class is speed," will allow us to accurately determine whether this horse can rise in claiming price successfully.

Inherent in class drops are two opposite logics. Is the drop positive? Is this the level at which the horse is going to be competitive? Or is the drop negative? Are the horse's human connections trying to unload damaged goods? These are essential distinctions that we must make with a high degree of accuracy if we're going to be able to take advantage of the legitimate descents and forswear the fire sales. The key to determining the virtue of a class drop is to identify the trainer's intent. A drop in itself isn't enough. We need further evidence that the trainer is earnestly trying with the horse. Look for evidence of positive trainer intention. Favorable signs include: a positive jockey switch to a leading rider or to a rider that has won with the horse previously; newfound early speed; improving ability time; the addition of Lasix first or second time; fitting with blinkers; recent gelding. These changes are significant because they can make inferior recent numbers irrelevant. The changes can practically usher in a new spirit of winning competitiveness for a horse. A class dropper without any of these positive indicators should be viewed with suspicion.

Conversely, class rises usually provide no room for negative maneuvering. The numbers at the lower level unequivocally speak for themselves. A good last race at the lower level with actual times close to the pars for today's level make a successful rise possible. Be on the lookout for horses rising to a claiming level at which they have failed repeatedly. The horse may have strongly competitive numbers at the $25,000 level, but if he's rising to $32,000 today and his record indicates that he's never won at $32,000 after similar rises, he probably won't handle the rise again today. Remember the Peter Principle: People rise to their level of incompetence. The same is true for most claiming horses.

The speed and pace components of adjusted fractional times and ability times constitute the decisive factors in claiming races. The win pars and pace bias are crucial. If a horse hasn't demonstrated that he can run to the pars and profile, he's not a contender. Your first job is to separate the contenders from the pretenders. It's done using standards.

Additionally, we can eyeball the sum of the *Form's* speed rating and track variant or Beyer speed numbers to get a gestalt for each horse's final-time abilities. As was previously mentioned, these numbers can also trace the trend of a horse's form cycle. When an older horse throws "a personal best" figure, it most likely has reached the peak of its form cycle. It's typically downhill from there. Don't expect a repeat of the sterling number, and definitely don't project continued improvement. This is an excellent way to identify false and vulnerable favorites that'll be overbet on the basis of that top effort, which likely has taken too much out of the horse for today's race. Younger, still developing two-year-olds and three-year-olds confront us with the opposite dilemma: they've yet to reach the upper limits of their performance capabilities. They repeatedly run successively better numbers. The operative question to ask of these precocious juveniles is: How much further improvement should we project?

Value criteria include each horse's closing odds in its last race and morning-line odds in today's race. This gives us an indication of how well-regarded this horse is. The public is a damn good handicapper; the accuracy of the morning line varies from track to track. Horses that were 40-to-1 in their last race and are less than 6-to-1 on the morning line today after showing no apparent improvement should cause us a wee bit of apprehension. Why? It doesn't make economic sense! Proceed with caution.

Ability, form factor, angle, and value considerations are nearly impossible to manage within the tight confines of our *Daily Racing Form* pages. Similar to the "maidenform" that we devised for maiden races, a "claiming form" allows us to organize and codify the essential factors contributing to the outcomes of claiming races. Again, the idea is to note decisive patterns that frequently isolate the contenders and winners of these races. By handicapping the horses, the racetrack, and ourselves, we'll know exactly what wins claiming races particular to our own situation. Even better, we can begin to see the Achilles' heels that cause favorites to lose. The overarching objective is to get in touch with what's winning and bet on those factors; and to learn what's losing, and totally avoid those factors. Let's now apply these principles to the following race:

The critical information is as follows:

Race Pars (in tenths):	21.80	44.60	115.60
Turn-Time Par:	22.80		
Ability Par:	67.40		

Final Odds According to Chart:

Cadillac Red	9.8	Big Daddy Kohr	5.2
Damelo	6.5	Planogram	16.9
Rippling Deal	2.2	Screen Tale	38.8
Proudnesian	16.6	Chief Sassafras	10.0
S.S. Picante	15.9	Burn And Turn	4.0

Cadillac Red Nice try at this level last time, although he didn't flash the razor-sharp interior speed essential to shortening up successfully; however, he has shown he can handle the sprint, winning at today's distance in his July 29 Del Mar race. Marginal contender. Let the computer figure out if his last race can cut it with his competition today. I suspect not.

Damelo A perfect example of the sharp interior route fractions that signal a winning shorten-up. The pars for the Oct. 19 race are 47^1 $1:12^2$. This guy ran almost seven lengths faster than par. Don't be concerned that he lost six lengths in the stretch. He was on the lead for more than three-fourths of the race. Strong chance. The June 2 Hollywood Park race at seven furlongs represents the pressing style he'll most certainly employ today. Using that paceline, he throws a fantastic ability time that's almost a full second faster than par. Don't worry about the slow projected final time. The profile is king in claiming races.

S. S. Picante

DELAHOUSSAYE E
Own.—Gallaher E J & Evelyn
$25,000
Ch. c. 3(Feb), by Sauce Boat—Catch Some Rays, by Gold L B
Br.—Owens K E (Md)
Tr.—
115

Speed Index: Last Race: -2.0   3-Race Avg.: -1.3   9-Race Avg.: -0.8   Overall Avg.: -0.8
LATEST WORKOUTS

Big Daddy Kohr

STEVENS G L
Own.—Silber M
$25,000
B. c. 3(Apr), by World Appeal—Classic Queen, by Minnesota Mac
Br.—Kohr E B (Fla)
Tr.—Stein Roger
118

Speed Index: Last Race: +5.0   3-Race Avg.: +4.6   7-Race Avg.: +2.2   Overall Avg.: -0.3

Planogram

VALENZUELA P A
Own.—Harrington L B
$25,000
Ro. g. 3(Mar), by Drone—Nimbus Star, by Grey Dawn II
Br.—Glen Hill Farm (Fla)
Tr.—Dutton Jerry
115

Speed Index: Last Race: -6.0   3-Race Avg.: -5.1   8-Race Avg.: -5.1   Overall Avg.: -7.0
LATEST WORKOUTS

Screen Tale

PEDROZA M A
Own.—Sczulick J
$25,000
Ch. g. 3(Feb), by Silent Screen—Regency Tale, by Vice Regent
Br.—Greensleeves Limited (Md)
Tr.—Stute Warren
115

Speed Index: Last Race: 0.0   3-Race Avg.: -4.0   3-Race Avg.: -4.0   Overall Avg.: -5.6
LATEST WORKOUTS

Chief Sassafras

CEDENO E A
Own.—Sonnier Brenda
$25,000
Dk. b. or br. c. 3(Feb), by Sassafras (Fra)—K's Folly, by Indian Chief II
Br.—Hollingsworth Catherine (Ky)
Tr.—Stute Gary
115

Speed Index: Last Race: -3.0   3-Race Avg.: -3.6   6-Race Avg.: -5.2   Overall Avg.: -5.2
LATEST WORKOUTS

Burn And Turn

FLORES D R
Own.—Mamakos J L
$22,500
B. g. 3(Mar), by TH Up—Blaze a Trail, by Nantequos
Br.—Mamakos J L (Ky)
Tr.—Mamakos Jason
113

Speed Index: Last Race: -1.0   3-Race Avg.: -5.0   4-Race Avg.: -6.7   Overall Avg.: -6.7
LATEST WORKOUTS

Claiming Form

race pars

Date 11/16/91   Distance 6.5 f Dirt   Win Pars This Type Race:

Race # 5   Class C25-22.5 K   /   21.80 44.60 115.80

Turn Time Par 22.80

PP	Name of Horse	Jockey Status	Age	# Races Since Layoff	Surface Distance Suitable S	D	Win Ratio Wins/Races	Recency Works Form Cycle R	W	FC
1	CAPILLAC RED	⊏	3	7	+	+	2/21	13	0	↗
2	DAMELO	=	3	5	+	−	2/13	28	1	OK
3	RIPPLING PEAL	=	3	9	+	+	4/11	22	2	OK
4	PROUDNESIAN	+	3	0	+	−	4/14	51	4	OK
5	S.S. PICANTE	+	3	3	+	+	1/9	22	2	↓
6	BIG DADDY KOHR	+	3	10	+	+	7/30	10	0	OK
7	PLANOGRAM	+	3	0	+	+	1/12	62	4	↓
8	SCREEN TALE	=	3	10	+	−	2/18	28	4	↓
9	CHIEF SASSAFRAS	−	3	1	+	+	2/13	22	3	↓
10	BURN AND TURN	=	3	1	+	+	1/4	44	2	?
11										
12										
13										
14										
15										
16										

Please note: Ability Time is different for turf.

Dirt Ability Time = TT + 2F
Turf Ability Time = FF + 3F

Ability Time Par 67.40

Class	Pace Fractions			TT	Ability Time	SR + TV	Odds Last Race	Morn Line Odds	L	B	G
	1st Call	2nd Call	Final								
SAME	23.20	45.50	116.80	22.30	67.80	100	2.60-1				
RISE	21.42	44.02	118.35	22.60	66.62	89	2.00-1				
DROP	22.60	45.50	116.10	22.90	68.40	102	2.90-1				
DROP	23.60	46.30	118.40	22.70	69.00	102	5.40-1				
DROP	22.00	45.00	117.00	23.00	68.00	98	8.20-1		1X		
DROP	22.70	45.50	115.80	22.80	68.30	105	2.50-1				
RISE	23.60	45.90	117.50	22.30	68.20	94	8.50-1				
RISE	22.30	44.80	116.81	22.50	67.30	100	10.70-1				
DROP	22.60	45.90	117.30	23.10	69.00	97	15.00-1				
RISE	21.80	44.60	115.65	22.80	67.40	100	7.00-1				

Rippling Deal He's an automatic throw-out. Just five weeks ago he barely won for $32,000 and last race he was in striking position for $40,000. He's worth at least $32,000. Dropping to $25,000 today, so soon after two good efforts for a higher price, is not a good sign. The numbers close the case: He can't run to the pars or profile, and his turn-time and ability time are much slower than par.

Proudnesian Has never won sprinting. Doesn't have the sharp interior route speed needed to turn back to sprint; he's got the slowest projected times at all three calls. Throw out.

S. S. Picante Has lost ground in both of his major-circuit races. This guy was competitive in the stretch at $40,000, but drops anyway. He's the kind of suicidal need-to-lead type that runs as fast as he can for as far as he can. He wins only when unmolested on a clear lead, but his projected times at the first and second calls show him behind other early speed types in here. Throw out.

Big Daddy Kohr High win percentage and very game. Will be pressing or stalking the pace throughout. A winner at this level on the turf, he has enough class. Contender. The numbers, however, say he doesn't fit the pace profile.

Planogram Maiden-claiming graduate at a lesser circuit has found little success in the big leagues. Has a very competitive turn-time, but it's the result of his pedestrian projected times of 23.60 45.90, figures way outside of the pace profile. Outclassed too, as he's never shown he can be competitive at this level.

Screen Tale After winning for $25,000 in August, he took the rise and was crushed. The subsequent drops back to this level and the next lower level have not resulted in success. Form cycle going the wrong way. Not suited to the distance, either. Toss out.

Chief Sassafras Very negative jockey switch from Solis (who's the only rider to have won with him) to Cedeno (who wins less than 5 percent of the time). Also, this horse began the year by winning a race for $50,000 claimers. He's definitely damaged goods as he drops for the second straight race. Elimination.

Burn And Turn Turned in a quitting-rat performance in his last, finishing second, beaten slightly more than a length after opening up three lengths on the field at the second call. Nonetheless, he returns to the site of his lone win and could be a horse-for-course in the making. Fits the profile perfectly. Don't use the Hollywood Park paceline, as it was achieved against a lowly band of maiden-claimers who failed to put any pressure on him. The last race is more representative of the horse's current form and the level of competition he'll be meeting today.

A typical competitive race with four contenders, none of them really standing out. Several possible outcomes are equally likely, so we must shop around and compare these possible outcomes with their respective values. We're likely to get a few overlays in the win pool since we've thrown out a false favorite who's going off at around 2-to-1.

Below is a copy of our computer printout using Cynthia Publishing's excellent computer program FIVE-IN-ONE.

Horse name	# ST	# W	# P	# S	$'S Earned	Date	Trk	Dist.	S	1st C time	2nd C time	Final time
CADILLAC RED	11	1	1	2	28750	3NOV91	SA	6.000	D	21.1	44.1	109.1
DAMELO	13	2	4	1	53120	2JUN91	HOL	7.000	D	21.4	44.2	124.1
BIG DADDY KOHR	20	5	1	5	58715	6NOV91	CRC	7.000	D	23.0	46.0	124.2
BURN AND TURN	4	1	1	0	12550	30OCT91	SA	6.500	D	21.4	44.4	116.1

Horse name	Class Lvl	1st C B.L.	2nd C B.L.	Final B.L.	SR	Var
CADILLAC RED	C32,000	10.00	7.50	4.00	86	14
DAMELO	C40,000	0.10	0.10	4.75	78	11
BIG DADDY KOHR	NW2	1.50	1.50	2.00	91	14
BURN AND TURN	C20,000	0.00	0.00	1.25	88	11

16NOV91   HOL   6.5 furlongs dirt
RACE #5   10 starters
Class C25,000   Class on

Horse name	PEH	H-I	THAAI	P-H	ESP	Rating	Betting Line	Fair Place $	Fair Show $
DAMELO	1	3	2	1	1	86.79	7-2		
BIG DADDY KOHR	2	1	1	2	3	82.86	4-1		
CADILLAC RED	4	2	4	4	2	75.83	6-1		
BURN AND TURN	3	4	3	3	4	75.79	6-1		

Our computer-generated odds line is:

Damelo	7-to-2
Big Daddy Kohr	4-to-1
Cadillac Red	6-to-1
Burn And Turn	6-to-1

The public's odds line was:

Damelo	6.5-to-1
Big Daddy Kohr	5.2-to-1
Cadillac Red	9.8-to-1
Burn And Turn	4.0-to-1

Burn And Turn is a definite underlay at public odds of 4-to-1. By throwing out the false favorite Rippling Deal, we are left with three win overlays. Our edge on Damelo is 65 percent; on Cadillac Red, 55 percent; and on Big Daddy Kohr, 24 percent. All meet our 20 percent minimum edge requirement. It's quite typical to have three strong win overlays in a race in which we have completely dismissed a false favorite. Damelo, at the top of our line, is our strongest bet because he offers us the largest edge. But it would not be incorrect to also bet Big Daddy Kohr and Cadillac Red to win. If you bet all three horses, you should have bet them proportional to their edge-to-odds ratio. In other words,

FIFTH RACE
Hollywood
NOVEMBER 16, 1991

6 ½ FURLONGS. (1.14²) CLAIMING. Purse $17,000. 3-year-olds. Weight, 121 lbs. Non-winners of two races since September 21 allowed 3 lbs.; a race since then, 6 lbs. Claiming price $25,000; if for $22,500 allowed 2 lbs. (Races when entered for $20,000 or less not considered.)

Value of race $17,000; value to winner $9,350; second $3,400; third $2,550; fourth $1,275; fifth $425. Mutuel pool $304,705. Exacta pool $434,424.

Last Raced	Horse	M/Eqt.A.Wt	PP	St	¼	½	Str	Fin	Jockey	Cl'g Pr	Odds $1
19Oct91 1SA4	Damelo	LB	3 115	2	4	4hd	2hd	1½	11	DesormuxKJ	25000	6.50
25Oct91 5SA4	Rippling Deal	LB	3 118	3	3	31	41	3½	2½	Sorenson D	25000	2.20
6Nov91 9Crc3	Big Daddy Kohr	LBb	3 118	6	6	5½	62	4½	3hd	Stevens G L	25000	5.20
15Sep91 8Fpx4	Planogram	LBb	3 116	7	10	8²½	7hd	6½	4½	ValenzuelPA	25000	16.90
19Oct91 1SA8	Screen Tale	Lb	3 115	8	7	6²	5hd	5¹	5nk	Pedroza M A	25000	38.80
25Oct91 5SA5	S. S. Picante	Lb	3 116	5	5	1hd	1hd	21	6²½	DelhoussyeE	25000	15.90
27Sep91 9EP4	Proudnesian	LB	3 117	4	9	10	10	7²	7hd	Pincay L Jr	25000	16.60
25Oct91 5SA6	Chief Sassafras	LBb	3 115	9	2	7hd	82	8½	82¾	Cedeno E A	25000	10.80
3Nov91 2SA3	Cadillac Red	LBb	3 115	1	8	9²	91	9¾	9⁶½	McCarron CJ	25000	9.80
30Oct91 3SA2	Burn And Turn	LBb	3 114	10	1	21½	31	10	10	Flores D R	22500	4.00

OFF AT 2:40. Start good. Won driving. Time, :21⁴, :44⁴, 1:09⁴, 1:16² Track fast.

$2 Mutuel Prices:	2-DAMELO	15.00	6.20	4.20
	3-RIPPLING DEAL		3.00	2.60
	6-BIG DADDY KOHR			3.60

$2 EXACTA 2-3 PAID $49.60.

Damelo gets the most money (40 %), Cadillac Red gets the second most (36%) and Big Daddy Kohr gets the least amount (24%). Damelo won straight and returned $15, a worthy price for our top pick in such a contentious field.

Most handicappers think that allowance races are easier than claiming races. As usual, they're not exactly correct. In fact, they aren't even close. You'll see why in the next chapter.

Chapter 10

Allowance and Stakes Races

MAIDEN RACES ARE reasonably predictable. Claiming races usually conform to the standards of speed, pace, and form. But allowance and stakes races are supposed to be the most formful. Sometimes they are. They're supposed to be relatively easy. Sometimes they are. But most of the time they are neither formful nor easy. Allowance races, particularly the non-winners series and the stakes menagerie, can regularly baffle the very best handicappers. They contain barbs, snares, and booby traps that can easily dupe the unwary. Consider the collision of conflicting class paradigms that confront us in these top-flight contests: claiming horses win allowance races, and allowance runners win stakes events; stakes horses lose allowance races, and allowance horses lose claiming events. How can we untwist these handicapping paradoxes and extract consistent profits from these non-claiming contests?

CHALLENGES OF NON-CLAIMING RACES

1. Claiming horses win allowance races.
2. Allowance runners win stakes races.
3. Stakes horses lose allowance races.
4. Allowance runners lose claiming races.
5. These races are supposed to be formful. They're not.

The myth pervading these races is that they're formful, that they run to the numbers. This isn't necessarily true. (A possible exception is the top of the top in non-winners allowance races that go on to win graded stakes.) The majority of runners in the non-winners series don't move up. They show form cycle variations similar to claiming horses. The old saw proclaims unequivocally, "Class will out." It ain't necessarily so. In fact, it's downright false! Witness the frequent occurrence of a proven $50,000 claimer who steps into the non-winners series against horses who've never raced for a tag and wins for fun. Truth is, the participants in these races should be subjected to the same four overarching criteria used to handicap maiden and claiming races: ability, form and condition, angles, and value.

UNIFYING PRINCIPLES

1. Ability (class, speed and pace) and form are the most meaningful factors.
2. You must be tuned in to your track bias.
3. You must be tuned in to what's winning at your track.
4. You must be tuned in to what's losing at your track.
5. Angles are secondary.
6. You must have a method to separate contenders from non-contenders.
7. The race favorite is the key to your betting strategy.
8. You must be able to make a betting line on every playable race.

It's very wise to structure your handicapping. It's really convenient to be able to look at all the pertinent data at a glance as opposed to trying to scan up and down the *Daily Racing Form*. That's why we use preprinted forms. The Allowance and Stakes Form will structure our handicapping and organize our analysis of the four significant criteria—ability, form, angles, and value. Patterns and general principles will emerge and allow us to construct a model of what kind of horse wins allowance and stakes races at our racetrack.

Take a look at the blank Allowance & Stakes Form on the next page. It puts all the important information right in front of you. It also guarantees that your handicapping will be structured. This form assumes that you have kept a "win profile" for your track. If you don't know what the winners at your track are doing, you are at a huge disadvantage.

Allowance & Stakes Form

Date _____   Distance _____   Win Pars This Type Race:

Race # ____   Class _____

Conditions _____   Purse _____   Ability Time Par _____

PP	Name of Horse	Jockey Status	A g e	# R S L	Surface Distance Suitable S D	W %	Recency Works Form Cycle R W FC	G S W	C R W	C
1										
2										
3										
4										
5										
6										
7										
8										
9										
10										
11										
12										
13										
14										
15										
16										

Please start keeping a winner's profile immediately. It's a good idea to enter the data for all the horses for at least 25 races. It's real important to get used to identifying horses that have very little or no chance to win today's race. After doing 25 races, you'll have a real feeling for which horses are contenders and which are pretenders.

After that, simply enter the data for your contenders only. After you have completed at least 50 races using this form, you'll

Please note: Ability Time is different
for turf.

Dirt Ability Time = TT + 2F
Turf Ability Time = 1F + 3F

Last Fraction Par _____

Pace Fractions			TT	Ability Time	SR + TV	Adj LF	O L R	M L O	L	B	G
1st Call	2nd Call	Final									

either convince yourself that it's an absolute necessity for winning non-claiming races or you'll be so familiar with what wins
that you'll be able to spot it in the *Racing Form* without help. In
either case, you'll be on your way to mastering these fairly difficult races.

The top part of the form contains the race data, and the bottom
part contains the data for each horse. Please also note the defini-
tions of "ability time." It's different from turf to dirt.

Date, Distance and **Race #** of the race are obvious.

For the **Class** blank, enter the type of race (allowance or stakes) and where it can be found on a par chart. Example: ALW NW2 or STK.

Conditions blank is for the conditions of the race, which includes the age restrictions and also the eligibility conditions. Example: 3 years ↑ NW2.

Purse Size blank is for the total purse size, not the winner's share. With respect to purse size, in general the higher the purse, the better the field. (The obvious exception is in state-bred races, which are typically augmented by additional monies from state breeding funds.)

Win Pars are taken directly from the win profile for your track. (If you don't have win pars for your track, the next best thing is the par times. I highly recommend Gordon Pine's Par Times because they give the times of all three calls. You need the first call to calculate "ability time.")

Ability Time Par is calculated from your win profile. Ability time is defined on the right-hand side of the form. (It's different for turf.) Last-fraction par is also calculated from your win profile. (Using the guidelines of the pace profile, in sprints allow approximately a two-length leeway when determining whether a horse can run to the win pars; in routes, a three-length allowance should be used. You also can use the concept of "Pace Contention Point." That's the maximum number of beaten lengths that winners were behind at the second call for 8 of the last 10 races at today's distance. An extra guideline we'll employ in our speed and pace analysis is the last-fraction par. This final fraction can be decisive. The reason the last fraction becomes important is that these higher-class horses can be rated. These races become tactical. (There's not much point in discussing tactical speed in maiden races. There's no such thing. They run as hard as they can for as long as they can.) Also, the higher-class horses tend to have the determination necessary to overcome the mild speed and pace biases that impair their lesser-grade counterparts.)

For each individual horse, we note the **Name** and **Post Position. Jockey Status** asks if the jockey is the same, better, or worse than the jockey that rode the horse last. As in the claiming game, the presence of a top jockey on a horse is a definite sign of positive trainer intent. Another positive sign is a switch to a rider who has won with the horse before. A negative jockey switch is one in which a leading rider abandons a horse in favor of another horse in the same field. The answers are filled in with a +, –, or = designation to indicate positive, negative, or same.

Age can be a significant factor. In the non-winners allowance series, the improving three-year-old has an advantage over older proven losers at the level. Beware of the late-maturing older horse who's been brought to the races slowly. In stakes races and classified allowances, prefer the older, more mature, more seasoned runners to still-developing three-year-olds, particularly during the spring and summer. Toward late fall and winter, three-year-olds race at no statistical disadvantage to older horses.

#RSL denotes the number of races since the most recent layoff. A layoff is defined as a 30-day or longer break between races. In this column the magic numbers to look for are 0, 1, and 2. A 0 in this category tells us to examine how the horse has performed immediately following previous layoffs. This is best accomplished by reading the past performances from bottom to top, noting gaps in racing activity. (The *Daily Racing Form* inserts a layoff line between consecutive races more than 45 days apart.) A 1 in this box suggests a form cycle that is still coming to fruition. Beware of a sterling but overtaxing effort in the first race back from a layoff; the "bounce" may cause a temporary regression in the second race back, notably for an older horse. A 2 in this category sets up the third race back today for the horse. Quirin's studies show that this third race following a layoff is magical; the typical horse will reach the peak of its form for this race. Unfortunately, the improvement is gradual and often noticeable in the past performances to your fellow handicappers. We'll try to anticipate improvement at least one race in advance of the crowd. In general, look for horses with 1 and 2 in the #RSL column to be on the upward swing of their form cycle.

Surface Distance Suitable boxes alert us to horses trying something new for the first time today. *S* is for surface and *D* is for distance. The most common examples concern sprinters stretching out and horses trying turf for the first time. Public favorites that have "no's" in either column must be considered vulnerable. These are favorites that we should bet against and try to beat. Horses must demonstrate they can handle the distance and the surface. It's not very wise to make a major bet on a horse that's being asked to do something that it's never done before. The answers can be "yes," "no," or "?" to indicate yes, no, or maybe. If a horse has run within one-half furlong of today's distance, it's suitable and gets a yes.

Win Percentage deals with consistency. Although this category should reflect a horse's performance for the past year, it's important to note the dramatic improvements shown by a late-blooming horse, whose record may be 3-for-12, but whose last three attempts are a perfect 3-for-3. Horses that are in the midst of one of these streaks deserve extra favor.

Recency Works Form Cycle information gives us an idea of the horse's current condition. *R* stands for recency. Recency involves the number of days since the horse's last race. *W* stands for workout pattern. If a horse doesn't lack recency, don't bother filling in this number. It's only when the horse lacks recency that we examine the workout pattern. The ratio of furlongs to days is the essential barometer of how well a horse has been training. Accept an allowance horse with a ratio of approximately .60; a stakes horse, .50. *FC* stands for form cycle. The form cycle question is quickly and easily answered by examining a horse's most recent numbers—use the Beyer speed number or the sum of the *Daily Racing Form's* speed rating and track variant. Five is the magic number. A fluctuation of 5 points up or down constitutes a noticeable improvement or decline. (For Beyer numbers, a 4-point swing is meaningful; however, make sure that an abnormally fast or slow pace didn't contribute to a correspondingly high or low figure.) Patterns become evident in the movement of these numbers. Simply mark an improving form cycle with a plus, a decline with a minus. For a horse that doesn't have a form cycle because he's returning from a layoff, check his previous performances when he returned from a similar layoff. As with the surface and distance suitability boxes, the form section will clearly point out false and vulnerable favorites that have form clouds or condition questions hanging over their heads.

GSW stands for graded stakes winner. Is the horse a graded stakes winner? The answer to this question has distinct implications in the two kinds of non-claiming races. In graded stakes, we always prefer horses that are previous graded stakes winners. They possess a class edge over non-graded stakes winners. However, a graded stakes winner entered in an allowance race, while wielding a similar advantage over the non-stakes winners, is usually not well-meant in the allowance race. Although this flies in the face of conventional class handicapping, the statistics of racing show that previous graded stakes winners throw unusually high negative ROIs when bet in allowance races. Because of future objectives, the trainer does not intend to push his graded stakes winner to the limit to win a relatively minor allowance purse. Most often, a horse will need a race against actual competition to be in peak form for the trainer's ultimate goal: winning another graded stakes race with the horse. The trainer will instruct the rider not to punish the horse with an all-out effort that may compromise the horse's ability to succeed in a future graded stake. The happy result is that our fellow bettors see only the obvious class domination. They fail to go beneath the surface to uncover the trainer's lack of intent to go fullbore to win the allowance race. The graded stakes winners are generally bet down to odds-on, and become very vulnerable or outright false favorites. By eliminating these classy but misplaced horses, we'll have a tremendous parimutuel advantage in the win pools. Another potential problem confronting graded stakes winners in allowance races is that they're typically entered in these events to answer questions about their current form and condition. The graded stakes winner may have declined, and its connections need to know the extent of the deterioration. Regardless of the particular situation, the general idea is to forswear graded stakes winners running in allowance races. They are not statistically profitable bets.

As with all horses moving up in class, allowance winners testing the graded stakes waters for the first time should possess numbers that are competitive in today's tougher field, if they are to have any hope of making a successful rise. In fact, it's wise to demand monster figures from allowance-to-stakes movers since we are dealing with unproven class commodities that will be trying to accomplish something that they have never done against graded stakes winners, which have proven their class.

Claiming race winners aren't automatic eliminations in allowance races. Consistent multiple claiming race winners can and do win allowance races. Especially in the non-winners series toward the end of the calendar year. That's when the genuine class items are noticeably absent, having already succeeded under these allowance conditions earlier in the season. Numbers earned in the claiming race that are competitive in today's allowance field give us the best evidence whether the horse can succeed. That's the litmus test.

Claiming race winners in graded stakes are usually toss-outs. They rate a look in lesser stakes. Incidentally, when determining the par times for stakes races, you should use the classified allowance (CLF) pars for non-graded stakes; use the stakes (STAKES) pars only for graded stakes. Unless the claiming race winner has numbers that totally dominate, don't expect it to be victorious in the stakes division. I usually fill in the GSW box with a "yes" or "no."

Class asks the question: Is this horse suitable to the class demands of today's race? We then note the class level of the paceline we have chosen for the horse. If the paceline race is an allowance race, simply enter the purse value. For a stakes paceline, differentiate graded from ungraded stakes. Graded stakes get the STK designation, while listed stakes, overnight stakes, and all non-graded stakes get a CLF designation. The proliferation of graded stakes has made Roman-numeral designations virtually interchangeable. Years ago, there was a distinct drop in quality from Grade 1 to Grade 2; now that graded stakes are carded almost daily and mostly attended by small fields, it's easier than ever for a Grade 2 horse to sneak in and win a Grade 1 race. Today, the two labels are virtually synonymous. Turf racing has managed to preserve these distinctions, mainly because there has not been as dramatic an increase in the number of graded turf races as there has in the number of graded dirt races. I usually put a "yes" or "no" in the class box. You may also choose to note pertinent class rises and drops here.

Pace Fractions are the most crucial data found on this form. Projected times for all three points of call, turn-times, and ability times are calculated by choosing a race to represent what the horse will do today and approximating the times by using one-fifth of a second per beaten length. It's not necessary that we demand rocket scientist accuracy. You'll get a good feel for this when we do some examples.

1st Call is the actual time, adjusted by beaten lengths, that it took the horse to run the first fraction. For a sprint it's the time for the first quarter of a mile, and for a route it's the time it takes to complete the first half-mile.

2nd Call is the adjusted time for the second fraction. For a sprint it's the time for the first half-mile, and for a route it's the time it takes to complete the first thee-quarters of a mile.

3rd Call is the adjusted time for the final fraction. This distance varies according to the length of the race.

TT stands for turn-time. This is the time it takes to run the second fraction. You calculate it by subtracting the 1st Call from the 2nd Call.

Ability Time is a very predictive factor, especially in the NW1 series. It's so important that it's defined on the form itself. Look in the upper right-hand corner.

SR + TV stands for speed rating plus track variant. You calculate this number by adding the two numbers that appear after the odds-last-race data in the *Daily Racing Form*. You can also use the *Beyer speed figure* if you like. The Beyer number, or the sum of the *Form* speed rating and track variant. (S.R. plus T.V.) can usually point out the true contenders at a glance. For instance, if you see a horse with a figure in the 80s while every other horse in the field has at least a 100, this low-rated horse probably doesn't belong.

Adj. LF (adjusted last-fraction time) is not terribly important except in turf races. Adjusted last fraction is helpful in finding late-running long shots that can sneak into the second and third slots of the exacta and trifecta. The public has forever believed that a strong track bias exerts an equal influence on all horses; that is, if the surface favors speed, all the top finishers must necessarily be speed horses. This usually isn't the case. Sartin has promoted the idea of "opposites attracting" in the exotics. Isn't it the case that in many trifectas, some bonkers high-odds horse will run on late and stick its ugly nose in either the place or show spots? Adjusted last fraction can pick out these spoilers.

OLR stands for odds last race. While not predictive, this information shows which horses have been well-regarded. There's a spot play using odds last race: a place bet on a favorite that was an even-money or odds-on favorite in its most recent outing but lost nonetheless, provided that today's race is under the same conditions (including distance) as the last race. Part of the logic behind the angle is that the horse that beat the favorite last time is not in the field today. Plus the bet is a place bet, not a win bet, just in case this horse is a chronic seconditis horse. This situation occurs mainly in the non-winners allowance series.

MLO stands for morning-line odds. When noting the morning-line odds, it's best to use the actual odds that appear in the track program, as they reflect the track handicapper's opinion of what the betting public will do. Newspaper selectors and the *Racing Form's* linemakers tend to give their own estimates of the winning probability for each horse; they don't assess how the crowd will bet. Again, the idea is to see if our evaluation strays wildly from the generally-valid view of the track handicapper. We really should think twice before dismissing a horse that we hate which the track handicapper has made his first or second pick. This MLO factor can be especially critical in our evaluation of horses running in this country for the first time. We have little information on these foreigners. The track handicapper has a better read on them than do we. His appraisal will tell us if the horse is a contender.

L asks if the horse is getting Lasix for the first or second time. We know that the second time on Lasix after a bid-and-hung effort the race before last shows a flat-bet profit on the West Coast. (Check it out for your track.)

B asks if the horse is getting an equipment change—either blinkers-on or -off. This information can be found in the front of the *Racing Form* under the graded handicap listing for today's races at your track. Blinkers-on indicates that the trainer is trying to improve the early speed of the horse. Blinkers-off indicates that the trainer is attempting to reduce the early speed in order to conserve energy.

G asks if this is the first or second race after being gelded.

Notations in the **L, B,** and **G** columns can land us some longshots that logically figure to wake up today with the addition of one or a combination of these positive changes.

By filling out the Allowance & Stakes Form for fifty or more races, you'll notice some very predictive trends. For example, my research has shown that in allowance or stakes races, the horses with the top five ability times will win over 90 percent of the time; the top three, 70 to 75 percent. (Please verify this fact for yourself.) Typically, however, no one factor will jump at you. You should instead look across the entire form for patterns that combine several factors. Once you acquire the habit of completing the form, you'll eventually be able to know at a glance which horses represent the true contention in a race. The number of contenders in a race can vary from a single horse to the entire field.

If we fill out and analyze this form for each allowance and stakes race we handicap, we'll have a solid wagering edge. The race favorite is the key to it all. A single look at the numbers can identify false favorites that can't run to the pars, or a legitimate favorite that has no "knocks" on its class, speed, pace, or current form and condition. Our job of uncovering value bets is made much easier with the Allowance & Stakes Form. Let's apply these principles to the following race. Handicap it using your present method, and note how you would have bet it. Then, follow along with our comments and method using the Allowance & Stakes Form. The critical information that you need is as follows:

Profile: Early   Pace Contention Point 1¼ lengths

Win Pars (in tenths):	47.4	1:11.5	1:43.2
Ability Par:	95.6		
Last Fraction Par:	31.7		

Distance Adjustments

Hollywood 7-furlong win profile	22.48	45.11	1:22.1

Final Odds According to Chart:

Me And Molly	3.4	Charisma	6.0
Tammy Lynn	4.5	Laurasia	9.5
Winglet	1.1	Stutz Cat	11.9

Me And Molly She's a contender off her last race. She can run to the profile.

Tammy Lynn She's a throw-out. A chronic beaten favorite. Horses laid off coming back into routes are disadvantaged. Plus her Santa Anita victory was in ordinary time. NW2 pars are 1:09.

Winglet Automatic throw-out. What's a graded stakes winner doing in an allowance race for $37,000?

Charisma She's a marginal contender at best because she doesn't fit the pace profile even though she's okay on adjusted final time. She should improve off her last race. But how much? Doesn't look bad for an exacta place horse.

Laurasia A throw-out. She's going the wrong way on form. Look at her second fraction times and ability times in her last two races. If you insist on leaving her in, you have to use her last race back and figure that's the best she's probably capable of in her present form.

Stutz Cat Throw out. Layoff into a route. Lack of early pace. Don't disregard as a place horse.

1 1/16 MILES. (1.40) ALLOWANCE. Purse $37,000. Fillies and mares. 3-year-olds and upward which have not won $3,000 twice other than maiden, claiming or starter. Weights, 3-year-olds, 115 lbs.; older, 122 lbs. Non-winners of two races other than claiming at a mile or over since April 15 allowed 2 lbs.; such a race other than maiden or claiming since then, 4 lbs.

LASIX—Me and Molly, Tammy Lynn, Winglet, Charisma, Laurasia, Stutz Cat.

Me And Molly
Dk. b. or br. f. 4, by Sloopy—Sweet Molly Malone, by Gemmo
Br.—Maendysland Farm (Ky)
Tr.—Whittingham Charles
Own.—Maendysland Farm
SOLIS A (207 24 23 34 .12)

120

Lifetime 1992 5 2 1 1 $46,350
7 2 1 1 1991 2 M 0 0 $3,000
$46,390 Turf 4 0 0 1 $4,250
Wet 1 0 1 0 $7,000

LATEST WORKOUTS Jun 11 Hol 3f fst :37¹ H Jun 2 Hol 3f fst :37² H May 24 Hol 5f fst 1:02¹ H May 19 Hol 5f fst 1:03² H

Tammy Lynn
B. f. 4, by Fappiano—Win Name, by Jacinto
Br.—Ky Heritage Tb Brd Prtnrs et al (Ky)
Tr.—Vogel George (3 0 0 0 .00)
Own.—Hughes B Wayne
DELANOUSSAYE E (131 25 16 23 .19)

118

Lifetime 1991 5 2 2 1 $46,350
5 2 2 1 1990 0 M 0 0
$46,390

LATEST WORKOUTS Jun 11 SA 4f fst :47² H Jun 4 SA 4f fst 1:33² Hg May 30 SA 4f fst :50 B May 23 SA 7f fst 1:30⁴ H

Winglet
B. f. 4, by Alydar—Highest Trump, by Bold Bidder
Br.—Paulson Allen E (Ky)
Tr.—Lundy Richard J (1 0 0 0 .00)
Own.—Paulson Allen E
VALENZUELA P A (105 21 27 12 .17)

118

Lifetime 1992 3 0 1 1 $51,475
8 2 1 3 1991 5 2 0 2 $98,950
$150,425 Turf 1 0 0 0 $4,625
Wet 1 0 0 0

LATEST WORKOUTS Jun 7 SLR tr.t 6f fst 1:13³ H May 19 SLR tr.t 4f fst :49² H May 14 SLR tr.t 5f fst 1:01² H Jun 9 SLR tr.t 6f fst 1:13 H

Charisma
Ch. f. 4, by Turkoman—Charisma-Ch, by Mr Long
Br.—Biaggio Carl J (Ky)
Tr.—Mayberry Brian A (30 11 7 3 .38)
Own.—Robbins Charles
PEDROZA M A (102 11 12 11 .08)

118

Lifetime 1992 3 2 0 1 $40,825
9 4 2 1 1991 4 2 0 1 $48,025
$57,100 Turf 1 0 0 0

LATEST WORKOUTS Jun 12 Hol 4f fst :48⁴ H May 21 Hol 4f fst 1:02³ H May 21 Hol 4f fst 1:02³ H

Laurasia
B. f. 3(Mar), by Pancho Villa—Anjolina, by Best Turn
Br.—Haynes Bros & Perkins (Ky)
Tr.—Lukas D Wayne (43 8 9 1 .19)
Own.—Rocachian Laura
FLORES D R (181 23 29 26 .13)

111

Lifetime 1992 5 2 0 1 $40,300
7 2 1 2 1991 2 0 1 1 $9,000
$49,300

LATEST WORKOUTS Jun 11 SA 4f fst :50² H May 26 SA 4f fst :49⁴ H May 12 SA 5f fst 1:02² H May 6 SA 3f fst :37² H

Stutz Cat
Ro. f. 3(Mar), by Vigors—Stuttering, by Ack Ack
Br.—Hava W E (Ky)
Tr.—MacDonald Mark (5 0 2 1 .00)
Own.—Sophel & Yavorski & Zanari
PINCAY L JR (159 25 22 18 .16)

111

Lifetime 1992 5 2 0 1 $42,075
11 2 2 2 1991 4 0 0 1 $17,700
$59,729 Turf 2 1 0 0 $6,300
Wet 1 0 0 0 $16,500

LATEST WORKOUTS Jun 12 SA 1 fst 1:45 H Jun 5 SA 3f fst 1:00⁴ H May 30 SA 1 fst 1:43³ H May 23 SA 7f fst 1:30⁴ H

Allowance & Stakes Form

Date 6/17/92   Distance 1 1/16

Race # 8   Class Nw 2

Conditions 3↑ F   Purse 37,000

Win Pars This Type Race:
47.4   111.5   143.

Ability Time Par   95.6

PP	Name of Horse	Jockey Status	A B c	# R S L	Surface Distance Suitable S	D	W %	Recency Works Form Cycle R	W	FC	G S W	C R W	Cl
1	ME AND Holly 3.4	=	4	2	Y	Y	2/5	21	OK	OK	No	No	+
2	TAMMY LyNN 4.5	=	4	O	Y	?	2/5	219	21/27	?	No	No	+
3	WINGLET 1.1	=	4	O	Y	Y	0/3	88	24/39	?	Yes		
4	CHARISMA 6	=	4	1	Y	Y	0/2	41	13/27	?	NO	NO	+
5	LAURASIA 9.5	=	3	4	Y	?	2/5	18	4/6	OK	No	NO	+
6	STUTZ CAT 11.9	+	3	O	Y	Y	2/5	52	28/35	?	No	NO	+
7													
8													
9													
10													
11													
12													
13													
14													
15													
16													

There's only one horse in this race that fits the profile and is in form and condition: Me And Molly. This is a wonderful situation. Your line on Me And Molly is either 2-to-1 or 5-to-2, at worst. Please note that all the *Daily Racing Form* selectors were faked out by Winglet. Horses like Winglet are money-sucking tempta-

Please note: Ability Time is different for turf.

Dirt Ability Time = TT + 2F
Turf Ability Time = 1F + 3F

Last Fraction Par __31.7__

Pace Fractions			TT	Ability Time	SR + TV	Adj LF	O L R	M L O	L	B	G
1st Call	2nd Call	Final									
47.8	111.4	143.4	23.6	95	99	32	2.3	7-2			
				Elimination	(C8F)			3			
Automatic	Throwout							9-5			
48.6	112.6	143.6	24	96.6	97	31	3.7	5			
47.4	111.9	144.8	24.5	96.4	97	32.9	43	5			
46.7	112.5	146.3	25.8	98.3	98	33.8	6.2	8			
ME AND MOLLY											

tions. Please, please resist. Bet against them. Will they beat you once in a while? Yes. (About 30 to 40 percent of the time.) If you bet all such horses, for every dollar that you bet, you can expect about 68 cents back.

Molly And Me was not the greatest score in thoroughbred

SELECTIONS

Consensus Totals Based on 5 points for First (7 for Best Bet), 2 for 2nd, 1 for 3rd. Best Bet in Bold Type.

	BRAD FREE	ANALYST	HERMIS®	SWEEP™	CONSENSUS	
1	Heartbreak Kid	Allawinir	Coverallbases	Heartbreak Kid	Heartbreak Kid	12
	So Ever Clever	Heartbreak Kid	Allawinir	So Ever Clever	Allawinir	8
	Allawinir	Coverallbases	Sofianna's Destiny	Buster's Brick	Coverallbases	6
2	Wood Spirit	Damelo	Wood Spirit	Damelo	Wood Spirit	14
	Damelo	Wood Spirit	Damelo	Wood Spirit	Damelo	14
	Great Event	Great Event	Great Event	Oscar Oscar Oscar	Great Event	3
3	DiamondbackDragon	DiamondbackDragon	DiamondbackDragon	DiamondbackDragon	DiamondbackDragon	20
	Twounder	Copeta	Intimate Kid	Intimate Kid	Intimate Kid	4
	Snow Perch	Snow Perch	Snow Perch	Twounder	Snow Perch	3
4	Her Royal Fox	Her Royal Fox	Her Royal Fox	Her Royal Fox	Her Royal Fox	20
	Decidedly Deborah	Decidedly Deborah	Decidedly Deborah	Decidedly Deborah	Decidedly Deborah	8
	Premier Engagement	Fabulous Val	Fabulous Val	Star Theme	Fabulous Val	2
5	Angel OfVengeance	Angel Of Vengeance	Knight Prospector	Knight Prospector	Knight Prospector	14
	Knight Prospector	Movie Cutie	Sharply	Movie Cutie	Angel Of Vengeance	12
	Sharply	Sharply	Movie Cutie	Sharply	Sharply	5
6	Patriotaki	You Are My Casey	Machote	Irish Recruit	Machote	10
	Machote	Vicious Faith	You Are My Casey	Machote	You Are My Casey	9
	You Are My Casey	Machote	Triskaideka Flyer	You Are My Casey	Patriotaki	5
7	Tanker Port	Tanker Port	Tanker Port	Tanker Port	Tanker Port	24
	Way Wild	Way Wild	Way Wild	Morlando	Way Wild	7
	Accesibility	Accesibility	Morlando	Way Wild	Morlando	3
8	Winglet	Winglet	Winglet	Winglet	Winglet	20
	Me And Molly	Tammy Lynn	Charisma	Laurasia	Charisma	4
	Charisma	Me And Molly	Laurasia	Charisma	Me And Molly	3
9	Ringaroundthefort	Torrissimmo	Ringaroundthefort	Union Audit	Ringaroundthefort	12
	Dame's Court	Dame's Court	Torrissimmo	Ringaroundthefort	Torrissimmo	8
	Torrissimmo	Akin Natural	Undilay	Akin Natural	Union Audit	5

EIGHTH RACE
Hollywood
JUNE 17, 1992

1 $\frac{1}{16}$ MILES. (1.40) ALLOWANCE. Purse $37,000. Fillies and mares. 3-year-olds and upward which have not won $3,000 twice other than maiden, claiming or starter. Weights, 3-year-olds, 115 lbs.; older, 122 lbs. Non-winners of two races other than claiming at a mile or over since April 15 allowed 2 lbs.; such a race other than maiden or claiming since then, 4 lbs.
Value of race $37,000; value to winner $20,350; second $7,400; third $5,550; fourth $2,775; fifth $925. Mutuel pool $225,431. Exacta pool $221,274.

Last Raced	Horse	M/Eqt.	A.	Wt	PP	St	¼	½	¾	Str	Fin	Jockey	Odds $1
27May92 ^{8}Hol^1	Me And Molly	LB	4	120	1	6	2^1	2^1	1^{hd}	1^{hd}	1^{hd}	Solis A	3.40
26Apr92 ^{8}GG^4	Stutz Cat	LB	3	117	6	3	6	6	6	$5^{\frac{1}{2}}$	2^{hd}	Pincay L Jr	11.90
21Mar92 ^{8}SA^4	Winglet	LBb	4	118	3	5	$3^{1\frac{1}{2}}$	$3^{\frac{1}{2}}$	$4^{\frac{1}{2}}$	4^{hd}	$3^{1\frac{1}{2}}$	Valenzuela P A	1.10
7May92 ^{8}Hol^2	Charisma	LB	4	118	4	4	$4^{1\frac{1}{2}}$	$4^{1\frac{1}{2}}$	$3^{1\frac{1}{2}}$	$3^{\frac{1}{2}}$	4^{hd}	Pedroza M A	6.00
30May92 ^{8}Hol^5	Laurasia	LB	3	114	5	2	5^3	5^3	$5^{1\frac{1}{2}}$	6	5^{hd}	Flores D R	9.50
11Nov91 ^{7}SA^1	Tammy Lynn	LB	4	118	2	1	$1^{1\frac{1}{2}}$	1^{hd}	2^{hd}	$2^{\frac{1}{2}}$	6	Delahoussaye E	4.50

OFF AT 4:34 Start good. Won driving. Time, :23^1, :47^1, 1:11^3, 1:36^1, 1:42^4 Track fast.

$2 Mutuel Prices:			
1-ME AND MOLLY	8.80	3.60	2.40
6-STUTZ CAT		7.80	3.00
3-WINGLET			2.20

$2 EXACTA 1-6 PAID $80.40.

handicapping at $8.80, but her race can teach us some important lessons.

This next race was won by my staff writer, Steve Unite. It's illustrative of the snares, barbs, and booby traps that are found in the non-winners series. His actual completed form along with his comments are included. The critical information is as follows:

Profile: Front	Pace Contention Point 1.2 lengths		
Win Pars	21.8	44.6	1:15.6
Ability Par	67.4		
Last Fraction Par	31.0		

Distance Adjustments			
Hollywood Park 6-furlong	22	45	1:09.6
	22.2	45	1:22.4

Final Odds According to Chart:

Manipulate	1.6	D'Or Ruckus	7.5
Exchange	2.3	Cara Carissima	2.7
Inner Peace	11.4	Cozzene's Queen	18.9

Exchange Broke maiden in claiming race, then followed that with all-out win for a $50,000 tag. Not exactly a perfect fit to Quinn's preferred class profile for lightly-raced NW1 candidates, which usually race exclusively in non-claiming company. However, her initial try at this level was a competitive second, so she deserves the benefit of the doubt. She doesn't fit the pace profile. Paceline is obviously last race.

7th Hollywood

6½ FURLONGS. (1.14²) ALLOWANCE. Purse $32,000. Fillies and mares. 3-year-olds and upward which have not won $3,000 other than maiden, claiming or starter. Weights, 3-year-olds, 115 lbs.; older, 121 lbs. Non-winners of a race other than claiming allowed 3 lbs.

LASIX—Exchange, Manipulate, Cozzene's Queen, D'Or Ruckus.

Exchange
Ch. f. 3(Feb), by Exploded—Wooly Willow, by Irish Stronghold
PINCAY L JR
Own.—Craig S H
Br.—Kinghaven Farms Ltd (Ont-C)
Tr.—Spawr Bill
112
Lifetime 1981 3 2 1 0 $32,000
3 2 1 0   1980 0 M 0 0
$32,000

Speed Index: Last Race: 0.0   3-Race Avg.: -1.3   3-Race Avg.: -1.3   Overall Avg.: -1.3
LATEST WORKOUTS

Manipulate
B. f. 3(Feb), by Clever Trick—Peppy's Lucky Girl, by Lucky Mel
DESORMEAUX K J
Own.—Four D Stb-Pep-Fay-Rick Sthts
Br.—Arnold & Pleiage (Ky)
Tr.—Hess R B Jr
112
Lifetime 1981 6 3 1 0 $43,250
6 3 1 0   1980 0 M 0 0
$43,250

Speed Index: Last Race: +0.3   3-Race Avg.: -0.3   5-Race Avg.: -6.0   Overall Avg.: -13.5
LATEST WORKOUTS

Cara Carissima
B. f. 3(Apr), by Caro—Reine Imperiale, by King Emperor
McCARRON C J
Own.—Evans E P
Br.—Skara Glen Stable (Ky)
Tr.—Lukas D Wayne
115
Lifetime 1980 4 1 2 1 $31,500
4 1 2 1 $31,500

Speed Index: Last Race: -5.0   3-Race Avg.: -2.6   4-Race Avg.: -3.5   Overall Avg.: -3.5
LATEST WORKOUTS

Cozzene's Queen
Gr. f. 3(May), by Cozzene—What's the Reason, by Hail to Reason
FLORES D R
Own.—Kenis & 3YU Stable
Br.—Lambholm (Ky)
Tr.—Luby Donn
115
Lifetime 1981 4 1 1 0 $7,000
4 1 1 0   1980 3 1 0 0 $16,650
$23,450

Speed Index: Last Race: -7.0   2-Race Avg.: -7.5   2-Race Avg.: -7.5   Overall Avg.: -4.7
LATEST WORKOUTS

D'Or Ruckus
Ch. f. 3(Mar), by Bold Ruckus—Pretense D'Or, by Medaille D'Or
BAZE R A
Own.—J B S Stable
Br.—Shefsky J (Ont-C)
Tr.—Moorman Gerald C
115
Lifetime 1981 12 1 2 2 $27,950
12 1 2 2   1980 3 M 1 1 $10,700
$38,650 Turf 1 0 0 0

Speed Index: Last Race: -1.0   3-Race Avg.: -6.0   8-Race Avg.: -6.0   Overall Avg.: -8.5
LATEST WORKOUTS

Inner Peace
B. f. 3(Mar), by Seattle Slew—Kathleen's Girl, by Native Charger
SANTOS J A
Own.—Everest Stables
Br.—Kentucky Select Bloodstock I (Ky)
Tr.—Fernandez Jose
115
Lifetime 1981 1 1 0 0 $15,400
1 1 0 0   1980 0 M 0 0
$15,400

Speed Index: Last Race: -5.0   1-Race Avg.: -5.0   1-Race Avg.: -5.0   Overall Avg.: -5.0
LATEST WORKOUTS

Manipulate Another who doesn't fit the class profile—has found her greatest success against claimers. Her one start at the NW1 level was a complete failure, although it did come at her first and only attempt around two turns. In her favor, she's demonstrated some versatility and a definite will to win, coming from the clouds in her last start while going wire-to-wire the race before. She doesn't fit the pace profile. The paceline chosen here is her last race, although all her other races seem to indicate she's an early speed type by nature.

Cara Carissima One that does fit the class profile, although she hasn't raced in seven months. But her ration of furlongs to days is within the .60 guideline. Additionally, Lukas works his finest magic with young fillies. She deserves a look. The last race is the proper paceline, as it was at the same racetrack and class level (and nearly the same distance) as today's race. She doesn't fit the pace profile.

Cozzene's Queen Like Cara Carissima, fits the class profile but has been away from the races for nearly six months. Furlongs-to-days ratio meets the acceptable limits, but she seems to prefer routing, never really getting into contention in her two sprints. Still, on class alone, she has a look at the race. Rate her off the Nov. 11 line, run at the same track and distance as today's race. She also doesn't fit the pace profile.

D'Or Ruckus Not really the lightly raced improving type that wins NW1 events, this one needed eight tries to break her maiden, and her subsequent starts in allowance company have been uncompetitive, though she picked it up a bit in her last race. She seems to be a proven loser at this level, but look at her ability time. It's the best in the race, and she does fit the pace profile.

Inner Peace Extremely game and classy performance to break her maiden at 34-to-1 in her debut. An exact fit to Quinn's class profile for a NW1 race. A "could be any kind" horse with loads of potential and promise. She also fits the pace profile.

This race is chaos. No horse can run to the final-time par; only two fit the pace profile. Anything can happen. The absolute best thing to do in this type of race is to line up the top four ability-time horses and consider any exacta combination paying over $66 among the following contenders:

D'Or Ruckus	66.80
Inner Peace	67.20
Manipulate	67.50
Exchange	67.50

Allowance & Stakes Form

Date 6/22/91

Distance 6,5f ?irt

Race # __7__

Class _NW1_

Conditions _Nw3000_

3?(F)

1XMCS

Purse _$32K_

yaa paws

Win Pars This Type Race:

21.80 44.60 115.60

Ability Time Par   67.40

PP	Name of Horse	Jockey Stable	Age	# RSL	Surface Distance Suitable S D	W %	Recency Works Form Cycle R W FC	GSW	CRW	Class
:	EXCHANGE	=	3	3	+	+	67	35	2	OFNN	Y	SAME
2	MANIPULATE	—	3	6	+	+	50	31	2	CKNN	Y	RISE
3	CARA CARISSIMA	=	3	0	+	+	25	214	16/29 ? 4/6 N	N	SAME
4	COZZENE's QUEEN	=	3	0	+	−	25	169	2/29 ? 4/6 N	N	SAM*
5	D'OR RUCKUS	=	3	9	+	+	8	13	1	1 ↑ N	N	SAM
6	INNER PEACE	=|	3	1	+	+	100	26	3	OFTN	N	RISE
7												
8												
9												
10												
11												
12												
13												
14												
15												
16												

This exacta strategy is the ultimate for securing consistent profits in wildly contentious and relatively unpredictable races. It's called the "Mitchell Matrix."

Next is to make a win bet on the top two overlays. Remember: this race is chaos! Hence a win bet on Inner Peace and D'Or Ruckus is an intelligent strategy, considering the odds. This race stands as a testament to the effectiveness of the NW1 contender-selection methods in James Quinn's *The Handicapper's Condition Book*. You didn't need to run this race through a computer.

Please note: Ability Time is different
for turf.

Dirt Ability Time = TT + 2F
Turf Ability Time = 1F + 3F

Last Fraction Par _31.00_

Pace Fractions			TT	Ability Time	SR + TV	Adj LF	O L R	M L O	L	B	G
1st Call	2nd Call	Final									
22.30	44.90	116.20	22.60	67.50	100	31.50	5.2-1				
24.40	45.95	116.00	21.55	67.50	103	30.05	3.40-1				
22.70	45.60	116.90	22.90	68.50	95	31.35	1.70-1				
23.10	45.90	118.15	22.80	68.70	93	32.25	8.10-1				
22.20	44.50	116.30	22.30	61.80	99	31.80	25.6-1	12X			
21.60	44.40	117.20	22.80	67.70	95	32.50	34.34				

You really didn't have to make an odds line, either. The class
factor alone would have been sufficient to "kill" this race.

In non-claiming races, especially the preliminary non-winners allowance series, sometimes the old saw "class will out"
gets the job done. Potential often counts more than previous
racetrack performance. Horses with genuine class and ability will
run through these NW1 and NW2 races with little difficulty.
The truly good horses will win these races almost at will. They
certainly don't lose repeatedly under these conditions, and they

most definitely don't get trounced. They're so much better than their opponents that they will routinely race through their conditions unbeaten, or with only one or two failures.

The class stickout here is Inner Peace. She really could be any kind. The others have each already lost at least once at today's level. The public's first two betting choices, Manipulate (3-to-2) and Exchange (2-to-1), both broke their maidens in claiming races, for crying out loud. They're not the genuine class articles handicappers should favor in these events.

Already questionable on the handicapping considerations of the class and pace profiles, Manipulate and Exchange fail the all-important value test as well. Cara Carissima also is overbet. We're left with a mammoth overlay on Inner Peace and a modest overlay on D'Or Ruckus. Our edge is a huge 175 percent on Inner Peace. Not bad. But the best bet of all is the exacta bet using the Mitchell Matrix. Either choice proved wonderful. A win price of $24.80 or an exacta price of $82.80, or both.

SEVENTH RACE	6 ½ FURLONGS. (1.14²) ALLOWANCE. Purse $32,000. Fillies and mares. 3-year-olds and

Hollywood
JUNE 22, 1991

6 ½ FURLONGS. (1.14²) ALLOWANCE. Purse $32,000. Fillies and mares. 3-year-olds and upward which have not won $3,000 other than maiden, claiming or starter. Weights, 3-year-olds, 115 lbs.; older, 121 lbs. Non-winners of a race other than claiming allowed 3 lbs.

Value of race $32,000; value to winner $17,600; second $6,400; third $4,800; fourth $2,400; fifth $800. Mutuel pool $290,085. Exacta pool $282,429.

Last Raced	Horse	M/Eqt.A.Wt	PP St	¼	½	Str	Fin	Jockey	Odds $1
27May91 2Hol1	Inner Peace	B 3 115	6 2	3²	2½	23½	1¹½	Santos J A	11.40
18May91 6Hol2	Exchange	LBb 3 117	1 5	5¹½	4hd	31½	2³	Pincay L Jr	2.30
22May91 7Hol1	Manipulate	LB 3 113	2 3	1¹	11½	1hd	3²	Desormeaux K J	1.60
9Jun91 6Hol3	D'Or Ruckus	LBb 3 115	5 1	4¹	51½	42½	41¾	Baze R A	7.50
3Jan91 3SA2	Cozzene's Queen	LB 3 115	4 6	6	6	51½	5⁹	Flores D R	18.90
18Nov90 7Hol2	Cara Carissima	B 3 115	3 4	2¹	33½	6	6	McCarron C J	2.70

OFF AT 4:24 Start good. Won ridden out. Time, :21³, :44 , 1:09¹, 1:15⁴ Track fast.

$2 Mutuel Prices:	6-INNER PEACE	24.80	7.60	3.20
	1-EXCHANGE		3.80	2.40
	2-MANIPULATE			2.40

$2 EXACTA 6-1 PAID $82.80.

Allowance and stakes races are tough, but they offer wonderful opportunities. Your job is to master them. Unfortunately, this is done by making a lot of mistakes. Pity. If you'll stick to the unifying principles and practice, you'll be able to make these races one of your most profitable investment vehicles. My best wishes go with you.

If you hadn't noticed, I'm presenting the different categories of races in order of difficulty. One of the most difficult races on any race card is a turf race. That's the bad news. The good news is that we can achieve outstanding profits if we learn to master these demanding races.

Chapter 11

Turf Races

No one should doubt the significance of class handicapping on the turf. Early speed is incidental, and often suicidal. Early pace can be irrelevant, or self-defeating. Final time can be entirely misleading, and so, too, the accompanying figures. . . . Late speed, and the capacity to prolong a late burst without let-up against horses of comparable or superior ability, is the distinguishing attribute. . . . Modern speed handicappers endure as many headaches on the turf as anybody, and probably more. No surprise. *Conventional speed methods do not apply*. Early speed, brilliance even certainly if slightly out of control, regularly tires, and regularly loses. Final times fluctuate abnormally, pace times madly. Daily track variants are unreliable commonly, and at times impossible to calculate. The resulting speed and pace figures cannot distinguish grass horses accurately enough.

—JAMES QUINN, *Recreational Handicapping*

I HAD ALWAYS CONSIDERED MYSELF to be a poor turf handicapper. This belief sprung from the fact that I hung around with James Quinn. He's one of the best turf handicappers in the country. Whenever we were in disagreement, his selection would usually win. It wasn't until I started to use THE BETTING ANALYST (a record-keeping program for handicappers) that I realized that even though my win percentage was below normal, my return on investment (ROI) was spectacular. Financially, my turf performance exceeded my dirt performance. It always disturbs me when the top pick of my program doesn't win more than any other selection. Imagine my consternation when I discovered that the fourth pick of FIVE-IN-ONE won as often as the first choice. In fact, the top four picks were indistinguishable. My first conclusion was that the program was not effective on turf. David Okamoto and I struggled with this problem for over a year. We tried all sorts of speed and pace algorithms, only to come to the conclusion that the top three or four choices were, in fact, indistinguishable. Our first conclusion was that speed and pace methods didn't work too well on the turf. In the meantime, however, we were getting a very healthy turf ROI. The only subset that showed a normal winning percentage was those races in which we could isolate the "class of the field" which didn't have any form knocks. Remember the old saw that "class laughs at pace on the turf"? David and I proved to ourselves the truth of that statement.

It's very fortunate that our betting strategy insists that you bet on overlays, because in this category you would have been wiped out trying to select the winner instead of betting the value. The above results suggest the optimum winning turf strategy: focus on the contentious races. Simply bet the top two horses among the top four that are going off at the highest odds. More on that later. For now, let's look at the significant handicapping factors that work on the grass.

Turf races are complicated by foreign invaders who have no history on American tracks. They are further complicated by good dirt horses going onto the turf for the first time. Will they be able to run to their dirt numbers? Another complication: bad dirt horses with good turf breeding. We must learn to cope with all these unknowns.

FIRST TIME ON THE GRASS

Bill Quirin has solved the problem of first-time turf starters. He has proven that you can make a flat-bet profit by betting on all the progeny of certain sires the first two times they run on the grass. Those sires and their ROIs are listed in Appendix B. Whenever a first-time turf horse is entered, you simply look at the name of its daddy. It's the first name after the color, sex, and age of the horse in the *Daily Racing Form* past performances. The following is a wonderful example of this play. This was the sixth race at Hollywood Park on Kentucky Derby day.

6th Hollywood

1 MILE. (Turf). (1.32⅘) 12th Running of THE SPOTLIGHT BREEDERS' CUP HANDICAP. $100,000 added ($75,000 added, Plus $25,000 from Breeders' Cup Fund). 3-year-olds. By subscription of $100 each, which shall accompany the nomination, $750 additional to start, with $75,000 added and an additional $25,000 from the Breeders' Cup Fund for Cup nominees only, the host associations added monies to be divided 55% to the winner, 20% to second, 15% to third, 7.5% to fourth and 2.5% to fifth. Breeders' Cup monies also correspondingly divided providing a Breeders' Cup nominee has finished in an awarded position. All fees to the winner. Any Breeders' Cup monies not awarded will revert to the fund. Weights: Monday, April 30. Starters to be named through the entry box by closing time of entries. This race will not be divided. Preference will be given in the following order: Breeders' Cup nominated highweights (including scale of weights); Breeders' Cup nominees; Non-Breeders' Cup nominated highweights (including scale of weights); total earnings in 1990 will be used in determining the order of preference of horses assigned equal weights on the scale. Failure to draw into this race at scratch time cancels all fees. A trophy will be presented to the owner of the winner. Breeders' Cup nominees preferred. Closed Wednesday, April 25, 1990 with 28 nominations.

Mehmetori

PATTON D B 112
Ch. c. 3(Feb), by Mehmet—Sonori, by Jungle Savage
Br.—Vallone Mr-Mrs G (Ky) 1990 5 1 0 0 $22,275
Tr.—Mulhall Richard W 1989 0 M 0 0
Own.—Arnold & Miller Lifetime 5 1 0 0 $22,275

14Apr90-7SA 1 :453 1:103 1:37 ft 16 118 817 89½ 48 46½ Baze R A3 Aw37000 76-17 Big Bass, Toby Jug, Honor Clef 8
14Apr90—Bumped 3/16
17Mar90-7SA 1 1/16 :474 1:122 1:433ft 8½ 118 65 66½ 55½ 89½ McCarronCJ8 Aw37000 76-12 HwnPss,FutureCrer,NuitsStGorgs 8
17Mar90—Bobbled start
4Mar90-4SA 7f :224 :461 1:25 ft 2½ 118 84¾ 53½ 31 11 McCarron C J5 Mdn 78-19 Mehmetori,FestiveColony,RsSyng 12
4Mar90—Bumped 3/16
4Feb90-2SA 6½f :214 :451 1:17 m 4½ 118 63½ 75½ 66 55½ Delahoussaye E9 Mdn 79-15 H'sLkThWind,SportsVw,FuturCrr 10
4Feb90—Broke slowly
14Jan90-6SA 6f :222 :453 1:103m *2¾ 118 813 813 59½ 44½ Delahoussaye E3 Mdn 78-14 HonorClef,Cox'sEnchnte,SpnishStl 9

Speed Index: Last Race: (—) 3-Race Avg.: (—) 12-Race Avg.: (—) Overall Avg.: -7.0
Apr 30 Hol 6f ft 1:144 H Apr 25 Hol 5f ft 1:011 H Apr 8 SA 4f ft :484 H ●Apr 2 SA 5f ft :59 H

Warcraft

DAVIS R G 120
B. c. 3(May), by Ack Ack—Became a Lark, by T V Lark
Br.—Bradley-Whittingham et al (Ky) 1990 6 2 1 1 $145,200
Tr.—Whittingham Charles 1989 0 M 0 0
Own.—Bradley-Chndler-Whittinghm Lifetime 6 2 1 1 $145,200

7Apr90-5SA 1⅛ :462 1:102 1:49 ft 5 122 42 32 35 35 McCrrCJ8 S A Dby 86-15 MisterFrisky,VideoRanger,Warcraft 8
7Apr90—Grade I
18Mar90-8SA 1 1/16 :463 1:11 1:42 ft 9½ 117 31 2hd 23 25½ Davis RG6 Sn Flpe H 87-16 RealCash,Wrcrft,MusicProspector 12
18Mar90—Grade II; Wide 7/8 turn
4Mar90-3SA 1 1/16 :483 1:13 1:441ft *3-2 120 1hd 1hd 13½ 16 McCarronCJ7 Aw37000 82-18 Warcraft, Apprised, Oh Wow 8
18Feb90-7SA 1 :46 1:103 1:361sy *4-5 120 75¼ 79¼ 817 730 McCarronCJ2 Aw37000 56-18 Flying Reb, Elikos, Oh Wow 9
18Feb90—Rank 7 1/2
4Feb90-4SA 1 1/16 :471 1:12 1:442gd *7-5 117 2½ 2½ 11 13 McCarron C J3 Mdn 81-18 Warcraft, HawaiianPass,LtdEdition 9
21Jan90-6SA 7f :222 :453 1:233ft 2 118 33 32 42½ 43½ McCarron C J5 Mdn 82-19 FrvOnFrv,H'sLikThWind,LtdEdton 12
21Jan90—Broke slowly

Speed Index: Last Race: (—) 3-Race Avg.: (—) 12-Race Avg.: (—) Overall Avg.: -3.6
May 1 Hol 5f ft :592 H Apr 26 Hol 7f ft 1:251 H ●Apr 20 SA 5f ft :594 H Apr 15 SA 3f ft :362 H

College Green

ALMEIDA G 114
B. c. 3(Feb), by Erins Isle (Ire)—Bold Stephanie, by Bold Bidder
Br.—Speelman & Sweeney (Ky) 1990 3 1 0 0 $19,830
Tr.—Sweeney Brian 1989 4 1 1 0 $15,400
Own.—Speelman & Sweeney Lifetime 7 2 1 0 $35,230 Turf 2 1 1 0 $25,430

21Apr90-8GG 1⅛ :444 1:083 1:464ft 25 114 65 55½ 816 1025½ HnsenRD3 Cal Dby 65-14 StlwrtChrgr,MscPrspctr,Ts'sDnng 12
21Apr90—Grade III; Ducked out start
25Mar90-7GG 1 1/16 Ⓣ:471 1:11 1:432fm 2½ 116 43 31½ 2hd 1nk Almeida G7 HcpO 95-07 CollegeGreen,Makaleha,FallingStar 7
4Mar90-3SA 1 1/16 :483 1:13 1:441ft 9 120 63½ 63¼ 89¼ 814½ Pincay L Jr3 Aw37000 67-18 Warcraft, Apprised, Oh Wow 8
15Nov89-9Hol 1 Ⓣ:47 1:113 1:361fm 15 120 54¼ 1½ 12½ 22 Solis A4 Aw28000 81-17 SilverEnding,CollegGrn,HroWorkr 10
15Nov89—Broke in a tangle
1Nov89-3BM 1 :452 1:103 1:37 ft *3 118 34½ 13 12 1½ Frazier R L8 Mdn 87-09 CollgGrn,MissionSttion,FrmSchool 8
15Oct89-6SA 1 1/16 :463 1:121 1:434ft 15 117 1½ 1hd 35½ 415 McCarron C J4 Mdn 67-16 SilverEnding,Dchi'sFolly,Riflemker 9
4Oct89-6SA 1 :463 1:112 1:37 ft 35 117 32 1hd 62¾ 612 Pedroza M A8 Mdn 70-20 HroWorkr,PowrLnch,HtchcckWds 10

Speed Index: Last Race: +2.0 2-Race Avg.: 0.0 2-Race Avg.: 0.0 Overall Avg.: -9.5
●May 1 SA 5f ft :584 H ●Apr 12 SA Ⓣ 5f fm 1:01 H (d) Apr 7 SA Ⓣ 7f fm 1:28 H (d) Apr 2 SA 5f ft :593 H

Green's Leader

DELAHOUSSAYE E 114
B. g. 3(Feb), by Fatih—Amberina, by Amber Rama
Br.—Parrish S G (Ky) 1990 2 0 1 0 $10,000
Tr.—Sadler John W 1989 7 4 0 2 $34,912
Own.—Petropolis Stable Inc Lifetime 9 4 1 2 $44,912 Turf 9 4 1 2 $44,912

4Apr90-7SA 1 Ⓣ:463 1:111 1:354fm 4½ 114 2½ 1hd 1½ 21 Davis R G6 Aw50000 83-16 Somthingdiffrnt,Grn'sLdr,OhWow 10
15Mar90-8SA a6½f Ⓣ:21 :431 1:133fm *2½ 120 73¾ 87¼ 76¼ 66¼ Davis R G10 Aw50000 87-05 SolrLnch,DToThKng,Conflctfntrst 10
15Mar90—Wide last 3/8

14Oct89♦1Ascot(Eng) 1 1 434gd 12 123 Ⓣ 31¼ HillsM RedOaksAutumn NoblePtrirch.Hrbourbr,Green'sLdr 10

6Oct89♦5Newmarket(Eng) 7f 1 28 gd 8 128 Ⓣ 12½ Hills M Rcng PstSer Fn H Green'sLdr,FcilityLttr,PrmirMoon 20

14Sep89♦2Doncaster(Eng) 1 1 42 gd 4½ 127 Ⓣ 53½ Hills M Holsten Nrsy H Pltonique,PrtingMomnt,EirLthScl 12

18Aug89♦2Sandown(Eng) 1 1 45 gd *3½ 131 Ⓣ 1½ Hills M Megatop Nrsy H Green'sLedr,FlmingGlory,ChssPic 12

28Jly89♦4Thirsk(Eng) 7f 1 263fm*3-2 128 Ⓣ 1no Day N Tatrsls Sasy Auc Green'sLeader,FinlShot,TrojnExcel 7

30Jun89♦1Doncaster(Eng) 7f 1 282gd 6 126 Ⓣ 1hd Hills M Mrgret Auc Green'sLeder,SnGreco,SnPirNicto 20

6Jun89♦4Yarmouth(Eng) 6f 1 152fm 10 120 Ⓣ 3¾ Hills M Rcng Pst Ser RoseofMimi,StisDncer,Green'sLdr 10

Speed Index: Last Race: -1.0 1-Race Avg.: -1.0 1-Race Avg.: -1.0 Overall Avg.: -4.5

Apr 27 Hol 6f ft 1:16 H Apr 20 SA 5f ft 1:014 H Apr 13 SA Ⓣ 5f fm 1:033 H (d) Mar 31 SA 5f ft 1:024 H

Somethingdifferent

B. c. 2(Feb), by Green Forest—Try Something New, by Hail The Pirates

Br.—Jonabell Farm Inc (Ky) 1990 1 1 0 0 $27,500

BAZE R A 121 Tr.—Mandella Richard 1989 9 4 4 0 $173,800

Own.—Jonabell Farm Inc Lifetime 10 5 4 0 $201,300 Turf 10 5 4 0 $201,300

4Apr90-7SA 1 Ⓣ:4631:1111:354fm*3-5 120 73 72½ 3½ 11 McCarronCJ8 Aw50000 84-16 Somthingdiffrnt,Grn'sLdr,OhWow 10

5Nov89-6GP 1 Ⓣ:4911:1221:37 gd*8-5 115 52½ 33 2½ 13½ McCarron C J6 Manila 89-15 Somethingdifferent,Lituniem,Swdus 8

14Oct89♦4Ascot(Eng) 5f 1 02 gd 6½ 131 Ⓣ 26 Carson W Crnwlls(Gr3) Argntum,Somthngdffrnt,DncngMsc 9

23Sep89♦4Newbury(Eng) 6f 1 12 gd 8 127 Ⓣ 21½ StarkeyG Mill Reef(Gr2) Welney,Somethingdiffrnt,OldAllinc 7

1Sep89♦5BadenBAden(Ger) a6f 1 103gd 7-5 128 Ⓣ 1no CrsnW MtChdRn(Gr2) Somthingdiffrnt,DuxAns,Shmshoon 5

14Aug89♦1Windsor(Eng) 6f 1 133gd 7-5 131 Ⓣ 1hd CrsnW Newhomle Grad Somethingdifferent,Barakish,Arny 10

11Jly89♦2Newmarket(Eng) 5f :592gd*7-5 124 Ⓣ 2½ Cauthen S Chesterfield DcAndDv,Smthngdffrnt,CrftImprl 12

24Jun89♦4Ascot(Eng) 6f 1 153fm 3 130 Ⓣ 2nk CrsonW SthrnCmfrtGd Makbul, Somethingdifferent,Daawi 5

17Jun89♦5Nottingham(Eng) 5f :59 fm*3-2 126 Ⓣ 110 CthnS Sherwood (Mdn) Somthngdffrnt,MyLdyTrs,ScndTNn 7

6Jun89♦1Yarmouth(Eng) a5f 1:032fm 3½ 126 Ⓣ 512 CuthnS J Holdrh(Mdn) WveMster,Shmshoon,DrytonSpecil 8

Speed Index: Last Race: 0.0 2-Race Avg.: +2.0 2-Race Avg.: +2.0 Overall Avg.: +2.0

May 1 Hol 5f ft 1:002 H Apr 26 Hol 7f ft 1:294 H Apr 20 SA 6f ft 1:142 H Apr 2 SA 4f ft :484 H

Short Timer

Dk. b. or br. c. 3(Apr), by Bates Motel—Cheddar Pink, by Olden Times

Br.—Ransom R K & Lynn A et al (Ky) 1990 3 0 0 1 $9,450

GARCIA J A 113 Tr.—Tinsley J E Jr 1989 6 2 0 0 $27,125

Own.—Trys Partners Lifetime 9 2 0 1 $36,575 Turf 3 1 0 1 $24,850

23Apr90-3SA a6½f Ⓣ:22 :4421:133fm 6¾ 116 54 54½ 35½ 34¾ Baze R A 1 Aw38000 88-07 Conflctofntrst,SolrLunch,ShortTmr 7

4Apr90-7SA 1 Ⓣ:4631:1111:354fm 17 114 52½ 51¾ 52 43¾ DesormuxKJ 2 Aw50000 80-16 Somthingdiffrnt,Grn'sLdr,OhWow 10

4Apr90—Boxed in 3/8

7Feb90-8SA 1 1/16 :472 1:113 1:433ft 25 114 64¾ 68½ 69½ 611¾ Davis RG 5 Ⓡ Sta Ctlna 73-24 MusicProspctor,Snglis,Tsu'sDwnng 6

28Dec89-3Hol 1 1/16 Ⓣ:4731:1131:421fm 29 116 53½ 52¾ 43 11¼ Davis R G 6 Aw28000 83-16 ShortTimer,Lituanien,TimelessJuan 7

22Nov89-2Hol 1 1/16 :464 1:122 1:451ft 7 117 76 67½ 33 1¾ Solis A 7 M32000 74-19 Short Timer, Power Base, Jestic 12

22Nov89—Wide into stretch

27Oct89-2SA 1 1/16 :471 1:124 1:453ft 19 117 1211 74½ 63¼ 45¼ Solis A 4 M32000 71-23 Cub One, ReasonToFight,WestArt 12

27Oct89—Broke slowly

28Aug89-6Dmr 6½f :221 :451 1:171ft 19 117 74¼ 1011 1114 1120¼ Olivares F 10 M50000 62-14 Z. Trump, Ash Hab, Hesmybaby 12

28Aug89—Wide into drive

2Aug89-6Dmr 6f :22 :452 1:102ft 14 1125 66¼ 87⅓ 88½ 812¾ Nakatani C S8 M50000 73-15 FrnchSvntf,WndDbnr,Cnflctfntrst 12

2Aug89—Broke in; bumped

7Jly89-6Hol 6f :221 :454 1:102ft 43 117 46 45½ 54¾ 47 Solis A10 M50000 82-13 MonsrMsn,TxFrmTxs,Cnflctfntrst 11

Speed Index: Last Race: -4.0 2-Race Avg.: -2.5 2-Race Avg.: -2.5 Overall Avg.: -7.4

May 1 Hol 4f ft :48 H Apr 21 SA 3f ft :354 H Apr 11 SA 4f ft :473 H Mar 28 SA 5f ft 1:002 H

*Balla Cove

B. c. 3(Mar), by Ballad Rock—Coven, by Sassafras

Br.—McCalmont Mrs V (Ire) 1990 3 1 0 0 $33,087

FLORES D R 118 Tr.—McAnally Ronald 1989 7 2 1 1 $146,004

Own.—KingBrsSt-Rechna-RoyalTSt Lifetime 10 3 1 1 $179,091 Turf 6 2 1 1 $146,004

7Apr90-5SA 1⅛ :462 1:102 1:49 ft 36 122 66½ 57 817 820¼ Baze R A2 S A Dby 71-15 MisterFrisky,VideoRanger,Warcraft 8

7Apr90—Grade I

3Mar90-8SA 1 :464 1:111 1:363ft 5 118 68 58½ 611 515½ Pincay LJr1 Sn Rfl 68-22 Mister Frisky, TightSpot,LandRush 7

3Mar90—Grade II; Rank 7/8

10Jan90-8SA 1 :454 1:094 1:351ft 2¾ 118 2½ 2hd 2hd 1no ♦ Pincay L Jr3 Ⓡ Ls Flz 91-15 Balla Cove, Land Rush, Top Cash 4

♦10Jan90—Dead heat; Broke in a tangle

4Nov89-8GP 1 1/16 :464 1:111 1:433ft 32 122 11½ 21 34 76¾ StvnsGL8 Br Cp Juv 86-01 Rhythm, Grand Canyon, Slavic 12

4Nov89—Grade I

5Oct89♦4Newmarket(Eng) 6f 1:11 gd 20 126 Ⓣ 12 CuthenS Midle Prk(Gr1) BallaCove, RockCity, Cordoba 6
18Aug89♦4Sandown(Eng) 7f 1:291gd 12 123 Ⓣ 33 3/4 Eddery P Solario(Gr3) BeMyChief, Robellation, BallaCove 3
10Aug89♦4Salisbury(Eng) 7f 1:274gd 12 120 Ⓣ 12 CuthenS Whitchurch BllCove,Digression,FrontLinRomnc 8
13Jly89♦1Newmarket(Eng) 7f 1:263gd 14 123 Ⓣ 35 1/2 EddryP Brnrd Vn Cutsm BeMyChief, LongIsland, BallaCove 6
10Jun89♦5Haydock(Eng) 6f 1:134gd 4 123 Ⓣ 58 1/2 Quinn J Strtfrd(Mdn) HarbourBar,SirArthurHobbs,Mitki 16
27May89♦1Doncaster(Eng) 6f 1:113gd 8 126 Ⓣ 23 RbrtsM Zetland(Mdn) BeMyChief, BallaCove, ShoutOut 8
Speed Index: Last Race: (—) 3-Race Avg.: (—) 12-Race Avg.: (—) Overall Avg.: -7.7
●Apr 29 Hol 6f ft 1:122 H Apr 23 SA 5f ft 1:013 H Apr 17 SA 4f ft :473 H ●Apr 4 SA 5f ft :592 H

Itsallgreektome
Gr. c. 3(Feb), by Sovereign Dancer—Sans Supplement, by Grey Dawn II
NAKATANI C S **112**
Br.—Sugar Maple Farm (Fla) 1990 3 0 0 0 $7,875
Tr.—Dollase Wallace 1989 2 1 0 0 $14,850
Own.—Jhayare Stables
Lifetime 5 1 0 0 $22,725
4Mar90-3SA 1 1/16 :483 1:13 1:441ft 2 3/4 118 41 1/2 51 3/4 46 1/2 47 3/4 Davis R G6 Aw37000 74-18 Warcraft, Apprised, Oh Wow 8
4Mar90—Broke awkwardly
9Feb90-7SA 6f :213 :443 1:101ft 6 1/2 120 85 1/2 86 3/4 59 49 1/2 Davis R G1 Aw34000 75-23 BurntHills,OneMoreWork,TlntdPirt 8
9Feb90—Broke in, bumped
6Jan90-5SA 6f :213 :434 1:084ft 9 1/2 120 52 1/4 41 3/4 42 41 1/4 Davis R G2 Aw34000 91-09 PhntomX.,BurntHills,DuToThKing 10
6Jan90—Bumped at 5 1/2
21Sep89-9LaD 7f :223 :461 1:26 ft *7-5 116 66 1/2 55 1/2 713 720 1/2 DavisRG7 Spr Dby Juv 57-25 CopperKnny,RocktGibrltr,LCounty 8
26Aug89-6Dmr 6f :214 :45 1:10 ft 28 117 64 1/2 44 33 1nk Davis R G6 Mdn 88-13 Itsllgreektome,Dchi'sFolly,JetWst 11
Speed Index: Last Race: (—) 3-Race Avg.: (—) 12-Race Avg.: (—) Overall Avg.: -5.4
May 3 Hol Ⓣ 4f fm :482 H (d) Apr 28 Hol 7f ft 1:274 H Apr 22 Hol 5f ft :593 H Apr 16 Hol 3f ft :361 H

Robyn Dancer
Ro. c. 3(May), by Crafty Prospector—Double Dancer, by Sword Dancer
OLIVARES F **115**
Br.—Cohen O A (Ky) 1990 3 0 0 1 $11,250
Tr.—Vienna Darrell 1989 9 5 2 1 $187,108
Own.—Herrick & No ProblemStable
Lifetime 12 5 2 2 $198,358 **Turf 3 2 0 1 $86,250**
21Apr90-8GG 1 1/8 :444 1:083 1:464ft 39 117 53 76 3/4 1123 1129 1/2 Baze G6 Cal Dby 61-14 SilwrtChrgr,MscPrspctr,Ts'sDnng 12
21Apr90—Grade III
28Mar90-8SA a6 1/2f Ⓣ:21 :431 1:134fm 6 1/2e 117 53 1/4 31 1/2 42 1/2 31 1/2 Solis A11 Bldwn 90-08 FarmWy,ImTheIcemn,RobynDncer 12
28Mar90—Wide 3/8 turn
18Mar90-8SA 1 1/16 :463 1:11 1:42 ft 21 117 42 64 1/4 68 1/2 815 1/4 VlnzulPA2 Sn Flpe H 78-16 RealCash,Wrcrft,MusicProspector 12
18Mar90—Grade II; Jostled start
4Nov89-8GP 1 1/16 :464 1:111 1:433ft 25 122 31 1/2 52 1/2 912 912 1/2 CordrAJr6 Br Cp Juv 80-01 Rhythm, Grand Canyon, Slavic 12
4Nov89—Grade I
21Oct89-10Lrl 1 1/16 :48 1:124 1:44 ft *6-5 122 11 1/2 11 2hd 2hd Stacy A T1 Futurity 93-15 GoAndGo,RobynDancer,SuperCholo 9
21Oct89—Grade II; Bore out
1Oct89-8Pim 1 Ⓣ:483 1:133 1:40 yl 5 1/2 116 2 1/2 2hd 12 1/2 11 1/4 StacyAT8 Vanlandham 75-27 RobynDncer,Duke'sCup,SuperCholo 9
16Sep89-10Pim 5f Ⓣ:233 :484 1:012yl 2 119 1 1/2 12 12 11 Stacy A T2 Jet Pilot 79-21 RobynDncr,‡SprCholo,ExplosvFshn 7
4Sep89-8Med 6f :214 :443 1:09 ft 9-5 121 52 3/4 41 1/2 35 38 3/4 Stacy A T6 J Dayton 88-08 RichardR.,HiMountain,RobynDncer 7
19Aug89-9Atl 5 1/2f :213 :45 1:042gd *3-2 117 54 1/2 54 1/2 34 11 1/2 StcyAT4 Wrld Playgrd 91-11 RobynDncr,PrimryElction,IcPowr 10
8Aug89-9Lrl 6f :223 :463 1:12 ft 3 1/4 120 2hd 11 13 18 Stacy A T3 Aw18000 83-21 RobynDncer,AncientArchie,Nscrm 10
Speed Index: Last Race: +2.0 1-Race Avg.: +2.0 1-Race Avg.: +2.0 Overall Avg.: -4.0
May 3 Hol 3f ft :363 H Apr 14 SA 7f ft 1:271 H Apr 9 SA 6f ft 1:14 H Apr 4 SA 4f ft :491 H

Warcraft was a prohibitive favorite at 8-to-5 on the morning line. He's a monster on the dirt and has weak turf breeding. His daddy is Ack Ack, whose progeny win less than 10 percent on the turf the first two times. They return $1.45 for each two dollars invested. Not too good. The longest shot in the field was Itsallgreektome at 30-to-1. His daddy, Sovereign Dancer, sires 19 percent turf winners the first two times and returns $6.52 for every two dollars invested. Handicappers should reject Warcraft, regardless of dirt performance, because he doesn't have a productive turf sire. Ack Ack is a less than 10 percent sire. Don't be fooled. Think of the first time on turf as running on a different planet. All bets are off regarding dirt performance. Stay strictly with the daddy's record. You'll only win about one race in every five or six, but the very generous mutuels will more than compensate for your losing streaks. You'll hit some monster-priced horses using this strategy.

SIXTH RACE
Hollywood
MAY 5, 1990

1 MILE.(Turf). (1.32⅘) 12th Running of THE SPOTLIGHT BREEDERS' CUP HANDICAP. $100,000 added ($75,000 added, Plus $25,000 from Breeders' Cup Fund). 3-year-olds. By subscription of $100 each, which shall accompany the nomination, $750 additional to start, with $75,000 added and an additional $25,000 from the Breeders' Cup Fund for Cup nominees only, the host associations added monies to be divided 55% to the winner, 20% to second, 15% to third, 7.5% to fourth and 2.5% to fifth. Breeders' Cup monies also correspondingly divided providing a Breeders' Cup nominee has finished in an awarded position. All fees to the winner. Any Breeders' Cup monies not awarded will revert to the fund. Weights: Monday, April 30. Starters to be named through the entry box by closing time of entries. This race will not be divided. Preference will be given in the following order: Breeders' Cup nominated highweights (including scale of weights); Breeders' Cup nominees; Non-Breeders' Cup nominated highweights (including scale of weights); total earnings in 1990 will be used in determining the order of preference of horses assigned equal weights on the scale. Failure to draw into this race at scratch time cancels all fees. A trophy will be presented to the owner of the winner. Breeders' Cup nominees preferred. Closed Wednesday, April 25, 1990 with 28 nominations. Breeders' Cup Awards to ITSALLGREEKTO ME, WARCRAFT, ROBYN DANCER, SOMETHINGDIFFERENT and MEMMETORI.
Value of race $109,550; value to winner $64,550; second $20,000; third $15,000; fourth $7,500; fifth $2,500. Mutuel pool $514,681. Exacta pool $579,995.

Last Raced	Horse	Eqt.	A.	Wt	PP	St	¼	½	¾	Str	Fin	Jockey	Odds $1
4Mar90 ^{3}SA^{4}	Itsallgreektome		3	112	8	5	$8^{3\frac{1}{2}}$	$7^{2\frac{1}{2}}$	$6^{\frac{1}{2}}$	2^{hd}	1no	Nakatani C S	31.90
7Apr90 ^{5}SA^{3}	Warcraft		3	120	2	7	5^{hd}	$6^{1\frac{1}{2}}$	$7^{1\frac{1}{2}}$	$7^{1\frac{1}{2}}$	2^{nk}	Davis R G	1.60
21Apr90 ^{8}GG^{11}	Robyn Dancer		3	115	9	1	$4^{1\frac{1}{2}}$	$4^{\frac{1}{2}}$	$3^{1\frac{1}{2}}$	3^{1}	$3^{\frac{1}{2}}$	Olivares F	16.60
4Apr90 ^{7}SA^{1}	Somethingdifferent		3	121	5	8	6^{1}	5^{1}	4^{1}	1^{hd}	4^{nk}	Baze R A	1.70
14Apr90 ^{7}SA^{4}	Mehmetori	b	3	112	1	9	9	9	8^{2}	$6^{\frac{1}{2}}$	$5^{2\frac{1}{2}}$	Patton D B	100.10
23Apr90 ^{3}SA^{3}	Short Timer	b	3	113	6	6	7^{hd}	8^{hd}	9	9	6^{hd}	Garcia J A	26.50
7Apr90 ^{5}SA^{8}	Balla Cove		3	118	7	3	2^{1}	$2^{\frac{1}{2}}$	$2^{\frac{1}{2}}$	$4^{\frac{1}{2}}$	$7^{1\frac{1}{2}}$	Flores D R	5.60
4Apr90 ^{7}SA^{2}	Green's Leader		3	116	4	2	1^{hd}	3^{1}	5^{hd}	8^{2}	$8^{3\frac{1}{2}}$	Delahoussaye E	10.50
21Apr90 ^{8}GG^{10}	College Green		3	114	3	4	$3^{1\frac{1}{2}}$	$1^{1\frac{1}{2}}$	$1^{1\frac{1}{2}}$	5^{1}	9	Almeida G	12.30

OFF AT 4:52. Start good. Won driving. Time, :23, :45⅘, 1:09⅘, 1:34⅘ Course firm.

$2 Mutuel Prices:				
	8-ITSALLGREEKTOME	65.80	19.20	8.00
	2-WARCRAFT		4.00	3.80
	9-ROBYN DANCER			6.80

$2 EXACTA 8-2 PAID $246.40.

If you want another example of this principle, consider the second race at Santa Anita on April 14, 1990.

2nd Santa Anita

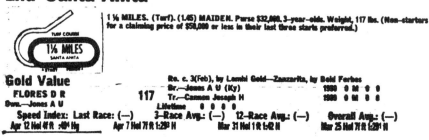

1⅛ MILES. (Turf). (1.45) MAIDEN. Purse $32,000. 3-year-olds. Weight, 117 lbs. (Non-starters for a claiming price of $50,000 or less in their last three starts preferred.)

Gold Value
FLORES D R — 117
Own.—Jones A U

Ro. c. 3(Feb), by Lombi Gold—Zanzarita, by Bold Forbes
Br.—Jones A U (Ky) — 1990 0 M 0 0
Tr.—Cannon Joseph H — 1989 0 M 0 0
Lifetime 0 0 0 0

Speed Index: Last Race: (—) 3-Race Avg.: (—) 12-Race Avg.: (—) Overall Avg.: (—)

Apr 12 Hol 4f ft :48^{4} Hg Apr 7 Hol 7f ft 1:29^{3} H Mar 31 Hol 1 ft 1:42 H Mar 25 Hol 7f ft 1:29^{1} H

Bel Air Paster — B. c. 3(Apr), by Flying Paster—Rieshamma, by Riverman
SORENSON D 117 — Br.—Cardiff Stud Farm (Cal) — 1990 2 M 0 0
Tr.—Russell John W — 1989 1 M 0 0
Own.—Friendly E — Lifetime 3 0 0 0
24Mar90-6SA 1 :46 1:113 1:383ft 70 117 74¼ 78½ 611 612½ Baze R A7 Mdn 61-21 TobyJug,PeerlssCurrnt,LtdEdition 10
24Mar90—Steadied 3 1/2
4Mar90-4SA 7f :224 :461 1:25 ft 17 118 96¼ 96 107¾1011¾ Baze R A4 Mdn 66-10 Mehmetori,FestiveColony,RsSyng 12
4Mar90—Stumbled at start
9Oct89-6SA 6f :214 :451 1:10 ft 4¼ 117 11101093¾11111017 Pincay L Jr2 [S]Mdn 71-13 Fidgety, Shantin O.,AssyrianPirate 12
9Oct89—Broke slowly
Speed Index: Last Race: (—) 3-Race Avg.: (—) 12-Race Avg.: (—) Overall Avg.: -16.3
Apr 8 Hol 5f ft 1:022 H — Mar 31 SA 6f ft 1:194 H — Mar 28 SA 5f ft 1:012 H — Mar 14 SA 6f ft 1:171 H

Officer Hawk — B. c. 3(Feb), by Silver Hawk—Dancing Lt, by San Feliou
ALMEIDA G 117 — Br.—Jones B C (Ky) — 1990 2 M 0 0
Tr.—McAnally Ronald — 1989 2 M 0 1 $1,825
Own.—Jones B C — Lifetime 4 0 0 1 $1,825
24Mar90-6SA 1 :46 1:113 1:383ft 11 117 42½101210211 925¾ McCarron C J10 Mdn 48-21 TobyJug,PeerlssCurrnt,LtdEdition 10
24Mar90—Steadied 3/8
8Jan90-4Aqu 1 70 [•]:482 1:151 1:471ft 9¾ 122 55 88¾ 816 921½ Migliore R2 Mdn 47-30 Dr. Root, Battle Fox, Junie James 9
24Dec89-6Aqu 6f [•]:231 :481 1:142ft 3½ 118 2½ 2½ 55 98 Cordero A Jr8 Mdn 66-22 MinstrelAlley,Udino,ExecutiveChief 9
23Nov89-4CD 6½f :23 :47 1:192ft *6-5 120 11 11 11½ 31½ Allen K K8 Mdn 83-17 Silver Future, Pignoli, OfficerHawk 8
Speed Index: Last Race: (—) 3-Race Avg.: (—) 12-Race Avg.: (—) Overall Avg.: -16.5
Apr 8 SA 5f ft :593 H — Apr 2 SA 4f ft :464 H — Mar 23 Hol 3f ft :37 H — Mar 18 Hol 1 ft 1:414 H

***Secret Witness** — Gr. c. 3(Feb), by Busted—Secret Gill, by Most Secret
SOLIS A 117 — Br.—Hall Miss S E (Eng) — 1990 1 M 0 0
Tr.—Sweeney Brian — 1989 0 M 0 0
Own.—Joy Cathryn — Lifetime 1 0 0 0
1Apr90-6SA 7f :222 :451 1:234ft 63 118 1½ 3½ 56 913½ Almeida G4 Mdn 70-17 ProForSure,FrOutStr,SmokJumpr 12
Speed Index: Last Race: (—) 3-Race Avg.: (—) 12-Race Avg.: (—) Overall Avg.: -13.0
Apr 9 SA 5f ft 1:002 H — Mar 29 SA 3f ft :364 Hg — Mar 24 SA 6f ft 1:123 H — Mar 19 SA 4f ft :484 Hg

River Dacer — Ch. c. 3(Mar), by Irish River (Fra)—Dacertina (Fra), by Concertino
DESORMEAUX K J 117 — Br.—Gann E A (Ky) — 1990 1 M 1 0 $6,400
Tr.—Frankel Robert — 1989 0 M 0 0
Own.—Gann E A — Lifetime 1 0 1 0 $6,400
18Mar90-4SA 1 1/16 :473 1:124 1:45 ft 11 117 1hd 2hd 1hd 21¼ McCarron C J5 Mdn 77-16 ChiefOnTheRun,RiverDcer,BtesCstl 9
18Mar90—Brushed 1/16
Speed Index: Last Race: (—) 3-Race Avg.: (—) 12-Race Avg.: (—) Overall Avg.: -7.0
Apr 10 SA 6f ft 1:133 H — Apr 5 SA 6f ft 1:163 H — Mar 30 SA 5f ft 1:011 H — Mar 25 SA 4f ft :471 H

Cranmer — Dk. b. or br. c. 3(Apr), by Seattle Song—Ivorinska, by Sir Ivor
NAKATANI C S 117 — Br.—Asta-Ltvk-FlxmnHoldngsLtd (Ky) — 1990 2 M 0 0 $4,500
Tr.—Moreno Henry — 1989 0 M 0 0
Own.—Jiles E W — Lifetime 2 0 0 0 $4,500
1Apr90-6SA 7f :222 :451 1:234ft 49 118 87¾ 88¾ 78 46 Davis R G1 Mdn 78-17 ProForSure,FrOutStr,SmokJumpr 12
18Mar90-6SA 7f :222 :452 1:241ft 96 118 810 911 810 48¾ Davis R G7 Mdn 75-13 Asia, Pendleton Ridge, Hoku 11
18Mar90—Green backstretch
Speed Index: Last Race: (—) 3-Race Avg.: (—) 12-Race Avg.: (—) Overall Avg.: -8.5
Apr 13 SA 3f ft :362 H — Apr 7 SA 5f ft 1:02 H — Mar 31 SA 3f ft :354 H — Mar 25 SA 4f ft :501 H

Teddy's Pick — B. g. 3(Apr), by Pirate's Bounty—River Festival, by Grenfall
CASTANON J L 1125 — Br.—Marden B (Cal) — 1990 4 M 0 0 $800
Tr.—Speckert Christopher — 1989 0 M 0 0
Own.—Dick R N — Lifetime 4 0 0 0 $800
17Mar90-6SA 7f :224 :46 1:234ft 114 118 31 53¾ 66 69 Black C A9 [S]Mdn 75-17 Akrokermi,BlzeO'Brin,ALittlRgtim 11
25Feb90-3SA 1 :471 1:123 1:381ft 83 117 3nk 53¼ 59½ 516¼ Black C A7 [S]Mdn 60-24 HawaiianPass,TobyJug,BlzeO'Brien 7
3Feb90-2SA 6½f :22 :452 1:173ft 79 118 94¾ 88 710 612¾ Dettori L F2 [S]Mdn 69-18 North'sTime,MaxTheBaker,Itsthefx 9
14Jan90-6SA 6f :222 :453 1:103m 28 118 67½ 59 612 613 Dettori L F2 Mdn 78-14 HonorClef,Cox'sEnchnte,SpnishStl 9
Speed Index: Last Race: (—) 3-Race Avg.: (—) 12-Race Avg.: (—) Overall Avg.: -13.2
Apr 10 SA 6f ft 1:143 H — Apr 5 SA 3f ft :363 H — Mar 30 SA 5f ft 1:004 H — Mar 15 SA 4f ft :512 B

Friend's First — Ch. c. 3(May), by Kris S—Merry Graustark, by Graustark
OLIVARES F 117 — Br.—Meadowbrook Farms Inc (Cal) — 1990 3 M 0 0 $2,400
Tr.—Niemetz Cindy N — 1989 1 M 0 0 $1,725
Own.—D C Stable — Lifetime 4 0 0 0 $4,125
17Mar90-6SA 7f :224 :46 1:234ft 10 118 117½ 99¾1014 1024½ DesormeauxKJ2 [S]Mdn 59-17 Akrokermi,BlzeO'Brin,ALittlRgtim 11
17Feb90-4SA 1 1/16 :47 1:122 1:451sy 5¾ 117 42 43 46½ 49¾ Desormeaux K J7 Mdn 67-21 TarnishedHlo,CoveDncer,BtesCstle 8
17Feb90—Lugged in late
7Jan90-4SA 6½f :214 :442 1:153ft 13 118 117½107 78¼ 68¼ Black C A6 [S]Mdn 83-09 ForMyFriends,PssThBlm,TobyJug 12
16Dec89-6Hol 6f :214 :45 1:103ft 4¼ 117 76¾ 68½ 47 48¾ Gryder A T6 [S]Mdn 79-09 Devine Force, Wild Too, Toby Jug 11
Speed Index: Last Race: (—) 3-Race Avg.: (—) 12-Race Avg.: (—) Overall Avg.: -14.0
Apr 9 SA 6f ft 1:143 H — Apr 4 SA 5f ft 1:021 H — Mar 31 SA 4f ft :51 H — ●Mar 14 SA 3f ft :343 H

High Rank B. g. 3(Mar), by Lord at War (Arg)—Queen to Conquer, by King's Bishop
DELAHOUSSAYE E 117 Br.—Wimborne Farm Inc (Ky) 1990 2 M 0 0 $750
Own.—Wimborne Farm Tr.—Whittingham Charles 1989 0 M 0 0
Lifetime 2 0 0 0 $750
18Mar90-4SA 1 1/16 :473 1:124 1:45 ft 5½ 117 97¼ 812 79¼ 716¼ Davis R G1 Mdn 62-16 ChiefOnTheRun,RiverDcer,BtesCstl 9
24Feb90-6SA 6f :214 :45 1:104ft 62 118 99¾ 88½ 79¾ 68½ Davis R G10 Mdn 73-16 StrOfRlity,‡CndymnB,LIBtO'Lrcny 11
24Feb90—Placed fifth through disqualification
Speed Index: Last Race: (—) 3–Race Avg.: (—) 12–Race Avg.: (—) Overall Avg.: –16.5
Apr 13 SA 3f ft :354 H Apr 8 SA 5f ft 1:004 H Apr 3 SA 7f ft 1:251 H Mar 29 SA 5f ft 1:003 H

Desert Lover B. c. 3(Mar), by Desert Wine—Diamond Lover, by Shecky Greene
BAZE R A 117 Br.—Agnew D J (Ky) 1990 5 M 0 2 $5,100
Own.—Shajay Stables Tr.—Canani Julio C 1989 0 M 0 0
Lifetime 5 0 0 2 $5,100
18Mar90-9GG 1 1/16 :464 1:113 1:443ft 6½ 118 2½ 42¼ 31 3nk Castanon A L 4 Mdn 75-19 Darglow, Raggle, Desert Lover 10
1Mar90-6GG 1 :463 1:111 1:371ft 6 118 21½ 1hd 33 35½ Castanon A L4 Mdn 73-31 WildNRoyl,GelicIntuition,DesrtLovr 6
4Feb90-4SA 1 1/16 :471 1:12 1:442gd 22 117 51½ 55 48½ 616 Delahoussaye E2 Mdn 65-18 Warcraft, HawaiianPass,LtdEdition 9
21Jan90-6SA 7f :222 :453 1:233ft 136 118 68½ 57 610 612 Olivares F7 Mdn 73-19 FivOnFiv,H'sLikThWind,LtdEdton 12
6Jan90-6SA 6½f :212 :441 1:16 ft 42 118 109¾ 1013 913 812¼ Davis R G5 Mdn 78-09 IndinWind,LtdEdition,SqureCreek 12
Speed Index: Last Race: (—) 3–Race Avg.: (—) 12–Race Avg.: (—) Overall Avg.: –8.0
Apr 7 SA 4f ft :481 H Apr 1 SA 5f ft 1:004 H Mar 26 SA 3f ft :354 H Mar 15 SA 4f ft :492 H

Interflip Ch. g. 3(Feb), by Interco—Flip Over Me, by Handsome Boy
STEVENS G L 117 Br.—Creaser&Warwick (Cal) 1990 3 M 0 1 $7,500
Own.—Stevens R (Lessee) Tr.—Stevens Ron 1989 1 M 1 0 $6,000
Lifetime 4 0 1 1 $13,500
17Mar90-6SA 7f :224 :46 1:234ft 12 118 84¾ 64¼ 54½ 46½ Stevens G L10 Ⓢ Mdn 77-17 Akrokermi,BlzeO'Brin,ALittlRgtim 11
21Feb90-3SA 6f :212 :443 1:094ft 8½ 118 57 46½ 48½ 39½ Stevens G L6 Ⓢ Mdn 78-13 Damazar, Akrokerami, Interflip 7
3Feb90-2SA 6½f :22 :452 1:173ft 5 118 63½ 58 68¾ 511¾ Stevens G L8 Ⓢ Mdn 78-18 North'sTime,MaxTheBaker,Itsthefx 9
3Feb90—Wide final 3/8
26Dec89-6SA 6f :221 :451 1:094ft 13 118 21 22½ 23½ 25½ Stevens G L5 Ⓢ Mdn 83-11 Wild Too, Interflip, Tex FromTexas 8
Speed Index: Last Race: (—) 3–Race Avg.: (—) 12–Race Avg.: (—) Overall Avg.: –8.2
Apr 12 SA 3f ft :352 H Apr 7 SA 5f ft 1:011 H Mar 31 SA 7f ft 1:263 H Mar 24 SA 4f ft :48 H

Cove Dancer Dk. b. or br. c. 3(Feb), by Sovereign Dancer—Turtle Cove, by Dr Fager
VALENZUELA P A 117 Br.—Tartan Farms Corp (Fla) 1990 3 M 1 0 $9,550
Own.—Tucker Paula J Tr.—Mayberry Brian A 1989 1 M 0 0 $1,020
Lifetime 4 0 1 0 $10,570
18Mar90-4SA 1 1/16 :473 1:124 1:45 ft 8½ 117 62½ 52½ 53¾ 46 Pedroza M A4 Mdn 72-16 ChiefOnTheRun,RiverDcer,BtesCstl 9
17Feb90-4SA 1 1/16 :47 1:122 1:451sy 5½ 117 77½ 53½ 32½ 21¾ Pedroza M A8 Mdn 75-21 TarnishedHlo,CoveDncer,BtesCstle 8
21Jan90-6SA 7f :222 :453 1:233ft 18 118 911 911 58½ 58¾ Pedroza M A2 Mdn 76-19 FivOnFiv,H'sLikThWind,LtdEdton 12
2Sep89-4AP 6f :224 :464 1:114ft 14 122 98½ 86¾ 78½ 49½ Bruin J E7 Mdn 71-20 Insurrection,TheGrtCrl,HomAtLst 12
Speed Index: Last Race: (—) 3–Race Avg.: (—) 12–Race Avg.: (—) Overall Avg.: –7.5
Apr 5 SA 4f ft :48 H Mar 16 SA 3f ft :37 H Mar 8 SA 5f ft 1:011 H

As usual, the public made the good-looking dirt performer a prohibitive favorite. We know better. We consider turf racing as if it were run on a different planet. There's no relationship between dirt performance and first-time turf performance. In this race there were no experienced turf performers. In such cases you simply bet on the two horses that have the most productive sires. A glance at your sire list shows that the top two sires are Silver Hawk and Sovereign Dancer. The nice part about this race is that Officer Hawk looked terrible. His recent dirt races were abysmal. Once again, forget about dirt performance when it comes to a horse's first and second time on the grass. You'll be handsomely rewarded if you keep this principle in mind.

SECOND RACE **1 ⅛ MILES.(Turf). (1.45) MAIDEN. Purse $32,000. 3-year-olds. Weight, 117 lbs. (Non-starters for a claiming price of $50,000 or less in their last three starts preferred.)**

Santa Anita

APRIL 14, 1990

Value of race $32,000; value to winner $17,600; second $6,400; third $4,800; fourth $2,400; fifth $800. Mutuel pool $637,364.

Last Raced	Horse	Eqt.	A.	Wt	PP	St	¼	½	¾	Str	Fin	Jockey	Odds $1
24Mar90 ^{6}SA^{9}	Officer Hawk		3	117	3	1	1^{3}	1^{7}	1^{8}	$1^{3\frac{1}{2}}$	1^{1}	Almeida G	29.10
1Apr90 ^{6}SA^{9}	Secret Witness		3	117	4	12	$5^{\frac{1}{2}}$	5^{2}	$2^{\frac{1}{2}}$	2^{4}	2^{3}	Solis A	15.60
18Mar90 ^{4}SA^{7}	High Rank		3	117	9	4	$6^{1\frac{1}{2}}$	7^{hd}	$7^{1\frac{1}{2}}$	$6^{\frac{1}{2}}$	3^{2}	Delahoussaye E	6.70
24Mar90 ^{6}SA^{6}	Bel Air Paster		3	117	2	3	2^{hd}	$2^{\frac{1}{2}}$	3^{hd}	$3^{1\frac{1}{2}}$	$4^{\frac{3}{4}}$	Sibille R	52.50
	Gold Value		3	117	1	9	11^{6}	$10^{\frac{1}{2}}$	$9^{1\frac{1}{2}}$	$7^{\frac{1}{2}}$	$5^{1\frac{3}{4}}$	Flores D R	67.80
17Mar90 ^{6}SA^{4}	Interflip	b	3	117	11	6	7^{1}	$6^{1\frac{1}{2}}$	$5^{\frac{1}{2}}$	$5^{1\frac{1}{2}}$	6^{nk}	Stevens G L	6.80
18Mar90 ^{4}SA^{4}	Cove Dancer		3	117	12	11	10^{1}	$8^{\frac{1}{2}}$	$8^{\frac{1}{2}}$	8^{4}	$7^{1\frac{1}{2}}$	Valenzuela P A	6.80
18Mar90 ^{4}SA^{2}	River Dacer		3	117	5	2	3^{1}	$3^{1\frac{1}{2}}$	4^{4}	4^{1}	$8^{1\frac{1}{4}}$	Desormeaux K J	1.30
1Apr90 ^{6}SA^{4}	Cranmer		3	117	6	8	9^{1}	11^{6}	11^{2}	10^{4}	9^{hd}	Nakatani C S	8.00
17Mar90 ^{6}SA^{6}	Teddy's Pick		3	112	7	7	$8^{\frac{1}{2}}$	$9^{1\frac{1}{2}}$	10^{5}	$9^{\frac{1}{2}}$	10^{7}	Castanon J L^{5}	95.00
18Mar90 ^{9}GG^{3}	Desert Lover	b	3	117	10	5	$4^{1\frac{1}{2}}$	4^{hd}	6^{hd}	11^{5}	11^{5}	Baze R A	10.30
17Mar90 ^{6}SA^{10}	Friend's First	b	3	117	8	10	12	12	12	12	12	Olivares F	35.40

OFF AT 1:35 Start good for all but SECRET WITNESS. Won driving. Time, :22⅘, :45⅘, 1:09⅗, 1:34⅘, 1:47⅘ Course firm.

$2 Mutuel Prices:				
	3–OFFICER HAWK	60.20	26.80	12.80
	4–SECRET WITNESS		14.60	9.80
	9–HIGH RANK			6.00

FOREIGN INVADERS

The next type of horse that we must learn to deal with is the foreign invader. Some writers will tell you to prefer horses from England and France to South American horses. This is probably good advice but it's not specific enough for our purposes. Remember, we are trying to find the "class of the field." We must have a method to evaluate the level of competition that a foreign invader succeeds against. There are two source materials that I recommend. The first is the *Statistical Review of 1993*, published each year by Thoroughbred Times and Thoroughbred Record and available through Bloodstock Research of Lexington, Kentucky. The second is James Quinn's *International Stakes Catalogue*. You can use these resources to answer the class question. They'll let you know the purse values of named races. The *Statistical Review* will also rank the horse by weighted handicap. Especially watch for fillies and mares that have run successfully against the boys in Europe.

Another technique that I have found to be quite effective is to use the morning-line odds printed in the racing program. After all, it's the track handicapper's job to keep track of these things. If the foreign invader is within the top three morning-line choices, he automatically becomes a contender and I'll use the morning-line odds as my betting line. This technique works well on both turf and dirt. The only thing that you must remember is to very seriously downgrade a surface switch. For example, if a foreign horse has only run on the grass and now it's entered in a dirt race—be leery. If he's the morning-line favorite, you have to respect that. If he's outside the top three morning-line favorites— forget him. If he beats you, he beats you, but I've seen too many of these horses run up the track because they didn't immediately adjust to the new surface. When dirt horses go onto the turf for the first time, we have Quirin's Grass Stallion Statistics (see Appendix B)—a powerful method to help us deal this switch. The reverse situation, when turf horses go onto dirt for the first time, are throw-outs regardless of class, unless they have shown early speed on the turf. Without the evidence of early speed, I simply wait to see how such a horse does his first time on the dirt and then evaluate it accordingly.

The technique of using the foreign invader's morning-line odds, providing that he's not switching surfaces, has worked out very well for me. Try it, you'll like it. Here's a typical example. It was the fifth race on Nov. 16, 1990, at Hollywood Park. The morning line was as follows:

Jungle Pioneer	3–1
Really Brilliant	7–2
Patchy Groundfog	4–1
Davon	4–1
Racing Rascal	5–1
Hot And Smoggy	8–1
Yucca	12–1
Romantic Prince	20–1

I suspected that Really Brilliant was going off form and would be made the false favorite. Hot And Smoggy was a horse-for-course. He loved Hollywood Park. He had never run out of the money on this course at this distance. But he had never won, either. He seemed to be the quintessential place horse. My problem was the win horse. According to my numbers, only Patchy Groundfog and Really Brilliant could run to the pars for this race. Both horses had big knocks. Patchy was 0 for 9 this year, and Really Brilliant was going the wrong way. The only logical win candidate was Jungle Pioneer. Why would the track handicapper put him at 3-to-1 in this field? The public let him go off at 5-to-1.

As a handicapper, you're wise to consider the top five choices of the morning line. The winner is usually found among these

5th Hollywood

1 1/16 MILES. (Turf). (1.38%) CLAIMING (Chute start). Purse $37,000. 3–year–olds and upward. Weights, 3–year–olds, 119 lbs.; older, 122 lbs. Non–winners of two races at a mile or over since September 15 allowed 3 lbs.; such a race since then, 6 lbs. Claiming price $100,000; for each $5,000 to $90,000 allowed 2 lbs. (Races when entered for $80,000 or less not considered.)

Coupled—Yucca and Kaif.

Really Brilliant

DESORMEAUX K J	**119**	
Own.—Golden Eagle Farm		

Ch. c. 4, by Riverman—Waterlot, by Buckpasser
Br.—Mabee Mr–Mrs J C (Ky)
Tr.—Mandella Richard $100,000
Lifetime 12 4 2 2 $81,064

1990 7 2 2 1 $66,650
1989 3 0 0 1 $4,037
Turf 12 4 2 2 $81,064

1Nov90-7SA	1 ①:46 2 1:10 1:34 1fm*6-5	LB 119	86 2/3 75 1/4 76 1/2 66 1/2	DsormxKJ2	Aw45000	85-08	Trebizond,PrudntLdr,GulfStr-Br 10

1Nov90—Wide trip

18Oct90-8SA	1 1/8 ①:45 1:09 11:45 3fm*9-5	LB 115	33 1/2 31 1/2 1 1/2 11 1/2	DsormxKJ7	Aw40000	97-03	ReallyBrilliant,Sartogn,ChrgingRj 7
7Sep90-7Dmr	1 ①:47 21:10 31:34 3fm*8-5	LB 116	31 1/2 3 1/2 2nd 1nk	DesormuxKJ5	80000 101	—	ReilyBrillint,J.T.'sPet,ElegntBrgin 8
9Aug90-8Dmr	1 1/16 ①:48 31:12 21:42 2fm 5 2/3	L 116	2 1/2 2hd 11 1/2 2 3/4	DsormxKJ2	Aw41000	94-05	Chief'sImge,RellyBrillint,Ertone 10
15Jly90-9Hol	1 1/16 ①:47 1:10 1:47 fm*6-5e	115	77 75 1/4 64 3/4 66 1/2	StevensGL7	Aw39000	86-04	GulfStr,Chief'sImge,Ventriloquist 9

15Jly90—Steadied late

17Jun90-9Hol	1 1/8 ①:46 1:10 1:47 fm 3	116	78 76 63 1/2 2 2	StevensGL2	Aw39000	91-04	Shotiche,ReilyBrillint,RiverWrden 9
3Jun90-10Hol	1 1/8 ①:45 41:09 11:46 fm*3	114	76 1/2 76 1/2 34 1/2 33 1/2	Garcia J A2	Aw37000	94-07	FlyTillDwn,Chif'sImg,RllyBrillint 10
20Jun89 ◆5Ascot(Eng)	1 1/2	2:29 3fm 6	120	① 69 3/4	CcrR	KngEdwrdVII(Gr2)	Cacoethes, Zayyani, SpringHay 6
24May89 ◆3Goodwood(Eng)	1 1/4	2:06 4fm 6	124	① 32	CchrnR	Predominate	Wrrshn,GrenwichPpillon,RllyBrillint 8
15Apr89 ◆3Newbury(Eng)	7f	1:31 3gd*8-5	126	① 9 18	CchrR	Greenham(Gr3)	Zayyani, Lunar Mover, Batshoof 12

Speed Index: Last Race: -7.0   3–Race Avg.: -2.0   7–Race Avg.: -3.0   Overall Avg.: -3.0
Nov 14 Hol 4f ft :50 3 H   Oct 14 SA 5f ft 1:02 1 B   Oct 1 SA 5f ft :58 3 H   Sep 25 SA 4f ft :48 H

Romantic Prince-Ir

PEDROZA M A	**116**	
Own.—Charles & ClearValleyStables		

Ch. h. 6, by Henbit—Supremely Royal, by Crowned Prince
Br.—Allen I (Ire)
Tr.—Shulman Sanford $100,000
Lifetime 26 4 3 4 $148,736

1990 6 0 0 1 $13,825
1989 7 0 1 0 $23,375
Turf 24 4 3 4 $148,736

20Oct90-7SA	1 ①:47 1:10 21:33 4fm 19	LB 116	21 21 32 1/2 74 1/2	PedrozMA4	Aw50000	90-07	Desptch-Fr,Trebizond,Individuiist 7
13Oct90-7SA	a6 1/2 f ①:21 3 :43 11:14 4fm 26	LB 115	41 1/2 53 1/2 89 1/2 8 11	DsormxKJ8	Aw50000	91	—	Shirkee, Oraibi, Sam Who 9

13Oct90—5-wide stretch

4Aug90-7Dmr	1 ①:46 21:10 31:35 2fm 16	L 116	74 1/2 84 1/2 85 1/2 87 1/2	Meza R Q5	Aw52000	90-07	RoylRch,BonVnt,HollywoodRprtr 8
21Jly90-7Hol	1 1/16 ①:46 31:10 11:40 4fm 6 1/2	L 116	11 1/2 11 11 31 1/2	VlenzulPA5	Aw55000	90-09	NotoriousPlsr,Colson,RomntcPrnc 6
3Jun90-8Hol	1 1/16 ①:46 21:10 21:40 fm 11	L 116	21 21 1/2 32 45 1/2	PedrozMA7	Aw60000	90-07	Bosphorus,JustAsLucky,TheMdic 7
24May90-8Hol	1 1/16 ①:49 11:13 21:42 3fm 12	114	52 1/2 62 1/2 62 1/2 55 3/4	DsormxKJ2	Aw43000	76-18	PlesntVriety,SudiDesrt,GyBursim 6

24May90—Troubled trip

24May89-8Hol	1 1/8 ①:48 1:11 31:41 fm 4 1/2	117	11 11 1/2 31 45 1/2	Pincay LJr5	Aw45000	83-11	FairJudgment,Paskos,LoylDouble 6
24Apr89-8SA	1 1/4 ①:46 21:35 42:03 4fm 27	115	43 83 1/2 10 11 914 1/2	GrrWA2	Sn Jcnt H	64-19	MsterTrety,SilntPrincII,ThMdic 10

24Apr89—Crowded 3/8 turn

6Apr89-8SA	1 ①:46 1:10 11:34 4fm 8 1/2	115	46 1/2 42 52 1/2 45 3/4	StevensGL3	Aw60000	91-03	AstrntPrnc,RNrmnd,HppysirkTms 7
24Mar89-8SA	1 ①:47 21:10 41:35 3fm 5	115	21 21 21 1/2 43	StevensGL2	Aw60000	91-10	PoliticlAmbition,TheMedic,Neshd 6

Speed Index: Last Race: -3.0   3–Race Avg.: -2.3   9–Race Avg.: -4.7   Overall Avg.: -5.2
Nov 10 Hol 7f ft 1:28 2 H   Oct 31 SA 5f ft :58 H   Oct 7 SA 4f ft :46 2 H   Sep 30 SA 4f ft :47 3 H

Hot And Smoggy

BLACK C A	**116**	
Own.—Abtahi & Stute		

Ch. h. 6, by Singular—Marselar, by Selari
Br.—Siegel Jan (Fla)
Tr.—Stute Melvin F $100,000
Lifetime 50 8 12 8 $437,405

1990 15 1 5 1 $72,155
1989 9 2 3 0 $35,075
Turf 21 2 8 2 $195,525

2Nov90-4SA	1 1/8 ①:47 2:00 32:24 3fm 16	LB 115	2hd 43 57 511 1/2	Black C A8	105000	79-09	Putting-Fr,Mshkour,OrneryGuest 8
13Oct90-5SA	1 1/8 ①:45 31:34 11:58 2fm 14e	LB 118	2 1/2 1hd 2hd 44 1/2	Black C A4	70000	92-04	Mashkour, Putting-Fr, Novelty 9
23Sep90-12Fpx	1 1/8 ①:47 1:11 1:42 ft 7 1/2	LB 122	84 1/2 97 1/2 915 917 1/2	LpAD9	CBAfflrbgh	84-05	MySonnyBoy,H'sASrs,StylshStd 10

23Sep90—Wide trip

7Sep90-7Dmr	1 ①:47 21:10 31:34 3fm 8	LB 120	1hd 2hd 31 1/2 84	Black C A3	80000	97	—	RellyBrillint,J.T.'sPet,ElegntBrgin 8

7Sep90—Took Up 1/16

18Aug90-5Dmr	1 1/16 ①:49 41:13 41:50 2fm 5	LB 116	11 11 1hd 1hd	Black C A8	80000	86-10	HotAndSmoggy,Novlty,DysGonBy 9
5Aug90-5Dmr	1 1/16 ①:48 41:12 41:42 3fm 12	L 116	11 1hd 1hd 21 1/2	DelhoussyeE2	90000	93-04	Trig,HotAndSmoggy,GrnJudgmnt 8

5Aug90—Lost whip 1/16

22Jly90-10Hol	1 ①:47 41:11 11:40 4fm 3 1/2	L 116	2 1/2 1hd 11 1/2 21 1/2	Solis A8	62500	90-12	Treig, Hot And Smoggy, Neskimo 8
1Jly90-5Hol	1 1/16 ①:46 21:09 41:34 fm 17	L 116	31 1/2 33 1/2 33 1/2 33 1/2	Solis A4	80000	91-08	BrvCpd,PtchGrndfg,HtAndSmgg 10
3Jun90-5Hol	1 1/8 ①:49 21:13 11:48 3fm 4 1/2	116	2hd 21 1/2 1hd 22	Solis A7	80000	83-07	Mshkur,HtAndSmggy,SngsFrstDnc 7

3Jun90—Broke slowly

19Mar90-8CD	1 1/16 ①:48 31:13 1:46 1sy 5	115	11 1/2 11hd 45 1/2 410	Gryder A T1	Aw32000	73-24	LuckyPch,LunchADrm,SprSolton 7

Speed Index: Last Race: -12.0   3–Race Avg.: -6.3   8–Race Avg.: -4.3   Overall Avg.: -4.9
Nov 9 Hol 3f ft :36 3 H   Oct 28 SA 5f ft 1:01 4 H   Oct 21 SA 3f ft :35 2 H   Oct 8 SA 5f ft 1:02 4 H

Racing Rascal — Dk. b. or br. g. 4, by Oh Say—O Mandy, by Buck's Bid
SOLIS A — 116 — Br.—Gatti R J (Fla) — Tr.—Lewis Craig A — $100,000
Own.—Gatti R J
Lifetime 35 6 8 7 $158,160 — 1990 10 3 1 1 $77,975 — 1989 17 2 5 6 $64,942 — Turf 12 2 2 4 $73,874

1Nov90-7SA 1 ⓣ:4621:10 1:341fm 9¾ LB115 97¼ 85¾ 87 55¼ Solis A Aw45000 87-08 Trebizond,PrudntLdr,GulfStr-Br 10
1Nov90—Wide trip
10Oct90-7SA 1⅛ ⓣ:4711:1111:461fm 4 LB119 41¼ 31½ 33 34¼ Solis A Aw45000 90-06 PortWshngtn,GlfStr-Br,RcngRscl 7
10Oct90—Wide 7/8 turn
29Aug90-7Dmr 1 1/16 ⓣ:47 1:1141:424fm 6 LB120 87 62¼ 11 13½ Solis A 62500 93-10 RacingRascl,Lordlik,GretReltions 9
29Aug90—Wide 3/8 turn
18Aug90-5Dmr 1⅛ ⓣ:4941:1341:502fm 8 LB120 76½ 65½ 76¾ 88 Meza R Q 80000 78-10 HotAndSmoggy,Novlty,DysGonBy 9
18Aug90—Rank early
5Aug90-5Dmr 1 1/16 ⓣ:4841:1241:423fm 8½ L 117 53 61¾ 85 64 Solis A 85000 90-04 Trig,HotAndSmoggy,GrnJudgmnt 8
5Aug90—Hit rail 3/16
25Jly90-2Dmr 1 1/16 ⓣ:49 1:1311:424fm 10 L 118 63½ 53 3½ 1hd Solis A Aw41000 93-05 RacingRscl,MjorMoment,Ertone 10
14Jly90-7Hol 1 :45 1:093 1:341ft 9½ L 116 66 64½ 44 45½ Garcia J A 80000 88-07 SnstonlStr,DkothThundr,SlvrCrcs 7
10Jun90-9Hol 1 ⓣ:4611:10 1:344fm 13 119 118¾119 96½ 31 Solis A 62500 89-10 ‡Sperry,CarolinNorth,RcingRscl 12
10Jun90—Placed second through disqualification; Wide into stretch
28May90-5Hol 1 1/16 :462 1:11 1:433gd *2½ 116 58 711 712 817½ Davis R G Aw37000 64-18 WellAwre,AbrgwunLd,Mr.KlnKut 8
4May90-3Hol 1 :45 1:093 1:351ft *9-5 116 53½ 52¾ 5¾ 13½ Davis R G 62500 88-16 RcngRscl,Wtch'nWn,Prt'sAdvntr 5
4May90—Steadied start
Speed Index: Last Race: -5.0 3-Race Avg.: -2.0 7-Race Avg.: -3.8 Overall Avg.: -4.6
Nov 18 Hol 5f ft 1:021 H Oct 28 SA 7f ft 1:284 H Oct 21 SA 4f ft :48 H Oct 5 SA 5f ft 1:004 H

Jungle Pioneer — B. c. 4, by Conquistador Cielo—Untitled, by Vaguely Noble
MCCARRON C J — 116 — Br.—Flaxman Holdings Ltd (Ky) — Tr.—Jones Gary — $100,000
Own.—Lima M
Lifetime 12 4 3 0 $28,241 — 1990 4 1 1 0 $8,714 — 1989 5 2 0 0 $8,809 — Turf 12 4 3 0 $28,241

14Aug90♦1Clairefont'e(Fra a1⅛ : gd — 126 ⓣ 2nk AsmssnC Px dsFrrsCtl JetJens,JunglePioner,BrownChick 14
14Aug90—No time taken
29Jly90♦1Vittel(Fra) a1 : yl *1-2 129 ⓣ 110 BohyP PxBonneSource JunglePioneer,ForTheRod,Pretdnt 10
29Jly90—No time taken
17Jun90♦4Strasbourg(Fra) a1 1/16 : gd — 130 ⓣ 45¼ DbrcqG Gr Px deStrsbrg Ardasher,RowanTree,ManildeSanon 8
17Jun90—No time taken
5Apr90♦4StCloud(Fra) a1 1:402gd — 123 ⓣ 13 DbrcG PxEdmBlc(Gr3) ValdesBois,MisterSicy,SharpYouth 13
19Nov89♦4Toulouse(Fra) a1½ : yl — 115 ⓣ 15 LScrllC PxMaxSicard Sigmaringen, Mercalle, Pestrained 15
19Nov89—No time taken
25Sep89♦6Nottingham(Eng) a1½2:042fm*2-3 124 ⓣ 13 CauthenS Bentinck Jungle Pioneer, Neatfoot, Bex 9
13Jun89♦5Pontefract(Eng) 1¼ 2:104fm 3-2 136 ⓣ 17 CthS MexboroughGrad Jungle Pioneer,MarineDiver,Willilov 3
Speed Index: Last Race: (—) 3-Race Avg.: (—) 12-Race Avg.: (—) Overall Avg.: (—)
Nov 11 Hol 7f ft 1:263 H Nov 4 Hol 6f ft 1:131 Hg Oct 29 Hol 5f ft 1:004 H Oct 23 Hol 4f ft :474 H

Patchy Groundfog — Ch. h. 7, by Instrument Landing—Tea At Five, by Olden Times
DELAHOUSSAYE E — 116 — Br.—Wooden Horse Investments (NY) — Tr.—Canani Julio C — $100,000
Own.—Fisher-Isom-Moore
Lifetime 56 14 7 10 $607,155 — 1990 9 0 2 2 $66,300 — 1989 9 4 3 1 $270,600 — Turf 40 11 6 6 $536,375

25Oct90-5SA a6½f ⓣ:212 :4331:123fm 7 LB116 108½ 96¾ 54½ 31¾ DelhoussyeE2 80000 96-02 PsnoPt,MjorCrrnt,PtchyGrndfg 10
25Oct90—Broke slowly
29Aug90-7Dmr 1 1/16 ⓣ:47 1:1141:424fm 9-5 LB116 2½ 2hd 65¾ 712½ McCarron CJ5 62500 80-10 RacingRascl,Lordlik,GretReltions 9
29Aug90—Checked 1/4
5Aug90-5Dmr 1 1/16 ⓣ:4841:1241:423fm 3¾ L 115 42½ 41½ 52 53 Black C A3 85000 91-04 Trig,HotAndSmoggy,GrnJudgmnt 8
1Jly90-5Hol 1 ⓣ:4621:0941:34 fm 2¾ L 116 21½ 21½ 22 22 ValenzuelPA9 80000 92-08 BrvCpd,PtchGrndfg,HtAndSmgg 10
11May90-9Hol 1 ⓣ:47 1:1021:341fm*7-5 117 55½ 42½ 42½ 32½ Black C A7 150000 91-07 CrmsonSlw,Somrmj,PtchyGrndfg 7
21Apr90-8SA a6½f ⓣ:211 :43 1:121fm 2½ 117 33 33 22½ 22¾ PcLJr2 Sn Smn H 97 — CostlVoyg,PtchyGrndfg,RsAStnz 4
21Apr90—Grade III
24Mar90-8GG 1 ⓣ:4641:1011:354fm 13 117 21½ 2½ 2½ 42¾ SibilleR5 S F Mi H 90-07 ColwyRlly,RiverMstr,MiswkiTrn 10
24Mar90—Grade III
4Mar90-5SA 1 ⓣ:45 1:09 1:342fm 11 117 713 78¾ 87¼ 54 BlckCA4 Arcadia H 87-18 Prized, Happy Toss, On TheMenu 9
4Mar90—Grade III; Broke slowly
3Feb90-5SA 1 ⓣ:46 1:10 1:341fm*2-3 118 2½ 2hd 2hd 41 ShrW8 Lg Lst Rd H 91-11 ExemplaryLeder,HppyToss,Oribi 11
31Dec89-8SA 1⅛ ⓣ:4631:1011:461fm 7½ 117 32½ 43 32½ 21 BlckCA5 Sn Gbrl H 100 — Wrthm,PtchyGrondfg,InExtrms 10
31Dec89—Grade III; Rank early
Speed Index: Last Race: -10.0 3-Race Avg.: -5.0 8-Race Avg.: -1.6 Overall Avg.: -1.8
Nov 9 Hol 4f ft :492 H Nov 3 SA 3f ft :353 B Oct 29 SA 4f ft :481 H Oct 14 SA 6f ft 1:124 H

Davon-Br — B. h. 5, by Shangamuzo—Danitie, by Tom Poker
SANTOS J A — 115 — Br.—Haras Morumbi (Brz) — Tr.—Nor Fabio — $90,000
Own.—Maggiore S
Lifetime 15 5 1 2 $68,131 — 1990 4 2 0 0 $37,325 — 1989 5 1 1 0 $24,925 — Turf 13 4 1 1 $67,080

24Oct90-6BM 1 1/16 ⓣ:4641:1141:443fm*4-5 L 117 47 41½ 41½ 12 Hansen RD 3 Aw25000 82-18 Davon-Br, Coax Me Clyde, Zin 5
24Oct90—Lacked room 1/4

9Sep90-7Dmr	1 1/16 Ⓣ:47 1:104 1:412fm	23	LB116	65½	43	3½	12	VlenzulPA 9	Aw41000	100-02	Davon, Predecessor,Ventriloquist	9
9Sep90—Bumped 1/8												
26Aug90-5Dmr	1 1/16 Ⓣ:502 1:152 1:444fm	10	LB116	64½	52¼	55¼	55¼	Meza R Q 1	Aw41000	78-14	Timdala, High Rank,Ventriloquist	9
26Aug90—Boxed In 1/2 1/4												
5Aug90-5Dmr	1 1/16 Ⓣ:484 1:124 1:423fm	20	L 115	31	3nk	3½	84¾	Hansen R D 1	85000	89-04	Trig,HotAndSmoggy,GrnJudgmnt	8
5Aug90—Rank early												
15Oct89-5SA	1¼ Ⓣ:47 1:352 1:59 fm	7	116	97¼	105½	86	53	Stevens G L10	80000	89-08	Novelty,Timefighter,LmmonJuic	10
15Oct89—Wide 3/8 turn												
3Sep89-7Dmr	1 1/16 Ⓣ:482 1:122 1:432fm	*2¾	117	56	54	53½	51½	StevensGL5	Aw38000	81-19	GrgHbrt,SvnRvrs,EghtyEghtKys	10
3Sep89—Wide 3/8 turn												
5Aug89-7Dmr	1⅛ Ⓣ:483 1:13 1:493fm	14	119	32½	51¼	21½	2½	StevensGL3	Aw38000	84-17	Rogue'sRealm,Davon,MindMaster	9
9Jly89-9Hol	1⅛ Ⓣ:481 1:124 1:49 fm	9	120	32	73¼	75¾	65¾	Davis R G 9	Aw33000	77-14	Wrethm,ImpossiblStrm,Wroquir	10
9Jly89—Crowded 1/4												
3Jun89-9Hol	1⅛ Ⓣ:474 1:121 1:493fm	4¼	116	42½	42	2hd	1nk	Davis R G5	Aw28000	80-15	Davon, Johnny Bear, The M. V. P.	8
3Jun89—Rank early												
7Sep88♦6CidJardin(Brazil	a1 1:353fm	—	123	Ⓣ 10					Gr Pr Iprng (Grl)		Further, information, unavailable	22

Speed Index: Last Race: 0.0 3–Race Avg.: –2.0 9–Race Avg.: –3.2 Overall Avg.: –3.2

Nov 10 Hol 5f ft 1:01 H Nov 5 Hol 5f ft 1:034 H ●Oct 13 Hol 3f ft :342 H Oct 7 Hol 1 ft 1:393 H

Yucca
VELASQUEZ J **112**
Own.—Sommer Viola

Gr. h. 6, by Vigors—Bold Brat, by Boldnesian
Br.—Hunt N B (Ky)
Tr.—Martin Frank **$90,000**
Lifetime 54 10 9 7 $322,580

1990	13	3	3	3	$75,114
1989	5	2	1	0	$37,719
Turf	38	8	9	4	$270,419

6Oct90-2Bel	1¼ Ⓣ:483 1:364 2:011fm	*2¾	115	75	73	55½	68½	Antley C W3	47500	85-05	DndyCndy,MyBbysFst,SyrinStngr	9
6Sep90-4Bel	1 Ⓣ:451 1:091 1:342fm	2¾	113	69	66½	65	57	Santos J A3	75000	87-07	SwordChrger,IRejoice,BrvelyBold	8
26Aug90-5Sar	1⅛ Ⓣ:482 1:124 1:504yl	*6-5	119	42½	41½	33½	21¼	Cordero AJr7	c50000	88-22	MyBabysFast,Yucca,DonMarioII	10
18Aug90-2Sar	1 3/16 Ⓣ:474 1:113 1:55 fm	2½	112	64	53	42	31¼	Cordero A Jr2	75000	94-07	I Rejoice, ExplosiveDancer,Yucca	8
3Aug90-9Sar	1 1/16 Ⓣ:463 1:10 1:402fm	4¼	115	42	41	21	1nk	Cordero A Jr5	47500	94-09	Yucca, D. White, Don Mario II	9
29Jun90-2Bel	1 Ⓣ:452 1:092 1:333hd	4	117	63½	73½	85¾	107	Migliore R7	75000	91-08	D.Whit,Finngn'sPrid,SyrinStingr	12
2May90-7Aqu	1 1/16 Ⓣ:481 1:132 1:454yl	*4-5	116	44	2½	2hd	2hd	Migliore R6	85000	85-15	D. White, Yucca, Sword Charger	6
1Apr90-9FG	a1⅛ Ⓣ:50 1:142 1:522gd	10	115	64¼	62¼	63¼	75½	MlrR11	Life Gold Cp	90 —	TowrAbov'Em,Alljb,ForgnSrvvor	12
17Mar90-9GP	1 Ⓣ:464 1:102 1:35 hd	*8-5	122	61¾	42½	31½	1nk	Migliore R1	Aw30000	99-04	Yucca, Racing Star, Green Book	12
3Mar90-9GP	a1 Ⓣ 1:392fm	3	112	75½	64¼	31½	2nk	Migliore R4	Aw28000	82-18	GreenBook,Yucca,HandsomeSon	11

Speed Index: Last Race: –10.0 3–Race Avg.: –2.0 10–Race Avg.: –1.0 Overall Avg.: –1.0

Nov 12 Hol 5f ft 1:004 H Nov 2 Bel tr.t 4f ft :492 B Oct 3 Bel tr.t 4f ft :484 B Sep 24 Bel tr.t 4f ft :49 B

FIFTH RACE
Hollywood
NOVEMBER 16, 1990

1 1/16 MILES.(Turf). (1.39⅘) CLAIMING (Chute start). Purse $37,000. 3-year-olds and upward. Weights, 3-year-olds, 119 lbs.; older, 122 lbs. Non-winners of two races at a mile or over since September 15 allowed 3 lbs.; such a race since then, 6 lbs. Claiming price $100,000; for each $5,000 to $90,000 allowed 2 lbs. (Races when entered for $80,000 or less not considered.)

Value of race $37,000; value to winner $20,350; second $7,400; third $5,550; fourth $2,775; fifth $925. Mutuel pool $236,947. Exacta pool $257,542.

Last Raced	Horse	M/Eqt.	A.Wt	PP	St	¼	½	¾	Str	Fin	Jockey	Cl'g Pr	Odds $1
14Aug90 1Cla2	Jungle Pioneer	LB	4 116	5	7	8	7hd	7hd	4½	12½	McCarronCJ	100000	5.30
2Nov90 4SA5	Hot And Smoggy	LBb	6 116	3	1	21	21	21½	11	2¾	Black C A	100000	11.60
24Oct90 8BM1	Davon-Br	Lb	5 115	7	5	51½	51½	4hd	3hd	3hd	Santos J A	90000	3.80
1Nov90 7SA6	Really Brilliant	LB	4 119	1	3	4hd	4½	3hd	2hd	41¼	DsormuxKJ	100000	2.50
6Oct90 2Bel6	Yucca	LB	6 112	8	4	6hd	6½	61	61	51¼	Velasquez J	90000	13.20
1Nov90 7SA5	Racing Rascal	LBb	4 116	4	8	7½	8	8	71½	64½	Solis A	100000	4.20
25Oct90 5SA3	Patchy Groundfog	LB	7 116	6	6	31	3½	5½	8	7nk	Davis R G	100000	6.40
20Oct90 4SA7	Romantic Prince-Ir	LB	6 116	2	2	1½	1½	1½	51½	8	Pedroza MA	100000	15.10

OFF AT 2:55. Start good. Won ridden out. Time, :23⅖, :46⅗, 1:10⅘, 1:34⅘, 1:40⅘ Course firm.

$2 Mutuel Prices:

5–JUNGLE PIONEER	12.60	7.00	6.00
3–HOT AND SMOGGY		10.40	6.60
7–DAVON–BR			4.40

$2 EXACTA 5–3 PAID $122.80.

choices. At some racetracks the winner is found within the top five more than 80 percent of the time. You're also wise to consider the top five choices of the public. The winner is usually found among these on the order of 90 percent of the time. When you're betting on a horse that isn't among the top five, you must have a good reason. In this case you had every reason to make a win bet on Jungle Pioneer.

EXPERIENCED TURF RUNNERS

Thus far we have handled the issues of first-time-on-the-turf runners and foreign invaders. We have used the factors of breeding, class, and morning line. What remains is the issue of evaluating turf performances for experienced runners and isolating the winning factors. James Quinn cuts the Gordian knot when he says that the three most important factors in turf handicapping are **class, late speed**, and **pedigree**.

We have already discussed the first and third point. We'll define class as the ability to succeed at the highest level of competition. That is, a horse's class will be a function of where he's able to win or just miss. Most handicappers make the mistake of defining class by the level of the horse's previous races regardless whether it succeeded or not. For example, a horse last ran in a claiming $32,000 event. He's now entered in a claiming $25,000 race. This is mistakenly considered a class drop. It's not, according to our definition, unless the horse had a victory or at least ran within a length or two of the winner at the $32,000 level. To determine the class of a horse, simply scan its past performances for all wins or close seconds. The highest level you find represents its class. Once a horse's class is determined, we then ask whether its current form and condition will allow it to perform at the level of today's race. This is particularly useful in stakes races. Fortunately, there are relatively few turf stakes races in comparison to dirt stakes. This tends to better preserve the turf stakes hierarchy. Unlike the dirt, where there's very little distinction among Grade 1, Grade 2, and Grade 3 races, turf races maintain a stricter conformity to the graded designations. If today's turf race is a Grade 2 event, we must first look for Grade 2 and above winners as our likely win candidates. We must always be on the lookout for improving horses, especially two- and three-year-olds. This is true on dirt as well as turf. In a graded stakes race you must include all graded stakes winners as contenders regardless of recent failures. Next, we look for horses moving through their conditions. (For a better understanding of this concept, please read or reread James Quinn's *The Handicapper's Condition Book*.) We'll insist that improving horses demonstrate their ability to run within two lengths of the par time of today's race on today's surface.

The typical turf route race looks like the following: The bell rings, and as the gates open, each horse looks at its neighbor and says "After you"; its neighbor responds, "No, no. After you." It seems that nobody is interested in breaking alertly. Depending upon post position and length of run down to the first turn, the horses sort themselves out with only one or two horses going extremely wide. On the backside they spread out while the pace remains moderate to slow. As the horses reach the far turn they start to bunch up and the pace starts to quicken. At the top of the stretch you can throw a blanket around the top five or six horses. They race down the stretch, the finish usually involving as many as six horses in an all-out charge to the wire. It's the only type of race where you see strange things in the past performances like 4^{nk} or $5^{1/2}$. It's easy to see that late speed is the key to pace analysis on the turf. Unfortunately, it's not as simple as evaluating the last fraction for each horse. Again, we are looking for the "class of the field." If we define class as speed (which isn't a bad definition), we'll then look for horses that can run fast early and have the ability to sustain their speed until late in the race. The trick is to use the first fraction and the adjusted last fraction for today's distance. The purpose of using this combination is to find horses who have the best late speed combined with early speed. It's actually very logical. We prefer horses that have endured a brisk early pace and still maintained a good final fraction to horses who have had an easy early fraction and the same closing fraction. You adjust the first and third fraction times of the horses by beaten lengths and then you add them together. The smaller the better.

Turf variants are practically a joke. Tom Brohamer is one of the best pace handicappers in the country and makes very sophisticated variants. He'll be the first to admit that turf variants are both inaccurate and unusable.

Unless there's a standout—that is, a horse that figures three or more lengths ahead of the field—we'll concentrate our efforts on all the horses that are within two lengths of the top-rated horse. We'll bet the **two** horses that have the longest odds. The reason that we mostly bet on two horses is because of the low probability associated with a single choice. In a study of 240 turf races using the method described here, my top figure horse regardless of odds only won 24 percent of the time. The fourth top horse won 18 percent of the time. The top two horses won 43 percent of the time. Our conclusion was that the top four picks were statistically more distinguishable than using FIVE-IN-ONE but still a little too unpredictable for betting with complete confidence. With a little creativity, we can use these results to our benefit. A good winning strategy is to bet on the two longest-odds horses among our top choices, except when there's a standout. We should win approximately 40 percent of our races at average odds of 5-to-1 or better. It doesn't take a genius to see that this is a profitable strategy. Our minimum mathematical expectation is as follows:

$$E(X) \ = \ .4(\$8) \ - \ .6(\$4) \ = \ \$.80$$

That's 80 cents profit for each $4 invested, or a 20 percent ROI. Not bad. If you're confused by the above calculation, it's explained by the fact that you're betting $4 per race. If you have a winner at 5-to-1, your profit for the race is $8. If you lose the race, you lose $4. Hence 40 percent of the time you collect an $8 profit. (Your 5-to-1 shot paid $12 and you bet $4, leaving $8.) You lose your $4 bet 60 percent of the time. If you did this one hundred times, you would have profits of $320 and losses of $240 for a final profit of $80. You would have invested $400 and got back $480 for a 20 percent profit. In reality, my actual average mutuel for the turf is between $14 and $15. My win percent is also higher than this example. My ROI on the turf is around 50 percent.

The way to deal with a standout is to bet him to win at odds of 5-to-2 or better, or else look for a place or show overlay or use him in the exacta or quinella. ***Don't bet against a standout.*** It's death on the bankroll.

TURF ROUTES "ABILITY TIME"

What now remains is to detail how to calculate "turf ability time." The last fraction is complicated by the distance of the race and the points of call. Consider the following table:

Race Distance	Dist. to 1st Call	Dist. of Last Fraction
1 mile	½ mile	¼ mile
1¹⁄₁₆ miles	½ mile	⁵⁄₁₆ mile
1⅛ miles	½ mile	⅜ mile
1³⁄₁₆ miles	½ mile	⁷⁄₁₆ mile
1¼ miles	½ mile	¼ mile
1⁵⁄₁₆ miles	½ mile	⁵⁄₁₆ mile
1⅜ miles	½ mile	⅜ mile
1½ miles	½ mile	¼ mile

The one mile, 1¼ mile, and 1½ mile races are treated the same with regard to computing "turf ability times." The 1¹⁄₁₆ and the 1⁵⁄₁₆ distance are grouped together, as is the 1⅛ and the 1⅜, which leaves the 1³⁄₁₆ distance as an oddball. The first fraction time is significant in that it usually determines the final time of a horse. If the horse blisters the first fraction, it usually depletes its energy supply and scores a poor last fraction time. Conversely, if you let a horse walk the first fraction, it will often run a very impressive last fraction. We are balancing a horse's final time with its energy allocation.

We must always adjust the distance of the last fraction of the chosen race to the distance of today's race. Let's see how we would go about making these adjustments. Consider a mythical racetrack that has par times (in fifths) as follows:

Distance	1st Call	2nd Call	Final
1 mile	45^4	1:10	$1:34^2$
1¹⁄₁₆	47	$1:10^3$	$1:41^2$
1⅛	47	1:11	1:48

The first thing that you should do is convert these times to tenths of seconds to allow for half-lengths. Our table now looks as follows:

Distance	1st Call	2nd Call	Final
1 mile	45.8	1:10	1:34.4
1¹⁄₁₆	47	1:10.6	1:41.4
1⅛	47	1:11	1:48

The distance adjustments suggest themselves from the above. The mile race runs faster early, hence the mile times must be downgraded by 1.2 seconds for the first call and .6 seconds for the second call in the 1¹⁄₁₆ case, and a full second for the second call in the 1⅛ distance. Final times are adjusted similarly. The mile to 1¹⁄₁₆ adjustment is 7 seconds; the mile to 1⅛ adjustment is 13.6 seconds; and the 1¹⁄₁₆ to 1⅛ adjustment is 6.6 seconds.

Jim Quinn advises a 6.3 second per sixteenth of a mile approximate final-time adjustment, and it has served him well. Since I am a computer person, I prefer to use the actual adjustment to the nearest tenth of a second. Let's take a look at a typical turf route race and make the necessary adjustments. This was the fifth race at Hollywood Park on November 24, 1990. The Hollywood turf pars (in tenths) for this level of racing were:

Distance	1st Call	2nd Call	Final
1 mile	46	1:10.4	1:35
1¹⁄₁₆	47	1:11	1:42
1⅛	47	1:11.4	1:48.6

The Santa Anita turf pars (in tenths) for this level of racing were:

Distance	1st Call	2nd Call	Final
1 mile	45.4	1:09.8	1:33.6
1⅛	46.2	1:10	1:46

The contenders were:

Quick Step Slewpy Using her last race, her adjusted times are 47.3 1:10.8 1:48.4. These are arrived at by adding one-tenth of a second for each one-half beaten length. She was behind by 1½ lengths at the first call; hence we must add .3 seconds to her time. We make no adjustment for nose, head, or neck; therefore, she gets her actual time for the second call. Her final beaten lengths were zero because she won the race, so she gets her final time with no adjustments. Since this race was at Hollywood Park, we now need only adjust the distance. After doing so, Quick Step Slewpy's projected times for the

5th Hollywood

1 MILE. (Turf). (1.32⅘) ALLOWANCE. Purse $34,000. Fillies and mares. 3-year-olds and upward, which have not won $3,000 twice other than maiden, claiming or starter. Weights, 3-year-olds, 118 lbs.; older, 121 lbs. Non-winners of two races other than claiming at a mile or over since Sept. 15 allowed 3 lbs.; a race other than maiden or claiming since then, 6 lbs.

Coupled—Justoneofthegirls and Lovlier Laura.

Quick Step Slewpy

BAZE R A **115**
Own.—Dance Hall Stable

Ch. f. 3(Apr), by Slewpy—Paradise Lost, by Fleet Nasrullah
Br.—Ky Thoroughbred Associates (Ky) 1990 13 2 2 5 $72,950
Tr.—Lewis Craig A 1989 1 M 0 0
Lifetime 14 2 2 5 $72,950 Turf 4 1 0 2 $28,250

9Nov90-8Hol	1⅛ (T):47 1:104 1:482fm	4	LB115	31½	2hd	11½	13½	Solis A 2	(F)Aw32000	86-14	QckStpSlpy,Csy'sRmnc,AdrblVc	10
26Oct90-7SA	1⅛ (T):4611:1031:473fm	7¾	LB114	21½	2½	32½	34	Solis A 5	(F)Aw35000	83-13	SongStylst,MtsDlly,QckStpSlwpy	8
6Oct90-7SA	1 :451 1:101 1:353ft	8½	LB118	55	53	23½	36½	DsrmxKJ 3	(F)Aw35000	82-09	LfthhThCrss,ScrtAl-En,QcStpSlp	9
6Sep90-8Dmr	1 1/16 (T):48 1:1211:42 fm	10	LB115	68	62¾	55	36½	DsrmxKJ 7	(F)Aw36000	90-03	Bequest,Ce'sSong,QuickStpSlwpy	9
6Sep90—4-wide stretch												
24Aug90-5Dmr	1 (T):47 1:1211:371fm	12	LB117	44	31	54	66	DsrmxKJ 1	(F)Aw36000	82-12	Shinko'sLss,Virtully,MediclMrvl	10
24Aug90—Steadied at 1/8												
29Jly90-5Dmr	6½f :214 :442 1:154ft	18	L 116	97¾	1012	97¾	96¾	StvnsGL 3	(F)Aw33000	82-07	Nordicn,TessOfHemt,TntPhyllis	10
29Jly90—Checked 1/8												
22Jun90-4Hol	7f :222 :452 1:233ft	2½	116	21½	2½	1½	13½	Stevens G L 6	(F)Mdn	87-10	QckStpSlwpy,AdorblVc,MtsDolly	6
26May90-4Hol	1 1/16 :471 1:113 1:423ft	3¼	115	21½	31	31½	34¾	Garcia J A 3	(F)Mdn	82-16	Raiatea,Atrevid,QuickStepSlewpy	6
5May90-2Hol	1 :452 1:103 1:354ft	5¼	115	42½	43½	43½	24½	Nakatani CS 7	(F)Mdn	80-09	SyrinWntr,QuckStpSlwpy,Clssclc	8
5May90—Wide 3/8												
21Apr90-6SA	1 :46 1:103 1:364ft	13	114	43½	57¾	29	211	Garcia J A 5	(F)Mdn	72-17	WrCmmndrss,QcStpSlp,FllDArnt	9
21Apr90—Wide final 5/16												

Speed Index: Last Race: 0.0 3-Race Avg.: -3.6 4-Race Avg.: -4.2 Overall Avg.: -6.4

Nov 21 Hol 3f ft :363 H Oct 21 SA tr.t 5f ft 1:004 H Oct 15 SA 5f ft 1:022 H Oct 1 SA 4f ft :504 H

Somethingmerry

STEVENS G L **112**
Own.—Johnston E W-Betty-Judy

B. f. 3(May), by Somethingfabulous—My Mary, by Rising Market
Br.—Old English Rancho (Cal) 1990 6 2 1 2 $103,075
Tr.—Warren Donald 1989 1 M 1 0 $4,600
Lifetime 7 2 2 2 $107,675 Turf 3 1 1 1 $80,200

3Nov90-5SA	a6½f (T):212 :4331:123fm	4¾	LB117	41¾	41¾	33	33¾	PcLJ4	(F)(S)CCpDstfH	94-02	LindCrd,Survive,Somethingmrry	13
3Nov90—4-wide stretch												
11Apr90-8SA	1⅛ (T):4631:1041:472fm	*2	120	63½	63	1½	2no	PcLJr5	(F)(R)Prvdncia	88-10	Mtrco,Somthngmrry,Njnsky'sLvr	9
11Apr90—Bumped start												
14Mar90-5SA	a6½f (T):204 :4311:14 fm	7½	117	58	57½	43½	12	PncLJr6	(F)La Habra	91-10	Smthngmrry,BrghtTMnd,FrstFlt	11
14Mar90—Run in divisions												
3Mar90-6SA	7f :221 :452 1:24 ft	2½	117	56½	55¾	11½	13½	Pincay L Jr2	(F)Mdn	83-24	Somthngmrry,IslndSplndor,DdHt	9
12Feb90-8SA	1 1/16 :464 1:114 1:453ft	36	114	75¼	76½	79½	511½	HwlyS5	(F)(R)Sta Ysbl	63-25	BrghtCndls,HvnForBd,AnnulRnon	7
12Feb90—Broke slowly												
21Jan90-4SA	6½f :221 :453 1:173ft	2½e	117	54	33½	34	34¼	Hawley S7	(F)Mdn	78-19	AutumnButy,VMy,Somthngmrry	11
9Dec89-4Hol	6f :22 :453 1:104ft	3½e	117	85	65½	42	21	PincyLJr10	(F)(S)Mdn	86-13	Slewrena,Somethingmerry,Azus	11
9Dec89—Wide into stretch												

Speed Index: Last Race: -2.0 1-Race Avg.: -2.0 1-Race Avg.: -2.0 Overall Avg.: -2.0

Nov 18 SA 7f ft 1:271 H Nov 12 SA 5f ft 1:003 H Nov 1 SA HC 3f fm :38 H ●Oct 25 SA (T) 5f fm :58 H (d)

Justoneofthegirls

NAKATANI C S **115**
Own.—Behar-Cohen-Recachina etal

Dk. b. or br. f. 4, by Floriano—Chrissy Lou, by Aegean Isle
Br.—Roub-Stewart-Truman (Cal) 1990 5 2 1 0 $38,250
Tr.—Cenicola Lewis 1989 2 M 0 0 $400
Lifetime 7 2 1 0 $38,650 Turf 4 1 1 0 $27,800

5Nov90-5SA	1 (T):4521:0931:344fm	2¾	LB118	86¼	118	119¼	1112¾	Solis A8	(F)Aw40000	76-11	JoLo'sJoy,Virtually,GrandAward	11
5Nov90—Bumped early												
30Oct90-5SA	1⅛ (T):4641:1021:461fm	8¼	B 119	11	11	12	21¾	Solis A9	(F)Aw40000	92-06	Orlnov,Jstonofthgrls,SmrtDcpton	9
23Aug90-8Dmr	1⅛ (T):4831:1331:511fm	35	B 119	1hd	1hd	1hd	11¼	Solis A2	(F)Aw36000	82-18	Jstonofthgrls,C'sSong,Wodly'sF	10
2Aug90-5Dmr	1 (T):4721:12 1:363fm	8½	116	42½	51¾	74¼	74½	StvnsGL5	(F)Aw36000	86-09	Cozzy, Cash In Now, Virtually	9
12Jly90-2Hol	6½f :214 :443 1:163ft	3¾	122	41½	31½	1½	15½	StvnsGL12	(F)M32000	92-10	Jstonofthgrls,PlcSt,MchosMtny	12
12Jly90—Wide early												
16Aug89-4Dmr	6f :22 :451 1:104ft	19	116	87½	610	611	812½	VlnzlPA 6	(F)(S)M28000	71-14	Btsy'sThm,Luvlomx,HughtyDncr	12
16Aug89—Wide 3/8 turn												
31Jly89-2Dmr	6f :22 :452 1:11 ft	58	116	108½	96¼	67	59¼	VlnzulPA 7	(F)M28000	74-16	Belle Mo,MissRockTalk,HiSailor	12
31Jly89—Wide into stretch												

Speed Index: Last Race: -13.0 3-Race Avg.: -5.0 4-Race Avg.: -5.0 Overall Avg.: -6.1

Nov 21 Hol 5f ft 1:012 H Nov 14 Hol 4f ft :503 H Oct 31 SA 5f ft 1:023 H Oct 25 SA 5f ft 1:023 H

Virtually — Gr. f. 3(Mar), by Spectacular Bid—Lady Face, by Proud Clarion
MCCARRON C J — 112 — Br.—Franks J & Hancock A B (Ky) — 1990 7 1 2 1 $41,325
Own.—Franks & Hancock III — Tr.—Whittingham Charles — 1989 6 1 4 0 $21,810
Lifetime 13 2 6 1 $63,135 — Turf 5 1 2 1 $40,400

5Nov90-5SA 1 Ⓣ:452 1:093 1:344fm *2¾ B 115 53¾ 62¾ 63¾ 2hd McCrrC11 ⒻAw40000 89-11 JoLo'sJoy,Virtually,GrandAward 11
5Nov90—Broke slowly
30Oct90-5SA 1⅛ Ⓣ:464 1:102 1:461fm *2 115 52½ 63½ 97 67 McCrrCJ6 ⒻAw40000 87-06 Orlnov,Jstonofthgrls,SmrtDcpton 9
30Oct90—Checked 1/16
8Sep90-5Dmr 1$\frac{1}{16}$ Ⓣ:492 1:133 1:432fm*4-5 117 63½ 42 21½ 11½ McCrrCJ7 ⒻAw36000 90-06 Virtully,SousEntendu,Shirly'sSvn 9
8Sep90—Shuffled back
24Aug90-5Dmr 1 Ⓣ:47 1:121 1:371fm *2½ B 1125 87½ 83¾ 42½ 2no BelvoirV8 ⒻAw36000 88-12 Shinko'sLss,Virtully,MediclMrvl 10
24Aug90—5-wide stretch
2Aug90-5Dmr 1 Ⓣ:472 1:12 1:363fm 9½ 1085 62¾ 3nk 3nk 3½ BelvoirV3 ⒻAw36000 90-09 Cozzy, Cash In Now, Virtually 9
2Aug90—Wide early
19Jly90-8Hol 1 :45 1:094 1:351ft 12 115 52¼ 41½ 51¾ 53¼ Baze RA4 ⒻAw37000 85-11 NorthernGlnc,LonlyDov,Lrkishnss 6
28Jun90-7Hol 6½f :214 :442 1:153ft 19 116 63¼ 85¼ 77 710 Baze RA1 ⒻAw35000 87-06 MttnsAndMnk,‡Orrfor,LttrsOfLv 8
28Jun90—Placed sixth through disqualification
18Nov89-6CD 6f :214 :46 1:11 ft 4 115 41¾ 43½ 48 615¾ McDllM3 ⒻAw22150 72-17 ScreenProspect,Urbnett,BoFostr 9
31Oct89-7CD 6f :223 :48 1:14 sy *2-3 112 2½ 21½ 23½ 21 Day P3 ⒻAw22150 72-26 RowdyDixi,Virtully,FigndAffction 6
11Oct89-4Kee 7f :232 :464 1:25 ft 2 115 31 31 2hd 23 Bruin JE7 ⒻAw20300 78-11 Crowned,Virtually,RisingMoment 7
Speed Index: Last Race: 0.0 3–Race Avg.: –3.6 5–Race Avg.: –2.4 Overall Avg.: –4.7
Nov 20 Hol 5f ft 1:012 H Nov 13 Hol 3f ft :36 H Nov 1 SA 4f ft :471 H ●Oct 26 SA 7f ft 1:264 H

Splendor Forever * — Dk. b. or br. f. 4, by Bates Motel—Embrujada Diez, by Cannonade
MEZA R Q — 115 — Br.—Chahin A (Ky) — 1990 7 3 0 3 $18,753
Own.—Chahin A — Tr.—Marquez Alfredo — 1989 8 5 0 2 $7,975
Lifetime 15 8 0 5 $26,728 — Turf 1 0 0 1 $5,100

14Nov90-8Hol 1$\frac{1}{16}$ Ⓣ:474 1:12 1:413fm 26 LB115 21 11 2hd 34 Meza RQ2 ⒻAw34000 83-15 Kikl-En,Mrsh'sDncr,SplndorForvr 7
31Oct90-4SA 6½f :22 :45 1:161ft 4 LB115 2½ 44½ 35 35¼ Meza R Q2 Ⓕ 32000 84-15 LTropcn,BoldFcd-Ar,SplndorFrvr 8
31Oct90—Bumped start
10Oct90-5SA 6f :212 :442 1:09 ft 22 117 61 74¾ 1111 911½ MezRQ10 ⒻAw36800 79-12 MamaSimba,WandaKye,LdyKite 12
10Oct90—Wide trip
9Jun90-8Mex 1⅛ :464 1:11 1:54 ft 7-5 114 34 24 31½ 36½ CsllsE 1 ⒻDmsgdo Cl 74 — Scarlett,Alemni,SplendorForever 6
9Jun90—Grade I
27May90-4Mex 1$\frac{1}{16}$:46 1:11 1:443ft *2-5 114 2hd 12 12 11½ CsllsE 5 ⒻCl Rafina 92 — SplendorForever,Jaiminh,Boldsty 8
27May90—Grade III
6May90-8Mex 1 :49 1:14 1:39 m *3-5e 103 12½ 11 12 19 Mora C 2 Aw 88 — SplendorForever,Ejmplo,Sonsont 6
28Apr90-6Mex 6½f :223 :453 1:163ft 2½ 108 1hd 13 14 14 Casallas E 6 Aw 97 — SplendorForever,Provence,Monet 7
16Dec89-8Mex 5½f :22 :443 1:031ft 3½ 107 44 47 412 38½ AlferzJ 6Cl Windsor 90 — Lobo,Lr'sPrince,SplendorForever 6
16Dec89—Grade III
3Dec89-6Mex 6f :222 :454 1:11 ft *3-5 105 1hd 1hd 11½ 16 Casallas E 2 Aw 91 — SplndorForvr,SomdyJck,MdoSglo 8
20Nov89-8Mex 7f :224 :454 1:24 ft 3½ 106 31 31½ 22 39 CsllsE 1 ⒻCl 20 Nov 85 — Alemni,Scrlett,SplendorForever 10
20Nov89—Grade II
Speed Index: Last Race: –2.0 1–Race Avg.: –2.0 1–Race Avg.: –2.0 Overall Avg.: –9.5
Oct 25 SA 5f ft 1:001 H Oct 4 SA 6f ft 1:133 Hg Sep 27 BM 6f ft 1:151 H

Majestic Sound — B. f. 4, by Majestic Light—Decision, by Resound
VELASQUEZ J — 115 — Br.—Post Time Inc (Ky) — 1990 14 2 2 0 $58,975
Own.—Power M S — Tr.—Haynes Jack B — 1989 11 1 2 0 $15,500
Lifetime 27 3 4 0 $74,475 — Turf 19 2 3 0 $69,175

10Sep90-9Dmr 1$\frac{1}{16}$ Ⓣ:48 1:12 1:43 fm 7½ LB117 11½ 11½ 1hd 43 MRQ8 ⒻⓇSndcstleH 89-05 FruleinMri,Grndiflor,PnicStrickn 10
30Aug90-3Dmr 1$\frac{1}{16}$ Ⓣ:47 1:12 1:434fm 7¼ LB116 21½ 21½ 68½ 618¾ DsormuxKJ6 Ⓕ 75000 69-12 Softscpe,Dncingintheprk,Quyfeor 6
30Aug90—Wide down chute
15Aug90-5Dmr 1$\frac{1}{16}$ Ⓣ:483 1:123 1:431fm 4 LB118 21½ 1hd 2½ 55 Meza R Q3 Ⓕ 55000 86-09 BoldCosta,FrauleinMri,Softscpe 10
19Jly90-9Hol 1$\frac{1}{16}$ Ⓣ:464 1:103 1:413fm 4 L 115 11½ 11 11½ 12¾ Meza R Q9 Ⓕ 45000 87-16 MjsticSound,FrulinMri,RdThCrds 9
28Jun90-5Hol 1$\frac{1}{16}$ Ⓣ:47 1:11 1:41 fm 6½ 116 12½ 11½ 11½ 21¼ Meza R Q5 Ⓕ 55000 89-08 Sonilla,MjesticSound,CsPetrone 10
7Jun90-8Hol 1$\frac{1}{16}$ Ⓣ:463 1:103 1:413fm 10 116 11½ 11½ 11½ 11¼ Meza RQ6 ⒻAw35000 87-13 MjsticSound,C'sSong,T.V.Listing 9
25May90-8Hol 1 Ⓣ:462 1:103 1:352fm 7¾ 116 22½ 2hd 2hd 53½ Meza RQ9 ⒻAw35000 83-11 Camisverde,Cee'sSong,CshInNow 9
12May90-9Hol 1⅛ Ⓣ:473 1:112 1:481fm 12 116 11½ 11 2hd 22½ Meza RQ1 ⒻAw32000 84-10 TafftShwl,MjesticSound,StrPster 7
28Apr90-9Hol 1$\frac{1}{16}$ Ⓣ:47 1:111 1:42 fm 58 1085 2hd 2½ 42½ 87¾ DvnportCL2 Ⓕ 70000 77-15 Nimes, Belle Poitrine, Seaside 12
12Apr90-5SA a6½f Ⓣ:211 :434 1:133fm 105 118 64½ 64¼ 64¼ 63¼ Solis A2 ⒻAw34000 90-07 PlumePoppy,RadintStr,TfftShwl 12
Speed Index: Last Race: –6.0 3–Race Avg.: –10.0 9–Race Avg.: –5.5 Overall Avg.: –5.3
Nov 18 SA 7f ft 1:264 H Nov 8 SA 1 ft 1:401 H Nov 1 SA 5f ft 1:002 H Oct 24 SA 4f ft :483 H

Nordican-Ir
B. f. 3(May), by Nordico—Angor, by Lorenzaccio
FLORES D R 112
Br.—BaronessThyssen-Bornemisza (Ire) 1990 7 1 0 1 $26,225
Tr.—Gonzalez Juan 1989 5 2 0 1 $10,173
Own.—McCaffery & Toffan Lifetime 12 3 0 2 $36,398 Turf 9 2 0 2 $16,498

5Nov90-5SA 1 Ⓣ:4521:0931:344fm 9 LB113 75¾ 73 53½ 62¼ FlorsDR9 ⒻAw40000 87-11 JoLo'sJoy,Virtually,GrandAward 11
5Nov90—Boxed in 3/16
24Oct90-7SA a6½f Ⓣ:213 :4321:131fm 14 L 113 54 44 44 32½ FlorsDR10 ⒻAw36000 92-05 Belr-Fr,SingingPirte,Nordicn-Ir 10
24Oct90—4-wide stretch
10Oct90-5SA 6f :212 :442 1:09 ft 10 LB117 92 85 53 57 PincyLJr4 ⒻAw36000 84-12 MamaSimba,WandaKye,LdyKite 12
29Jly90-5Dmr 6½f :214 :442 1:154ft 3¾ L 117 74¾ 75¾ 42 1½ PncLJr10 ⒻAw33000 89-07 Nordicn,TessOfHemt,TntPhyllis 10
29Jly90—Wide early
27Jun90-8Hol 1 1/16 Ⓣ:47 1:11 1:413fm 4 117 11½ 2hd 21 77 VlnzlPA1 ⒻAw37000 80-13 Jefforee,BiddrCrm,Tny'sTuition 10
14Jun90-8Hol 1⅛ Ⓣ:4721:1141:483fm 3¾ 117 2½ 1hd 1½ 52½ VlnzlPA4 ⒻAw37000 82-15 Cat'sAir,PleasureBought,Raiatea 10
14Jun90—In tight 1/16
14Apr90-3SA 6f :22 :444 1:092ft 7 120 55½ 56 47½ 59¾ DsrmxKJ5 ⒻAw34000 79-20 Barronette, Red Halo, Orrefor 6
23Sep89♦4Curragh(Ire) 1 1:412yl 6 119 Ⓣ 51½ Roche C Futurity(Gr3) TechDhMhil,AnniLuri,Hro'sWlcom 10
2Sep89♦5PhoenixPk(Ire) 7f 1:202gd 10 122 Ⓣ 63¾ Roche C ⒻSilvrFlash TheCretker,MissingYou,EndlssJoy 14
19Aug89♦4Curragh(Ire) 7f 1:253gd *2 120 Ⓣ 33¾ Roche C Tyros Go And Go, Pictorial, Nordican 8
Speed Index: Last Race: -2.0 3-Race Avg.: -4.0 3-Race Avg.: -4.0 Overall Avg.: -3.4
Nov 19 Hol 5f ft 1:002 H ●Nov 2 Hol 4f ft :462 H Oct 19 SA 5f ft :594 H Oct 3 SA 5f ft :59 H

Vaguely Charming
Dk. b. or br. f. 3(Mar), by Tim the Tiger—Vaguely's Charm, by Vaguely Noble
DELAHOUSSAYE E 112
Br.—Backer J W DVM (Ky) 1990 9 2 1 3 $62,425
Tr.—Cross Richard J Turf 1 0 0 1 $9,000
Own.—Dick-Ellis-Hamilton et al Lifetime 9 2 1 3 $62,425

7Nov90-8Hol 1 1/16 Ⓣ:46 1:1031:411fm 15 B 118 44¼ 32½ 33½ 38 PcLJr8 ⒻⓇAlFrncH 81-11 AnnulRunion,Mhsk,VgulyChrming 8
20Oct90-8SA 1 1/16 :462 1:101 1:42 ft 11 B 114 86½ 99¼ 912 812½ DsrKJ3 ⒻLnd Vst H 81-14 A Wild Ride, Orlanova, Mahaska 9
20Oct90—Grade III; Broke slowly
7Sep90-8Dmr 1 1/16 :452 1:102 1:424ft *2¼ B 118 43½106 101310224 PncLJr9 ⒻⓇTry Pns 65-10 OhSwtThing,ErthAngl,SrosTrsur 10
18Aug90-7Dmr 1 1/16 :462 1:102 1:413ft *9-5 B 117 11½ 11½ 11½ 12½ PincyLJr3 ⒻAw36000 93-07 VglyChrmng,OhSwtThng,SssySlw 6
3Aug90-6Dmr 1 1/16 :461 1:104 1:422ft *1 117 11½ 1hd 1½ 11 Pincay L Jr7 ⒻMdn 89-12 VgulyChrmng,ErthAngl,AdorblVc 9
12Jly90-6Hol 1 1/16 :47 1:111 1:432ft 5½ 117 11½ 1½ 11½ 21½ Pincay L Jr6 ⒻMdn 82-15 Orlnov,VguelyChrming,AdorblVic 6
9Jun90-2Hol 6f :22 :451 1:094ft *3 116 98 77½ 612 514½ Black C A8 ⒻMdn 76-07 Undeniably,MyPrayer,SartogLss 11
9Jun90—Wide backstretch
19May90-5Hol 1 :451 1:103 1:362ft 3¾ 115 1hd 2hd 1hd 3hd Black C A5 ⒻMdn 82-12 MissTris,Orlanov,VguelyChrming 9
6May90-4Hol 6f :213 :443 1:084ft 53 115 54½ 55½ 36½ 37 Black C A7 ⒻMdn 89-05 FldsOfGold,MmSmb,VglyChrmng 8
6May90—Wide backstretch
Speed Index: Last Race: -8.0 1-Race Avg.: -8.0 1-Race Avg.: -8.0 Overall Avg.: -7.6
Nov 19 Hol 5f ft :592 H Nov 3 Hol 5f ft :594 H Oct 29 Hol 4f ft :494 H Oct 15 Hol 5f ft :593 H

Highland Tide
Dk. b. or br. f. 3(Mar), by Highland Blade—Maytide, by Naskra
GARCIA J A 112
Br.—Elmendorf Farm Inc (Ky) 1990 11 2 4 1 $54,460
Tr.—Robbins Jay M Turf 6 0 4 0 $29,580
Own.—Cooke J K Lifetime 11 2 4 1 $54,460

27Sep90-7Bel 1 Ⓣ:4531:1021:352fm*8-5 113 74½ 42 21½ 42½ SntsJA11 ⒻAw31000 87-12 QueensWild,HotPillow,FirstView 12
6Sep90-6Bel 1 1/16 Ⓣ:4731:11 1:42 fm*9-5 113 75 75 41¾ 2nk SntosJA6 ⒻAw31000 95-07 StgeSet,HighlndTide,DncingPrty 10
19Aug90-7Sar 1⅜ Ⓣ:4711:1131:551fm 4 112 63 41½ 11 2nk ChvezJF5 ⒻAw31000 94-06 BeExclusiveII,HighlndTid,StgSt 11
20Jly90-2Bel 1 1/16 Ⓣ:4621:10 1:403fm 7 111 42 21 2½ 23¾ ChvezJF9 ⒻAw33000 98-03 Songlines, Highland Tide,LeFamo 9
30Jun90-4Bel 1 1/16 Ⓣ:4721:11 1:42 fm 27 109 74½ 23 1½ 2hd ChvezJF9 ⒻAw31000 91-15 SnorTippy,HighlndTid,QunOfSvns 9
11Jun90-7Bel 1 Ⓣ:4441:0911:34 fm 12 109 75¾ 88 710 915¾ CrugutJ3 ⒻAw31000 80-05 Srolucy,PlentyOfGrc,QunOfSvns 12
16May90-5Bel 6f :22 :45 1:094m 7¾ 116 33 33 37½ 39¾ BaileyJD5 ⒻAw31000 80-14 PrimlForc,VoodooLily,HighlndTid 5
4Apr90-9GP 7f :222 :454 1:26 ft 7¾ 112 33 47 622 625¾ BlJD4 ⒻDavona Dale 50-27 Big Pride, Crowned, Sonic Gray 6
25Feb90-5GP 7f :223 :464 1:252ft 9-5 121 1½ 11 13 13 BaileyJD1 ⒻAw19000 79-18 HghlndTd,JoLo'sJoy,DmstcGddss 7
3Feb90-3GP 7f :223 :46 1:251ft 22 121 2hd 11 17 110½ Bailey J D9 ⒻMdn 80-17 HghlndTd,FshonSttr,OfthMomnt 11
Speed Index: Last Race: -1.0 1-Race Avg.: -1.0 1-Race Avg.: -1.0 Overall Avg.: -1.0
Nov 20 SA 5f gd 1:002 H Nov 14 SA 5f ft :594 H Nov 7 SA 4f ft :462 H Oct 21 Bel 5f ft 1:01 H

Sonata Slew
Ch. f. 4, by Nodouble—Miss Slewfonic, by Seattle Slew
DESORMEAUX K J 115
Br.—Irongate Farm (Ky) 1990 5 1 0 1 $28,075
Tr.—Nickerson Victor J 1989 4 1 0 0 $17,500
Own.—Wygod Mr-Mrs M J Lifetime 9 2 0 1 $45,575 Turf 7 1 0 1 $28,925

21Jly90-9Hol 1⅛ Ⓣ:4721:1041:473fm 9¼ L 118 58 65 87½ 810 GarciaJA4 ⒻAw39000 80-09 GirlOfFrnce,SpectculrFce,DedHet 8
21Jly90—Wide into drive
22Jun90-3Hol 1⅛ Ⓣ:4731:1211:491fm*8-5 119 54 51¾ 32 1no Davis RG7 ⒻAw37000 82-15 SonataSlew,Cee'sSong,CshInNow 7
22Jun90—Wide 3/8 turn
25May90-8Hol 1 Ⓣ:4621:1031:352fm 3¾ 119 44½ 52½ 52½ 43½ McCrrCJ5 ⒻAw35000 84-11 Camisverde,Cee'sSong,CshInNow 9
25May90—Checked 1/8

18Mar90-5SA 1 Ⓣ:4541:1011:361fm 6¼ 120 1011 108½ 85¾ 64 DvisRG10 ⒻAw37000 78-16 ‡Dlght'sTrbut,LstGlnc,Grn'sSscp 10
18Mar90—Wide throughout
11Feb90-5SA a6½f Ⓣ:212 :44 1:134fm 13 120 118¾ 95¾ 54½ 33 Davis RG6 ⒻAw34000 89-08 WhtHsBeen,Gren'sSscp,SontSlw 12
26Nov89-7BM 1 1/16 :461 1:111 1:453gd 19 112 58½ 46 45 52¾ CrtAC11 ⒻCarmel H 66-29 LdyMichele,TchYou,ColletivJoy 11
13Nov89-9SA 1⅛ Ⓣ:46 1:1011:474fm *2 118 98½ 96¾ 76 54½ Davis RG4 ⒻAw34000 89 — Dncngnthpr,ImprlGm,RpAtThDr 12
14Oct89-6SA 1 :464 1:114 1:372ft 3½ 117 36 31½ 1½ 12 Davis R G1 ⒻMdn 80-19 Sonata Slew, LoveBeat,Rapsinger 8
13Sep89-6Dmr 1 1/16 Ⓣ:4911:1321:441fm 17 1095 75¾ 73¾ 53½ 62½ Jauregui L H3 Mdn 77-16 Petrl'sFlight,OnThMnu,RulThOcn 9
Speed Index: Last Race: -11.0 3-Race Avg.: -6.3 6-Race Avg.: -7.1 Overall Avg.: -5.7
Nov 17 Hol 6f ft 1:152 H Nov 10 Hol 6f ft 1:134 H Nov 4 SA 5f ft 1:004 H Oct 27 SA 5f ft 1:003 H

Nu Myoozik **B. f. 3(Mar), by Cure The Blues—Holiday Dancer, by Masked Dancer**
PEDROZA M A **112** **Br.—Moss Mr-Mrs J S (Ky)** **1990 9 0 0 0 $5,934**
Own.—Moss Mr-Mrs J S **Tr.—Stute Melvin F** **1989 6 2 0 2 $40,200**
Lifetime 15 2 0 2 $46,134 **Turf 2 0 0 0 $1,050**
2Nov90-7SA 6f :211 :434 1:091ft 45 LB112 54 54½ 44½ 55¾ Solis A 3 ⒻAw36000 84-17 LongLongTril,BitO'Dip,CntnnlTm 7
10Oct90-5SA 6f :212 :442 1:09 ft 79 LB114 3½ 41¾ 76½ 1112¾ Solis A 11 ⒻAw36000 78-12 MamaSimba,WandaKye,LdyKite 12
10Oct90—Wide trip
31May90-3Hol 6½f :222 :453 1:163ft 7½ 112 1½ 3½ 65½ 612½ Solis A 6 ⒻAw35000 79-11 Decora,CascadingGold,AWildRide 6
21Apr90-3SA 6½f :213 :441 1:162ft 22 114 21 45 514 523¼ FlrsDR 3 ⒻCrwngGly 65-17 SpclHppnng,FrstFlty,BrghtTMnd 5
21Apr90—Steadied 3/8
29Mar90-8SA 1 Ⓣ:4621:1121:362fm 23e 116 56 44½ 44½ 59¾ DlhssyE 1 ⒻAw42000 71-18 Njnsky'sLvr,BrghtTMnd,SndyBst 7
29Mar90—Veered in start
14Mar90-5SA a6½f Ⓣ:204 :4311:14 fm 36 116 1116 1116 79 64¾ DlhssyE1 ⒻLa Habra 86-10 Smthngmrry,BrghtTMnd,FrstFlt 11
14Mar90—Run in divisions
19Feb90-9OP 6f :212 :453 1:11 ft 15 112 914 811 76¾ 510¼ KtzD4 ⒻMrtha Wsh 78-18 ClssyIrene,LovelyHeiress,FerniBll 9
19Feb90—Forced back
2Feb90-8OP 5½f :214 :454 1:061gd 6½ 115 45½ 58½ 1016 1015¼ Kutz D4 ⒻDixie B 70-17 BrezyMcbr,MissPrsto,LovlyHirss 13
17Jan90-8SA 1 :463 1:12 1:383gd 14 114 21½ 73½ 76 710 SolisA2 ⒻⓇLa Cntla 64-26 FtToScout,AnnulRunon,NsrsPrd 10
17Jan90—Lugged out 3/8
10Dec89-8BM 6f :221 :45 1:10 ft 8-5 117 32½ 21 32 44¾ GrdrAT4 ⒻB M Deb 87-06 ScorAndTll,BrginDoll,PuffOLuck 5
Speed Index: Last Race: -11.0 1-Race Avg.: -11.0 1-Race Avg.: -11.0 Overall Avg.: -8.6
Nov 20 Hol 5f ft :59 H Nov 14 Hol 5f ft 1:031 H Oct 30 SA 4f ft :462 H Oct 24 SA 5f ft :591 H

Marsha's Dancer **B. f. 4, by Northern Dancer—Ivorlanche, by Sir Ivor**
DELAHOUSSAYE E **115** **Br.—Windfields Farm (Md)** **1990 7 2 3 2 $56,212**
Own.—Paulsen A E **Tr.—Lundy Richard J** **1989 3 M 1 0 $7,747**
Lifetime 10 2 4 2 $63,959 **Turf 10 2 4 2 $63,959**
14Nov90-8Hol 1 1/16 Ⓣ:4741:12 1:413fm 2¼ LB118 31½ 21 3½ 22¾ DlhssyE7 ⒻAw34000 84-15 Kiki-En,Mrsh'sDncr,SplndorForvr 7
14Sep90-4Med 1 1/16 Ⓣ:47 1:1031:412fm *2-3 L 116 52½ 31 1½ 14¾ BaileyJD6 ⒻAw16500 90-09 Mrsh'sDncer,Whinhny,IsoltdLdy 11
28Jly90-9AP 1⅜ Ⓣ:4841:1241:552fm 8½ L 114 21 21 33½ 3¾ FiresE2 ⒻMdsty 98-02 GailyGaily,Coolwin,Mrsh'sDncer 11
28Jly90—Grade III
7Jly90-8AP 1 1/16 Ⓣ:4711:1221:432fm 4½ L 110 24½ 31½ 32 21½ VlszJ2 ⒻBar Hills H 89-11 GodExmpl,Mrsh'sDncr,MystclLss 7
28Jun90-3AP a1 Ⓣ:5021:1511:39 gd *1-3 122 1½ 11 14 16 Velasquez J1 ⒻMdn — — Mrsh'sDncr,FrnchQll,Mrs.Ncholls 7
2Jun90-8AP 1⅛ Ⓣ:5031:14 1:503gd 5 110 52½ 45½ 46½ 32½ BrdET2 ⒻEstrapdeH 88-09 LittlBrinn,MysticlLss,Mrsh'sDncr 7
14Apr90-9Kee 1 1/16 Ⓣ:4731:1341:453yl 17 112 1013 73 22 23 BaileyJD7 ⒻAw28000 84-15 TThLghths,Mrsh'sDncr,MnclMss 10
15Oct89♦6Longchamp(Fra) a1¼ 2:04 gd 10 116 Ⓣ 43½ Cruz A S Px d Rnlgh Garm, Torcecuellos, Rainibik 8
7May89♦2Longchamp(Fra) a1¼ 2:043gd *4-5 128 Ⓣ 63¼ BfD ⒻPx D Mnt Vlrn(Mdn) BbblngDnss,Bobby'sDrmr,Hlnthmm 6
23Apr89♦1Longchamp(Fra) a1¼ 2:161sf 2 123 Ⓣ 2¾ BoufD ⒻPx d Chllt(Mdn) Krill, Marsha's Dancer, Green Moon 7
Speed Index: Last Race: -1.0 3-Race Avg.: -0.6 6-Race Avg.: -1.0 Overall Avg.: -1.0
Nov 9 SA 6f ft 1:16 H Nov 3 SA 6f ft 1:162 H Oct 29 SA 6f ft 1:17 H Oct 24 SA 5f ft 1:013 H

mile are 46.3 1:09.8 1:34.8. To calculate her "turf ability time," we simply add 46.3 to her adjusted last fraction time of 25 (1:34.8 minus 1:09.8) for a rating of 71.3.

Somethingmerry Using her second race back—because we almost never use a sprint time in a route race—we must make both a track adjustment and a distance adjustment. You always make the track-to-track adjustment first. We see that the 1⅛ mile Santa Anita turf runs .8 faster in the first fraction, 1.4 seconds faster for the second fraction, and 2.6 seconds faster in final time than Hollywood Park. We now calculate her adjusted time for Santa Anita and convert it into Hollywood

Park time. Her adjusted Santa Anita time is 47.3 1:11.4 1:47.4. To convert to Hollywood Park times we add .8 seconds to the first call, 1.4 seconds to the second call, and 2.6 seconds to the final time. Somethingmerry's projected Hollywood Park times for the 1⅛ mile distance are 48.1 1:12.8 1:50. We now convert these to one mile times by subtracting a full second from the first call time, a full second from the second call time, and 13.6 seconds from the final time. Her adjusted times are 47.1 1:11.8 1:36.4. Her turf route ability time is 47.1 plus a final fraction of 24.6 to give a 71.7 rating.

Justoneofthegirls Using the Oct. 3 race, we see that her Santa Anita adjusted times (in tenths) are 46.8 1:10.4 1:46.6. We convert to Hollywood Park one mile times by deducting 2 tenths from the first call, adding 4 tenths to the second call, and subtracting 11 seconds from the final call. Her adjusted Hollywood times are 46.6 1:10.8 1:35.6. Her turf route ability time is 46.6 plus a final fraction of 24.8 to give a 71.4 rating.

Virtually Using the Nov. 5 race, we see that her Santa Anita adjusted times (in tenths) are 46.2 1:10.2 1:34.8. We convert to Hollywood Park one mile times by adding 6 tenths to the first call, adding 6 tenths to the second call, and adding 1.4 seconds to the final call. Her adjusted Hollywood times are 46.8 1:10.8 1:35.2. Her turf route ability time is 46.8 plus a final fraction of 24.4, to give a 71.2 rating.

Splendor Forever Using the Nov. 14 race, we see that her adjusted times (in tenths) are 48.0 1:12.0 1:42.4. We convert to one mile times by deducting 1 second from the first call, subtracting 6 tenths from the second call, and subtracting 7 seconds from the final call. Her adjusted Hollywood one mile times are 47.0 1:11.4 1:35.4. Her turf route ability time is 47.0 plus a final fraction of 24.0 to give a 71.0 rating.

Marsha's Dancer Using the Nov. 14 race, we see that her adjusted times (in tenths) are 48.1 1:12.2 1:42.2. We convert to one mile times by deducting 1 second from the first call, subtracting 6 tenths from the second call, and subtracting 7 seconds from the final call. Her adjusted Hollywood one mile times are 47.1 1:11.6 1:35.2. Her turf route ability time is 47.1 plus a final fraction of 23.6 to give a 70.7 rating.

FIFTH RACE
Hollywood
NOVEMBER 24, 1990

1 MILE.(Turf). (1.32⅘) ALLOWANCE. Purse $34,000. Fillies and mares. 3–year–olds and upward, which have not won $3,000 twice other than maiden, claiming or starter. Weights, 3–year–olds, 118 lbs.; older, 121 lbs. Non–winners of two races other than claiming at a mile or over since Sept. 15 allowed 3 lbs.; a race other than maiden or claiming since then, 6 lbs.
Value of race $34,000; value to winner $18,700; second $6,800; third $5,100; fourth $2,550; fifth $850. Mutuel pool $396,781. Exacta Pool $462,334.

Last Raced	Horse	M/Eqt.	A.	Wt	PP	St	¼	½	¾	Str	Fin	Jockey	Odds $1
14Nov90 ^{8}Hol^{2}	Marsha's Dancer	LB	4	116	12	10	1^{2}	1^{2}	1^{2}	6½	1½	Delahoussaye E	4.30
3Nov90 ^{5}SA^{3}	Somethingmerry	LB	3	114	2	12	4½	3^{1}	1^{hd}	1^{2}	$2^{1\frac{1}{4}}$	Stevens G L	1.80
14Nov90 ^{8}Hol^{3}	Splendor Forever	LB	4	115	5	4	$5^{1\frac{1}{2}}$	$5^{1\frac{1}{2}}$	5^{hd}	2^{hd}	3^{1}	Meza R Q	33.30
27Sep90 ^{7}Bel^{4}	Highland Tide	B	3	112	9	9	11^{4}	9^{1}	9½	9^{1}	4^{2}	Garcia J A	8.60
5Nov90 ^{5}SA^{2}	Virtually	B	3	114	4	11	6½	6^{hd}	6^{1}	5½	$5^{1\frac{1}{4}}$	McCarron C J	3.60
5Nov90 ^{5}SA^{11}	Justoneofthegirls	LB	4	115	3	2	2^{2}	2^{hd}	$2^{1\frac{1}{2}}$	4½	$6^{1\frac{1}{4}}$	Nakatani C S	11.90
5Nov90 ^{5}SA^{6}	Nordican-Ir	LB	3	113	7	5	7^{1}	7^{hd}	7^{hd}	7^{hd}	7no	Flores D R	20.10
9Nov90 ^{8}Hol^{1}	Quick Step Slewpy	LBb	3	115	1	3	1^{hd}	$1^{1\frac{1}{2}}$	3^{1}	$3^{1\frac{1}{2}}$	8no	Baze R A	14.10
7Nov90 ^{8}Hol^{3}	Vaguely Charming	B	3	112	8	8	10^{1}	$11^{3\frac{1}{2}}$	11½	10^{1}	9no	Hansen R D	20.30
2Nov90 ^{7}SA^{5}	Nu Myoozik	LB	3	113	11	6	8^{1}	8½	8^{1}	8^{hd}	$10^{1\frac{1}{4}}$	Pedroza M A	99.30
21Jly90 ^{9}Hol^{8}	Sonata Slew	LB	4	115	10	7	9½	$10^{1\frac{1}{2}}$	10^{1}	11^{hd}	11½	Desormeaux K J	50.20
10Sep90 ^{9}Dmr^{4}	Majestic Sound	LB	4	115	6	1	3^{1}	4½	4^{hd}	1^{2}	1^{2}	Velasquez J	36.50

OFF AT 3:02 Start good. Won driving. Time, :23⅕, :47, 1:11, 1:35⅕ Course firm.

$2 Mutuel Prices:			
12–MARSHA'S DANCER	10.60	4.60	3.20
2–SOMETHINGMERRY		3.60	3.00
5–SPLENDOR FOREVER			9.60

$2 EXACTA 12–2 PAID $36.00.

When we sort the turf ability ratings, we have:

Marsha's Dancer	70.7
Splendor Forever	71.0
Virtually	71.2
Quick Step Slewpy	71.3
Justoneofthegirls	71.4
Somethingmerry	71.7

In this case we only have two horses to consider. The top rating is 70.7, hence we look at all horses that have ratings up to 71.1 (.4 equals 2 lengths). This means that we only have to consider Marsha's Dancer and Splendor Forever. Marsha's Dancer went off at 4-to-1 and Splendor Forever was 30-to-1. The strategy calls for a win bet on each horse. In this case our $4 bet returned $10.60.

Suppose for a moment that the top ratings were:

Marsha's Dancer	70.7
Splendor Forever	70.8
Virtually	70.9
Quick Step Slewpy	71.0
Justoneofthegirls	71.1
Somethingmerry	71.7

We now have a very contentious situation. Five horses that cannot be separated by as much as two lengths. The strategy says to bet the two horses that are offering the longest odds. In this case we would make a win bet on ***Splendor Forever*** and ***Quick Step Slewpy***.

TURF SPRINTS "ABILITY TIME"

A turf sprint isn't as tactical as a turf route, but it's handled in the same way. We are still looking for the "class of the field" as defined by speed. Again we use the combined speeds of the adjusted first fraction and the adjusted last fraction. Turf first fractions tend to be slower than dirt first fractions for the same class of horse, and yet final times in most cases are faster than the dirt final times. This again demonstrates the importance of late speed in turf racing. Again, we must consider the early fraction to see if a horse can sustain its speed. Let's look at the contenders in the fifth race at Santa Anita on October 14, 1990. It was a 6½-furlong turf sprint. The reason that the par times are so fast is because this course is downhill for a good part of the race. The Santa Anita turf pars (in tenths) for this level of racing were:

Distance	1st Call	2nd Call	Final
6½ fur.	21.0	43.0	1:12.4

The Hollywood turf six-furlong pars (in tenths) for this level of racing were:

Distance	1st Call	2nd Call	Final
6 fur.	21.8	44.2	1:08.4

The contenders were:

Eratone This horse is basically a router. The reason that I used it as a contender was because it was the top pick of Sweep and Hermis. Normally I would throw this horse out, but I'll include it to make the point of how to compare turf

5th Santa Anita

ABOUT 6 ½ FURLONGS. (Turf). (1.11⅘) ALLOWANCE. Purse $36,000. 3 year olds and upward which are non winners of $3,000 twice other than maiden, claiming or starter. Weights, 3 year olds, 118 lbs.; older, 121 lbs. Non winners of two races other than claiming since August 1 allowed 2 lbs.; of a race other than maiden or claiming since then, 4 lbs. (Horses eligible only to the above conditions are preferred.) (Non starters for a claiming price of $25,000 or less in their last three starts preferred.)

Eratone
MCCARRON C J 119
Own.—Segal-Segal-Xitco
Ch. g. 5, by Exclusive Era—Last Bell, by Nicaray
Br.—Two Ton Tony Farm (Cal)
Tr.—Canani Julio C
Lifetime 19 5 2 5 $120,170
1990 11 3 2 4 $98,850
1989 7 2 0 1 $21,320
Turf 7 3 0 3 $86,450

9Sep90-9Dmr 1$\frac{1}{16}$ ⓣ:4831:1221:422fm*6-5 LB121 97 86½ 32½ 1nk StnsGL 9 [R]Snshrk H 95-02 Erlone,AskTheMn,BoldlyExcellnt 9
9Aug90-8Dmr 1$\frac{1}{16}$ ⓣ:4831:1221:422fm*7-5 L 116 86½ 85½ 63½ 31½ StevensGL 9 Aw41000 93-05 Chief'sImge,RellyBrillint,Erlone 10
9Aug90—Troubled trip
25Jly90-2Dmr 1$\frac{1}{16}$ ⓣ:49 1:1311:424fm *3½ L 118 84½106½ 42 31½ StevnsGL 10 Aw41000 92-05 RacingRscl,MjorMoment,Erlone 10
25Jly90—Rough Trip
13Jly90-9Hol 1⅛ ⓣ:4721:1131:481fm*7-5 L 120 64 52½ 1hd 13 Stevens G L 2 H25000 87-11 Eratone,Shirkee,SwingsFirstDnce 9
23Jun90-6Hol 1$\frac{1}{16}$ ⓣ:4821:12 1:414fm 3 115 42½ 52½ 53 43½ BlckCA 1 [S]Khaled H 82-14 RiverMstr,ElgntBrgin,StylishStud 5
18May90-8Hol 1⅛ ⓣ:4741:1121:472fm 3½ 120 52½ 52 21½ 3nk Black C A 3 Aw37000 91-12 Kanatiyr,AdvocateTrining,Erlone 7
18May90—Jostled at break
3May90-9Hol 1$\frac{1}{16}$ ⓣ:4631:1021:404fm 7½ 116 74½ 62½ 11½ 16 Black C A 6 Aw32000 91-10 Eratone, King Armour, Rejim 8
15Apr90-9SA 1$\frac{1}{16}$:47 1:113 1:423ft 4½ 116 85½ 65½ 34½ 24½ Davis R G 6 c25000 85-12 TheMhrsCs,Erton,HurryAndSpdy 9
15Apr90—Wide
24Mar90-9SA 1$\frac{1}{16}$:464 1:12 1:434ft 4 116 63½ 32½ 2½ 22 VlenzuelPA 7 c20000 82-21 Buckland'sHalo,Erlone,Vysotsky 11
24Mar90—Wide in stretch
8Mar90-5SA 7f :224 :452 1:231ft *2½ 116 54 55 34½ 33 Davis R G 5 20000 84-16 Lark'sLegacy,RumboSet,Erlone 11
8Mar90—Broke slowly

Speed Index: Last Race: (—) 3–Race Avg.: (—) 12–Race Avg.: (—) Overall Avg.: -1.0
Oct 8 SA 5f ft 1:01¹ H Oct 2 SA 4f ft :47² H Sep 26 SA 5f ft :59¹ H Sep 20 SA 4f ft :51² H

Roman Avie
DESORMEAUX K J 117
Own.—Friendly Natalie B
Ch. g. 4, by Lord Avie—Yoda, by Proudest Roman
Br.—Hillbrook Farm Inc (Ky)
Tr.—Sadler John W
Lifetime 14 2 3 3 $81,000
1990 6 0 1 2 $22,050
1989 8 2 2 1 $42,450
Turf 1 0 1 0 $7,400

1Sep90-3Dmr 6½f :214 :441 1:143ft 4½ B 115 42 52½ 55 57½ McCrrnCJ 7 Aw37000 88-10 On ARoll,C SamMaggio,Petrolero 7
1Sep90—Wide into drive
19Aug90-7Dmr 1 :44 1:083 1:332ft 2½e B 116 79 76½ 715 722 Davis R G 9 Aw41000 77-12 Cee's Tizzy, Asia, Lazy Boy 9
5Aug90-7Dmr 6½f :212 :44 1:153ft 3 116 52½ 53 42 31 DsormxKJ 8 Aw37000 89-10 AbergwunLd,T.V.Scren,RomnAvi 11
5Aug90—Wide stretch
6Jly90-8Hol 6f ⓣ:214 :4411:082fm 3 116 86 74½ 62½ 2hd Davis R G 7 Aw37000 97-03 Cove Way, Roman Avie,HeftyFee 8
6Jly90—Wide trip
23Jun90-3Hol 6f :22 :443 1:084ft 7 116 2hd 2½ 21½ 35½ VlenzulPA 1 Aw37000 90-09 Thirty Slews, Asia, Roman Avie 6
23Jun90—Broke slowly
9Jun90-5Hol 6f :221 :451 1:091ft 5½ 116 3nk 2½ 32 45½ VlenzulPA 7 Aw35000 89-07 Siroccan, Jacodra, Trebizond 7
9Jun90—Bobbled start
26Apr89-8Hol 7f :22 :441 1:213ft *1e 116 41½ 42½ 86½ 810½ VlnzulPA 6 Debonair 86-10 Sbulose,Mr.Bolg,TimelessAnswr 10
14Apr89-8SA 6f :212 :434 1:082ft 8 120 31½ 32 21 2½ VlenzulPA 1 Aw37000 95-12 ValintPete,RomnAvie,YesI'mBlue 5
17Mar89-7SA 6f :212 :444 1:094ft 4½ 120 31½ 21½ 12 12½ VlenzulPA 7 Aw32000 89-20 RomnAvie,BigConviction,Jotcro 10
5Feb89-5SA 1 :463 1:123 1:401sy *8-5 116 52½ 75½ 816 724½ StevensGL 6 Aw35000 43-28 Bbyitscoldoutsid,Copt.BrirticChif 9
5Feb89—Broke out, bumped

Speed Index: Last Race: 0.0 1–Race Avg.: 0.0 1–Race Avg.: 0.0 Overall Avg.: -3.6
●Oct 8 SA 7f ft 1:254 H Oct 2 SA 6f ft 1:13 H Sep 26 SA 6f ft 1:13² H Sep 14 SA 4f ft :46² H

Top Cash
SOLIS A 114
Own.—Lukas & Mathis
Dk. b. or br. c. 3(Apr), by Stalwart—Exceptional Value, by Hold Your Peace
Br.—Churn Thoroughbred Farm (Neb)
Tr.—Lukas D Wayne
Lifetime 13 2 1 2 $121,222
1990 7 0 0 2 $26,250
1989 6 2 1 0 $94,972
Turf 1 0 0 0

8Oct90-5SA 1 ⓣ:4511:0921:331fm 26 LB116 54 51½109 1013½ Solis A 5 Aw40000 84-03 ProForSw,Prfcssor,BrlonDn-Ir 10
8Oct90—Wide trip
1Sep90-3Dmr 6½f :214 :441 1:143ft 4e B 112 75½ 77½ 79½ 716 Solis A 3 Aw37000 79-10 On ARoll,C SamMaggio,Petrolero 7
5Aug90-7Dmr 6½f :212 :44 1:153ft 8½ 112 2hd 1hd 53 109½ Solis A 3 Aw37000 80-10 AbergwunLd,T.V.Scren,RomnAvi 11
17Mar90-9RP 1$\frac{1}{16}$:453 1:101 1:43 ft 3½ 122 33 35 55 811 CordrAJr 6 Rem Dby 74-21 WickedDestiny,Sesbb,Pnthouse 11
21Feb90-8SA 6f :213 :443 1:091ft 8-5e 122 65 53½ 57 68½ FlrsDR 3 [R]Blsa Chca 81-13 Burnt Hills, Shantin O.,KeepClear 9
21Feb90—Impeded early
10Feb90-8SA 7f :221 :444 1:223ft 7½ 120 2hd 1hd 32 39 VlnzulPA 2 Sn Vcnte 81-20 Mister Frisky, Tarascon, TopCash 6
10Feb90—Rough start

10Jan90-8SA 1 :454 1:094 1:351ft 3-2e 118 1½ 1hd 1hd 3no McCrrnCJ 1 [R]Ls Flz 91-15 Balla Cove, Land Rush, Top Cash 4
29Dec89-8SA 6f :213 :441 1:083ft 3 122 72¾ 62¼ 64½ 47 PincyLJr 2 Sn Miguel 88-13 Tarascon, Express It, Shantin O. 9
29Dec89—Broke slowly
6Dec89-8Hol 7f :214 :442 1:221ft 8 122 1hd 1hd 1hd 22½ PncyLJr 2 Hol Prv 91-11 Individualist I, TopCash,Tarascon 6
6Dec89—Grade III
25Nov89-8BM 1$\frac{1}{16}$:453 1:103 1:441sy *4-5 118 2½ 3½ 32½ 47 Doocy T T 1 L Stnfrd 69-19 RstlssCon,GoldFinl,ChmpgnNJuls 5
Speed Index: Last Race: (—) 3-Race Avg.: (—) 12-Race Avg.: (—) Overall Avg.: -4.7
Oct 3 SA 5f ft 1:012 H Sep 26 SA 5f ft 1:002 H Sep 19 SA 4f ft :482 H Sep 11 Dmr 4f ft :492 H

Carolina North — **B. g. 6, by Far North—Carolina Saga, by Care**
BLACK C A **117** **Br.—Evans T M (Ky)** **1990 9 2 1 0 $51,125**
Tr.—Copland Jeffrey **1989 10 2 2 1 $56,775**
Own.—Accardy-Nadel-Snyder **Lifetime 45 5 6 3 $155,770** **Turf 30 4 5 3 $132,260**

9Aug90-8Dmr 1$\frac{1}{16}$ (T):483 1:122 1:422fm 6 L 116 42 41¾ 51¾ 74¼ Black C A10 Aw41000 91-05 Chief'sImge,RellyBrillint,Ertone 10
9Aug90—Wide early
25Jly90-2Dmr 1$\frac{1}{16}$ (T):49 1:131 1:424fm 3¾ L 118 2½ 1hd 2½ 43¼ Black C A9 Aw41000 89-05 RacingRscl,MjorMoment,Ertone 10
1Jly90-9Hol 1$\frac{1}{16}$ (T):46 1:093 1:403fm 6 L 115 21½ 21 1hd 2nk Solis A3 Aw39000 92-08 LegerCt,CrolinNorth,Chief'sImge 8
1Jly90—Lugged out early
10Jun90-9Hol 1 (T):461 1:10 1:344fm 3¾ 119 31½ 31½ 11½ 2nk Black C A5 62500 90-10 ‡Sperry,CarolinNorth,RcingRscl 12
10Jun90—Placed first through disqualification
16May90-9Hol 1 (T):46 1:092 1:334fm 6¾ 116 32 21½ 21½ 11¾ Black C A4 80000 95-06 Carolina North, Neskimo, Treig 8
6May90-9Hol 1⅛ (T):472 1:11 1:464fm 16 116 52 3½ 53 65½ Black C A10 80000 88-04 Simjour, Sperry, Cannon Bar 11
7Apr90-6SA 1 (T):453 1:092 1:341fm 17 116 77½ 75 76¼ 76½ Patton DB5 Aw42000 85-11 Shirkee, Fly Till Dawn,LegerCat 10
7Apr90—Broke out, bumped
25Mar90-5SA a6½f (T):21 :431 1:134fm *3½ 117 1011 1011 107½ 72½ DlhoussyE6 Aw38000 89-08 WonderDncr,Bshyr,Pt'sPocktful 10
25Mar90—Wide
7Mar90-3SA a6½f (T):212 :432 1:132fm 8¾ 117 77½ 76¼ 75¼ 4½ DlhoussyE4 Aw38000 93-06 AskTheMan,AlAzim,MajesticCper 9
21Dec89-5Hol 1 (T):453 1:093 1:34 fm 8 113 46½ 53¾ 74¾ 78¾ Meza R Q3 90000 85-11 GorgHobrt,NrthrnPrvdr,RctlnSpn 7
Speed Index: Last Race: -3.0 2-Race Avg.: -2.0 2-Race Avg.: -2.0 Overall Avg.: -2.9
Oct 11 SA 4f ft :472 H Oct 6 SA 5f ft 1:02 H Sep 30 SA 5f ft 1:011 H Sep 19 SA 3f ft :362 H

Into The Moat — **Dk. b. or br. g. 4, by The Irish Lord—Cunningly, by Decidedly**
MEZA R Q **117** **Br.—Pope G A Jr (Cal)** **1990 9 1 0 0 $22,400**
Tr.—Ravin Robert W **1989 10 1 2 4 $37,475**
Own.—Muter Ann **Lifetime 19 2 2 4 $59,875** **Turf 5 1 0 0 $18,700**

26Aug90-5Dmr 1$\frac{1}{16}$ (T):502 1:152 1:444fm 37 LB 116 11½ 2hd 66½ 811¾ Patton DB 5 Aw41000 71-14 Timdala, High Rank, Ventriloquist 9
5Aug90-7Dmr 6½f :212 :44 1:153ft 66 L 116 63¼ 85¼ 97½ 96 Meza R Q 10 Aw37000 84-10 AbergwunLd,T.V.Scren,RomnAvi 11
5Aug90—Wide trip
6Jly90-8Hol 6f (T):214 :441 1:082fm 31 L 116 41¾ 64½ 75 79½ Black C A 2 Aw37000 87-03 Cove Way, Roman Avie,HeftyFee 8
9Jun90-5Hol 6f :221 :451 1:091ft 19 116 2hd 3½ 55½ 613¼ Baze R A 3 Aw35000 81-07 Siroccan, Jacodra, Trebizond 7
9Jun90—Veered out break
6Apr90-7SA 6½f :222 :454 1:17 ft 14 118 11½ 11 2hd 42½ DlhoussyE 4 Aw38000 82-20 Petrolero,ChperrlMotel,JustDeds 7
6Apr90—Veered out start
25Mar90-5SA a6½f (T):21 :431 1:134fm 9 119 11 1½ 1½ 62½ VlenzulPA 2 Aw38000 89-08 WonderDncr,Bshyr,Pt'sPocktful 10
7Mar90-3SA a6½f (T):212 :432 1:132fm 5½ 119 32 51¾ 86¾ 99 McCrrnCJ 1 Aw38000 85-06 AskTheMan,AlAzim,MajesticCper 9
7Mar90—Hopped in air
9Feb90-8SA a6½f (T):212 :44 1:134fm 5¾ 116 11 1½ 14 11 McCrrnCJ 3 Aw34000 92-08 IntoTheMoat,Litigted,SwingShift 9
5Jan90-7SA 6f :213 :442 1:084ft 8¼ 116 2½ 31 33 56½ Patton DB 1 Aw34000 86-12 SilentHrmony,PorD.J.,HolySmoly 8
22Dec89-3Hol 6f :22 :444 1:094ft 4 115 2½ 2hd 22 32½ PttonDB 8 [S]Aw27000 89-09 Overidge, Navy Cut,IntoTheMoat 7
Speed Index: Last Race: -10.0 3-Race Avg.: -7.3 4-Race Avg.: -5.5 Overall Avg.: -5.7
Sep 26 Hol 4f ft :47 H Sep 4 Dmr 5f ft :582 H Sep 1 Dmr 5f ft 1:004 H Aug 28 Dmr (T) 5f fm 1:032 H (d)

routes to turf sprints. I'll use its May 3 race to illustrate. *Inside each route paceline is a sprint.* To approximate the quarter-mile call, take the first fraction time (in tenths), cut it in half and then subtract .4 (2 ticks). His raw times (in tenths) were 47.5 1:11 1:40.8. The way I arrived at these numbers was as follows: Since he was 4½ lengths behind a 46.3 (in fifths), this translates to 9 tenths behind a 46.6, for a total of 47.5 (in tenths). He then was 2¾ lengths behind a 1:10.2, which means that he was 5.5 tenths behind a 1:10.4, for a total of 1:10.95, rounded to 1:11. Now, to project his quarter-mile time, we divide 45.5 by 2 and subtract .4, for a projected time of 23.35, rounded to 23.4. We take his route first call and second call times as is, and use them as our projected sprint second call and final times. You'll see that 23.4 47.5 1:11 in a six-furlong Hollywood Park turf race is quite slow. To convert these times to Santa Anita 6½-furlong times, we compare the pars and adjust the difference. In this case we must subtract .8 from the first fraction, subtract 1.2 seconds from the second call, and add 4 seconds to the final time. His adjusted Santa Anita times are 22.6 46.3 1:15. His ability time is 22.6 plus 28.7 (75 minus 46.3) which is 51.3.

Roman Avie Although this is only his second turf start, he has proven his turf prowess. Using his July 6 race, we see that he ran within a whisker of par the first time asked. His adjusted Hollywood Park times are 23 45.2 1:08.4. These are converted into Santa Anita 6½-furlong times by the usual adjustment procedure—compare the pars and adjust the difference. In this case we must subtract .8 from the first fraction, subtract 1.2 seconds from the second call, and add 4 seconds to the final time. His adjusted Santa Anita times are 22.2 44.0 1:12.4. This means that this performance equates to a par performance at Santa Anita with a spectacular final fraction and a so-so first fraction. His turf ability time is 22.2 plus 28.4 (72.4 minus 44.0) for a total of 50.6.

Carolina North We'll use his July 1 race. His adjusted Hollywood Park times are 46.3 1:09.8 1:40.6. We then look at the sprint within the route, which gives us 22.8 46.3 1:09.8. These convert to 22.0 45.1 1:13.8 Santa Anita 6½-furlong times. His turf ability time is 50.7.

Into The Moat We'll use his July 6 race. His adjusted Hollywood Park times are 22.2 45.1 1:10.3. These convert to 21.4 43.9 1:14.3 Santa Anita 6½-furlong times. His turf ability time is 51.8.

When we sort the turf ability ratings we have:

Roman Avie	50.6
Carolina North	50.7

Eratone	51.3
Into The Moat	51.8

Roman Avie has a small advantage. Unfortunately, the race is complicated by Top Cash. He has an excellent turf sire. Stalwart's progeny win 19.4 percent of the time and show an over 40 percent ROI of $2.81 for every two dollars invested. This means that we must bet both horses. Roman Avie paid a generous $9.60. Had the race not contained Top Cash, we would have bet both Roman Avie and Carolina North.

FIFTH RACE
Santa Anita
OCTOBER 14, 1990

ABOUT 6 ½ FURLONGS.(Turf). (1.11⅘) ALLOWANCE. Purse $36,000. 3-year-olds and upward which are non-winners of $3,000 twice other than maiden, claiming or starter. Weights, 3-year-olds, 118 lbs.; older, 121 lbs. Non-winners of two races other than claiming since August 1 allowed 2 lbs.; of a race other than maiden or claiming since then, 4 lbs. (Horses eligible only to the above conditions are preferred.) (Non-starters for a claiming price of $25,000 or less in their last three starts preferred.)

Value of race $36,000; value to winner $19,800; second $7,200; third $5,400; fourth $2,700; fifth $900. Mutuel pool $428,873. Exacta Pool $494,274.

Last Raced	Horse	M/Eqt.A.Wt	PP St	¼	½	Str	Fin	Jockey	Odds $1
1Sep90 3Dmr5	Roman Avie	B b 4 117	2 6	5hd	2hd	2hd	1no	Desormeaux K J	3.60
26Aug90 9Lga9	Way Wild	L B b 4 117	9 1	62½	3hd	31½	21	Baze R A	15.20
9Sep90 9Dmr1	Eratone	L B b 5 119	1 9	9	9	5½	3nk	McCarron C J	2.40
30Sep90 10Fpx2	Kipper Kelly	B	3 116	7 2	1½	11½	11½	42	Valenzuela P A	2.60
9Aug90 8Dmr7	Carolina North	L B	6 117	5 4	31½	41	41½	5½	Black C A	5.50
8Oct90 5SA10	Top Cash	L B b	3 114	4 5	41	61½	62	63	Solis A	12.80
9Sep90 7Dmr9	Curio	L B	5 117	3 8	7hd	7hd	72½	73½	Flores D R	24.20
26Aug90 5Dmr8	Into The Moat	L B b	4 117	6 3	2hd	51½	81	81½	Meza R Q	19.50
13Oct89 7SA3	Sizzlin' Sharp	L B b	5 112	8 7	82½	8hd	9	9	Berrio O A5	36.10

OFF AT 1:52. Start good. Won driving. Time, :21⅘, :43⅘, 1:06½, 1:13 Course firm.

$2 Mutuel Prices:

2–ROMAN AVIE	9.20	5.20	3.60
10–WAY WILD		13.80	4.80
1–ERATONE			2.80

$5 EXACTA 2–10 PAID $300.50.

When a race contains more than one turf sire plus experienced turf horses who run within two ticks of par, I usually bet both the top turf "ability time" horse who offers value plus the first-time grass horse who has the most productive sire. The key is to bet the top horse in each category. If all three categories are represented, you bet all three horses if the odds permit—otherwise choose the top two that offer the longest odds.

SUMMARY

The key to handicapping on the turf is the ability to find the "class of the field." We have to deal with the first-time grass runner, whether a maiden first-time starter or an experienced dirt horse going onto the turf for the first or second time. We accomplish this by the use of the Quirin's Grass Stallion Statistics. The first and most important figure is the stallion's ROI ($ NET). We should insist that the $ NET be well above the two-dollar break-even figure. Secondarily, we must consider the win percentage. If two horses have daddies with similar ROIs, then the win percentage becomes vitally important. When the horse's daddy is a less than 10 percent sire, we aren't terribly impressed. A high ROI for a less than 10 percent sire is usually explained by one or two monster mutuels. Whether you realize it or not, we're defining class by breeding when it comes to first and second time on turf.

Foreign horses who have no North American experience can be handled in one of two ways. The first is to judge their class by the company that they kept at home. At what level did they succeed? The *Statistical Review* or Jim Quinn's *International Stakes Catalogue* are valuable resources in helping make this determination. A second quick and practical method is to use the horse's morning-line odds as a yardstick. If the horse is within the top three on the morning line, it deserves your attention. I tend to be xenophobic (fearful of foreigners) when it comes to foreign horses coming from well-respected trainers, especially when a leading rider has the mount. In the case of foreign horses, we are judging its class by the company it keeps or by how well it's regarded by the track handicapper.

Experienced turf runners are judged by their ability to run fast both early and late. This is the meaning of class, as defined by speed. In turf races we use the adjusted first fraction time added to the adjusted last fraction time. (The lower the number, the better.)

The challenge of turf racing is that we rarely have the commonalities that we do in dirt racing. It's not unusual to have a dirt race where all the contenders have had a recent race on this surface at this distance. It's most unusual to have these commonalities in a turf race. It's quite usual to deal with distance switches, track switches, a foreign horse or two, and perhaps a few first-time starters on grass runners in the same race.

Please heed the warning of the next paragraph. It'll save you a lot of money and grief.

Pay attention to track bias. Most turf tracks are contained inside a dirt track. The turns are steeper. This creates a natural bias for inside post positions. Sometimes temporary fences known as "dogs" are erected, which makes all the horses in the race run wide. These fences are put up to protect the inside portion of the turf course. Outside horses that have just missed with the "dogs up" coming back at inside post positions are dangerous. Similarly, inside horses moving to the outside should be downgraded a bit. It's always important to study the **Winning Post Positions** table printed in the *Racing Form* or in your track program. Obvious post position biases will be easy to see. You must upgrade horses that performed well against a bias, and downgrade horses that were favored by the bias and don't have it in their favor today.

I recommend betting on more than one horse except where there's a horse with at least a 6-point ability-time advantage (three lengths). The reason: low percentage of any single choice in a turf race. In a contentious race, you may have as many as four or five horses that can run within two ticks of each other. Even if such a group were to contain the winner 100 percent of the time, any single selection would only have a 20 to 25 percent chance to win.

When you have a race in which there are multiple categories such as first-time turf horse running against experienced turf horses, you bet the top horse in each category if the odds permit. Sometimes you'll be betting on three horses, but most of the time you'll bet on two horses. When you have a standout, you'll be betting on only one horse. You'll bet to win if the odds are 5-to-2 or greater, else you'll look for a place or show bet. This turf standout is also a wonderful exacta top horse.

Quirin's Grass Stallion Statistics, through 1991, can be found in Appendix B. Please be warned that by the time you read this book, this list will be obsolete. The list is updated annually and is available from Cynthia Publishing Company (see Appendix A).

Thus far, we have learned how to handicap each different type of race, plus we've learned the importance of a betting line. Now we're going to move into the land of big profits. If you'll master exacta wagering, you'll catapult yourself to a new level of earning power. I'm very proud to say that for every dollar that I invest in exactas, my return is almost two dollars. Please pay close attention to the next chapter.

Chapter 12

Exacta Wagering

EXACTAS (PERFECTAS) ARE THE MOST misplayed bet in thoroughbred wagering. If there's one area that offers almost unlimited opportunity, this is it. I'm very proud of my ROI in exacta wagering. It's close to 100 percent. That is, for every dollar that I wager on exactas, I get back almost two. There are two parts to exacta wagering. The first is the selection component, and the second is the decision component. They're like body and soul. Neither one can be the most important because they're inseparable. We'll look at the selection aspect of exactas first.

Most handicappers really don't understand this bet. It's a compound bet. You are picking the winner plus the place horse. If you learn nothing else from this chapter, please memorize this: **The second-best win horse rarely comes in second**. In other words, the place horse is not the second-best win horse. On average, the favorite should win and the second favorite should complete the exacta around 12 percent of the time. Most empirical studies cluster between 8 and 10 percent. How often does the favorite/second-favorite exacta pay more than $20 for a two-dollar bet? Seldom, if ever. It doesn't take a genius to see that you shouldn't buy this exacta combination. Not only does the public overload on this combination in every race, they usually "send it in" on the reverse combination as well. The reversal is usually a sucker bet, too.

Typically, exacta pools are larger than the straight mutuel pools. What a lovely situation. The public bets more money where they're least proficient. Here's your opportunity to plunder and pillage. Master this chapter and Chapter 26 of my book *Winning Thoroughbred Strategies*. You'll be very well compensated for your time and energy.

The quintessential handicapping skill that you need to crush the exacta is the ability to pick the place horse. The way you acquire any skill is practice—practice with feedback. (As an aside, the old saw that "practice makes perfect" is a lie. Practice without feedback just means that you continue to perfect the wrong way to do things. This aphorism should read "practice makes permanent.") Fortunately, for us, we have the best feedback system ever invented: the mutuel windows. Every time you handicap a race, try to pick the horse that will come in second. Write down all the place contenders, no matter how many. You should have the place horse listed within your contenders at least 80 percent of the time, the same as your win contenders.

There are four basic paradigms of the place horse. They are:

1. The Unbalanced Horse
2. The Anti-bias Horse
3. The Seconditis Horse
4. The Favorite

THE UNBALANCED HORSE

This is the horse that doesn't quite have it together. He either has high class and inferior speed or low class and superior speed. In order to be a legitimate favorite, the horse must have both class and speed superiority. Have you noticed how often a recent maiden graduate with good numbers manages to come in second in non-winners allowance races? This is especially true for recent maiden-claiming graduates dramatically moving up in class.

THE ANTI-BIAS HORSE

This is the front runner on a track favoring closers, or a closer on a track favoring front runners. This is the horse coming from the one-post when the rail is dead. This is the turf horse coming from the twelve-hole in a two-turn mile race. Despite the negative situation, there's one thing the anti-bias horse has going for him—superior numbers. This horse usually has the best adjusted final time of any horse in the race, but has to deal with a strong negative bias.

THE SECONDITIS HORSE

This is the kind of horse that reads the *Racing Form*—a very intelligent creature. He figures out a way to come in second most of the time. The seconditis horse is easy to spot. His record will look something like this: 7 1 4 0. In seven outings he managed to come in second four times. God bless these horses. They make wonderful candidates for the second spot on any exacta ticket.

THE FAVORITE

This includes three types of favorites. The first is the betting favorite of the crowd. The second is the morning-line favorite. Most of the time, these horses are the same. When they aren't, consider both horses as second-place candidates. The third type of favorite is the *Daily Racing Form*'s consensus horse, which has bold type. This kind of favorite wins over 40 percent of the time and places over 60 percent of the time, meaning if he doesn't win, he's the place horse around 20 percent of the time. The public favorite also comes in second around 20 percent of the time. Keep in mind that the favorite is involved in the exacta around 52 percent of the time. The public favorite or the second favorite is involved in the exacta at least 75 percent of the time— that is, either one or both are involved in the exacta three out of four times.

The exacta can be used strategically. There are three strategies that make wonderful use of the exacta pools. The first is what I call "the exacta as a win bet." The second is "the exacta as a place bet." The third is the "Mitchell Matrix."

You must understand that an exacta wheel is essentially the same bet as a win bet—you're just using different pools to make the bet. You should always check to see if the win bet is paying more than the exacta top wheel. It's rare, but it does happen. It's our job to get the most value for our money. Most often it happens that if the favorite is our first choice, it's usually underlayed in the win pool. Typically, our line reads 2-to-1 and the horse is going off at 8-to-5 or less. Suppose this is the case and we also notice that the exacta payoffs to the three most logical place horses are $18, $19.20, and $22. By wagering on this horse in the exacta, you'll now be getting at least 2-to-1. Your straight $6 win bet would return $15.60, assuming that the horse paid 8-to-5 or $5.20. By playing your top pick in the exacta, he'll pay at least $18 for your $6 bet. The downside is, of course, that one of your three choices must come in second. I find myself using this strategy mostly in maiden races and graded stakes races.

Place and show bets are for strong favorites only. Place and show bets on longshots are dumb. Very dumb. Please see Chapter 19 of *Winning Thoroughbred Strategies* for a thorough explanation. Place and show betting on longshots is for living brain donors and those who possess less intelligence than a tree. Trust me, it's a dreadful way to bet. Given that this is true, a question arises: How can we prosper when a longshot runs second? Answer: the exacta. Whenever you bet a long shot (9–2 or over) to win, also play him second in the exacta to the horse(s) most likely to beat him. Usually the most likely horse to beat your longshot is the favorite, unless it's a false favorite. So it's a good idea to play your longshot second to the favorite in the exacta and make a straight win bet on him as well. If the race is contentious, it's a good idea to use your longshot second to a few horses.

The Mitchell Matrix is a technique that one of my students used to purchase a brand new $9000 car for cash. This is a technique that takes a small amount of cash and turns it into a huge pile. This is a crush technique that can earn you your season's profits in a single race. The idea is simple. You find a contentious race with three or more win and place contenders. I'll demonstrate using four contenders and give you a general formula for any number of contenders. If you have a race that contains four contenders that you can't separate, then your betting line is 4-to-1 on each contender and 4-to-1 on the rest of the field. The probability of any exacta combination involving these four horses is the same. The probability of a 4-to-1 shot finishing on top of another 4-to-1 shot is found by multiplying the win probability by the dependent probability of the place horse coming in second. This is mighty fancy verbiage to describe the following: a 4-to-1 shot has a 20 percent chance to win the race. Another 4-to-1 shot has a 20 percent chance to win the rest of the race, given that another horse won. His 20 percent is not 20 percent of 100 percent, it's 20 percent of 80 percent because we already know that another horse won the race. His probability of coming in second was dependent on who won the race. The probability of winning this exacta is 20 percent of 25 percent, which is 5 percent. This result generalizes. It's always the reciprocal of n times n + 1; where n represents the number of contenders. In this case, $1/(4 \times 5)$ or $\frac{1}{20}$, which is 5 percent. In the case of five contenders, it's $\frac{1}{30}$, or 3.3 percent. For six contenders it's $\frac{1}{42}$, or 2.4 percent.

The trick to the Mitchell Matrix is to write down the probable exacta payoffs in a table or matrix. You then circle the highest-paying combinations. If you have four contenders, you circle the top four highest-paying combinations. If you have five contenders, you circle the top five highest paying combinations, and so on. In the case of four contenders, we have a 20 percent chance to hit this exacta. That is, we have four combinations which each have a 5 percent chance of hitting. It should be apparent that these combinations must pay over a certain minimum or you don't bet them. If you have a 5 percent chance of winning a bet, then you must be paid 19-to-1 for it to be a fair bet. But who wants fair bets? We insist on a 50 percent premium, so the minimum must be $57.

Mitchell Matrix Table

# of contenders	P(W) single bet	P(W) entire bet	Minimum $2 Payoff
3	8.3%	25%	$ 35
4	5.0	20	57
5	3.3	17	87
6	2.4	14	123
7	1.8	13	165
8	1.3	11	213
9	1.1	10	267

This table tells us the probability of any single combination winning the exacta, the total chances that one of our combinations will win, plus the minimum price to accept. If any combination falls below this minimum, we'll leave it out. The table ends with nine contenders for a very good reason. It's not a good idea to use this technique when your total win probability is less than 10 percent. Try this method. It's dynamite. But go slow at first. Test it with two bucks on each combination. When you're convinced, accelerate your bets to your maximum comfort level.

Let's now take a look at the decision aspect of exacta wagering. It's no secret that you should bet on overlays only. That's the secret to winning. You only bet when you have a positive expectation. How can we tell if an exacta combination is an overlay or not? The answer is easy if we make a betting line or if we accept the public's win odds as our probability estimates. Andy Beyer tells the story of the "Doc." He's a guy who makes his living by betting exacta races and does no handicapping whatsoever. He simply compares the fair exacta payoffs to the offered payoffs and bets only on the overlaid combinations. He's got a medical degree and could be making a ton of money practicing medicine. Instead, he makes his living on the ignorance of the betting public. They really don't play exactas anywhere near efficiently, as we already know.

If you use your own betting line, the formula for the fair price is:

$$\text{Fair Price} = \text{Bet Size} \times \text{Odds1} \times (\text{Odds2} + 1)$$

The above formula tells you to multiply three numbers: the bet size; the win odds of your top choice; and the number 1 added to the win odds of your place horse. For example, assume your betting line was as follows:

Horse A	2-to-1
Horse B	3-to-1
Horse C	4-to-1

Let's figure the $2 and $5 exacta fair prices for all six possible exacta combinations.

AB = $2 × 2 × (3 + 1) = $16
AC = $2 × 2 × (4 + 1) = $20
BA = $2 × 3 × (2 + 1) = $18
BC = $2 × 3 × (4 + 1) = $30
CA = $2 × 4 × (2 + 1) = $24
CB = $2 × 4 × (3 + 1) = $32

AB = $5 × 2 × (3 + 1) = $40
AC = $5 × 2 × (4 + 1) = $50
BA = $5 × 3 × (2 + 1) = $45
BC = $5 × 3 × (4 + 1) = $75
CA = $5 × 4 × (2 + 1) = $60
CB = $5 × 4 × (3 + 1) = $80

If you use the public's odds line as your betting line, the formula is the same except you must divide by the square of the track payback. (The track payback is the one's complement of the track take. In other words, track payback = 1 − track take.) The track payback is the amount of the bettor's dollar that's returned in the win pool. In California the track take is 15.33 percent, therefore the track payback is 84.67 percent, or .8467 expressed as a decimal.

$$\text{Fair Price} = \frac{\text{Bet Size} \times \text{Odds1} \times (\text{Odds2} + 1)}{(\text{Track Payback})^2}$$

The above formula tells you to divide the results of the first formula by the track payback multiplied by itself. Let's figure the $2 exacta fair prices in California for all six possible exacta combinations using the above example.

AB = [$2 × 2 × (3 + 1)]/(.7169) = $16/.7169 = $22.31
AC = [$2 × 2 × (4 + 1)]/(.7169) = $20/.7169 = $27.89
BA = [$2 × 3 × (2 + 1)]/(.7169) = $18/.7169 = $25.15
BC = [$2 × 3 × (4 + 1)]/(.7169) = $30/.7169 = $41.84
CA = [$2 × 4 × (2 + 1)]/(.7169) = $24/.7169 = $33.47
CB = [$2 × 4 × (3 + 1)]/(.7169) = $32/.7169 = $44.63

Note that .7169 is $(.8467)^2$. If the "Doc" happened to be in California, that's how he would generate the fair prices. Naturally, he didn't want fair prices. He wanted a premium. I'm not sure exactly what premium was necessary. Barry Meadow suggests 50 percent as the acceptable premium. This is good advice. (Barry's been a consistent winner for the past twenty years.)

You now know how to calculate the price necessary to make the exacta combination yield an acceptable overlay. The way you play the exacta is simple. You write down all your win horses and your place horses. You draw the grid or matrix that represents all the possibilities. You then calculate the acceptable overlay price for each combination. Next, you write down the probable pay from the monitors at the track. Circle all the combinations that offer good value. Make sure that you deduct the effect of losing two-dollar bets. For example, suppose you have four combinations circled as overlays. You must subtract $6 from each payoff to compensate yourself for your losing bets. You then bet on all combinations in proportion to their respective probabilities. You definitely want to have more money on those combinations with the higher probabilities. (The best way to play exacta races is to order a pocket computer from Cynthia Publishing called THE BETTOR-HANDICAPPER. It automates this whole process. It also automates all the other betting propositions, such as win betting, place and show betting, daily double, serial triple, and any serial bet. In addition, it contains a class and pace calculator. The truth is—betting is complicated and you really need a computer to do it correctly. I wouldn't go to the track without my pocket computer with these betting programs installed.)

Here are some exacta wagering guidelines:

1. Never bet an exacta when you can make more money by betting to win.
2. Each exacta combination must carry a positive edge.
3. When wagering on more than one exacta combination, you must be compensated for your guaranteed losing bets.
4. Unless a race is a Mitchell Matrix type, you should have no more than two win horses and three place-horse contenders.

Exacta wagering offers the investor a wonderful opportunity to earn substantial profits. These wagers can be strategic as well. They can be used to convert an underlay into an overlay. They offer us wide latitude for making intelligent betting choices. Please take advantage of the fact that only a small number of bettors understand how to make these wagers properly.

If your personal financial goal exceeds $200 per day, you must master the exacta. In order to win a lot of money at thoroughbred wagering, you must bet a lot of money. It's a sad fact that the parimutuel system penalizes you for making large bets. The only way around this difficulty is to invest in low-probability/high-payoff wagers such as the exacta.

Treat the next section as a workshop. Try the races yourself and compare your conclusions to the conclusions of Kitts Anderson, Steve Unite, and ALL-IN-ONE.

Chapter 13

Workshop: Putting It All Together

WE'RE NOW READY TO do battle against the odds. We've learned how to use the four overarching criteria of ability, form, angles, and value to evaluate the merits of each horse. We've also learned how to apply these four criteria variously to maiden races, claiming events, allowance and stakes contests, and turf racing. In this chapter we're going to put it all together. We're going to use everything we've learned so far to handicap and wager on an actual day at the races.

My staff chose the December 1, 1991, program at Hollywood Park because it included the four types of races we've discussed: three maiden races, a couple of mid-to-low-range claiming races, a top-level claiming race, a classified allowance, and three turf stakes. These races give you a near-perfect exercise in applying all the concepts I've covered in the book. Treat this chapter as a workshop so you can put into practice the lessons in this book. Handicap the races based on the knowledge you've gained up to this point, construct your own betting line and wagers, then consult our narrative and betting lines.

Before we begin, let's discuss the way the contenders were chosen. Staff handicapper Kitts Anderson is a devoted user of the Cynthia Publishing program ALL-IN-ONE, which contains a win profile feature that automates the record-keeping essential to maintaining the win profiles promoted in the book. Kitts had the huge edge of knowing exactly what was winning at Hollywood Park during the time leading up to our day at the races; he was able to choose contenders based on how closely they fit the corresponding win profile. Kitts then subjected potential contenders to current form and condition guidelines. In short, he applied everything he knows about handicapping in his contender and paceline selection process. It's necessary, but not sufficient, for a horse to fit the win profile; the horse must also show some evidence that he'll be able to run today to the paceline that fits the win profile. The win profiles influence his decisions, but a more comprehensive style guides them overall. If you don't have the benefit of a current win profile, it's not the end of the world. I'm convinced that much of the time the real contenders jump up and bite you in the neck off their paper form anyway. The win profile simply confirms this strong first impression. If you do have a current win profile, the first question you should always ask of a horse is: Does it fit the win profile? Horses that do fit the win profile are considerably advantaged. Kitts then ran his contenders and pacelines through ALL-IN-ONE and got tons of information crucial to making intelligent handicapping and wagering decisions.

You'll first see the past performances, followed by the narratives for each horse in each race. You'll then be given ALL-IN-ONE's output, which includes the critical information of the win profile, Pace Contention Point, Win Pars, and Ability Time Par, plus the Betting Line, Exacta Grid, Speed/Pace Summary, and Pace Graph. Give yourself the wonderful learning opportunity of handicapping and constructing your own betting lines first before consulting our opinions.

Tanker Port The last race definitely fits the pace profile. However, though he won at this level last time, he doesn't step up today. That puts a form cloud over his head. He was also in a graded stakes earlier in the year, but has descended to the claiming ranks. On the numbers alone, he's a contender.

Conflictofinterest Takes mandatory but logical step up in class after the claim and has won at this level. He's also a "loves-to-win" type whose last race puts him squarely in the pace profile.

Maxibob Very dull form against slightly better in NW2 allowance. Only shows wins at NW1 and claiming $32,000 levels, significantly lower than today's $50,000 claimer. His previous races suggest that he runs his best races from way off the pace at the second call, which isn't the style that's been winning. Non-contender.

1st Hollywood

6 FURLONGS. (1.07) CLAIMING. Purse $26,000. 3-year-olds and upward. Weights, 3-year-olds, 120 lbs.; older, 122 lbs. Non-winners of two races since October 6 allowed 3 lbs.; of one since Oct., 5 lbs. Claiming price $50,000 for each $2,500 to $45,000, 2 lbs. (Races when entered for $40,000 or less not considered.)

LASIX—Tanker Port, Conflictofinterest, Maxibob, Movinglikeawinner, Indian Wind.

Tanker Port ✷
PINCAY L JR

Conflictofinterest
VALENZUELA P A

Maxibob
McCARRON C J

Movinglikeawinner
PEDROZA M A

Ready To Launch
NAKATANI C S

Indian Wind
ALVARADO F J

Movinglikeawinner Ran in the same race as Tanker Port last time and finished within 2½ lengths of that contender and a neck in front of another of today's contenders, Conflictofinterest, so should be rated off that tandem race Nov. 10 at Santa Anita.

Ready to Launch A classic "need-to-lead" type that won't get it in this race. Throw out.

Indian Wind Can't win sprinting. Toss out.

Candyman Bee Finished within a head of contender Conflictofinterest, so we've obviously got to rate him. I've chosen his next-to-last race back for a paceline.

Callide Valley Granted, his last win came in a race limited to three-year-old $40,000 claimers, but remember that this late in the year, three-year-olds are at no statistical final-time disadvantage to their older rivals. And don't be suckered by the old business of the taxing stretch drive being a negative form pattern; it's just the opposite. This one's got really sharp form. Also, he's been freshened for 37 days off that last one, and his training pattern is perfectly spaced: four works in four weeks, one per week. There's no form cloud over him. Delahoussaye stays on, a good sign. Right on the pace profile. Very strong contender. Obviously use his last race.

Five live contenders in a very contentious race. Tanker Port could be a class standout, but the fact that he stays at the same level after a win puts a form cloud over him. We also have to deal with three class risers: Conflictofinterest, Callide Valley, and Candyman Bee. Movinglikeawinner stays at the same class after a competitive second last time. The interesting thing about this race is that the four older contenders have all finished within three lengths of each other at some point in their careers. Since they're all pretty much of equal ability, this race should be wildly contentious. Whose turn will it be today? Callide Valley is literally the "new kid on the block" and just might have enough to break up the status quo.

A look at the ALL-IN-ONE's Speed/Pace Summary clearly shows how contentious this race is. Four contenders are within the Pace Contention Point and Ability Time Par. The Pace Graph shows three horses in a dead heat at the wire. This closeness in ability is reflected in ALL-IN-ONE's Betting Line:

Callide Valley	9-to-2
Tanker Port	9-to-2
Candyman Bee	9-to-2
Conflictofinterest	5-to-1

On the basis of an uncompetitive ability time in combination with falling outside the pace contention point, Movinglikeawinner was dismissed by the program at win odds of above 8-to-1. Most authors will tell you that trying to pick the winner in a contentious race such as this one isn't worth it. True, picking the eventual winner is very difficult, but picking the win bets is child's play. In a race this close, to take a short price would be unwise. Since this race is a practical toss-up with the top pick having no better than an 18 percent chance to win, whoever is favored will be hugely overbet and definitely vulnerable. This is the type of race we pray for. There is absolutely no way you can make any of these horses lower than 9-to-2. But the public, bless 'em, has to make somebody a favorite. And in a race this competitive, the public will most likely be confused.

Public line:

```
1DEC91                        HOL                      6 furlongs dirt
Race #1                                                     8 starters
C50,000                                          Age: 3+years, Male
```

---------------------------------------INPUT DATA-----------------------------------

Horse name	# ST	# W	# P	# S	$'S Earned	Date	Trk	Dist.	S	1st C time	2nd C time	Final time
Tanker Port	12	4	0	2	143900	10NOV91	SA	6.500	D	22.2	45.1	115.4
Conflictofinterest	12	4	1	2	68200	23NOV91	HOL	6.000	D	22.0	45.1	109.1
Movinglikeawinner	8	1	1	3	30950	10NOV91	SA	6.500	D	22.2	45.1	115.4
Candyman Bee	12	5	2	2	71490	11NOV91	SA	6.500	D	22.0	45.0	116.0
Callide Valley	5	3	0	1	47200	25OCT91	SA	6.000	D	22.0	45.1	109.4

Horse name	Class Lvl	1st C B.L.	2nd C B.L.	Final B.L.	SR	Var
Tanker Port	C50,000	0.00	0.10	0.00	91	13
Conflictofinterest	C40,000	3.50	1.00	0.00	94	9
Movinglikeawinner	C50,000	1.50	2.00	2.50	88	13
Candyman Bee	C32,000	0.00	0.00	0.00	90	16
Callide Valley	C40,000	0.10	0.10	0.00	87	18

-------------------------------------BETTING LINE-----------------------------------

Horse name	PEH	H-I	THAAI	P-H	ESP	Rating	Betting Line	Fair Place $	Fair Show $
Callide Valley	1	4	2	1	3	84.31	9-2		
Tanker Port	3	1	1	2	4	83.54	9-2		
Candyman Bee	2	3	3	3	2	82.47	9-2		
Conflictofinterest	4	2	4	4	1	80.82	5-1		
Movinglikeawinner	5	5	5	5	5	68.41			

-------------------------------------EXACTA GRID-----------------------------------

	Callide Valley	Tanker Port	Candyman Bee	Conflictofinter
Callide Valley	. . . .	42 104	44 109	47 117
Tanker Port	42 105	. . . .	46 113	49 122
Candyman Bee	45 111	46 114	. . . .	52 129
Conflictofinte	49 121	50 125	53 131	. . . .

---------------------------------SPEED/PACE SUMMARY---------------------------------

```
Race Profile:    22.59   45.47  109.62   Winners' Pace Profile: EARLY
Ability Par:     68.35                    Pace Contention Point: 2.53 lengths
```

Projected Times:	1st C	2nd C	Fin C	Ability Balance Time	Time	Last Frac	Proj Pace	Con-tender
Callide Valley	22.11	45.18	108.80	68.25	67.60	23.62	FRONT	Y
Tanker Port	22.56	45.47	108.80	68.38	67.08	23.33	EARLY	Y
Candyman Bee	22.14	45.17	108.80	68.20	67.23	23.63	FRONT	Y
Conflictofinterest	22.68	45.31	109.00	67.94	67.05	23.69	EARLY	Y
Movinglikeawinner	22.86	45.85*	109.30	68.84	67.51	23.45	MID	N

------------------------------------PACE GRAPH------------------------------------

```
    Profile:            22.59            45.47             109.62
    Front Runner:       22.11            45.17             108.80
Horse name               1C               2C                    F
Callide Valley     ----------------X ---------------(--X -----------------X
Tanker Port        ---------------X-+ --------------(-X+ -----------------X
Candyman Bee       ----------------X ---------------(--X -----------------X
Conflictofinterest -------------X-+ --------------(-X+ -----------------X+
Movinglikeawinner  --------------X---+ -------------X(--+ --------------X--+
```

Callide Valley	12-to-1
Tanker Port	3-to-2
Candyman Bee	9-to-2
Conflictofinterest	7-to-2
Movinglikeawinner	7-to-1

The public jumped all over Tanker Port because of his "back class." But they neglected the equally salient point of current form. The favorite was going to be overbet to begin with, but on top of that, Tanker Port is actually a false favorite in terms of the form cloud over him. The obvious overlay is a win bet on Callide Valley. Please take my advice on contentious races: since your win-betting risk is going to be the same on your top horses, your potential reward should dictate which risk you take. It's no contest. Our edge on Callide Valley is 150 percent.

This same risk-reward principle could also be applied to the exacta in this race by using the Mitchell Matrix. Since the contenders are inseparable on our line at 9-to-2, the fair price on the two-dollar exacta is $50. Each of these exacta combinations has an equal likelihood of coming in, so again we'd be foolish not to buy the combinations that offer us the greatest reward. We circle the four highest-paying combinations. After all is said and done, a $152.60 exacta on two natural 9-to-2 horses is outstanding. After the first race, we're ahead $25.80 on win betting. We won't keep score on exactas, assuming you haven't yet mastered them.

FIRST RACE

Hollywood

DECEMBER 1, 1991

6 FURLONGS. (1.08) CLAIMING. Purse $26,000. 3-year-olds and upward. Weights, 3-year-olds, 120 lbs.; older, 122 lbs. Non-winners of two races since October 6 allowed 3 lbs.; a race since then, 5 lbs. Claiming price $50,000 for each $2,500 to $45,000; 2 lbs. (Races when entered for $40,000 or less not considered.) 15th DAY. WEATHER CLOUDY. TEMPERATURE 67 DEGREES.

Value of race $26,000; value to winner $14,300; second $5,200; third $3,900; fourth $1,950; fifth $650. Mutuel pool $242,306. Exacta pool $196,004.

Last Raced	Horse	M/Eqt.A.Wt	PP St	¼	½	Str	Fin	Jockey	Cl'g Pr	Odds $1
25Oct91 5SA1	Callide Valley	B 3 116	8 1	4hd	31	2hd	1hd	Delhoussye E	50000	12.90
23Nov91 5Hol2	Candyman Bee	Bb 4 117	7 2	1hd	1hd	1hd	21½	Smith M E	50000	4.90
10Nov91 2SA2	Movinglikeawinner	LB 5 117	4 7	61½	4hd	3hd	3½	Pedroza M A	50000	7.30
20Nov91 8Hol5	Maxibob	LB 4 117	3 8	8	61½	63	41½	McCarron C J	50000	10.20
10Nov91 2SA1	Tanker Port	LBb 6 119	1 3	21½	2½	43	5nk	Pincay L Jr	50000	1.50
6Oct91 8EP3	Indian Wind	LBb 4 117	6 6	51	53	51	64½	Alvarado F J	50000	18.90
23Nov91 5Hol1	Conflictofinterest	LB 4 119	2 5	72	72	75	71³	Valenzuel P A	50000	3.60
1Nov91 3BM1	Ready To Launch	4 119	5 4	3½	8	8	8	Nakatani C S	50000	13.10

OFF AT 12:32. Start good. Won driving. Time, :22¹, :45¹, :57², 1:10 Track fast.

Official Program Numbers \

$2 Mutuel Prices:

8-CALLIDE VALLEY		27.80	13.00	6.80
7-CANDYMAN BEE			6.20	4.20
4-MOVINGLIKEAWINNER				5.20

$2 EXACTA 8-7 PAID $152.60.

This next race is a baby maiden claimer.

2nd Hollywood

1 1-16MILES
HOLLYWOOD PARK
FINISH ▲ ▲START

1 1/16 MILES. (1.40) MAIDEN CLAIMING. Purse $17,000. 2-year-olds. Weight, 117 lbs. Claiming price $32,000; if for $28,000 allowed 2 lbs.

LASIX—Yargo, Bad Boy Butch, Polar Attraction, Joanie's Prince, The Last Thruway, Hunters Arrow, Mid Stretch.

Yargo Ch. g. 2(Mar), by Derilord—Idle Duchess, by Figonero Lifetime 1991 4 M 0 1 $3,825
TORRES H $32,000 Br.—Pulliam C N (Cal) 4 0 0 1
Own.—Pulliam C N Tr.—Pulliam Vivian M 112 5 $3,825
15Nov91- 4Hol fst 1 1/16 :481 1:124 1:452 Md 32000 8 10 1011 810 610 318 1/4 Torres H5 Lb 113 16.60 64-27 Tee Zee118 1 1/4 School Bend118 9 Yargo113no Carried wide 7/8 12
14Oct91- 6SA fst 6f :213 :444 1:102 [S]Md 32000 11 5 98 1/4 913 713 511 3/4 Torres H5 Lb 113 11.00 72-12 U.S.OfAmrc118 7 SchoolBnd118 4 OrMomntInTm118 1/2 Wide trip 11
23Aug91- 6Dmr fst 7f :233 :454 1:252 Md 40000 4 5 76 89 1/2 66 1/2 66 1/2 Pedroza M A LB 117 17.70 67-18 Sky Rider117 2 JonesIsland117 1/2 NineDimes117 1/2 4-wide stretch 10
11Aug91- 4Dmr fst 6f :221 :453 1:11 [S]Md Sp Wt 7 3 78 1/2 79 1/2 69 1/2 510 1/2 Pedroza M A L 117 30.20 73-13 VntgYr117 1 1/2 Blckbrd'sGhost117 5 1/2 StrngLdr117 1 3/4 Wide stretch 8
Speed Index: Last Race: -9.0 1-Race Avg.: -9.0 1-Race Avg.: -9.0 Overall Avg.: -13.5
LATEST WORKOUTS ●Nov 22 SA 3f fst :353 H ●Nov 8 SA 3f fst :35 H Nov 3 SA 4f fst :48 H Oct 25 SA 6f fst 1:153 H

Badger Bay B. c. 2(May), by Badger Land—Bay of Fundy, by Portsmouth Lifetime 1991 2 M 0 0
ALVARADO F J $28,000 Br.—Backer J W & Calumet Farm (Ky) 2 0 0 0
Own.—Awesome Stable Tr.—Cross David C Jr 115
15Nov91- 4Hol fst 1 1/16 :481 1:124 1:452 Md 32000 1 3 44 1215 1221 1232 1/4 Cedeno E A Bb 118 121.70 41-27 Tee Zee118 1 1/4 School Bend118 9 Yargo113no Gave way 12
4Oct91- 6SA fst 6f :214 :453 1:112 Md 32000 4 9 128 1/2 119 1/2 1011 812 1/4 Cedeno E A Bb 118 127.80 66-18 Merry Kris Marge118no HonorBoy118 2 Arp118 1/2 5-wide stretch 12
Speed Index: Last Race: -32.0 1-Race Avg.: -32.0 1-Race Avg.: -32.0 Overall Avg.: -24.0
LATEST WORKOUTS Nov 24 SA 6f fst 1:151 H Nov 6 SA 5f fst 1:032 H Oct 19 SA 7f fst 1:293 H Oct 13 SA 6f fst 1:17 H

Bad Boy Butch Gr. g. 2(Mar), by P Vik—Very Much the Lady, by Zein Lifetime 1991 2 M 0 0
SORENSON D $32,000 Br.—Velasquez R & Lydia (Cal) 2 0 0 0
Own.—Sinardi-Velasquez-Wooley Tr.—Bean Robert A 117
16Nov91- 6Hol fst 6 1/2f :222 :451 1:181 [S]Md Sp Wt 3 7 87 1/2 812 79 1/2 69 3/4 Torres H5 LB 113 40.50 71-12 CeseFiring118hd OhioChrmr118no Potisimo118 1 3/4 Bumped start 8
17Oct91- 2SA fst 6f :214 :454 1:123 Md 32000 11 6 64 3/4 66 57 89 Torres H5 B 113 16.20 64-17 GeeMrcus118hd GrowingBold118 7 ThDroullr118nk Steadied 1/16 12
Speed Index: Last Race: (—) 3-Race Avg.: (—) 12-Race Avg.: (—) Overall Avg.: -18.0
LATEST WORKOUTS Nov 28 SA 3f fst :364 H Nov 7 SA 5f fst 1:022 H Nov 1 SA 5f fst 1:013 H Oct 14 SA 4f fst :474 H

One Tough Saros Dk. b. or br. g. 2(Jan), by Saros—Fran's Missy, by Bicker Lifetime 1991 2 M 0 0 $360
ATKINSON P $32,000 Br.—Holland & Holland (Cal) 2 0 0 0
Own.—Holland G O & Dolly Tr.—Manzi Dominick 117 $360
17Oct91- 2SA fst 6f :214 :454 1:123 Md 32000 7 10 86 1/4 76 1/4 68 78 Patton D B 118 78.70 65-17 GeeMarcus118hd GrowingBold118 7 TheDrouller118nk Wide trip 12
28Sep91- 4Fpx fst 6f :223 :463 1:121 [S]Md 32000 7 6 79 611 612 614 3/4 Ceballos O F 118 23.80 70-11 Poppysros118 8 CssnDvsn118nk MntHvn118 3 1/2 Lugged out early 7
Speed Index: Last Race: (—) 3-Race Avg.: (—) 12-Race Avg.: (—) Overall Avg.: -18.5
LATEST WORKOUTS Nov 29 Hol 4f fst :474 H Nov 24 Hol 5f fst 1:012 H Nov 18 Hol 6f fst 1:16 H Nov 13 Hol 6f fst 1:152 H

Polar Attraction B. c. 2(Jun), by Eskimo—Southern Blush, by Washington County Lifetime 1991 2 M 0 0
NAKATANI C S $32,000 Br.—Franks John (Fla) 2 0 0 0
Own.—Whispering Woods Farm Tr.—Van Berg Jack C 117
17Oct91- 2SA fst 6f :214 :454 1:123 Md 32000 5 8 128 1211 1013 1012 1/4 Stevens G L B 118 7.10 61-17 GeMrcus118hd GrowingBold118 7 ThDroullr118nk 6-wide stretch 12
14Sep91- 3AP sly 5 1/2f :231 :48 1:07 Md 35000 2 3 31 1/2 31 1/2 713 720 Pettinger D R 120 12.30 63-18 Bid120 6 1/2 M. T. Foyt120hd Distinct Leader120hd Gave way 9
Speed Index: Last Race: (—) 3-Race Avg.: (—) 12-Race Avg.: (—) Overall Avg.: -20.5
LATEST WORKOUTS Nov 28 Hol 7f fst 1:273 H Nov 13 Hol 5f fst 1:013 Hg Nov 6 Hol 5f fst 1:013 Hg Oct 30 Hol 5f fst 1:012 H

Episodic Dk. b. or br. c. 2(Feb), by Hail Bold King—Poopydoodle, by Don B Lifetime 1991 4 M 1 0 $6,100
MCCARRON C J $32,000 Br.—Shahan E H (Cal) 4 0 1 0
Own.—Shahan E H Tr.—Headley Bruce 117 $6,100
30Oct91- 6SA fst 1 1/16 :47 1:12 1:434 Md 28000 8 5 53 3/4 42 33 25 McCarron C J B 115 8.20 79-14 PssoGeno117 5 Episodic115nk CommndTheFire115 4 1/2 No match 12
14Oct91- 6SA fst 6f :213 :444 1:102 [S]Md 32000 6 7 65 3/4 67 1/2 59 1/2 411 1/4 Solis A Bb 118 2.80 72-12 USOfAmrc118 7 SchlBnd118 4 OrMntInT118 1/2 Wide backstretch 11
28Sep91- 4Fpx fst 6f :223 :463 1:121 [S]Md 32000 5 3 44 1/4 33 1/4 47 512 1/4 Flores D R b 118 *1.00 73-11 Poppysros118 8 CssiniDivision118nk MontHevn118 3 1/2 Rough trip 7
30Aug91- 4Dmr fst 6f :221 :454 1:113 [S]Md 32000 1 11 1010 75 3/4 63 1/4 57 1/2 Solis A Bb 117 5.70 73-15 MaterialEyes117 5 PmFlyer117 2 Bossnov112hd Off slowly, wide 11
Speed Index: Last Race: -7.0 1-Race Avg.: -7.0 1-Race Avg.: -7.0 Overall Avg.: -12.7
LATEST WORKOUTS Nov 22 SA 5f fst 1:012 H Nov 17 SA 5f fst 1:00 H Nov 12 SA 3f fst :374 H Oct 26 SA 4f fst :47 H

Cielo Caballo Dk. b. or br. c. 2(May), by Conquistador Cielo—Our Trudy, by Grounded II Lifetime 1991 1 M 0 0
VALENZUELA P A $32,000 Br.—Beasley-Parker-Kennelot Stbs (Ky) 1 0 0 0
Own.—Gatti R J Tr.—Lewis Craig A 117
13Nov91- 6Hol fst 5 1/2f :22 :45 1:031 Md 62500 6 12 1215 1216 1118 1023 1/4 Valenzuela P A Bb 118 39.10 74-14 ZfiroDelmr118 4 1/2 OkForest118 6 StrtgicPowr118 1 1/2 Broke slowly 12
Speed Index: Last Race: (—) 3-Race Avg.: (—) 12-Race Avg.: (—) Overall Avg.: -12.0
LATEST WORKOUTS Nov 5 SA 5f fst 1:02 H Oct 29 SA 4f fst :484 H Oct 22 SA 4f fst :491 H Oct 16 SA 3f fst :362 H

Caviar 'N Dreams Ch. g. 2(Feb), by Hail Bold King—Trouble On The Run, by Flying Pastor Lifetime 1991 10 M 2 2 $14,200
MARTINEZ F F $32,000 Br.—Cardiff Stud Farms (Cal) 10 0 2 2
Own.—Brewer-Byrd-Ensley Tr.—Byrd Adolph 112 5 $14,200
15Nov91- 4Hol fst 1 1/16 :481 1:124 1:452 Md 32000 6 12 1213 913 811 511 Berrio O A b 118 7.70 63-27 Tee Zee118 1 1/4 School Bend118 9 Yargo113no Broke slowly 12
30Oct91- 6SA fst 1 1/16 :47 1:12 1:434 Md 32000 3 12 118 1/2 85 1/2 65 3/4 49 3/4 Berrio O A Bb 117 7.30 74-14 PssoGno117 5 Epsdc115nk CmmndThFr115 4 1/2 Passed tired ones 12
16Oct91- 6SA fst 1 :464 1:112 1:382 Md 32000 6 9 811 78 1/4 66 33 3/4 Berrio O A b 117 11.70 71-23 MyMnSh117 2 1/2 PssGn117 1 1/2 Cvr'NDrms117 3 1/4 Broke out,bumped 10
3Oct91- 4SA fst 1 1/16 :471 1:121 1:452 Md 32000 8 9 89 58 43 1/2 33 Berrio O A Bb 117 7.10 73-21 CarpenterBill117no PassoGeno117 3 Cavir'NDrems117hd Rallied 9
19Sep91- 9Fpx fst 1 1/16 :47 1:13 1:454 Md Sp Wt 10 9 99 3/4 78 3/4 69 1/4 58 1/4 Alvarado F J b 118 22.00 71-21 Thinkernot118hd Sevengreenpairs113 4 Starwtcher118hd No bid 10
1Sep91- 9Dmr fst 1 :464 1:12 1:384 Md 32000 8 10 1011 68 53 1/4 2no Martinez F F5 b 111 36.20 72-17 Kurtcly116no Cvir'NDrems111 1 1/2 MyMnSho116 1 3/4 5-wide stretch 10
23Aug91- 6Dmr fst 7f :233 :454 1:252 Md 40000 9 4 44 44 1/2 810 914 Castanon A L Bb 117 46.00 59-18 SkyRider117 2 JonesIslnd117 1/2 NineDims117 1/2 Wide backstretch 10
8Aug91- 7LA fst 6 1/2f :223 :464 1:183 Md 32000 7 8 54 1/2 55 35 26 1/4 Scott J M Bb 118 10.90 75-11 Maknit119 6 1/4 Cavir'NDrems118 2 HenryTheFox118 1/2 Well placed 10
25Jly91- 6Dmr fst 6f :222 :461 1:113 [S]Md 32000 12 8 105 3/4 98 1/4 810 814 1/4 Torres H5 Bb 112 30.70 67-17 ApcheTlismn117 1 3/4 FxNws117 6 GnitsocMiRglob117 1 3/4 Wide trip 12
11Jly91- 4Hol fst 6f :221 :453 1:122 Md 50000 11 11 1113 1112 1111 86 3/4 Berrio O A Bb 117 74.60 71-16 El Anelo117 2 NineDimes117nk LaMota117nk Wide backstretch 12
Speed Index: Last Race: -10.0 3-Race Avg.: -9.3 6-Race Avg.: -8.8 Overall Avg.: -11.9
LATEST WORKOUTS Nov 23 Hol 5f fst 1:011 H Nov 9 Hol 5f fst 1:013 H Oct 26 Hol 4f fst :493 H Oct 12 Hol 4f fst :49 H

Luisillo B. c. 2(Apr), by Morning Bob—Bubble Burster, by Effervescing Lifetime 1991 1 M 0 0 $1,200
DELAHOUSSAYE E $32,000 Br.—Farnsworth Fms & M & M Bloodstock (Fla) 1 0 0 0
Own.—Achar V Tr.—Lopez Patricia 117 $1,200
17Oct91- 2SA fst 6f :214 :454 1:123 Md 32000 8 5 108 1/4 109 3/4 810 47 1/4 Valenzuela P A B 118 12.00 66-17 GeeMarcus118hd GrowingBold118 7 TheDrouller118nk Wide trip 12
Speed Index: Last Race: (—) 3-Race Avg.: (—) 12-Race Avg.: (—) Overall Avg.: -17.0
LATEST WORKOUTS Nov 26 SA 7f fst 1:302 H Nov 21 SA 3f fst :354 H Nov 16 SA 6f fst 1:142 H Nov 10 SA 5f fst 1:024 H

Joanie's Prince Dk. b. or br. g. 2(Mar), by Ginistrelli—Joanie's Hunch, by Giboulee Lifetime 1991 3 M 0 0 $180
BERRIO O A $28,000 Br.—Falken Stable (Ky) 3 0 0 0
Own.—Mayer & Moore Tr.—Martinez Rafael A 115 $180
15Nov91- 4Hol fst 1 1/16 :481 1:124 1:452 Md 32000 5 8 88 1/4 79 1/4 710 712 1/4 Fuentes J A5 LB 113 82.90 62-27 Tee Zee118 1 1/4 School Bend118 9 Yargo113no Drifted out 7/8 12
21Sep91- 6Fpx fst 6f :221 :462 1:13 Md 32000 2 3 810 814 811 712 3/4 Martinez F F5 B 113 23.30 68-14 Rth'sVlntn118 4 Spot'sScrt113nk Poppysros118 2 Bolted 1st turn 10
6Sep91- 2Dmr gd 6f :223 :463 1:121 Md 45000 8 9 1216 1217 1115 1117 1/4 Alvarado F J B 115 58.70 61-18 Chief Snow117 1 1/2 WearsBuzzy117 3 LittleChester117 3 Wide trip 12
Speed Index: Last Race: -11.0 1-Race Avg.: -11.0 1-Race Avg.: -11.0 Overall Avg.: -16.6
LATEST WORKOUTS Oct 31 Hol 5f fst 1:013 H Oct 10 Hol 5f fst 1:02 H

Colonial Time B. c. 2(Mar), by Pleasant Colony—Green Magazine, by Green Forest Lifetime 1991 5 M 0 0 $3,600
FLORES D R $32,000 Br.—Evans T M (Ky) 5 0 0 0
Own.—Buckland Farm Tr.—Speckert Christopher 117 $3,600
15Nov91- 4Hol fst 1 1/16 :481 1:124 1:452 Md 32000 4 6 55 44 46 1/2 410 1/4 Flores D R Bb 118 22.00 64-27 Tee Zee118 1 1/4 School Bend118 9 Yargo113no Mild bid 12
16Oct91- 6SA fst 1 :464 1:112 1:382 Md 28000 5 7 75 1/2 88 1/4 89 1/4 69 Nakatani C S Bb 115 18.40 66-23 MyManShoe117 2 1/2 PssoGeno117 1 1/2 Cvir'NDrems117 3 1/4 Gave way 10

20Oct91- 6SA fst 1 :464 1:111 1:382 Md Sp Wt 6 7 88½ 67 67½ 610½ Solis A B 117 39.90 64-15 RngdKing117hdCoco'sMinMn1172½CurrntRcption1173½ No bid 8
25Sep91- 6Dmr fst 1 :454 1:102 1:363 Md Sp Wt 4 7 714 714 711 413 Solis A B 116 20.90 70-17 Natural Nine1166½ Thinkernot1164 Canal1162½ No bid 7
3Aug91- 6Dmr fst 6f :213 :443 1:103 Md Sp Wt 2 10 1019 1016 1017 715½ Davenport C L5 B 112 85.90 70-11 StrRcruit117noCpotMgiqu1172Thinkrnot1172½ Off very slowly 10
Speed Index: Last Race: -9.0 3-Race Avg.: -13.6 4-Race Avg.: -13.5 Overall Avg.: -14.6
LATEST WORKOUTS Nov 26 SA 4f fst :504 H Nov 12 SA 4f fst :484 H Nov 7 SA 5f fst 1:014 H Nov 1 SA 5f fst 1:022 H

Dick's Prospect Ch. c. 2(Feb), by Allen's Prospect—Bletcha Lass, by Bletchingly Lifetime 1991 3 M 0 0 $2,460
DESORMEAUX K J $32,000 Br.—Paulsen A E (Ky) 117 3 0 0 0
Own.—Paulsen A E Tr.—Lundy Richard J $2,460
21Nov91- 2Hol fst 6f :22 :454 1:11 Md 32000 10 8 128½ 109 88¾ 410½ Desormeaux K J B 118 14.40 74-12 Cndoslew1181½GrndAdvntur118nkThLstThruwy1189 Wide trip 12
16Sep91- 5Fpx fst 6f :221 :462 1:123 Md 32000 7 8 79½ 77½ 56½ 46 Torres H5 B 113 4.80 77-12 LaMota1183RemrkbleWill1181JeffKing1182 Bumped at break 9
1Sep91- 6Dmr fst 6f :214 :442 1:084 Md Sp Wt 3 5 1119 1118 1118 724¾ Torres H B 117 40.10 70-08 Bag11716FabulousPosition117¾Starwtcher1172 6-wide stretch 11
Speed Index: Last Race: (—) 3-Race Avg.: (—) 12-Race Avg.: (—) Overall Avg.: -15.6
LATEST WORKOUTS Nov 18 SA 5f fst 1:04 H Nov 13 SA 6f fst 1:162 H Nov 3 SA 5f fst 1:022 H Oct 29 SA 4f fst :52 H

Also Eligible (Not in Post Position Order):

The Last Thruway Ch. g. 2(Feb), by Kris S—Thruway, by Clem Lifetime 1991 3 M 1 1 $5,600
MCCARRON C J $32,000 Br.—Meadowbrook Farms Inc (Fla) 117 3 0 1 1
Own.—Meadowbrook Farms Inc Tr.—La Croix David $5,600
21Nov91- 2Hol fst 6f :22 :454 1:11 Md 32000 11 2 3½ 31½ 21 31½ McCarron C J Lb 118 *1.60 83-12 Cndoslw1181½GrndAdvntur118nkThLstThrwy1189 Outfinished 12
31Oct91- 4SA fst 6f :213 :452 1:11 Md 32000 7 4 51½ 52½ 21 22¾ Frontiere V S5 LBb 113 129.00 78-13 RooTl1182¾ThLstThruwy1131½FlyngBlprnt1181½ Bumped 5/16 12
31Jly91- 6Dmr gd 6f :22 :461 1:113 Md 50000 10 10 89 810 1018 1024½ Nakatani C S Bb 117 28.80 57-20 OcnNt-Mx11711LttlChstr1172½CmmndThFr1174 Broke slowly 12
Speed Index: Last Race: (—) 3-Race Avg.: (—) 12-Race Avg.: (—) Overall Avg.: -12.3
LATEST WORKOUTS Nov 17 Hol 4f fst :494 H Nov 10 Hol 5f fst 1:042 H ●Oct 25 Hol 6f fst 1:15 H Oct 19 Hol 5f fst 1:022 H

Hunters Arrow Gr. c. 2(Feb), by Mr Paul—Buffalark, by Buffalo Lark Lifetime 1991 3 M 0 0
BERRIO O A $28,000 Br.—Elkins H (Cal) 115 3 0 0 0
Own.—Leschi A N Tr.—Donato Robert A
21Nov91- 2Hol fst 6f :22 :454 1:11 Md 28000 3 9 107¾ 1111 1012 1019½ Castanon A L LBb 116 17.00 65-12 Cndoslw1181½GrndAdvntur118nkThLstThrwy1189 Bumped 1/2 12
17Oct91- 2SA fst 6f :214 :454 1:123 Md 28000 4 4 76½ 55 46½ 67¾ Castanon A L Bb 116 76.70 65-17 GeMrcus118hdGrowingBold1187ThDroulr118nk No late punch 12
5Jly91- 4Hol fst 5½f :222 :451 1:051 Md 28000 11 1 108¾ 107½ 1012 911¾ Soto J F5 110 82.20 75-10 FntstcPr1174½GntscMRlb117½CrpntrBll1172 Wide backstretch 11
Speed Index: Last Race: (—) 3-Race Avg.: (—) 12-Race Avg.: (—) Overall Avg.: -18.6
LATEST WORKOUTS Nov 15 SA 5f fst 1:00 H Nov 4 SA 3f fst :353 H Oct 25 SA 3f fst :351 H Oct 10 SA 5f fst 1:014 Hg

Mid Stretch Dk. b. or br. c. 2(May), by Romeo—Grecian Mid-Ar, by Snow Ball Lifetime 1991 3 M 0 0 $396
PEDROZA M A $32,000 Br.—Braam J R (Cal) 117 3 0 0 0
Own.—Braam J R Tr.—West Ted $396
22Nov91- 4Hol fst 7½f :223 :453 1:293 Md 45000 2 10 1111 1113 1112 1117½ Alvarado F J LB 116 27.00 — — Hudlam'sSidekick1187BlinkingLights118hdChapar118½ Outrun 11
2Nov91- 9TuP gd 6f :22 :46 1:132 Md Sp Wt 5 3 75¾ 77¾ 77½ 41¾ Jauregui L H 120 5.00 71-17 R.AndE.'sG.P.1201DmndMor120nkFirstCond120½ With interest 8
20Oct91- 6TuP fst 6f :214 :443 1:102 Md Sp Wt 8 10 87¾ 911 88¾ 48 Jauregui L H 120 15.90 80-11 Rider1204HighStorm1201OfficeExchequr1203 Squeezed break 12
Speed Index: Last Race: (—) 3-Race Avg.: (—) 12-Race Avg.: (—) Overall Avg.: -10.5
LATEST WORKOUTS Nov 19 SA 3f fst :371 H Nov 13 TuP 3f fst :344 H Oct 31 TuP 3f sl :382 H Oct 17 TuP 4f fst :48 H

Dubious Dancer Ch. g. 2(Feb), by Dance in Time—Rose Du Soir, by Dewan Lifetime 1991 7 M 0 2 $8,765
SOLIS A $32,000 Br.—Freeman S (Cal) 117 7 0 0 2
Own.—Freeman Annetta Tr.—Stute Melvin F $8,765
22Nov91- 4Hol fst 7½f :223 :453 1:293 Md 50000 6 2 33 33 54 510 Solis A B 118 6.70 — — Hudlm'sSidkick1187BlnkngLghts118hdChpr118½ Bumped start 11
30Oct91- 4SA fst 6f :212 :45 1:102 [S]Md 32000 9 1 55¾ 47 47 37 Solis A B 118 *2.50 77-14 HppyDydrem1184½ThDroulr118¾DubiousDncr1181 No threat 9
11Oct91- 6SA fst 6f :214 :45 1:102 Md 50000 5 7 75 75¾ 67 610½ Flores D R Bb 118 12.00 73-16 SouthrnWish118½OkForst118nkKrmChrm118no 5-wide stretch 12
27Sep91- 9Fpx fst 6f :221 :46 1:12 [S]Md Sp Wt 9 5 44 45 45 46 Castanon A L Bb 118 14.00 80-14 SimpleKing1132Bckbrd'sGhost1182PwderPrnc1182 Evenly 10
13Sep91- 9Fpx fst 6½f :22 :461 1:184 [S]Md Sp Wt 10 4 31½ 44½ 45½ 35½ Flores D R Bb 118 3.20 76-13 PowrSlyd1133½PrncJnstr1182DubiousDncr118¾ 4-wide stretch 10
28Jly91- 4Dmr fst 5½f :213 :451 1:043 [S]Md Sp Wt 10 2 52½ 53 76½ 710½ Pedroza M A Bb 117 17.00 81-11 [illegible]Dr.Agst117nkSorrowfSn117nkBckbrd'sGhst117nk Faltered 10
21Jly91-10Hol fst 5½f :214 :452 1:034 Md Sp Wt 12 5 63½ 64 57½ 610 Torres H5 B 112 114.40 84-14 Ovrstock1173PoliticlRlly1171½Spdbr117¾ Wide backstretch 12
Speed Index: Last Race: (—) 3-Race Avg.: (—) 12-Race Avg.: (—) Overall Avg.: [illegible]
LATEST WORKOUTS Nov 29 Hol 4f fst :48 H ●Nov 19 Hol 4f fst :472 H Nov 12 Hol 4f fst :482 H ●Nov 6 SA 4f fst :471 H

Badger Bay The pace contention point says he's an automatic throw-out.

Bad Boy Butch Dropping from maiden special weight to maiden claimer, but he's already lost (badly) at this level. Remember, the elevator only goes in one direction in maiden races: down. It doesn't magically change direction. No stretch-out potential, either. Elimination.

One Tough Saros Lost twice already at this level. Using the six-furlong time from his last race, he projects to be far behind the win par of 1:12.31. Out.

Polar Attraction Looks identical to One Tough Saros. Elimination.

Episodic Really took to the route last out and fits the model snugly. Even though he's lost at this level four times, at least he's showing some improvement. Mild contender on the strength of his last line.

Cielo Caballo Not much going for him. Toss out.

Luisillo Don't be fooled by this one. Even though he rallied in the stretch in a sprint, he won't even see a sniff of the pace in today's route. Remember, the preferred stretch-out pattern is an even sort of run, not one king-hell finish. Elimination.

Joanie's Prince Field filler. Out.

Colonial Time Doesn't fit the model, yet showed some signs of life last out, actually tracking the pace more closely than in any of his other races. Use his last line.

Dick's Prospect Not the proper stretch-out pattern. Elimination.

The Last Thruway Very even with the pace in his last race, a sprint, so stretching out shouldn't be a problem. His rapid sprint fractions fit well within the model and put him right on the lead, exactly where he needs to be in order to win this maiden race for two-year-olds. Contender. Rate him off the sprint performance of his last race.

Hunters Arrow Very dull. Very little chance.

We've got a classic case of the lone front runner in a paceless field. Sprinters stretching out after showing even mild early speed always figure to contest or set the pace in the route, especially at this level. The Last Thruway has been right on some brisk fractions in his shorter races. Not one of his rivals figures to be able to go with him early. Toss in the fact that the race is for maidens and two-year-olds, and the case for The Last Thruway is closed. Maidens are honest. They run one way. They rarely change position. Two-year-olds are loath to be rated. They don't yet know how to close strongly. Look at ALL-IN-ONE's Speed/ Pace Summary and Pace Graph. The Last Thruway's domination early in the race is unmistakable. He figures to be almost six lengths clear of the field after four furlongs and three lengths ahead after six furlongs. ALL-IN-ONE's Betting Line reflects this

```
1DEC91                              HOL                    8.5 furlongs dirt
Race #2                                                          12 starters
MCL                                                      Age: 2 years, Male
```

```
------------------------------INPUT DATA-----------------------------------
            #   #   #   #   $'S                          1st C  2nd C  Final
Horse name  ST  W   P   S   Earned Date   Trk Dist. S    time   time   time
---------------------------------------------------------------------------
Episodic    0   0   0   0     0 30OCT91 SA  8.500 D  47.0  112.0  143.4
Colonial Time  0 0  0   0     0 15NOV91 HOL 8.500 D  48.1  112.4  145.2
The Last Thruway 0 0 0  0     0 21NOV91 HOL 6.000 D  22.0   45.4  111.0
```

```
                              1st C  2nd C  Final
Horse name        Class Lvl   B.L.   B.L.   B.L.    SR    Var
------------------------------------------------------------------
Episodic          MCL         3.75   2.00   5.00    79    14
Colonial Time     MCL         5.00   4.00  10.00    64    27
The Last Thruway  MCL         0.50   1.50   1.50    83    12
```

```
----------------------------BETTING LINE-----------------------------------
                  -------Rankings--------         Betting   Fair    Fair
Horse name        PEH H-I THAAI P-H ESP  Rating   Line    Place $ Show $
-------------------------------------------------------------------------
The Last Thruway   1   2   2    1   2    89.84    2-1      3.80    2.80
Episodic           2   1   1    2   1    78.24    4-1
Colonial Time      3   3   3    3   3    61.80
```

```
----------------------------EXACTA GRID------------------------------------
              |The Last Thruwa|  Episodic  |
--------------+---------------+-------------+
The Last Thruw|  . . . . . . .|   19    47  |
              |  . . . . . . .|            |
              |  . . . . . . .|            |
--------------+---------------+-------------+
Episodic      |    23    56   |  . . . . . .|
              |               |  . . . . . .|
              |               |  . . . . . .|
--------------+---------------+-------------+
```

```
----------------------------SPEED/PACE SUMMARY-----------------------------
Race Profile:    47.68  112.31  145.91   Winners' Pace Profile: EARLY
Ability Par:     96.95                    Pace Contention Point:  2.22 lengths

Projected Times:                         Ability Balance  Last  Proj  Con-
                 1st C   2nd C   Fin C    Time    Time     Frac  Pace  tender
--------------------------------------------------------------------------
The Last Thruway 47.30  112.57  145.87   97.84  103.52   33.30  FRONT  Y
Episodic         48.59  113.10* 146.33   97.60  103.35   33.24  MID    N
Colonial Time    49.16  113.55* 147.43   97.95  104.23   33.87  LATE   N
```

```
------------------------------PACE GRAPH------------------------------------
       Profile:               47.68          112.31           145.91
       Front Runner:          47.30          112.57           145.87
Horse name                     1C             2C                 F
The Last Thruway -------------------X --------------(--X ----------------X
Episodic         -----------X--------+ -------------X--+ ------------X-+
Colonial Time    ---------X--------+ ------------X-(--+ ----------X------+
```

superiority. It recognized that The Last Thruway was the only horse advantaged by fitting the win profile and being well within the Pace Contention Point at the second call. The Last Thruway's commanding lead early should be enough to put away this field of gutless young maidens who give up if they're not on the lead and don't yet know how to close. ALL-IN-ONE's Betting Line translates the Speed/Pace Summary's logic into an elegant expression of value:

The Last Thruway 2-to-1
Episodic 4-to-1

Recognizing his awesome early pace advantage, ALL-IN-ONE ranked The Last Thruway a strong top pick at 2-to-1. Episodic was rated at 4-to-1, and Colonial Time was given no chance. Let's examine the morning line and actual closing odds to see if there are any bet-downs:

Horse	Morning Line	Public Line
Badger Bay	30	80
Bad Boy Butch	30	40
One Tough Saros	30	70
Polar Attraction	30	7
Episodic	8–5	6–5
Cielo Caballo	20	9
Luisillo	8	11
Joanie's Prince	30	60
Colonial Time	5	16
Dick's Prospect	6	14
The Last Thruway	7–2	5–2
Hunter's Arrow	30	99

Considering the advantage held by bet-downs in maiden races, only Polar Attraction, Episodic, Cielo Caballo, and The Last Thruway deserve our attention. Episodic is an underlay, and a vulnerable favorite in terms of position at the first call. ALL-IN-ONE considers The Last Thruway a fair bet at 2-to-1. He's going off at 5-to-2. This is a positive expectation play. In fact, it's the best of both worlds: a bet-down that's also an overlay. From a win-betting standpoint, this is an extremely easy race.

Incidentally, Kitts was at the track and made a nice score on the early daily double. The key to it was, of course, the sweet overlay on Callide Valley in the first. Kitts didn't use a rigorous mathematical overlay-finding approach to determine what the fair daily double price should have been. He simply asked the question: How can I make money from this race? He knew beforehand that the second race would be no bargain in terms of a win overlay (it turned out that it actually was); however, he did know about the dominance of front runners in maiden races. (Especially in routes for two-year-olds.) The daily double from the huge overlay Callide Valley in the first race to the probable (lone) front runner in the second race was an excellent bet. All he did then was identify which horse would be on the lead in the second race. It was The Last Thruway. Kitts was rewarded handsomely: the two-dollar daily double paid $130.60.

SECOND RACE
Hollywood
DECEMBER 1, 1991

1$\frac{1}{16}$ MILES. (1.40) MAIDEN CLAIMING. Purse $17,000. 2-year-olds. Weight, 117 lbs. Claiming price $32,000; if for $28,000 allowed 2 lbs.

Value of race $17,000; value to winner $9,350; second $3,400; third $2,550; fourth $1,275; fifth $425. Mutuel pool $277,048. Exacta pool $301,836.

Last Raced	Horse	M/Eqt.	A.Wt	PP	St	¼	½	¾	Str	Fin	Jockey	Cl'g Pr	Odds $1
21Nov91 ^{2}Hol^{3}	The Last Thruway	LBb	2 117	11	1	$1^{1\frac{1}{2}}$	$1^{1\frac{1}{2}}$	$1^{1\frac{1}{2}}$	1^{2}	$1^{2\frac{1}{2}}$	Pincay L Jr	32000	2.90
16Nov91 ^{6}Hol^{6}	Bad Boy Butch	LB	2 117	2	4	4^{1}	$4^{2\frac{1}{2}}$	$3^{\frac{1}{2}}$	$2^{1\frac{1}{2}}$	$2^{3\frac{1}{2}}$	Sorenson D	32000	40.40
15Nov91 ^{4}Hol^{4}	Colonial Time	Bb	2 117	9	11	$11^{1\frac{1}{2}}$	9^{1}	5^{1}	$4^{1\frac{1}{2}}$	$3^{2\frac{1}{2}}$	Flores D R	32000	16.50
17Oct91 ^{2}SA^{10}	Polar Attraction	LBb	2 117	4	5	$3^{1\frac{1}{2}}$	2^{hd}	2^{1}	$3^{\frac{1}{2}}$	$4^{2\frac{3}{4}}$	Nakatani C S	32000	7.60
15Nov91 ^{4}Hol^{12}	Badger Bay	Bb	2 115	1	7	$7^{1\frac{1}{2}}$	8^{hd}	7^{hd}	7^{2}	5^{nk}	Alvarado F J	28000	89.10
15Nov91 ^{4}Hol^{7}	Joanie's Prince	LB	2 115	8	3	$5^{1\frac{1}{2}}$	5^{hd}	4^{2}	5^{2}	$6^{2\frac{3}{4}}$	Berrio O A	28000	61.10
17Oct91 ^{2}SA^{4}	Luisillo		2 117	7	8	9^{hd}	12	12	$8^{2\frac{1}{2}}$	7^{nk}	DelhoussyeE	32000	11.40
17Oct91 ^{2}SA^{7}	One Tough Saros	B	2 117	3	10	$8^{2\frac{1}{2}}$	6^{2}	$6^{3\frac{1}{2}}$	$6^{1\frac{1}{2}}$	8^{6}	Atkinson P	32000	79.60
21Nov91 ^{2}Hol^{4}	Dick's Prospect	B	2 117	10	6	$6^{1\frac{1}{2}}$	7^{1}	8^{1}	9^{3}	$9^{3\frac{1}{2}}$	DesormuxKJ	32000	14.20
30Oct91 ^{6}SA^{2}	Episodic	B	2 117	5	12	12	$11^{2\frac{1}{2}}$	$10^{1\frac{1}{2}}$	$10^{3\frac{1}{2}}$	10^{7}	McCarron CJ	32000	1.20
21Nov91 ^{2}Hol^{10}	Hunters Arrow	LBb	2 115	12	2	$2^{\frac{1}{2}}$	$3^{1\frac{1}{2}}$	9^{hd}	12	11no	Castanon J L	28000	113.80
13Nov91 ^{6}Hol^{10}	Cielo Caballo	Bb	2 117	6	9	10^{hd}	$10^{1\frac{1}{2}}$	$11^{1\frac{1}{2}}$	$11^{\frac{1}{2}}$	12	ValenzuelPA	32000	9.40

OFF AT 1:03. Start good. Won driving. Time, :23 , :47 , 1:12^{1}, 1:38^{2}, 1:45^{1} Track fast.

$2 Mutuel Prices:			
11–THE LAST THRUWAY	7.80	5.00	4.40
2–BAD BOY BUTCH		28.60	18.40
9–COLONIAL TIME			7.20

$2 EXACTA 11–2 PAID $332.80.

We've won the first two races, and our running profit/loss is plus $31.60.

Major Launch Classic sucker horse. Four second-place finishes in a row. Nine races in all, six times a bridesmaid. However, he does fit the profile, and his running style is advantaged. Obviously, use his last line.

Penrod Mild bid in his first time at the route, finishing within three lengths of Major Launch. Small chance, but comes from too far out of it to be a strong contender. Use last race for paceline.

Our Genius Improving for Whittingham, but why did they risk losing him in a maiden claimer? Tough call, but the current improvement outweighs the loss in the maiden claimer, and he shows the gradual progression of the typical Whittingham maiden. Contender. Rate him off the Oct. 9 race.

Deduction Automatic elimination on the basis of a no-win jockey.

3rd Hollywood

1 1-16MILES
HOLLYWOOD PARK
FINISH ▲ ▲ START

1 1/16 MILES. (1.40) MAIDEN. Purse $30,000. 3-year-olds and upward. Weights, 3-year-olds, 117 lbs.; older, 121 lbs.

LASIX—Deduction, Terrific Trip, Gas Man, Reno City.

Major Launch Gr. g. 3(Mar), by Relaunch—Gamberta, by Roberto
PINCAY L JR Br.—Cabin Creek Farm (Ky) 117 Lifetime 9 0 6 1 $36,700 1991 7 M 5 0 $27,600 1990 2 M 1 1 $9,100
Own.—Summa Stable Tr.—Cross Richard J
20Nov91- 6Hol fst 1 1/16 :464 1:112 1:432 3↑Md Sp Wt 7 5 54½ 53 74¼ 31 Pincay L Jr B 118 3.60 83-16 DQ El Travieso118¾ Alybenbo118nk MajorLaunch118¾ Wide bid 9
20Nov91-Placed second through disqualification
1Nov91- 2BM fst 1 1/16 :48 1:122 1:442 3↑Md Sp Wt 2 3 42½ 43½ 33½ 21½ Baze R A B 118 *.90 73-18 AlwaysKris1181½MajorLunch118¾SkyGenerl1185 Wide stretch 8
30Aug91- 6Dmr fst 1 1/16 :463 1:112 1:431 3↑Md Sp Wt 8 5 52½ 31 31 22 Nakatani C S Bb 117 3.70 83-18 RghtBrght1172MjorLnch117¾VctryPrk1171½ Wide to far turn 12
16Aug91- 6Dmr fst 1 1/16 :46 1:11 1:431 3↑Md Sp Wt 6 4 58 43½ 31½ 2no Solis A Bb 117 25.60 85-16 Rum Isle117noMajorLaunch1172¾HotDate1171½ Checked 6 1/2 12
3Aug91- 4Dmr fst 6f :22 :45 1:102 3↑Md Sp Wt 5 7 1013 1110 99¼ 89 McCarron C J Bb 116 3.50 78-11 FvortPth116nkBordrRun1162¾Mr.Lovbl116½ Wide backstretch 12
6Jly91- 6Hol fst 6½f :221 :444 1:162 3↑Md Sp Wt 2 3 41½ 64¾ 34½ 24 Delahoussaye E Bb 116 5.70 86-11 Consultant1164MajorLunch116½NeverSubtle116½ Bumped 1/4 9
14Jun91- 6Hol fst 1 1/16 :462 1:104 1:424 3↑Md Sp Wt 10 7 99½ 1014 1015 1014½ Santos J A Bb 115 8.70 72-13 For Sure122nk Majestic Twoeleven115¾ Medium Cool115hd 10
14Jun91-Reared break, lugged out
2Dec90- 3Hol fst 6½f :214 :443 1:17 Md Sp Wt 6 6 67¾ 56 44½ 33 McCarron C J b 118 *1.20 87-09 CoastalCondo118hdBrronNijinsky1183MjorLunch118¾ Greenly 9
12Nov90- 6Hol fst 6½f :214 :444 1:163 Md Sp Wt 9 7 76¾ 67 57 26½ McCarron C J Bb 119 7.90 85-11 CienFuegos1196½MjorLunch1191¾TrucFlg119hd 4-wide stretch 11
Speed Index: Last Race: -1.0 3-Race Avg.: -3.0 5-Race Avg.: -4.6 Overall Avg.: -5.0
LATEST WORKOUTS Nov 28 Hol 3f fst :361 H Nov 12 Hol 5f fst 1:012 H Nov 8 Hol 3f fst :372 H

Penrod Dk. b. or br. c. 3(Apr), by Mr Prospector—Batucada, by Roman Line
SOLIS A Br.—Robinson J M (Ky) 117 Lifetime 2 0 0 0 1991 2 M 0 0 1990 0 M 0 0
Own.—Paulson A E Tr.—Lundy Richard J
20Nov91- 6Hol fst 1 1/16 :464 1:112 1:432 3↑Md Sp Wt 6 6 711 77 64½ 74 Solis A B 118 15.20 80-16 DQ El Travieso118¾ Alybenbo118nk Major Launch118¾ Mild bid 9
31Oct91- 6SA fst 6f :213 :441 1:084 3↑Md Sp Wt 6 7 713 615 511 611½ Solis A B 117 5.40 81-13 Sinag117½ Alybenbo1171½ Ivyleaguer1174½ Broke awkwardly 8
Speed Index: Last Race: -4.0 1-Race Avg.: -4.0 1-Race Avg.: -4.0 Overall Avg.: -5.0
LATEST WORKOUTS Nov 29 SA 3f fst :384 H Nov 24 SA 4f fst :494 H Nov 18 SA 3f fst :354 H Oct 26 SA 4f fst :474 Hg

Our Genius Ch. g. 3(Mar), by Greinton—Be Along, by Berzoi
MCCARRON C J Br.—Fishback W D & BWW Syndicate (Ky) 117 Lifetime 6 0 1 2 $13,900 1991 6 M 1 2 $13,900 1990 0 M 0 0 Turf 1 0 0 0
Own.—Bradley-Bradley(Lse)-Wynne Tr.—Whittingham Charles
8Nov91- 6SA fst 1 :472 1:123 1:382 3↑Md Sp Wt 3 5 53 63½ 32 31½ Stevens G L b 117 2.70 73-26 Standard1171½ El Travieso117hd Our Genius117nk Brushed 1/8 9
9Oct91- 6SA fst 1 1/16 :462 1:11 1:431 3↑Md Sp Wt 8 8 76¾ 56½ 45 33½ Stevens G L b 117 3.30 83-15 Flytorio1171½ El Travieso1172 Our Genius117½ 4-wide stretch 8
23Aug91- 9Dmr fst 6f :214 :45 1:11 3↑Md 50000 5 10 910 97½ 55 22¾ Stevens G L Bb 117 5.40 81-18 Somebt1172¾OurGnius1171¾BusyCircuits1152 12
23Aug91-Broke slowly, 5-wide into lane
5Jun91- 8Hol fm 1 1/16 Ⓣ:471 1:104 1:41 Alw 35000 4 6 66½ 89½ 89½ 816¾ Santos J A b 115 *1.30e 73-10 Heavy Rain1191 TruceFlag1153½TidyColony110½ Broke slowly 8
19May91- 3Hol fst 1 1/16 :47 1:112 1:423 3↑Md Sp Wt 4 7 75½ 73¾ 59½ 59½ Santos J A Bb 115 3.80e 78-10 KngTrk1151¾Prospctor'sRdg1153½MjstcTwlvn1151¾ Wide trip 9
6Apr91- 4SA fst 6½f :22 :443 1:164 Md Sp Wt 2 11 1118 1113 913 913¾ Santos J A 118 4.70e 73-13 Future Force1181 Mandon1183½ Mr. Melair118½ Rank early 11
Speed Index: Last Race: -1.0 3-Race Avg.: -5.0 3-Race Avg.: -5.0 Overall Avg.: -7.8
LATEST WORKOUTS Nov 25 Hol 6f fst 1:142 H Nov 19 Hol 5f fst 1:023 H Nov 14 Hol 3f fst :363 H Nov 6 SA 5f fst 1:02 H

Deduction B. c. 3(May), by Damascus—Resume, by Reviewer
SORENSON D Br.—Hancock A (Ky) 117 Lifetime 6 0 0 0 1991 5 M 0 0 1990 1 M 0 0
Own.—Lewis R B & Beverly Tr.—Veiga Frank
8Nov91- 6SA fst 1 :472 1:123 1:382 3↑Md Sp Wt 7 6 63½ 42 64¾ 75¾ Sorenson D LB 117 78.10 69-26 Standard1171½ El Travieso117hd Our Genius117nk No rally 9
30Mar91- 6SA fst 1 1/16 :471 1:112 1:423 Md Sp Wt 9 10 96½ 1211 1114 1120 Patton D B LB 117 194.40 70-07 Navarone1172 Worry Free1174 El Travieso1172¾ Wide 1/2 12
2Mar91- 6SA my 1 1/16 :483 1:133 1:461 Md Sp Wt 1 10 99½ 1010 911 812½ Sorenson D LB 117 104.60 59-28 Kng'sCnyon117¾BndngBck1173½NrthFrvr1173½ 5-wide stretch 11
10Feb91- 6SA fst 6½f :221 :451 1:162 Md Sp Wt 9 6 62½ 84½ 1013 1022½ Pincay L Jr LBb 118 29.00 66-18 Warfield118¾WhatAProspect1181¾MjesticClss118¾ Wide early 11
19Jan91- 6SA fst 1 1/16 :462 1:112 1:432 Md Sp Wt 7 4 5¾ 1112 1120 1234½ Velasquez J Bb 117 22.70 51-09 Conveyor1174 Interdance1171¾PoliticalAnimal1171 5-wide 7/8 12
3Dec90- 4Hol fst 6f :223 :46 1:101 Md Sp Wt 5 6 74½ 78½ 711 717 Santos J A B 119 4.20 72-08 BlueNeon1193PrfctlyProud1192WhtAProspct1191 Wide early 7
Speed Index: Last Race: -5.0 3-Race Avg.: -13.6 4-Race Avg.: -20.2 Overall Avg.: -20.8
LATEST WORKOUTS Nov 28 SA 3f fst :36 H Nov 23 SA 1 fst 1:431 H Nov 3 SA 5f fst 1:001 Hg Oct 26 SA 6f fst 1:133 Hg

Terrific Trip Dk. b. or br. c. 3(Feb), by Flying Paster—Quiet Flight, by Wing Out
FLORES D R Br.—Friendly E (Cal) 117 Lifetime 8 0 3 1 $20,675 1991 3 M 2 0 $9,775 1990 5 M 1 1 $10,900
Own.—Friendly E Tr.—Sadler John W
7Nov91- 6SA fst 6½f :22 :444 1:171 3↑Md 50000 11 3 52½ 42½ 42 21½ Flores D R LBb 118 *1.90 83-18 Stlvoy1181½TrrificTrip1181½Prospctor'sRidg1131½ Good effort 11
16Oct91- 4SA fst 6f :214 :444 1:10 3↑SMd 50000 4 4 22 21½ 21½ 2hd Flores D R LBb 117 2.70 86-12 MidnightSnow117hdTerrificTrip1174MacA'Wr1174½ Sharp try 9
31Aug91- 6Dmr fst 6f :22 :451 1:10 3↑Md Sp Wt 6 2 42 41½ 42½ 45¾ Flores D R LBb 117 11.40 83-13 Border Run1171¾ Mr. Lovable1171 Stalvoy1173 Weakened 9
3Oct90- 6SA fst 1 :452 1:102 1:371 Md Sp Wt 8 3 1hd 3nk 56½ 814 Valenzuela P A LBb 117 *2.30 67-15 Deputy Meister1171¾ Jet OfGold1171¾Conveyor117no Used up 10
12Sep90- 8Dmr fst 1 :461 1:101 1:352 Dmr Fut 11 10 96½ 1111 1118 1124½ Baze R A Bb 115 57.00 64-14 Best Pal1203½ Pillaring116hd Got To Fly1176 Bumped 7 1/2 11
12Sep90-Grade II
19Aug90- 2Dmr fst 1 :46 1:102 1:362 Md Sp Wt 5 1 11 2hd 2hd 2nk Stevens G L Bb 116 7.90 84-12 Pillaring116nk Terrific Trip116hd Rally Run1162½ Just missed 8
29Jly90- 4Dmr fst 5½f :213 :451 1:034 SMd Sp Wt 5 6 54¾ 53¾ 56 36 Stevens G L b 117 9.70 89-07 GtTFly1173½TnD.J.'sJmmn1172½TrrfcTrp1171½ 4-wide stretch 9
7Jly90- 6Hol fst 5½f :22 :451 1:044 SMd Sp Wt 4 7 97½ 78¾ 79½ 68¾ Stevens G L 117 18.00 85-06 Apollo1171 Warfare Prince1171½ Pillaring1173 Wide final 3/8 9
Speed Index: Last Race: -18.0 3-Race Avg.: -14.6 3-Race Avg.: -14.6 Overall Avg.: -7.7
LATEST WORKOUTS Nov 28 Hol 4f fst :482 H Nov 23 Hol 6f fst 1:133 H Nov 17 Hol 5f fst 1:002 H Nov 3 SA 6f fst 1:153 H

Gas Man Gr. c. 3(Apr), by Halo—Fancy Naskra, by Naskra
VALENZUELA P A Br.—Oak Cliff Bloodstock Ltd 85 (Cal) 117 Lifetime 8 0 2 2 $21,355 1991 8 M 2 2 $21,355 1990 0 M 0 0 Turf 3 0 2 0 $8,200
Own.—Oak Cliff Stable Tr.—Whittingham Michael
8Nov91- 6SA fst 1 :472 1:123 1:382 3↑Md Sp Wt 2 4 42½ 52½ 52½ 41¾ Valenzuela P A LBb 117 5.90 73-26 Standard1171½ El Travieso117hd Our Genius117nk In tight 1/4 9
30Aug91- 1AP yl *1 1/16 Ⓣ:474 1:121 1:443 3↑Md Sp Wt 1 6 68 58½ 42 23 Sellers S J Lb 117 1.60 72-25 City Ballet1223 GasMan1171½CarrickOnSur1173½ Lacked rally 8
10Aug91- 10AP gd 1 1/16 Ⓣ:474 1:133 1:451 3↑Md Sp Wt 2 8 910 77 34 23½ Velasquez J Lb 115 2.20 76-14 Ivor The Perfect1153½ Gas Man115¾ CityBallet1227 Mild rally 11
22Jly91- 9Hol fm 1 Ⓣ:47 1:104 1:36 3↑Md Sp Wt 12 9 85 84½ 72½ 6¾ Stevens G L LBb 116 17.00 84-11 YourInLuck116noStlyDwn117noElTrviso116hd Blocked in lane 12
23Jun91- 6Hol fst 6f :22 :444 1:11 3↑Md Sp Wt 2 8 610 78½ 97¾ 98 Stevens G L B 116 7.30 77-11 Chelsea's Pick116hd Consultant1161¾ Porgy116no No mishap 9
9Jun91- 2Hol fst 7½f :223 :46 1:29 3↑SMd Sp Wt 9 2 66½ 63 24 39 Stevens G L B 116 *2.20 — — Native Boundary1167 Right Bright1172GasMan1163 Wide trip 9
5May91- 6Hol fst 7½f :222 :452 1:29 3↑Md Sp Wt 10 2 64¾ 52¾ 35 35½ Nakatani C S B 115 6.20 — — EskyCrk115nkPrspctr'sRdg1155GsMn1152½ Wide backstretch 10
26Jan91- 6SA fst 6f :212 :441 1:093 SMd Sp Wt 1 12 1116 1010 68½ 46¾ Stevens G L B 118 12.70 81-14 WlkWthRylty1183½Slg'sRdg1182½SndsFbls118¾ Awkward start 12
Speed Index: Last Race: -1.0 1-Race Avg.: -1.0 1-Race Avg.: -1.0 Overall Avg.: -6.0
LATEST WORKOUTS Nov 25 SA 4f fst :484 H Nov 20 SA 3f fst :351 H Nov 15 SA 3f fst :371 H Nov 4 SA 4f fst :474 H

Reno City B. c. 3(Feb), by Fappiano—Sefa's Beauty, by Lt Stevens
SMITH M E Br.—Sefa & Santulli (Ky) 117 Lifetime 7 0 2 2 $23,425 1991 6 M 2 1 $19,525 1990 1 M 0 1 $3,900
Own.—Lukas & Overbrook Farm Tr.—Lukas D Wayne
20Nov91- 6Hol fst 1 1/16 :464 1:112 1:432 3↑Md Sp Wt 3 2 2hd 2½ 3½ 63¾ McCarron C J LB 118 4.20 80-16 DQ El Travieso118¾ Alybenbo118nk Major Launch118¾ 9
20Nov91-Placed fifth through disqualification; Steadied sharply 1/8
31Oct91- 6SA fst 6f :213 :441 1:084 3↑Md Sp Wt 3 5 32½ 33½ 45 46½ McCarron C J B 117 4.40 86-13 Sinag117½ Alybenbo1171½ Ivyleaguer1174½ No rally 8
17Oct91- 6SA fst 6½f :214 :444 1:16 3↑Md Sp Wt 7 3 2½ 21½ 24 24 McCarron C J B 117 4.00 86-17 TrkThShrk1174RnoCty1171½Prospctor'sRdg1122¾ Best of rest 9
3Oct91- 6SA fst 6f :214 :443 1:09 3↑Md Sp Wt 3 6 55 58 59 311½ McCarron C J B 117 2.40 79-11 Kennedy Factor117¾ Sinag11711 Reno City1174 7
3Oct91-Off awkwardly, 5-wide into stretch
17Feb91- 3SA fst 6f :213 :442 1:093 Md Sp Wt 7 1 43 33 34 24½ Stevens G L B 118 *1.00 83-11 Gray Slewpy1184½ Reno City1182 Multiengine1184 Wide early 7
3Feb91- 4SA fst 6f :212 :442 1:092 Md Sp Wt 6 3 32 31 33 44¾ Stevens G L B 118 *1.30 84-07 Smkstr118¾CmplingSnd1183Fghtcthll1181½ Bumped break 3/8 8
24Nov90- 6Hol fst 6f :221 :453 1:102 Md Sp Wt 1 8 2hd 2hd 31½ 35 Stevens G L B 119 3.00 83-06 Excavate1195PtienceOfJove119hdRenoCity1191½ Broke slowly 11
Speed Index: Last Race: -4.0 1-Race Avg.: -4.0 1-Race Avg.: -4.0 Overall Avg.: -5.4
LATEST WORKOUTS Nov 11 SA 5f fst 1:012 H Oct 28 SA 3f gd :373 B Oct 11 SA 5f fst 1:013 H

```
1DEC91                              HOL                    8.5 furlongs dirt
Race #3                                                          7 starters
MSW                                                   Age: 3+years, Male
----------------------------------INPUT DATA------------------------------------
                    #   #   #   #   $'S                         1st C 2nd C Final
Horse name          ST  W   P   S  Earned  Date    Trk Dist. S  time  time  time
--------------------------------------------------------------------------------
Major Launch        0   0   0   0     0  20NOV91 HOL 8.500 D   46.4 111.2 143.2
Penrod              0   0   0   0     0  20NOV91 HOL 8.500 D   46.4 111.2 143.2
Our Genius          0   0   0   0     0   9OCT91  SA 8.500 D   46.2 111.0 143.1
Gas Man             0   0   0   0     0   8NOV91  SA 8.000 D   47.2 112.3 138.2
Reno City           0   0   0   0     0  20NOV91 HOL 8.500 D   46.4 111.2 143.2

                              1st C 2nd C Final
Horse name          Class Lvl B.L.  B.L.  B.L.   SR   Var
--------------------------------------------------------------------------------
Major Launch        MSW        4.50  3.00  1.00   83   16
Penrod              MSW       11.00  7.00  4.00   80   16
Our Genius          MSW        6.75  6.50  3.50   83   15
Gas Man             MSW        2.50  2.25  1.75   73   26
Reno City           MCL        0.10  0.50  3.75   80   16

----------------------------------BETTING LINE----------------------------------
                    -------Rankings--------        Betting   Fair   Fair
Horse name          PEH H-I THAAI P-H ESP  Rating   Line   Place $ Show $
--------------------------------------------------------------------------------
Major Launch         1   2   2    1   1    88.78    9-2
Penrod               5   1   1    4   3    85.25    5-1
Reno City            2   5   5    3   2    82.19    6-1
Gas Man              3   4   4    5   4    81.27    6-1
Our Genius           4   3   3    2   5    81.14    6-1

----------------------------------EXACTA GRID-----------------------------------
             | Major Launch |    Penrod   |  Reno City  |   Gas Man   |
-------------+--------------+-------------+-------------+-------------+
Major Launch | . . . . . .  |  50   123   |  56   140   |  58   145   |
             | . . . . . .  |             |             |             |
             | . . . . . .  |             |             |             |
-------------+--------------+-------------+-------------+-------------+
Penrod       |  51   127    | . . . . . . |  66   163   |  68   170   |
             |              | . . . . . . |             |             |
             |              | . . . . . . |             |             |
-------------+--------------+-------------+-------------+-------------+
Reno City    |  59   147    |  67   167   | . . . . . . |  79   198   |
             |              |             | . . . . . . |             |
             |              |             | . . . . . . |             |
-------------+--------------+-------------+-------------+-------------+
Gas Man      |  62   154    |  71   176   |  80   199   | . . . . . . |
             |              |             |             | . . . . . . |
             |              |             |             | . . . . . . |
-------------+--------------+-------------+-------------+-------------+

----------------------------SPEED/PACE SUMMARY----------------------------------
Race Profile:       47.66 112.30 145.06   Winners' Pace Profile: EARLY
Ability Par:        96.94                  Pace Contention Point:  2.22 lengths

Projected Times:                          Ability Balance Last Proj  Con-
                    1st C  2nd C   Fin C    Time    Time  Frac Pace  tender
--------------------------------------------------------------------------------
Major Launch        47.64 111.98 143.63    96.32  100.83 31.65 EARLY  Y
Penrod              48.85 112.67* 144.21   96.49  100.87 31.54 LATE   N
Reno City           46.92 111.72 144.62    96.53  102.20 32.90 FRONT  Y
Gas Man             48.54 113.13* 145.62   97.72  102.69 32.49 REAR   N
Our Genius          48.94 113.51* 145.56   98.07  102.48 32.05 REAR   N

--------------------------------PACE GRAPH--------------------------------------
        Profile:             47.66             112.30            145.06
        Front Runner:        46.92             111.72            143.63
Horse name               1C                2C                       F
Major Launch    --------------X---+  ---------------(-X+  ------------------X
Penrod          --------X---------+  ---------------X-(--+  ----------------X--+
Reno City       ------------------X  ---------------(--X  ----------------X----+
Gas Man         ---------X-------+  -------------X---(--+  --------X---------+
Our Genius      --------X---------+  ----------X-----(--+  --------X---------+
```

Terrific Trip Loves to run second. Already finished there twice in maiden claimers. Remember, the elevator only goes one way in maiden races: down. It's not going back up for this guy. Out.

Gas Man Improving on dirt and had trouble last out. Second back from layoff, so he's eligible to continue his improvement. Contender off his last line.

Reno City Seven starts, two seconds, two thirds. Sucker-horse tendencies; however, this one seemed to relish the stretch-out and would have been closer if not for some serious traffic problems. Fits the pace profile nicely. He's a contender off that last race.

This could be the first race in history that doesn't have a winner. With the exception of Penrod, each of these horses has lost at this level or lower at least five times. What futility. Who's going to win? This is a definite "lesser-of-evils" race. Someone has to win it. You would be correct in guessing this is a wildly contentious race. ALL-IN-ONE's odds line:

Major Launch	9-to-2
Penrod	5-to-1
Reno City	6-to-1
Gas Man	6-to-1
Our Genius	6-to-1

ALL-IN-ONE correctly assessed this field as very contentious. It's a very weak field in which our top pick has no greater than an 18 percent chance to win. Three stragglers each rate a 14 percent win probability. Since this is a maiden race, it's essential to look for bet-downs:

Horse	Morning Line	Public Line
Major Launch	2	2
Penrod	10	13
Our Genius	3	4
Deduction	20	70
Terrific Trip	8	3
Gas Man	4	5
Reno City	7–2	7–2

The public made Major Launch a clear favorite, and ranked Reno City, Gas Man, and Our Genius pretty much equally as best of the rest. Interestingly, the only bet-down is Terrific Trip, whom we've already eliminated on the basis of being outclassed. We have a clear overlay on Penrod, so that becomes our bet. As you can see in the results chart, the first six finishers ran within three lengths of each other, an unmistakable sign of both a weak race and a contentious race. No horse was able to demonstrate any kind of superiority. Dismal.

THIRD RACE

Hollywood

DECEMBER 1, 1991

1 ¹⁄₁₆ MILES. (1.40) MAIDEN. Purse $30,000. 3-year-olds and upward. Weights, 3-year-olds, 117 lbs.; older, 121 lbs.

Value of race $30,000; value to winner $16,500; second $6,000; third $4,500; fourth $2,250; fifth $750. Mutuel pool $335,576. Exacta pool $353,940.

Last Raced	Horse	M/Eqt.A.Wt	PP St	¼	½	¾	Str	Fin	Jockey	Odds $1
8Nov91 6SA3	Our Genius	b 3 117	3 7	6½	4hd	42	3½	1¾	McCarron C J	4.30
20Nov91 6Hol5	Reno City	LB 3 117	7 2	2¹	21½	2½	1hd	2½	Smith M E	3.80
8Nov91 6SA7	Deduction	LB 3 117	4 1	1¹	11½	1hd	2½	3nk	Sorenson D	73.60
8Nov91 6SA4	Gas Man	LBb 3 117	6 4	5½	61½	31½	42½	4nk	Valenzuela P A	5.20
20Nov91 6Hol2	Major Launch	B 3 117	1 5	3¹	3hd	63	63	51½	Pincay L Jr	2.10
20Nov91 6Hol7	Penrod	B 3 117	2 6	4¹	5½	51½	51	66	Delahoussaye E	13.00
7Nov91 6SA2	Terrific Trip	LBb 3 117	5 3	7	7	7	7	7	Flores D R	3.30

OFF AT 1:34. Start good. Won driving. Time, :23³, :47³, 1:12 , 1:37³, 1:44 Track fast.

$2 Mutuel Prices:

3–OUR GENIUS	10.60	5.00	3.80
7–RENO CITY		6.00	4.80
4–DEDUCTION			10.80

$2 EXACTA 3–7 PAID $63.00.

Unfortunately, this maiden race wasn't as clear-cut as the previous maiden race. This race featured a horse that won even though it wasn't a bet-down. "Stuff happens." Pity. After three races, we're $29.60 to the good.

Silver Ray Second time turfward for this guy. Check Quirin's master turf sires list. Silver Hawk's offspring win 52 percent of their first or second grass starts and return $7.43 for each two dollars bet on them in those races. Those are positive and potentially decisive factors, made even stronger by a very good effort in Silver Ray's first turf start. Contender. Last line sticks out.

Al Sabin Another one making his second grass start. Closed furiously in lone turf try, albeit versus much softer preliminary non-winners allowance runners. That late-running style hasn't been winning, however, and Alydar isn't a prominent turf sire. The last one stamps this guy a mild contender. Last race is obvious paceline.

4th Hollywood

1 MILE
HOLLYWOOD PARK
FINISH   START

1 MILE. (Turf). (1.324) 10th Running of THE HOIST THE FLAG STAKES (1st Division) (Grade III). $112,500 added. 2-year-olds. (Allowance). By subscription of $150 each, which shall accompany the nomination, $1,500 additional to start, with $112,500 added, of which $22,500 to second, $16,875 to third, $8,438 to fourth and $2,812 to fifth. Weight, 121 lbs. Non-winners of $50,000 at any distance or $30,000 at one mile or over allowed 3 lbs.; of $25,000 or two races other than claiming at one mile or over, 5 lbs.; of $15,000 other than maiden or claiming, 7 lbs. Hollywood Park reserves the right not to divide this race. Should this race not be divided and the number of entries exceed the starting gate capacity, first preference will be given to graded or group stakes winners. Second preference will be given to those horses with the highest total earnings and an also eligible list will be drawn. Failure to draw into this race at scratch time cancels all fees. Trophies will be presented to the winning owner, trainer and jockey. No fees for remaining eligible (those kept eligible with the Wednesday, July 17 sustaining payment), to the 1991 Hollywood Futurity or Hollywood Park Starlet. Closed Wednesday, November 13, 1991 with 47 nominations.

LASIX—Hammer Man, Thinkernot, B. G.'s Drone.

African Colony — Dk. b. or br. c. 2(Mar), by Pleasant Colony—African Music, by Stop the Music
PINCAY L JR — Br.—Evans T M (Va)
Own.—Buckland Farm — Tr.—Speckert Christopher
114 — Lifetime 5 1 0 0 $21,350 — 1991 5 1 0 0 $21,350 — Turf 1 1 0 0 $16,500

15Nov91- 6Hol	fm	1 1/16 Ⓣ	:453	1:10	1:424	Md Sp Wt	3	7	714	78	1hd	1hd	Pincay L Jr	B	118	8.30	81-17	AfrcnColony118hdFbiosPoston[illegible]		Wide rally	9
20Oct91- 8SA	fst	7f	:224	:453	1:231	Sunny Slope	4	5	53	52	56	58¾	Solis A	Bb	113	15.90	79-13	RichrdOfEnglnd1151Ebonr116½B[illegible]1222½		Broke awkwardly	6
7Sep91- 6Dmr	fst	6½f	:224	:462	1:172	Md Sp Wt	11	2	64¾	31	21½	56	Solis A	B	117	36.50	76-15	RchrdOfEnlnd1173½WldHr117nkApprp[illegible]		Wide, lugged in	12
17Aug91- 6Dmr	fst	6f	:221	:451	1:102	Md Sp Wt	5	7	65	65¾	55½	46	Ortega L E	B	117	45.60	81-15	Dr.Scrto117½WldHrmny1173½StrOfThCrp1172		Lugged in drive	9
4Jly91- 6Hol	fst	6f	:22	:451	1:11	Md Sp Wt	6	8	1014	1013	1012	1016½	Davenport C L5	B	112	42.80	68-11	FrnklinSqure1173½Soudbkr117no[illegible]		4-wide stretch	10

Speed Index: Last Race: -2.0 1-Race Avg.: -2.0 1-Race Avg.: -2.0 Overall Avg.: -4.8
LATEST WORKOUTS Nov 26 SA 4f fst :504 H Nov 12 SA 4f fst :483 H Nov 7 SA 7f fst 1:272 H Oct 26 SA 4f fst :502 H

B. G.'s Drone — Ch. c. 2(Mar), by Full Choke—Flying B G, by Barachois
VALENZUELA P A — Br.—Callaway V J (NM)
Own.—Callaway W M & Martha T — Tr.—Grissom O Dwain
121 — Lifetime 10 5 3 0 $132,603 — 1991 10 5 3 0 $132,603

9Nov91-10Sun	fst	6f	:222	:443	1:101	Rui Sle Fut	8	1	2hd	21	1hd	12½	Krasner S	Lb	120	*.50	99-08	B.G.'sDrone1202½Vleme120[illegible]JosPoncho[illegible]		Handily, outside	12
25Oct91- 9Sun	fst	6f	:222	:443	1:103	Fut Trl	2	4	1hd	11	12	12½	Krasner S	Lb	120	*.80	97-13	B. G.'s Drone1202½ Valeme120[illegible]JosePoncho120[illegible]		Handily, rail	9
29Sep91-12Alb	fst	6f	:212	:441	1:102	ⓈG M Fut	7	1	31½	21½	21½	2nk	Corbett G W	Lb	120	*1.10	95-09	MchoEg120nkB.G.'sDrn120[illegible]JnAllmnd120[illegible]		Closing on winner	12
17Sep91-11Alb	fst	6f	:221	:452	1:112	ⓈFut Trl	4	4	12	14	15	16½	Corbett G W	Lb	118	*.70	90-14	B.G.'sDrone1186½HvMoreSherry[illegible]ApacheSummit1181		Easily	9
25Aug91-10Rui	fst	6f	:214	:444	1:131	Rui Fut	7	7	64¾	62½	63½	1½	Koyle K	Lb	120	6.00	83-13	B. G.'s Drone120½ Scalp[illegible]120[illegible]Valeme120[illegible]		5-wide driving	11
12Aug91- 9Rui	sly	6f	:213	:442	1:114	Fut Trl	8	1	12	11½	11	2½	Koyle K	Lb	120	6.10	89-14	MstrProspct120½B.G.'sDrn120[illegible]Scalp[illegible]120[illegible]		Game finish, rail	8
4Aug91-11Rui	sly	6f	:213	:45	1:124	ⓈRio Grde Fut	4	6	21	32	79	715	Ortiz M F Jr	Lb	120	4.20	70-20	JosPoncho120[illegible]JnAllmnd120[illegible]ApchSummit120[illegible]		Speed, tired	12
25Jly91-10Rui	sl	6f	:22	:464	1:143	ⓈFut Trl	9	7	76½	76½	89	714½	Ortiz M F Jr	L	120	*1.50	61-25	JosPoncho120½JnAllmnd120[illegible]ApchSummit120[illegible]		Stumbled start	10
12May91-11TuP	fst	5f	:212	:433	:571	Phoenix Fut	5	3	2hd	21½	34	24	Castro J M		119	1.90	99-06	To The Post1164 B. G.'s Drone119[illegible]		Came on again	11
1May91-13TuP	fst	4½f	:214	:442	:503	Fut Trl	3	4		16	18	114	Castro J M		119	2.00	103-04	B.G.'sDron11914ShmfulChf119[illegible]		Much the best	9

Speed Index: Last Race: (—) 3-Race Avg.: (—) 12-Race Avg.: (—) Overall Avg.: +1.2
LATEST WORKOUTS Nov 27 TuP 3f fst :35 H ●Nov 22 TuP 4f fst :461 H Nov 6 TuP 3f fst :381 H Oct 22 TuP 3f fst :38 H

Hammer Man Very much on the improve for D. Wayne Lukas, who is a master at striking while the iron is hot with two-year-olds. However, that old Lukas magic tends to disappear on the turf. First time on turf, and Quirin's grass stallions list doesn't mention Wild Again. We're truly stuck here. The horse is a contender, but we have the undesirable situation in which we're forced to project today's turf performance from a prior dirt paceline. This is to be avoided whenever possible. Comparisons and projections are not tenable between the two surfaces. Reluctantly, I used the last line.

Gold Desert Frankel is the master of bringing horses in from Europe and winning right off the plane in the United States. "Right off the plane" means right off the plane, however, and this one has been away for nearly three months without a single workout. There are also unanswered questions about this guy's stretch-out potential. The track oddsmaker's morning line on him is 5-to-1, making him the fourth choice. Remember that in order for a foreign invader to be a contender, he has to be among the track oddsmaker's top three morning-line choices. Out.

Dolly's Fortune All-out to beat maidens. Fortunate Prospect isn't even listed among Quirin's master turf sires. Unfavorable energy distribution that goes against turf-course profile. Noncontender.

Thinkernot Tandem race with Al Sabin, so must be rated off that paceline.

Vying Victor We're unable to evaluate him through our normal speed-and-pace standards. His morning line is 8-to-1, and he's the track oddsmaker's co-fifth choice, so he can be dismissed.

B. G.'s Drone Picked up minor stakes awards in the New Mexico bush leagues. Five wins in ten starts is impressive, but this one burns up too much energy too early to stay the longer and more grueling turf route today. Obscure sire closes case. Out.

Successfully predicting and betting on horses doing something they've never done before is one of the best ways to get an edge on the game. Because the public tends to think in terms of the past immutably repeating itself, you can stay a jump ahead of the crowd by betting on horses that project to do well their first or second times on turf, or around two turns, or over a distance of ground, or tackling a higher class level. This is precisely what this race offers us. Before you go out on a limb, however, make sure the "unknowns" offer correspondingly high odds to compensate for the associated risks. Conversely, actual betting favorites cannot be saddled with "unknowns." "No knocks," warns Ron Ambrose. Since none of these horses has won a turf route at the graded stakes level, we definitely know that whichever one the public makes the favorite is false. They make Al Sabin their choice. How false is Al Sabin? He's never won a route, never won on turf, never beaten winners. In fact, all he's done is break his maiden in a dirt sprint at another track. There's no way he should be even 5-to-1. Making him 8-to-5 is ridiculous, considering all the "unknowns" surrounding him. Looking for overlays becomes easier.

Public odds:

Silver Ray	9-to-2
African Colony	9-to-1
Al Sabin	8-to-5
Thinkernot	7-to-1

Silver Ray, African Colony, and Thinkernot offer wager value. However, Thinkernot is a marginal play, offering an edge of only 12 percent. African Colony gives us an edge of 60 percent, while the advantage on Silver Ray is 21 percent. The aggressive bettor

```
1DEC91                          HOL                      8 furlongs turf
Race #4                                                        9 starters
STAKES 1                                                 Age: 2 years, Male
---------------------------------INPUT DATA-------------------------------
```

Horse name	# ST	# W	# P	# S	$'S Earned	Date	Trk	Dist.	S	1st C time	2nd C time	Final time
Silver Ray	0	0	0	0	0	1NOV91	SA	6.500	T	21.2	43.3	113.1
Al Sabin	0	0	0	0	0	15NOV91	HOL	8.000	T	47.0	111.0	136.0
Hammer Man	0	0	0	0	0	10NOV91	SA	8.500	D	47.2	112.0	144.4
Thinkernot	0	0	0	0	0	15NOV91	HOL	8.000	T	47.0	111.0	136.0
African Colony	0	0	0	0	0	15NOV91	HOL	8.500	T	45.3	110.0	142.4

Horse name	Class Lvl	1st C B.L.	2nd C B.L.	Final B.L.	SR	Var
Silver Ray	CLF	0.20	1.50	1.50	91	7
Al Sabin	NW1	11.00	10.00	0.20	85	17
Hammer Man	MSW	2.00	0.00	0.00	79	19
Thinkernot	NW1	9.00	8.00	0.75	84	17
African Colony	MSW	14.00	8.00	0.00	81	17

```
------------------------------BETTING LINE--------------------------------
```

Horse name	PEH	H-I	THAAI	P-H	ESP	Rating	Betting Line	Fair Place $	Fair Show $
Silver Ray	1	1	1	1	1	91.79	7-2		
African Colony	2	2	2	4	5	82.36	5-1		
Al Sabin	5	3	3	2	2	81.36	5-1		
Thinkernot	3	4	4	3	3	81.08	6-1		
Hammer Man	4	5	5	5	4	76.86			

```
------------------------------EXACTA GRID---------------------------------
```

	Silver Ray	African Colony	Al Sabin	Thinkernot
Silver Ray	. . . .	42 104	44 109	44 110
African Colony	46 113	. . . .	67 167	68 169
Al Sabin	48 119	68 168	. . . .	72 178
Thinkernot	49 121	69 171	72 179	. . . .

```
----------------------------SPEED/PACE SUMMARY----------------------------

Race Profile:    47.63  111.70  134.89   Winners' Pace Profile: EARLY
Ability Par:     70.81                    Pace Contention Point: 1.85 lengths

Projected Times:                     Ability  Balance  Last  Proj  Con-
                 1st C   2nd C   Fin C   Time    Time    Frac  Pace  tender
```

Horse name	1st C	2nd C	Fin C	Ability Time	Balance Time	Last Frac	Proj Pace	Contender
Silver Ray	48.07	112.39*	135.76	71.44	92.71	23.37	LATE	N
African Colony	48.07	111.60	137.00	73.48	94.18	25.41	FRONT	N
Al Sabin	49.06	112.75*	136.04	72.35	92.55	23.29	REAR	N
Thinkernot	48.68	112.42*	136.14	72.40	92.88	23.72	LATE	N
Hammer Man	50.03	114.50*	138.49	74.01	94.99	23.98	REAR	N

```
-------------------------------PACE GRAPH---------------------------------

       Profile:               47.63            111.70              134.89
       Front Runner:          48.07            111.60              135.76
Horse name                      1C               2C                   F
Silver Ray       --------------------X -------------------X-(-+ ------------------X
African Colony   --------------------X ----------------(-X ------------X-----+
Al Sabin         -------------X----+ -------------X---(-+ ------------------X+
Thinkernot       --------------X--+ -------------X-(-+ -----X-------------X-+
Hammer Man       --------X----------+ ---X------------(-+ ----X-------------+
```

would choose the superior edge of African Colony; moderate and conservative bettors would support both Silver Ray and African Colony to win. Since this is a turf race, it's advised that you bet on two horses unless one has a distinct advantage. The keys to this race were spotting a false favorite and demanding a high price on horses that had yet to prove they could win at this combination of surface, distance, and class level.

FOURTH RACE
Hollywood
DECEMBER 1, 1991

1 MILE.(Turf). (1.32^4) 10th Running of THE HOIST THE FLAG STAKES (1st Division) (Grade III). $112,500 added. 2-year-olds. (Allowance). By subscription of $150 each, which shall accompany the nomination, $1,500 additional to start, with $112,500 added, of which $22,500 to second, $16,875 to third, $8,438 to fourth and $2,812 to fifth. Weight, 121 lbs. Non-winners of $50,000 at any distance or $30,000 at one mile or over allowed 3 lbs.; of $25,000 or two races other than claiming at one mile or over, 5 lbs.; of $19,000 other than maiden or claiming, 7 lbs. Hollywood Park reserves the right not to divide this race. Should this race not be divided and the number of entries exceed the starting gate capacity, first preference will be given to graded or group stakes winners. Second preference will be given to these horses with the highest total earnings and an also eligible list will be drawn. Failure to draw into this race at scratch time cancels all fees. Trophies will be presented to the winning owner, trainer and jockey. No fees to remaining eligible (those kept eiligible with the Wednesday, July 17 sustaining payment), to the 1991 Hollywood Futurity or Hollywood Starlet. Closed Wednesday, November 13, 1991 with 47 nominations.

Value of race $125,400; value to winner $74,775; second $22,500; third $16,875; fourth $8,438; fifth $2,812. Mutuel pool $331,493. Exacta pool $333,418.

Last Raced	Horse	M/Eqt.	A.Wt	PP	St	¼	½	¾	Str	Fin	Jockey	Odds $1
1Nov91 8SA3	Silver Ray	B	2 114	1	6	77	5hd	3hd	1 1½	1 1¼	Pedroza M A	4.60
15Nov91 8Hol3	Thinkernot	LB	2 115	6	8	84	84	6½	3hd	2hd	McCarron C J	7.20
15Nov91 6Hol1	African Colony	B	2 117	8	9	9	9	9	7 1½	3nk	Pincay L Jr	9.60
7Sep91 3Eng3	Gold Desert-Ir	B	2 114	4	3	4 1½	4½	4½	4 1½	41	Flores D R	6.80
10Nov91 6SA1	Hammer Man	LBb	2 114	3	4	21	1½	1hd	2½	5nk	Nakatani C S	9.70
15Nov91 8Hol2	Al Sabin	B	2 114	2	7	61	61	71	6hd	63	Smith M E	1.70
3Nov91 6SA1	Dolly's Fortune	B	2 116	5	5	1½	2 1½	22	51	7 3½	Delahoussaye E	8.80
21Oct91 3Eng1	Vying Victor	B	2 114	7	1	5½	7 1½	8 1½	8½	8¾	Desormeaux K J	33.70
9Nov91 10Sun1	B. G.'s Drone	LBb	2 121	9	2	3 2½	3 1½	5½	9	9	Valenzuela P A	12.00

OFF AT 2:09. Start good. Won driving. Time, :22^4, :46 , 1:10^1, 1:35 Course firm.

$2 Mutuel Prices:				
	1-SILVER RAY	11.20	6.60	4.60
	6-THINKERNOT		6.80	4.00
	8-AFRICAN COLONY			6.40

$2 EXACTA 1-6 PAID $87.80.

We have two bets—one on African Colony, the other on Silver Ray. Silver Ray wins and pays $11.20. Our race P/L is $7.20; our running P/L is plus $36.80.

Free And Equal Right kind of training pattern for comeback from a six-month layoff; however, he's already lost at odds-on, and is probably well on his way to becoming a proven loser/chronic beaten favorite at this level. He also figures to be well outside of the pace profile at the second call. Non-contender.

Chief's Key No problems with form, as workouts average exactly a furlong per day. But no signs of betting action in debut, and a negative jockey switch today wipe out the good form. Out.

START
5th Hollywood
6½ FURLONGS
HOLLYWOOD PARK
FINISH

6 ½ FURLONGS. (1.14²) MAIDEN. Purse $28,000. 2-year-olds. Weight, 117 lbs.

LASIX—Free and Equal, Boss of Bosses, Capistrano.

Free And Equal B. c. 2(Jan), by Nijinsky II—Fine Spirit, by Secretariat — Lifetime 1991 2 M 0 0 $2,100
PEDROZA M A — Br.—Mabee Mr-Mrs J C (Ky) — 117 — 2 0 0 0
Own.—Golden Eagle Farm — Tr.—Jones Gary — $2,100
19May91- 6Hol fst 5f :214 :452 :574 Md Sp Wt 1 6 69 67½ 56½ 46½ Nakatani C S B 117 7.40 86-08 Stolen Script117¾ Jer Kei1173 Top Senator1171 No bid 9
3May91- 6Hol fst 4½f :222 :452 :514 Md Sp Wt 4 8 815 611 610½ Garcia J A B 117 *.90e — — BurnshdBronz1171PrkLtnnt1174TopSntor117no Bumped 3 1/2 9
Speed Index: Last Race: -6.0 1-Race Avg.: -6.0 1-Race Avg.: -6.0 Overall Avg.: -6.0
LATEST WORKOUTS ●Nov 27 Hol 6f fst 1:131 H Nov 21 Hol 6f fst 1:14 Hg Nov 16 Hol 6f fst 1:143 H Nov 11 Hol 5f fst 1:01 H

Chief's Key B. c. 2(Mar), by Key to the Kingdom—Crossed Arrows, by Lydian — Lifetime 1991 1 M 0 0
ALVARADO F J — Br.—Arnold-Clark-Clearman-Kicker-Wiles (Ky) — 117 — 1 0 0 0
Own.—Arnold-Clearman-Wiles — Tr.—Mulhall Richard W
27Oct91- 6SA sl 6½f 214 :453 1:181 Md Sp Wt 8 5 63 86½ 913 931 Desormeaux K J B 117 23.70 48-24 A. P. Indy1174 Dr Pain117¾ Hickman Creek1172 Done early 9
Speed Index: Last Race: -28.0 1-Race Avg.: -28.0 1-Race Avg.: -28.0 Overall Avg.: -28.0
LATEST WORKOUTS ●Nov 28 SA 4f fst :463 B Nov 23 SA 4f fst :473 H ●Nov 18 SA 5f fst :592 H Nov 13 SA 5f fst 1:01 H

Boss Of Bosses B. c. 2(Feb), by Stalwart—Iron Crown, by Iron Ruler — Lifetime 1991 2 M 0 0 $700
DESORMEAUX K J — Br.—Yowell Renee (Fla) — 117 — 2 0 0 0
Own.—Cuicchi&EmeraldMeadowsRnch — Tr.—Hess R B Jr — $700
20Oct91- 4SA fst 6f 212 :443 1:102 Md Sp Wt 1 5 21½ 32½ 41½ 63 Mena F B 117 6.10 81-16 StarOfTheCrop117¾OldMaster117nkCpeRoyle1171½ Weakened 10
5Oct91- 6SA fst 6f :214 :444 1:094 Md Sp Wt 9 3 32½ 34 42¾ 56 Mena F B 117 13.70 81-14 Approprition117¾ChrokGry1171¾BuckOgygin117no Weakened 11
Speed Index: Last Race: -3.0 2-Race Avg.: -4.0 2-Race Avg.: -4.0 Overall Avg.: -4.0
LATEST WORKOUTS Nov 28 SA 3f fst :353 H Nov 22 SA 4f fst :494 H Nov 11 SA 4f fst :482 H Oct 30 Hol 4f fst :47 H

Lil Orphan Moonie Dk. b. or br. c. 2(Jan), by Basket Weave—Lover's Moon, by Roberto — Lifetime 1991 0 M 0 0
MENA F — Br.—Elgot & Murphy (Wash) — 117 — 0 0 0 0
Own.—Elgot & Murphy — Tr.—Jory Ian P B
Speed Index: Last Race: (—) 3-Race Avg.: (—) 12-Race Avg.: (—) Overall Avg.: (—)
LATEST WORKOUTS Nov 27 Hol 5f fst 1:013 Hg Nov 9 Hol 6f fst 1:18 H Nov 3 Hol 5f fst 1:024 H Oct 28 Hol 5f fst 1:033 H

Play Ten B. g. 2(Mar), by Play On—Ten Plus, by Judger — Lifetime 1991 0 M 0 0
MCCARRON C J — Br.—Kercheval R G (Ky) — 117 — 0 0 0 0
Own.—Knohl & Sigband — Tr.—Murphy Marcus J
Speed Index: Last Race: (—) 3-Race Avg.: (—) 12-Race Avg.: (—) Overall Avg.: (—)
LATEST WORKOUTS Nov 29 Hol 3f fst :36 H Nov 24 Hol 5f fst :591 H Nov 19 Hol 3f fst :352 Hg Nov 14 Hol 6f fst 1:14 H

Bold Assert Ch. c. 2(Apr), by Assert—Travertine, by Habitat — Lifetime 1991 0 M 0 0
FLORES D R — Br.—Bittersweet Farms Inc (Pa) — 117 — 0 0 0 0
Own.—Estrada E S & J — Tr.—Cenicola Lewis
Speed Index: Last Race: (—) 3-Race Avg.: (—) 12-Race Avg.: (—) Overall Avg.: (—)
LATEST WORKOUTS Nov 24 Hol 5f fst :593 H Nov 19 SA 7f fst 1:272 H Nov 13 SA 6f fst 1:163 H Nov 7 SA 6f fst 1:152 H

Old Master B. g. 2(Mar), by Classic Go Go—Nijimagic, by Sir Ivor — Lifetime 1991 2 M 2 0 $10,000
NAKATANI C S — Br.—Winchell V H (Ky) — 117 — 2 0 2 0
Own.—V H W Stables (Lessee) — Tr.—McAnally Ronald — $10,000
11Nov91- 6SA fst 6½f :213 :451 1:173 Md Sp Wt 1 5 64 63¼ 51¾ 2hd Nakatani C S 118 2.80 82-16 HickmanCreek118hdOldMster118nkCpistrno1181 Strong finish 12
20Oct91- 4SA fst 6f :212 :443 1:102 Md Sp Wt 5 8 811 88½ 63¼ 2½ Nakatani C S 117 14.10 83-16 StarOfTheCrop117½OldMaster117nkCapeRoyle1171½ Wide trip 10
Speed Index: Last Race: -2.0 2-Race Avg.: -1.5 2-Race Avg.: -1.5 Overall Avg.: -1.5
LATEST WORKOUTS ●Nov 29 SA 3f fst :351 H Nov 22 SA 4f fst :48 H ●Nov 8 Hol 3f fst :35 H Nov 1 Hol 4f fst :484 H

Call Me Wild Dk. b. or br. c. 2(Feb), by Wild Again—Negation, by Mongo — Lifetime 1991 1 M 0 0
PINCAY L JR — Br.—Shadowlawn Farm & Lundy (Ky) — 117 — 1 0 0 0
Own.—Gaillard M N Jr & Dr E — Tr.—Whittingham Charles
11Nov91- 6SA fst 6½f :213 :451 1:173 Md Sp Wt 11 7 106½ 95¾ 1012 812½ Pincay L Jr 118 32.60 69-16 HickmanCreek118hdOldMaster118nkCapistrano1181 Wide trip 12
Speed Index: Last Race: -15.0 1-Race Avg.: -15.0 1-Race Avg.: -15.0 Overall Avg.: -15.0
LATEST WORKOUTS Nov 27 Hol 5f fst 1:023 H Nov 22 Hol 5f fst 1:041 H Nov 17 Hol 3f fst :383 H Nov 9 SA 3f fst :363 Hg

Judge Hammer Dk. b. or br. g. 2(May), by Shadeed—Ma Biche, by Key to the Kingdom — Lifetime 1991 0 M 0 0
SMITH M E — Br.—Gainsborough Farm, Inc. (Ky) — 117 — 0 0 0 0
Own.—Maktoum Shkh MktmBnRshdAl — Tr.—Drysdale Neil
Speed Index: Last Race: (—) 3-Race Avg.: (—) 12-Race Avg.: (—) Overall Avg.: (—)
LATEST WORKOUTS Nov 25 Hol 5f fst 1:021 H Nov 20 Hol 4f fst :492 Hg Nov 15 Hol 4f fst :482 H Nov 5 SA 7f fst 1:302 H

Ruthless Monarch Ch. c. 2(Mar), by Wavering Monarch—Achaea, by Affirmed — Lifetime 1991 1 M 0 0 $4,365
DELAHOUSSAYE E — Br.—Swynford Farm (Va) — 117 — 1 0 0 0
Own.—Rubey M M — Tr.—Cannni Julio C — $4,365
30Oct91- 8SA fst 7f :223 :451 1:234 ⓈVy Stl DstW 11 5 2½ 3nk 2hd 52¼ Delahoussaye E B 116 7.30e 82-14 CpeRoyle113¾FrindshipForvr117nkMgiclMidn1141½ Weakened 11
Speed Index: Last Race: -4.0 1-Race Avg.: -4.0 1-Race Avg.: -4.0 Overall Avg.: -4.0
LATEST WORKOUTS Nov 25 Hol 6f fst 1:134 H Nov 20 Hol 5f fst :593 H Oct 24 SA 5f fst 1:001 Hg Oct 18 SA 7f fst 1:281 H

Capistrano B. c. 2(Apr), by Storm Bird—Ravine, by Sir Ivor — Lifetime 1991 1 M 0 1 $3,750
VALENZUELA P A — Br.—Huntington Interests Inc (Ky) — 117 — 1 0 0 1
Own.—Clark C W — Tr.—Rothblum Steve — $3,750
11Nov91- 6SA fst 6½f :213 :451 1:173 Md Sp Wt 5 1 2hd 1hd 1hd 3nk Desormeaux K J LB 118 26.10 82-16 Hickman Creek118hdOldMaster118nkCapistrano1181 Game try 12
Speed Index: Last Race: -2.0 1-Race Avg.: -2.0 1-Race Avg.: -2.0 Overall Avg.: -2.0
LATEST WORKOUTS Nov 26 SA 4f fst :50 H Nov 21 SA 3f fst :361 H Nov 6 SA 5f fst 1:021 H Oct 29 SA 5f fst 1:002 H

Boss Of Bosses Gets a positive jockey switch, but workouts have been unevenly spaced and too short to instill confidence in his current condition. Elimination.

Lil Orphan Moonie First-timer with low-win jockey. Also have to wonder about the 18-day gap in workouts, Nov. 9–27. Toss out.

Play Ten Perfect pattern of 18 furlongs in 16 days. McCarron on board is a plus. First-timer, so let's see if the experienced maidens can run to the pars.

Bold Assert Another perfect pattern of exactly a furlong per day. First-timer, so we must check ability of experienced maidens.

Old Master Despite showing sucker-horse tendencies in his two starts, he seems to embody Mark Cramer's "ascending numbers" theory more strongly, racing closer to the lead at every call of his last race. Also, his mid-pack running style fits the profile perfectly. Contender.

Call Me Wild No betting action in dismal debut, plus Whittingham tends to use his horses' first few races for educational purposes, teaching them how to rate in sprints so they'll take to the route. Out.

Judge Hammer Even though he shows only 20 furlongs in 26 days, remember that we can add five furlongs to the number of furlongs, making his new ratio 25 furlongs in 26 days. Another first-timer whose chances must be measured against the ability of the experienced maidens.

Ruthless Monarch Made debut in company way over his head in restricted stakes. Was nevertheless able to gamely force the pace all the way before tiring to fifth, beaten only slightly more than two lengths by the subsequent stakes winner Cape Royale. Has worked 11 furlongs in 10 days since returning to training, so form is acceptable. A strong contender who is well within the win pars, but whose pressing style goes slightly against the pace profile.

Capistrano Very gritty performance to contest the pace the entire trip and still finish third just a neck behind the eventual stakes winner Hickman Creek and Old Master, who is in today's field. He's well within the win pars, although his style looks a bit disadvantaged. Definite contender.

When you handicap a maiden race that features several first-time starters, you can reliably determine whether the first-timers

```
1DEC91                            HOL                        6.5 furlongs dirt
Race #5                                                         11 starters
MSW                                                      Age: 2 years, Male

---------------------------------INPUT DATA------------------------------------

                 #   #   #   #  $'S                           1st C  2nd C  Final
Horse name       ST  W   P   S  Earned Date    Trk Dist. S    time   time   time
-------------------------------------------------------------------------------
Old Master       0   0   0   0      0  11NOV91 SA  6.500 D    21.3   45.1   117.3
Ruthless Monarch 0   0   0   0      0  30OCT91 SA  7.000 D    22.3   45.1   123.4
Capistrano       0   0   0   0      0  11NOV91 SA  6.500 D    21.3   45.1   117.3

                              1st C  2nd C  Final
Horse name       Class Lvl    B.L.   B.L.   B.L.   SR    Var
---------------------------------------------------------------
Old Master       MSW          4.00   3.50   0.10   82    16
Ruthless Monarch MSW          0.50   0.20   2.75   82    14
Capistrano       MSW          0.10   0.00   0.20   82    16

------------------------------BETTING LINE-------------------------------------

                 -------Rankings--------        Betting   Fair    Fair
Horse name       PEH H-I THAAI P-H ESP  Rating  Line      Place $ Show $
-------------------------------------------------------------------------------
Ruthless Monarch  1   1   1   1   1     77.71   9-5       3.60    2.80
Capistrano        2   3   3   3   2     69.29   9-2
Old Master        3   2   2   2   3     64.33

------------------------------EXACTA GRID--------------------------------------

                |Ruthless Monarc| Capistrano |
----------------+---------------+------------+
Ruthless Monar  |. . . . . . .  |   19    47  |
                |. . . . . . .  |            |
                |. . . . . . .  |            |
----------------+---------------+------------+
Capistrano      |   24    59    |. . . . . . .|
                |               |. . . . . . .|
                |               |. . . . . . .|
----------------+---------------+------------+

-----------------------------SPEED/PACE SUMMARY--------------------------------

Race Profile:    22.71   45.73  117.36   Winners' Pace Profile: MID
Ability Par:     68.74                   Pace Contention Point:  4.24 lengths

Projected Times:                    Ability Balance  Last  Proj  Con-
                 1st C   2nd C  Fin C   Time   Time   Frac  Pace  tender
-------------------------------------------------------------------------------
Ruthless Monarch 22.80   45.56  118.12  68.32  74.91  32.56 EARLY N
Capistrano       22.53   45.93  118.20  69.32  75.12  32.28 FRONT N
Old Master       23.23   46.56* 118.18  69.89  75.32  31.62 LATE  N

------------------------------PACE GRAPH---------------------------------------

        Profile:           22.71            45.73              117.36
        Front Runner:      22.53            45.56              118.12
        Horse name          1C               2C                  F
Ruthless Monarch  -----------------X+ ------------(----X -------------------X
Capistrano        ------------------X -----------(--X-+ -------------------X
Old Master        ---------------X--+ ------------X----+ -------------------X
```

are contenders by checking whether the experienced horses can
run to the win pars of today's race. If the experienced horses have
shown in their previous races that they can run to the pars,

mark the first-timers down, as they will most likely have to show above-average speed and class to win today. Since most first-timers are ordinary at best, they can be eliminated. However, if the experienced runners have shown that they cannot run to the pars, then the first-timers' chances increase. Ordinary first-timers can often break through in fields lacking horses that can run to the pars. ALL-IN-ONE's speed/pace summary tells us the win pars for this race and the projected times each of the contenders should run today. When determining whether experienced maidens can run to the win pars, allow approximately a two-length (two-fifths of a second, or four-tenths of a second) leeway at each call. In this case, we're looking for the experienced maidens to run about 23.11 to the first call, 46.13 to the second call, and still be able to finish in 1:17.76 or thereabouts. Ruthless Monarch and Capistrano can run to the win pars. Therefore, we can safely eliminate the first-timers. When we look at the pace profile, Old Master has the advantage of being a mid-pack runner. The profile has not been kind to front and early horses, which Ruthless Monarch and Capistrano will be in today's field; the pace profile is mid, and this favors Old Master. ALL-IN-ONE's odds line was interesting. It disregarded Old Master, even though all three horses have identical final times. Let's identify the bet-downs:

Horse	Morning Line	Public Line
Free And Equal	15	17
Chief's Key	15	30
Boss Of Bosses	6	5
Lil Orphan Moonie	20	99
Play Ten	6	17
Bold Assert	15	13
Old Master	5–2	6–5
Call Me Wild	30	50
Judge Hammer	20	50
Ruthless Monarch	7–2	4
Capistrano	9–2	9–2

Our top three choices (contenders) are also the public's top three choices. Capistrano is a break-even bet; Ruthless Monarch offers us a big edge. There are three bet-downs: Boss of Bosses, Bold Assert, and Old Master. Boss of Bosses is a non-contender, Bold Assert is a first-time starter, and Old Master is an underlay. We bet Ruthless Monarch to win.

FIFTH RACE   6 ½ FURLONGS. (1.142) MAIDEN. Purse $28,000. 2-year-olds. Weight, 117 lbs.

Hollywood

DECEMBER 1, 1991

Value of race $28,000; value to winner $15,400; second $5,600; third $4,200; fourth $2,100; fifth $700. Mutuel pool $418,584.
Exacta pool $442,698.

Last Raced	Horse	M/Eqt.A.Wt	PP St	¼	½	Str	Fin	Jockey	Odds $1
11Nov91 6SA2	Old Master	2 117	7 6	7½	4hd	21½	12½	Nakatani C S	1.30
	Play Ten	LB 2 117	5 4	4hd	31½	3hd	22¾	McCarron C J	17.30
27Oct91 6SA9	Chief's Key	B 2 117	2 10	82	72	64	3hd	Alvarado F J	32.50
	Bold Assert	B 2 117	6 8	3½	52½	42½	4no	Flores D R	13.90
20Oct91 4SA6	Boss Of Bosses	LB 2 117	3 3	1½	1½	1hd	51½	Desormeaux K J	5.90
30Oct91 8SA5	Ruthless Monarch	B 2 117	10 5	51	2hd	51	65½	Delahoussaye E	4.20
11Nov91 6SA8	Call Me Wild	2 117	8 7	6½	6½	72½	74	Pincay L Jr	58.70
19May91 6Hol4	Free And Equal	LB 2 117	1 11	96	84	86	811	Pedroza M A	17.40
	Lil Orphan Moonie	B 2 117	4 2	21	91½	9	9	Mena F	140.30
	Judge Hammer	B 2 117	9 9	10	10	—	—	Smith M E	56.00
1Nov91 6SA3	Capistrano	LB 2 117	11 1	—	—	—	—	Valenzuela P A	4.50

Judge Hammer, Lost rider; Capistrano, Broke down.

OFF AT 2:42. Start good. Won driving. Time, :22², :45³, 1:10⁴, 1:17¹ Track fast.

$2 Mutuel Prices:

7–OLD MASTER	4.60	3.00	2.60
5–PLAY TEN		9.20	7.80
2–CHIEF'S KEY			10.40

$2 EXACTA 7-5 PAID $56.60.

We lose $2 on this race. Our profit is $34.80 midway through the card.

Turbulent Kris Kris S. is a monster turf-sire whose progeny return $5.15 for each two-dollar win bet in their first and second grass races. First turf try pushes him outside of the win pars, but he's eligible to improve today in his second grass start. Contender off the strong turf breeding. In order to make tenable comparisons, definitely use his lone turf line.

Fair Crack Placed in a listed stakes, but several others in here have either won a listed stakes or placed in a graded stakes. No way to project today's performance from foreign form, either. The track odds-maker rates him the morning line favorite at 5-to-2. We respect that assessment and make him a contender.

Casual Lies Followed NW1 win with game score in listed stakes. Lear Fan isn't among Quirin's turf sires. But not even a lack of grass breeding may be enough to stop him, as he's demonstrated a distinct will to overcome big odds in three longshot victories in his first four starts. Love-to-win type and a strong contender who fits the profile. We're stuck with using his last race, on dirt, for a paceline, but at least it's at the same

6th Hollywood

1 MILE. (Turf). (1.32⁴) 10th Running of THE HOIST THE FLAG STAKES (2nd Division) (Grade III). Purse $112,500 added. 2-year-olds. (Allowance). By subscription of $150 each, which shall accompany the nomination, $1,500 additional to start, with $112,500 added, of which $22,500 to second, $16,875 to third, $8,438 to fourth and $2,812 to fifth. Weight, 121 lbs. Non-winners of $50,000 at any distance or $30,000 at one mile or over allowed 3 lbs.; of $25,000 or two races other than claiming at one mile or over, 5 lbs.; of $19,000 other than maiden or claiming, 7 lbs. Hollywood Park reserves the right not to divide this race. Should this race not be divided and the number of entries exceed the starting gate capacity, first preference will be given to graded or group stakes winners. Second preference will be given to those horses with the highest total earnings and an also eligible list will be drawn. Failure to draw into this race at scratch time cancels all fees. Trophies will be presented to the winning owner, trainer and jockey. No fees to remaining eligibles (those kept eligible with the Wednesday, July 17 sustaining payment), to the 1991 Hollywood Futurity or Hollywood Starlet. Closed Wednesday, November 13, 1991, with 47 nominations.

LASIX—Turbulent Kris, Casual Lies, Dr. Secreto, Spudabaker.

Turbulent Kris

Dk. b. or br. c. 2(May), by Kris S—My Turbulent Miss, by My Bad George
SOLIS A
Own.—505 Fms—Nhm—Midwbrkt Fms Inc
Br.—Meadowbrook Farms Inc (Fla)
Tr.—La Croix David

Lifetime 1991 5 1 0 0 $29,419
5 1 0 0
$29,419   Turf 1 0 0 0 $825
114

Speed Index: Last Race: -4.0   1-Race Avg.: -4.0   1-Race Avg.: -4.0   Overall Avg.: -6.4
LATEST WORKOUTS   Nov 24 Hol ① 6f fm 1:11⁴ H   Nov 9 Hol 5f fst 1:01 H   Nov 3 Hol 4f fst :50⁴ H   Oct 8 SA 6f fst 1:13 H

Fair Crack-Ir

B. c. 2(Feb), by Fairy King—Have A Flutter, by Auction Ring
RAYMOND B
Own.—A F Budge Ltd
Br.—Hannon P J (Ire)
Tr.—Hannon Richard

Lifetime 1991 9 3 1 2 $759,454
9 3 1 2
$759,454   Turf 9 3 1 2 $759,454
114

Speed Index: Last Race: (—)   3-Race Avg.: (—)   12-Race Avg.: (—)   Overall Avg.: (—)

Casual Lies

B. c. 2(May), by Lear Fan—Morau-En, by Blakeney
PATTERSON A
Own.—Riley Shelley L
Br.—Meadowhill (Ky)
Tr.—Riley Shelley L

Lifetime 1991 4 3 0 0 $52,250
4 3 0 0
$52,250
121

Speed Index: Last Race: (—)   3-Race Avg.: (—)   12-Race Avg.: (—)   Overall Avg.: -1.0
LATEST WORKOUTS   Nov 29 Hol 3f fm :39⁴ H (d)   Nov 20 BM ① 7f fm 1:33 H (d)   Nov 5 Pln 5f fst 1:01 H   Oct 29 Pln 5f fst 1:02 H

Richard Of England

B. g. 2(Mar), by Tri Jet—Liz Taylor, by Worm Front
McCARRON C J
Own.—Chvr Rcg Stb—Crrgn—Crckt Etal
Br.—Mary E Tippett Estate (Va)
Tr.—Lukas D Wayne

Lifetime 1991 5 2 0 2 $76,505
5 2 0 2
$76,505
116

Speed Index: Last Race: (—)   3-Race Avg.: (—)   12-Race Avg.: (—)   Overall Avg.: -5.0
LATEST WORKOUTS   Nov 27 SA 4f fst :47⁴ H   Nov 22 SA 5f fst 1:01² H   Nov 16 SA 5f fst 1:00⁴ H   ● Oct 29 CD 5f fst 1:01 H

Dr. Secreto

Ch. c. 2(Apr), by Secreto—Bespangle, by Dr Fager
ALVARADO F J
Own.—Butter & Hazuherd
Br.—Brant P M (Ky)
Tr.—Bernstein James W

Lifetime 1991 8 1 3 0 $58,631
8 1 3 0
$58,631   Turf 1 0 0 0 $1,250
114

Speed Index: Last Race: (—)   3-Race Avg.: (—)   12-Race Avg.: (—)   Overall Avg.: -0.7
LATEST WORKOUTS   Nov 21 SA 7f fst 1:28 H   Nov 15 SA 7f fst 1:25³ H   ● Nov 9 SA 6f fst 1:13² H   Oct 25 SA 7f fst 1:01² H (d)

El Anelo

Ro. c. 2(May), by L'Enjoleur—Careful Glance, by Roberto
PINCAY L JR
Own.—Class M K
Br.—Burning Daylight Farms Inc (Ky)
Tr.—Martinez Rafael A

Lifetime 1991 5 1 1 0 $16,450
5 1 1 0
$16,450   Turf 1 0 0 0
114

Speed Index: Last Race: -8.0   1-Race Avg.: -8.0   1-Race Avg.: -8.0   Overall Avg.: -7.5
LATEST WORKOUTS   ● Nov 24 Hol 7f fst 1:26¹ H   Nov 7 Hol 7f fst 1:31⁴ H   Oct 30 Hol 5f fst 1:00⁴ H   Oct 13 Hol 7f fst 1:28² H

Sevengreenpairs Ch. c. 2(May), by Green Dancer—Bounces Over Seven, by Cannonade | Lifetime 1991 7 M 3 1 $23,840
MARTINEZ F F | Br.—Ransom R E (Ky) | 114 | 7 0 3 1
Own.—St Cyr & Tavoularis | Tr.—St Cyr Robert | $23,840

10Nov91- 6SA	fst	1 1/16	:472	1:12	1:444	Md Sp Wt	9	5	43½	32½	21½	22	Pincay L Jr	Bb	118	3.50	77-19	HmmrMn1182Svngrnpirs118nkBuckOgygn118hd	Veered in start	9
13Oct91- 4SA	fst	1 1/16	:474	1:121	1:434	Md Sp Wt	2	9	97½	86	55	34½	Solis A	B	117	3.60	80-16	FrndshpFrvr1172½Strtchr1171½Svngrnprs1171¾	6-wide stretch	9
26Sep91- 12Fpx	fst	1 1/16	:464	1:114	1:45	Gtwy To Glry	8	8	87	66½	44½	2no	Solis A	B	114	7.20	83-13	ProspctForFr117noSvngrnprs1142½FblsPstn1142½	Just missed	8
15Sep91- 9Fpx	fst	1 1/16	:47	1:13	1:454	Md Sp Wt	7	8	78	53½	43½	2hd	Martinez F F5	B	113	10.30	79-21	Thinkernot118hdSvngrnpirs1134Strwtchr118hd	4-wide stretch	10
18Aug91- 6Dmr	fst	1	:454	1:12	1:374	Md Sp Wt	7	9	94½	85½	87½	810¾	Pedroza M A		117	24.40	66-19	EnterThePlayer1172½Marfamtic1172RpMster117hd	Rough trip	10
13Jly91- 6Hol	fst	5½f	:22	:452	1:04	Md Sp Wt	11	10	108½	109½	610	611¾	Mercado P		117	77.30	81-12	Monrch'sPrd1172½StrRcrut1175Bustr'sBrck1173	Steadied 5/16	11
19May91- 6Hol	fst	5f	:214	:452	:574	Md Sp Wt	3	9	916	911	69½	69½	Faul R J	B	117	57.60	83-08	Stolen Script1172½ Jer Kei1173 Top Senator1171	Outrun	9

Speed Index: Last Race: (—) 3–Race Avg.: (—) 12–Race Avg.: (—) Overall Avg.: –6.1
LATEST WORKOUTS Nov 29 Hol ⓣ 4f fm :48 H (d) Nov 23 SLR tr.t 6f fst 1:16 H ●Nov 18 SLR tr.t 3f fst :364 H Nov 3 SLR tr.t 7f fst 1:292 H

Spudabaker Dk. b. or br. c. 2(Mar), by Northern Ringer—Acknofina, by Ruffinal | Lifetime 1991 8 1 2 2 $51,000
FLORES D R | Br.—Drakos C (Ky) | 114 | 8 1 2 2
Own.—Drakos C | Tr.—Smith Michael R | $51,000

26Oct91- 6SA	fst	1 1/16	:47	1:12	1:441	Md Sp Wt	8	1	11½	11	12	13½	Flores D R	L	117	5.70	82-20	Spudabaker1173½ Haloshine1171½ Rare Cat117¾	Driving	8
13Oct91- 4SA	fst	1 1/16	:474	1:121	1:434	Md Sp Wt	1	2	42	32½	43½	58½	Flores D R	L	117	*2.30	78-16	FrndshpFrvr1172½Strtchr1171½Svngrnprs1171¾	Saved ground	9
11Sep91- 8Dmr	fst	1	:46	1:102	1:362	Del Mar Fut	8	8	89½	78	710	410	Flores D R	LB	114	56.50	74-18	Bertrando1143½ Zurich1144½ Star Recruit1152	4-wide 7/8	10
11Sep91-Grade II																				
18Aug91- 6Dmr	fst	1	:454	1:12	1:374	Md Sp Wt	2	7	74½	74½	65	58½	Solis A	LB	117	6.80	71-19	EnterThePlayer1172½Marfmtc1172RpMster117hd	Checked 7/8	10
21Jly91- 10Hol	fst	5½f	:214	:452	1:034	Md Sp Wt	3	3	21½	31½	32	34½	Solis A	LBb	117	6.80	90-14	Overstock1173PoliticalRally1171½Spudabker117¾	Always close	12
4Jly91- 6Hol	fst	6f	:22	:451	1:11	Md Sp Wt	7	2	32	43½	33	23½	Flores D R	B	117	6.70	81-11	FranklinSquare1173½Spudabker117nkL'EnVivre1171½	2nd best	10
15Jun91- 6Hol	fst	5½f	:222	:454	1:043	Md Sp Wt	1	4	31½	32	24	28½	Pincay L Jr	B	117	4.10	86-10	SilverRay1178½Spudabaker1174PoliticalRally1171	Best of rest	9
17May91- 3Hol	fst	4½f	:223	:46	:52	Md 40000	10	6		53	54	33¾	Solis A	B	117	8.60e	— —	P. J. And Me117¾ KernelChris1173Spudabaker117hd	Wide trip	10

Speed Index: Last Race: (—) 3–Race Avg.: (—) 12–Race Avg.: (—) Overall Avg.: –4.2
LATEST WORKOUTS Nov 26 SA 4f fst :482 H Nov 20 SA 6f fst 1:151 H Nov 14 SA 5f fst 1:013 H Nov 3 SA 4f fst :531 B

Contested Bid Dk. b. or br. c. 2(May), by Alleged—Queens Only, by Marshua's Dancer | Lifetime 1991 3 1 0 1 $34,600
NAKATANI C S | Br.—Juddmonte Farms Inc (Ky) | 114 | 3 1 0 1
Own.—Juddmonte Farms | Tr.—Zilber Maurice | $34,600 | Turf 3 1 0 1 $34,600

3Nov91 ♦ 3StCloud(Fra)	sf*1⅝	2:281	ⓣ Criterium de StCloud(Gr1)	35	Eddery P	123	5.00	— —	Glleul123hd ClingCollct1235 ContstdBid123no	Prom,mild bid	9
7Oct91 ♦ 1StCloud(Fra)	gd*1	1:442	ⓣ Prix Victrix(Mdn)	1nk	Lequeux A	123	2.30	— —	Contested Bid 123nk Arctic Charm 1232 Mirsu 123¾	Rallied	12
18Sep91 ♦ 2Longchamp(Fra)	fm*1	1:45	ⓣ Prix de Villebon(Mdn)	44	Lequeux A	123	*.70	— —	Tertian 1232 Shivaree 1231 Seen Running 1231	Late rally	7

Speed Index: Last Race: (—) 3–Race Avg.: (—) 12–Race Avg.: (—) Overall Avg.: (—)

distance as today's race, and he tends to run his races pretty much identically.

Richard Of England Tri Jet appears on Quirin's list, but as a sire to stay away from. His progeny return $1.93 on each two-dollar win bet in their first and second grass starts. Nonetheless, that's probably a better showing than that of a no-name sire, and Richard Of England's races show he can run to the win pars at this level. Contender off his last race.

Dr. Secreto Secreto's sons and daughters throw a 69 percent loss in their first and second turf starts. Also, this one's going to be stretching out against proven route winners. He's never beaten winners, either. Too many questions in a field full of competitive horses. Out.

El Anelo First turf try was hardly surprising, as L'Enjoleur's offspring toss dollar losses. Broke maiden in maiden claimer, so how much potential could there have been? That race on the turf hardly fits the model, either. Expect no improvement second time on the turf against these kind. Elimination.

Sevengreenpairs Hasn't even broken his maiden, yet deserves to be a contender on the strength of his Green Dancer turf breeding, which tosses profits of more than 100 percent first and second starts on turf. Should move up on the grass, although he's shown a distinct sluggishness to the second call in his route races, contrary to the winners' pace profile. Rate him off his last race.

Spudabaker Just when practically everyone had him pegged as a sucker horse, this guy fooled them all and finally broke his maiden, no doubt benefiting from setting easy fractions in an uncontested wire-to-wire romp. Like Sevengreenpairs, he's used to setting or racing behind very pedestrian second call route fractions. He may have found his niche as a "need-to-lead" type. No turf breeding to mention, but his last race was a dramatically improved effort, so let's make him a contender off it.

Contested Bid Only horse in the field to have won a turf route, which was the same distance as today's race. Finished third in Grade 1 race at 1 ¼ miles, so there's a positive drop in class to a distance that seems to suit him. Very strong contender, as he's the only horse in the field who's won on the distance/surface combination of today's race. This foreign invader is listed as the 7-to-2 second choice on the morning line.

Foreign-raced horses running in the United States for the first time pose a potential problem for us. We obviously can't rate them by our usual means of par-time handicapping. However, this doesn't force us to relegate them to non-contender status. In fact, there is a recurring situation in which foreign shippers must always be considered contenders.

The track oddsmaker generally has a pretty good feel for how a foreign shipper will perform in its first American start. If a foreign-raced horse is among the top three morning-line horses, the track odds-maker has a high estimation of that horse. That horse is a contender. In addition, we can accept the track odds-maker's morning-line odds on that highly regarded foreign-raced horse as our own betting-line odds. Of the American-raced horses, ALL-IN-ONE saw the race this way:

Casual Lies	3-to-1
Richard Of England	4-to-1
Turbulent Kris	7-to-1

```
1DEC91                              HOL                        8 furlongs turf
Race #6                                                             9 starters
STAKES                                                  Age: 2 years, Male
```

```
-------------------------------INPUT DATA------------------------------------
```

Horse name	# ST	# W	# P	# S	$'S Earned	Date	Trk	Dist.	S	1st C time	2nd C time	Final time
Turbulent Kris	0	0	0	0	0	15NOV91	HOL	8.000	T	47.0	111.0	136.0
Casual Lies	0	0	0	0	0	12OCT91	BM	8.000	D	46.2	110.4	135.4
Sevengreenpairs	0	0	0	0	0	10NOV91	SA	8.500	D	47.2	112.0	144.4
Spudabaker	0	0	0	0	0	26OCT91	SA	8.500	D	47.0	112.0	144.1
Richard Of England	0	0	0	0	0	2NOV91	CD	8.000	D	45.1	111.1	137.4

Horse name	Class Lvl	1st C B.L.	2nd C B.L.	Final B.L.	SR	Var
Turbulent Kris	NW1	12.00	12.00	5.75	79	17
Casual Lies	CLF	1.50	0.50	0.00	91	11
Sevengreenpairs	MSW	3.50	2.50	2.00	77	19
Spudabaker	MSW	0.00	0.00	0.00	82	20
Richard Of England	STAKES	2.50	0.50	0.20	88	9

```
-------------------------------BETTING LINE----------------------------------
```

Horse name	PEH	H-I	THAAI	P-H	ESP	Rating	Betting Line	Fair Place $	Fair Show $
Casual Lies	3	1	1	1	1	79.13	3-1		
Richard Of England	1	2	2	2	2	76.02	4-1		
Turbulent Kris	2	3	3	3	4	69.67	7-1		
Spudabaker	4	4	4	4	3	65.44			
Sevengreenpairs	5	5	5	5	5	60.00			

```
------------------------------EXACTA GRID------------------------------------
```

	Casual Lies		Richard Of Engl		Turbulent Kris	
Casual Lies	. . . .		28	69	45	112
Richard Of Eng	29	73	. . . .		56	140
Turbulent Kris	52	130	62	155	. . . .	

```
----------------------------SPEED/PACE SUMMARY-------------------------------
```

```
Race Profile:      47.63  111.70  134.89   Winners' Pace Profile: EARLY
Ability Par:       70.81                    Pace Contention Point: 1.85 lengths

Projected Times:                         Ability  Balance  Last   Proj  Con-
                  1st C   2nd C   Fin C    Time     Time    Frac   Pace  tender
-----------------------------------------------------------------------------
Casual Lies       49.32  113.60* 136.29   72.01    92.51   22.69  REAR   N
Richard Of England 47.90 112.40  136.32   71.83    93.56   23.92  FRONT  N
Turbulent Kris    49.24  113.08* 137.05   73.21    93.71   23.97  MID    N
Spudabaker        49.23  114.50* 137.89   72.61    94.63   23.38  REAR   N
Sevengreenpairs   50.32  114.98* 138.86   74.20    95.28   23.88  REAR   N
```

```
-------------------------------PACE GRAPH------------------------------------
```

```
        Profile:              47.63             111.70              134.89
        Front Runner:         47.90             112.40              136.29
    Horse name              1C                2C                    F
    Casual Lies        -----------X------+  -----------X---(-+  -------------------X
    Richard Of England -----------------X  -----------(-X------  ----------------X
    Turbulent Kris     -----------X------+  -----------X(-+  -------------X---+
    Spudabaker         -----------X------+  -------X--------(-+  ----------X-------+
    Sevengreenpairs    ------X-----------+  -----X----------(-+  -----X------------+
```

Both foreign invaders were among the track odds-maker's top four morning-line choices: Contested Bid at 7-to-2; Fair Crack, 5-to-2.

The public's odds:

Casual Lies	13-to-1
Richard Of England	3-to-1
Turbulent Kris	8-to-1
Sevengreenpairs	37-to-1
Contested Bid	5-to-2
Fair Crack	2-to-1

Richard Of England is an underlay. Based on comparing the morning line to the actual public line, Contested Bid and Fair Crack are slight underlays. We are left with a huge overlay on Casual Lies and a marginal edge on Turbulent Kris. For the sake of illustration, we'll bet both Casual Lies and Turbulent Kris to win. As is often the case, the track handicapper's high estimation of the eventual winner, the foreign invader Contested Bid, was absolutely correct.

SIXTH RACE
Hollywood
DECEMBER 1, 1991

1 MILE.(Turf). (1.32⁴) 10th Running of THE HOIST THE FLAG STAKES (2nd Division) (Grade III). Purse $112,500 added. 2-year-olds. (Allowance). By subscription of $150 each, which shall accompany the nomination, $1,500 additional to start, with $112,500 added, of which $22,500 to second, $16,875 to third, $8,438 to fourth and $2,812 to fifth. Weight, 121 lbs. Non-winners of $50,000 at any distance or $30,000 at one mile or over allowed 3 lbs.; of $25,000 or two races other than claiming at one mile or over, 5 lbs.; or $19,000 other than maiden or claiming, 7 lbs. Hollywood Park reserves the right not to divide this race. Should this race not be divided and the number of entries exceed the starting gate capacity, first preference will be given to graded or group stakes winners. Second preference will be given to those horses with the highest total earnings and an also eligible list will be drawn. Failure to draw into this race at scratch time cancels all fees. Trophies will be presented to the winning owner, trainer and jockey. No fees to remaining eligibles (those kept eligible with the Wednesday, July 17 sustaining payment), to the 1991 Hollywood Futurity or Hollywood Starlet. Closed Wednesday, November 13, 1991, with 47 nominations.

Value of race $122,400; value to winner $71,775; second $22,500; third $16,875; fourth $8,438; fifth $2,812. Mutuel pool $368,642. Exacta Pool $409,745.

Last Raced	Horse	M/Eqt.A.Wt	PP	St	¼	½	¾	Str	Fin	Jockey	Odds $1
3Nov91 3Fra3	Contested Bid	B	2 114	9	5	5½	6¹	5²	23½	11½	Nakatani C S	2.80
15Nov91 8Hol5	Turbulent Kris	LBb	2 114	1	4	2hd	2hd	1hd	1²	2⁴	Desormeaux K J	8.30
10Nov91 6SA2	Sevengreenpairs		2 114	7	6	86	86	71½	4½	3hd	Martinez F F	37.80
12Oct91 8BM1	Casual Lies	•LB	2 121	3	3	4²	41½	41½	31½	43½	Patterson A	13.90
1Nov91 8SA5	Dr. Secreto	LB	2 114	5	7	6¹	5hd	6¹	71½	5³	Alvarado F J	9.20
26Oct91 6SA1	Spudabaker	LB	2 114	8	2	3⁴	35	2hd	51½	6³	Flores D R	22.80
2Nov91 9CD3	Richard Of England	B	2 116	4	1	1½	1hd	33½	6½	71½	McCarron C J	3.40
29Oct91 6Eng3	Fair Crack-Ir	B	2 121	2	9	7½	7½	86	86	85½	Raymond B	2.00
15Nov91 8Hol8	El Anelo		2 117	6	8	9	9	9	9	9	Pincay L Jr	36.20

OFF AT 3:14 Start good. Won driving. Time, :23 , :46¹, 1:10 , 1:34² Course firm.

$2 Mutuel Prices:

9-CONTESTED BID	7.60	5.00	4.00
1-TURBULENT KRIS		8.50	5.60
7-SEVENGREENPAIRS			7.80

$2 EXACTA 9-1 PAID $55.20.

We lost $4 in the sixth race, dropping our winnings to plus $30.80 for the day.

7th Hollywood

START
6½ FURLONGS
HOLLYWOOD PARK
FINISH

6 ½ FURLONGS. (1.14²) ALLOWANCE. Purse $50,000. 3-year-olds and upward which have not won $18,000 other than closed or claiming since June 25. Weights, 3-year-olds 119 lbs.; older, 121 lbs. Non-winners of $22,000 twice since April 25 allowed 3 lbs.; one such race since then, 5 lbs.; $15,500 twice since June 25, 7 lbs. (Claiming races not considered.)

LASIX—Exemplary Leader, Morlando, Dominated Debut, Profit Key, Sir Beaufort, Blue Eyed Danny, Past Prince.

Exemplary Leader — Dk. b. or br. h. 5, by Vigors—Paradigmatic, by Aristocratic — Lifetime 29 6 4 9 $330,618 — 1991 5 1 1 2 $84,900; 1990 6 1 0 1 $75,600; Turf 9 3 1 2 $168,986
DELAHOUSSAYE E — Br.—Kenwood Stable II (Ky) — **114**
Own.—Siegel M-Jan-Samantha — Tr.—Mayberry Brian A

4May91- 6CD fst 7f :231 :461 1:22 Chrchl Dns H 4 7 108¾ 109 811 810 Antley C W LB 113 14.80 93-05 Thirty Six Red117¾ Private School113nk Bratt's Choice1152 10
4May91-Bothered, shuffled back start
25Apr91- 8Kee fst 1⅛ :473 1:12 1:493 Ben Ali 1 3 42 42 33½ 37 Black C A LB 112 3.80 80-22 SportsViw119hdBrightAgin1137ExmplryLdr112¾ Flattened out 6
25Apr91-Grade III
12Apr91- 8Kee fst 7f :222 :452 1:214 3+Cmwth Br Cp 5 1 69 69 45½ 35 Black C A LB 115 18.40 96-12 BlcTAffr-Ir1241Hsbstr1244EmplrLdr115hd Improved position 6
12Apr91-Grade III
13Feb91- 7SA fst 1 :452 1:092 1:342 Alw 55000 6 8 813 79 54½ 2no Delahoussaye E LB 116 *2.30 95-15 TnkerPort117noExemplryLdr116½DrpuTricolor1151½ Wide trip 9
25Jan91- 8SA fst 6½f :22 :443 1:151 Alw 50000 7 4 76½ 67 45 11 Delahoussaye E LB 116 1.80 94-17 Exemplary Leader1161 Irish114¾ Snipledo1211 Wide early 7
4Aug90- 7Sar fst 1⅛ :484 1:122 1:483 3+Whitney H 5 2 21½ 46½ 511 516½ Garcia J A 115 14.80 78-06 CriminlType1261½DncingSpree1212½MiSlcto1177¾ Tired badly 6
4Aug90-Grade I
14Jly90- 8Hol fst 1 :45 1:084 1:341 3+Bel Air H 1 7 712 79 65½ 51½ Delahoussaye E L 116 2.30e 91-07 PrspctrsGbl1161MscPrspctr112nkAnnlDt117hd 4-wide stretch 7
14Jly90-Grade II
28May90- 7Hol gd 1 :46 1:101 1:353 Handicap 7 6 62¾ 64½ 65½ 34¾ Delahoussaye E 117 3.10 81-18 AnnualDte1143MusicMerci1201¾ExemplryLeder117nk Wide 3/8 7
24Mar90- 8GG fm 1 ⓣ:464 1:101 1:354 3+S F Mile H 9 8 98½ 87½ 74¾ 75 Pedroza M A 117 9.90 88-07 ColwyRlly116nkRiverMster1152MiswkiTern117½ Showed little 10
24Mar90-Grade III
4Mar90- 5SA fm 1 ⓣ:45 1:09 1:342 Arcadia H 6 5 610 67½ 66 64½ McCarron C J 118 5.70 87-18 Prized1241 Happy Toss115hd On The Menu1122¾ Never rallied 9
4Mar90-Grade III
Speed Index: Last Race: -2.0 3-Race Avg.: +5.6 3-Race Avg.: +5.6 Overall Avg.: +1.0
LATEST WORKOUTS Nov 22 SA 5f fst 1:004 H Nov 14 SA 5f fst 1:023 H Nov 6 SA 5f fst 1:003 H Oct 25 SA 4f fst :483 H

Morlando * — Dk. b. or br. g. 5, by Proud Appeal—Virgin Reef, by Unconscious — Lifetime 43 5 7 8 $214,610 — 1991 11 1 1 2 $68,935; 1990 15 2 3 2 $76,300; Turf 2 0 0 0 $1,375
SOLIS A — Br.—Hough J & S (Fla) — **114**
Own.—Freeman Annetta — Tr.—Stute Melvin F

6Jly91- 3Hol fm 1 ⓣ:453 1:093 1:332 Alw 55000 2 4 411 517 517 533¾ Solis A LBb 116 17.60 64-06 Mdjristn1162ExclusivPrtnr1151½JunglPionr1182 Bled nostrils 5
27May91- 7Hol fst 1 1/16 :461 1:093 1:411 3+Handicap 3 5 42 54½ 711 713½ Solis A LBb 116 8.10 82-15 RobynDncr1171½Trbizond118nkAgulucho-Ch1161 Jostled early 8
16May91- 8Hol fst 7½f :224 :451 1:27 Alw 50000 4 5 52½ 53½ 56 55½ Desormeaux KJ LBb 121 4.60 — — RbnDncr1172FrnchSvntfv1141½Stng'sTghr115½ 5-wide stretch 6
3May91- 8Hol fst 1 1/16 :461 1:094 1:413 Alw 55000 4 3 35 34 33½ 32½ Solis A LBb 119 12.00 91-22 Perforce1191½ Warcraft1171 Morlando1193 Gained in drive 5
14Apr91- 8GG fst 1 1/16 :463 1:10 1:402 3+Bd Br Cp H 2 7 73½ 53½ 56½ 56¾ Sibille R LBb 116 12.50 89-21 LouisCyphr-Ir1193PtchyGroundfog115¾Prforc1191½ Wide trip 8
30Mar91- 8SA fst 1⅛ :461 1:10 1:47 Sn Brndno H 2 9 97¾ 76¾ 77 57½ Pedroza M A LBb 112 53.50 87-07 Anshan-GB115noLouisCyphre-Ir1124PleasantTap116no No bid 9
30Mar91-Grade II
13Mar91- 7SA sly 1 :453 1:10 1:36 Alw 48000 4 5 59 53¾ 11 15½ Desormeaux KJ LBb 115 5.50 87-22 Morlando1155½ Tokatee1154 Graf1171½ Handily 5
28Feb91- 8SA sly 1 1/16 :463 1:111 1:424 ⓡAck Ack H 2 4 310 25 23 23½ Desormeaux KJ LBb 113 6.60 85-20 Ibero-Ar1153½ Morlando1134CoaxMeClyde1151½ Jostled start 4
13Feb91- 7SA fst 1 :452 1:092 1:342 Alw 55000 3 6 57½ 66 65 41¾ Desormeaux KJ LBb 115 27.00 93-15 TnkerPort117noExemplryLdr116½DrpuTricolor1151½ Came on 9
26Jan91- 3SA fst 1 :47 1:104 1:351 Alw 43000 4 4 44½ 41½ 31½ 32½ Solis A LBb 115 8.60 88-13 Graf1141¾ Shaynoor-Ir115¾ Morlando1155 4-wide 1/4 6
Speed Index: Last Race: (—) 3-Race Avg.: (—) 12-Race Avg.: (—) Overall Avg.: +0.7
LATEST WORKOUTS Nov 26 Hol 5f fst 1:012 H Nov 20 Hol 1 fst 1:401 H ●Nov 14 Hol 3f fst :353 H ●Nov 8 SA 7f fst 1:291 H

Dominated Debut * — Ch. h. 5, by Topsider—Sierra Vieja, by Exclusive Native — Lifetime 16 4 1 1 $89,625 — 1991 8 2 0 0 $50,625; 1989 8 2 1 1 $39,000; Turf 1 0 0 0
MARTINEZ F F — Br.—Camelot Thoroughbred (Ky) — **109⁵**
Own.—Cho M K — Tr.—Martinez Rafael A

3Nov91- 6BM fst 6f :221 :45 1:094 3+Rnng Luck H 4 2 1hd 2hd 32 610 Gonzalez R M Lb 118 *1.60 77-16 Makaleha1181KnightInSvnnh1172½FbulousGuy114½ Gave way 6
20Oct91- 8BM fst 6f :221 :443 1:09 3+Van Mar Fm H 1 1 11½ 12 11½ 11½ Gonzalez R M Lb 115 8.10 91-14 DomintedDbut1151½BurnAnni1223CrystlRun114½ Held gamely 6
4Oct91- 7SA fst 6f :211 :433 1:084 3+Alw 36000 4 2 1hd 1hd 1hd 43¾ Berrio O A Lb 117 44.00 88-18 Rushmore1171½ Xray1172 Baba Ran119½ Bumped 1/16 8
21Apr91- 7SA fst 5½f :22 :444 1:03 To B Or Nt H 3 4 1½ 1½ 43 49½ Nakatani C S LBb 113 10.40 90-12 NevusStr116hdSunnyBlossom1222½Doyousewhtis1147 Faltered 4
3Apr91- 8SA fst 6½f :214 :44 1:15 Ptro Grnd H 6 3 3nk 3½ 66½ 610½ Garcia J A LBb 108 39.00 84-13 Jacodra111¾ Answer Do1181½ Bruho117hd No whip, wide 6
3Apr91-Grade III
2Mar91- 8SA my 5½f :222 :451 1:051 El Conejo H 6 4 3nk 1hd 21½ 44 Baze R A LB 114 18.70 85-21 BlckJckRod115½LrnsQst1103L'sTnthm117½ Wide backstretch 6
31Jan91- 7SA fst 6½f :211 :433 1:142 Alw 36000 6 1 1hd 1hd 36½ 513½ Martinez F F5 LB 114 8.00 84-15 Navajo Storm1195 Jacodra1167½ Kleven Up114hd No whip 6
6Jan91- 5SA my 6½f :22 :45 1:172 Alw 34000 3 2 1½ 1hd 1hd 1no Martinez F F5 LB 113 13.30 83-18 Dominated Debut113no Naevus Star1212ElToreo1205 No whip 10
4Jly89- 7Hol fst 1 :44 1:081 1:334 3+Handicap 4 7 76¾ 76¾ 78 69 Jauregui L H 108 42.90 85-12 Rahy1145 Paramount Jet115nk Don's Irish Melody1142¾ 10
25Jun89- 3Hol fst 1 1/16 :453 1:102 1:441 3+Alw 31000 1 1 1½ 11 1½ 33¾ Nakatani C S5 109 *1.40 75-19 NpSonom112nkKennedy'sKnockout1223½DomintedDbut1095½ 7
Speed Index: Last Race: -7.0 3-Race Avg.: +1.3 8-Race Avg.: +1.1 Overall Avg.: 0.0
LATEST WORKOUTS ●Nov 24 Hol 6f fst 1:131 H Nov 2 Hol 5f fst 1:032 H Oct 13 Hol 5f fst 1:03 H

Profit Key — B. c. 4, by Desert Wine—Sharm a Sheikh, by New Policy — Lifetime 16 5 4 0 $368,918 — 1991 5 0 1 0 $40,000; 1990 9 5 1 0 $318,118
SMITH M E — Br.—Agnew D J (Ky) — **114**
Own.—Allen & Mathis — Tr.—Lukas D Wayne

17Nov91- 6Hol fst 1 1/16 :46 1:094 1:42 3+Handicap 5 4 49 613 78½ 710 Stevens G L LB 118 10.80 81-15 Perforce116hdBoldCurrent1151½FnticBoy-Ar1182½ Done early 7
23Oct91- 6Kee fst 6f :221 :454 1:10 3+Alw 27600 9 5 72¾ 85¾ 95½ 68¾ Day P LB 117 *1.40 84-12 TomCobbly1175IntownForThDy1172½FllingSky117¾ Wide trip 9
13Apr91- 8Aqu fst 6f :221 :452 1:094 3+Bold Ruler 6 6 55½ 54½ 65 65 Rojas R I 123 5.40 87-17 RousingPast119¾TruendBlue121hdSunshineJimmy1191 Outrun 6
13Apr91-Grade III
29Mar91- 8Aqu gd 1 :46 1:093 1:344 3+Westchstr H 8 4 54½ 56 612 617 Antley C W 118 *1.00 71-17 Rubiano1111¾ Senor Speedy1133 Killer Diller1158½ No threat 9
29Mar91-Grade III
16Feb91-11Lrl fst 7f :223 :451 1:224 3+Gen George 2 8 42 42½ 42½ 2no Santos J A L 118 *2.70 93-18 Star Touch-Fr118no Profit Key1181½ Fire Plug1182½ Gamely 11
16Feb91-Grade II
26Dec90- 8SA fst 7f :22 :441 1:213 Malibu 10 3 84½ 65¾ 67½ 67 Santos J A LB 126 2.90 88-10 PleasntTp1171½Bedeviled1201½DueToTheKing1171½ Wide trip 10
26Dec90-Grade II
18Aug90- 7Sar fst 1¼ :472 1:362 2:023 Travers 6 6 62¾ 66½ 77 58½ Santos J A 126 7.30e 82-09 Rhythm1263½ ShotGunScott126nkSirRichardLewis1263½ Tired 13
18Aug90-Grade I
28Jly90-10Mth fst 1⅛ :471 1:111 1:491 Haskell H 1 1 2½ 4nk 65¾ 67 Santos J A L 122 *1.40 82-10 RestlessCon1182½BrondVux117nkRhythm121hd Stumbled start 7
28Jly90-Grade I
30Jun90- 8Bel fst 1⅛ :462 1:094 1:472 Dwyer 1 1 11 11 11 11½ Santos J A 123 *.60 97-03 Profit Key1231½ Rhythm1231¾ Graf1142 Good handling 4
30Jun90-Grade II
27May90- 8Bel fst 1⅛ :453 1:093 1:471 Peter Pan 6 3 2hd 1½ 13 16½ Santos J A 117 *1.30 98-12 Profit Key1176½ CountryDay1142ParadiseFound1144 Drew off 8
27May90-Grade II
Speed Index: Last Race: -4.0 3-Race Avg.: +3.6 4-Race Avg.: +2.2 Overall Avg.: -1.4
LATEST WORKOUTS Nov 10 Hol 4f fst :491 H Oct 19 CD 4f fst :492 B

Sir Beaufort Gr. c. 4, by Pleasant Colony—Carolina Saga, by Caro (Ire) Lifetime 1991 9 2 1 4 $85,450
MCCARRON C J Br.—Buckland Farm (Va) 16 4 5 4 1990 6 2 2 0 $81,375
Own.—Calantoni Victoria Tr.—Whittingham Charles 118 $177,605 Turf 4 0 1 0 $7,800
2Nov91- 14SA fm *6½f ⓣ:214 :432 1:114 Morvich H 1 5 31 32½ 55 67 Nakatani C S LB 116 3.50 93 – Waterscape119¾ HollywoodReporter113¾Anjiz1151 Gave way 6
16Oct91- 8SA fst 6f :214 :443 1:083 3↑Anct Titl H 6 6 52½ 52 52½ 3½ Nakatani C S L 113 7.50 92-12 FrostFree119hdAnswrDo118½SirBufort113hd Wide,steadied3/8 7
16Oct91-Grade III
7Sep91- 3Dmr fst 6½f :224 :452 1:161 3↑Alw 50000 4 2 31½ 32 31½ 43½ Valenzuela P A LB 115 *1.90 83-15 PleasantTp1211DMediPln1171½AskTheMn115nk Took up 1/16 5
7Sep91-Placed third through disqualification
23Aug91- 7Dmr fst 6f :213 :442 1:09 3↑Alw 50000 3 7 78½ 41½ 41½ 3¾ McCarron C J L 115 4.80 93-10 Asia115½ Blue Eyed Danny116nk Sir Beaufort115½ Wide trip 7
1Aug91- 7Dmr fst 6½f :222 :451 1:161 3↑Alw 46000 3 6 53¾ 42 2hd 11½ McCarron C J LB 115 2.20 87-15 Sir Beaufort1151½ Blue Eyed Danny1161¾ BeirneStation118no 6
1Aug91-Bumped start, 4-wide stretch, ridden out
12Jun91- 3Hol fst 1⅛ :453 1:093 1:413 Alw 42000 5 3 31½ 3nk 31½ 37 Santos J A L 115 3.00 86-11 Aguilucho-Ch1175 Admirallus1152SirBeaufort1154 Weakened 5
9May91- 8Hol fm 1 ⓣ:47 1:104 1:341 Alw 42000 7 2 21½ 63½ 85¾ 87½ Flores D R LB 115 9.40 87-06 LxeyBy-Ir116noDoubleFound115nkOldAllince1151½ Rank early 8
6Apr91- 3SA fm *6½f ⓣ:213 :433 1:122 Alw 39000 5 3 45 43 25 26 Santos J A L 118 4.00 91-08 Forest Glow1146 Sir Beaufort1181 Qui Danzig118¾ 2nd best 6
17Mar91- 3SA fst 6½f :212 :434 1:15 Alw 36000 2 6 51½ 2½ 1½ 11½ Santos J A LB 115 4.50 95-10 SirBeufort1151½FutureCreer1152MstrLyphor119¾ Boxed in 1/8 7
23May90- 8Hol fm 1 ⓣ:463 1:103 1:352 Alw 37000 2 1 1½ 1hd 53½ 611¾ McCarron C J 117 *1.40 75-13 OldAllince1171CollegeGreen1152¾Predecessor1151½ Gave way 7
Speed Index: Last Race: +4.0 3–Race Avg.: +4.3 5–Race Avg.: +4.0 Overall Avg.: -1.0
LATEST WORKOUTS Nov 28 Hol 3f fst :35 H ●Nov 21 Hol 6f fst 1:122 H Nov 15 Hol 5f fst 1:011 H Nov 10 SA 3f fst :354 B

Blue Eyed Danny Ch. h. 5, by Blue Eyed Davy—Dora Maar, by Native Charger Lifetime 1991 11 1 6 1 $103,560
PEDROZA M A Br.—Tricar Sales Inc (Cal) 18 3 9 2 1990 4 1 1 1 $30,975
Own.—Tricar Stable Tr.—Feld Jude T 114 $157,235
9Nov91- 3SA fst 6f :212 :441 1:092 3↑[S]Cal Cp Spt H 2 4 42 64 86¾ 98 Baze R A LB 117 27.80 81-11 Ltthbighossroll118hdAnswrDo1214PstPrnc113hd Bobbled start 10
16Oct91- 8SA fst 6f :214 :443 1:083 3↑Anct Titl H 2 2 2hd 2hd 2hd 52¾ Valenzuela P A LB 116 5.30 90-12 Frost Free118hd Answer Do118½ Sir Beaufort113hd Weakened 7
16Oct91-Grade III
28Sep91- 8BM fst 6f :22 :444 1:091 3↑Bud Br Cp H 6 1 1hd 1hd 2½ 21 Baze R A LB 115 6.80 89-19 RobynDncr1191BlEydDnny115noLtthbghossroll1162 Game try 7
7Sep91- 8BM fst 6f :214 :441 1:09 3↑Saratoga H 2 1 2hd 2hd 2hd 31 Castanon A L LBb 115 3.70 90-14 CpeLudtke116noBlckJckRod1171BlueEydDnny115hd Good try 7
23Aug91- 7Dmr fst 6f :213 :442 1:09 3↑Alw 50000 1 5 2½ 2hd 1hd 2½ Valenzuela P A Lb 116 10.30 93-10 Asia115½ Blue Eyed Danny116nk Sir Beaufort115½ 7
23Aug91-Bumped hard, jostled badly early, rushed to contention, good try
1Aug91- 7Dmr fst 6½f :222 :451 1:161 3↑Alw 46000 2 3 1hd 1hd 1hd 21½ Valenzuela P A LBb 116 2.70 86-15 SirBeufort1151½BlueEyedDnny1161¾BirnSttion118no Held 2nd 6
29Jun91- 8Hol fst 7f :214 :434 1:21 3↑Trpl Bnd H 5 3 2hd 31½ 36½ 411½ Delahoussaye E LBb 116 7.50 88-09 Robyn Dancer118¾ Bruho1172 BlackJackRoad118¾ Gave way 6
29Jun91-Grade III
13Jun91- 8Hol fst 6f :22 :44 1:081 3↑Alw 39000 1 5 1hd 2hd 2hd 2nk Santos J A LBb 115 5.80 99-09 Asia115nk Blue Eyed Danny115¾ Nucleon1170 Broke slowly 5
24Apr91- 8GG fst 1 :454 1:101 1:354 Alw 28000 6 2 2hd 2hd 1hd 2hd Diaz A L LBb 117 *1.00 86-21 SrtogLd117hdBlEydDnny117¾WlcomDnSr117½ Drifted out late 6
13Apr91- 1GG fst 6f :213 :442 1:092 3↑[S]Montclair H 1 4 2hd 2hd 2hd 1no Diaz A L LBb 115 15.40[D] 91-13 [D]BlEdDnn115noDTThKn118¾FrnchSntf1154½ Drifted out late 5
13Apr91-Disqualified and placed second
Speed Index: Last Race: -8.0 3–Race Avg.: +0.6 9–Race Avg.: +3.0 Overall Avg.: +3.4
LATEST WORKOUTS Nov 24 SA 6f fst 1:131 H Nov 19 SA 4f fst :504 H Nov 5 SA 3f fst :353 H Oct 30 SA 6f fst 1:141 H

Past Prince Ch. g. 4, by Princely Native—Passion, by Distinctive Lifetime 1991 5 1 1 1 $47,285
TORRES H Br.—Fallon Nikki (Cal) 12 3 3 1 1990 7 2 2 0 $41,250
Own.—Fallon Nikki L Tr.—Fallon Thomas 109[5] $88,535 Turf 2 0 0 0
9Nov91- 3SA fst 6f :212 :441 1:092 3↑[S]Cal Cp Spt H 5 3 21 21½ 41¾ 34 Desormeaux K J LB 113 35.90 85-11 LtthbghssrII118hdAnswrD1214PstPrnc113hd Lugged out early 10
20Oct91- 3SA fst 6½f :221 :45 1:152 3↑Alw 36000 6 1 1½ 1hd 1hd 2¾ Nakatani C S L 115 6.90 92-16 Express It117¾ Past Prince115¾ Rushmore119¾ Game try 6
8Jun91- 3Hol fst 6½f :22 :443 1:16 3↑[S]Fty Sx In Rw 7 1 41½ 31½ 42½ 53½ Desormeaux K J LB 114 9.50 88-12 Gum118nkBurnAnnie1141½FrenchSevntyfiv114hd Bumped 5/16 7
19May91- 5Hol fm 5½f ⓣ:213 :441 1:013 Alw 50000 3 1 1½ 1½ 41½ 66¼ Desormeaux K J LB 114 14.50 — — DuckAndDiv-Ir116¾BurnAnni115hdRobnsk-NZ1161½ Gave way 6
25Apr91- 3Hol fst 6f :22 :451 1:094 3↑[S]Alw 36000 6 2 2hd 2hd 2½ 1½ McCarron C J LB 118 *1.60 91-10 Past Prince118½DanaweeProspector118½Andimo1181½ Driving 6
30Dec90- 7SA fst 6½f :214 :444 1:15 3↑Alw 38000 2 3 11 1hd 23 27 McCarron C J LB 115 3.50 88-12 Farma Way1147 Past Prince115¾ Express It117¾ Held 2nd 8
7Dec90- 5Hol fm 6f ⓣ:214 :441 1:073 3↑Alw 32000 11 1 1½ 1½ 2hd 61¾ Flores D R LB 113 12.70 99 – KipperKelly113¾Phrisien-Fr114noPureGnius1161 Bumped 1/16 12
16Nov90- 7Hol fst 7f :212 :44 1:213 Clm 62500 4 1 1½ 1hd 11 2½ McCarron C J LB 116 4.90 96-09 TimlssJun116½PstPrinc1162½Gundghi1161¾ Broke out,bumped 6
21Oct90- 9SA fst 7f :22 :442 1:21 3↑Alw 36000 7 1 1½ 31 816 819½ Flores D R L 116 20.60 79-13 Timebank1165½Greydar1141½Mr.DandyDncer1171½ Lugged out 9
26Aug90- 7Dmr fst 6½f :213 :443 1:153 3↑[S]Alw 33000 1 7 1hd 1hd 1½ 11 Desormeaux K J LB 114 17.50 90-12 PastPrince1141BlazeO'Brien117½LteDivorce1183 Broke slowly 7
Speed Index: Last Race: -4.0 3–Race Avg.: +1.3 8–Race Avg.: +0.5 Overall Avg.: +0.3
LATEST WORKOUTS ●Nov 28 Fpx 3f fst :352 H Nov 23 SA 5f fst :594 H ●Nov 3 SA 5f fst :593 H Oct 12 SA 5f fst 1:023 H

The conditions of eligibility for classified allowance races absolutely require a close reading. Examining the conditions will always help us identify which horses are well-meant, and often can assist us in determining for which horse the race was written. It's a fine point of class handicapping that James Quinn has promoted, first in his exceptional *The Handicapper's Condition Book*, and subsequently in his definitive *Recreational Handicapping*. Here we have a 6½ furlong dirt sprint for three-year-olds and up "which have not won $19,500 other than closed or claiming since June 25." The "closed" means the non-winners allowance series. A winner's share of $19,500 in southern California translates into a total purse of $35,454. Classified allowance and stakes purses start at $50,000. So today's race would effectively bar entry of any horse that had won a classified allowance or a stakes race since June 25. Horses that won a "closed" race—in other words, a non-winners allowance race—or a claiming race were eligible. Quinn would say that the conditions of this race were highly restrictive, and as such, superior class would bow to exceedingly sharp or peaking form, the reason being that really high-class animals—recent stakes winners and recent winners of other classified allowance races—couldn't run in today's highly restricted classified race. Thus, "inferior" non-claiming stock are given a better chance to knock down a large purse. Because of the time restriction in the conditions, the true class stickouts entered today are probably coming off layoffs or being raced into shape, their current form not allowing them to have won for the past five months. Be on the lookout for current-form-and-condition stickouts.

Exemplary Leader Several competitive placings in graded stakes, but he's been away for even longer than the specified June 25 date in the conditions, not having raced in seven months. He's in here for the conditioning. In terms of the profile, he's a confirmed late runner, positioned last at the second call of his two sprints. Elimination.

Morlando Recent form has been atrocious; hence the layoff from early July. Complete lack of sharp condition. Really not a sprinter, either. Out.

Dominated Debut Interestingly, he won a minor stakes at Bay Meadows within the time period specified in the conditions. We can tell it's a minor stakes because the conditions state that any horse entered today cannot have won a winner's share of more than $19,500. A contender, even though his wire-to-wire winning style hasn't been holding up at this distance recently. Use the Oct. 20 race.

Profit Key Might have displayed his best last year as a high-class, non-claiming three-year-old. Obviously those days are past, as his recent form in much lesser races has been awful. He's really gone south since that Feb. 16 race at Laurel, which forced him to lay off. He seems better-suited to front-running in route races, as well. Dismiss.

Sir Beaufort Throw out the last race, as it was on turf, a surface on which he's never won, and all his dirt sprints exhibit very good form. Yes, the August 1 race at Del Mar had a purse greater than $35,454; but that was a closed race for non-winners three times other than maiden or claiming. His confirmed running style of laying in mid-pack approximately two lengths off the lead at the second call is what's winning at this distance. Rate him off the Oct. 16 race.

Blue Eyed Danny The last race was not indicative of current form, as the horse bobbled at the start. Going back to the penultimate line, he ran within two lengths of Sir Beaufort. Blue Eyed Danny has finished in the money eight of his last ten, so there are no problems with this guy on current form. Like Dominated Debut, he's a habitual need-to-lead type whose style doesn't match that of recent winners at this distance. Use the Sept. 28 line.

Past Prince Another strong candidate on the basis of sharp current form. Like Dominated Debut and Blue Eyed Danny, he's a one-dimensional speedball who goes against the winners' pace profile. The paceline is the most recent race.

Who was the race written for? Only two of the entrants have won during the prescribed time period written in the eligibility conditions: Dominated Debut and Sir Beaufort. Of these two, Sir Beaufort scores higher on the current-form and condition test. He also is immensely advantaged by the winners' pace profile that has favored mid-pack runners. Dominated Debut is a wire-to-wire type, and that running style has been penalized lately. Here is how ALL-IN-ONE interpreted our data:

Dominated Debut	3-to-1
Sir Beaufort	3-to-1
Blue Eyed Danny	7-to-2

The public's odds:

Dominated Debut	12-to-1
Sir Beaufort	1-to-1
Blue Eyed Danny	7-to-1

The value horses in the win pool are Dominated Debut and Blue Eyed Danny. Notice how Sir Beaufort has the best final time on the Speed/Pace Summary and Pace Graph? Don't be alarmed. Remember, our job is to love bets, not horses. Most of your fellow

```
1DEC91                          HOL                       6.5 furlongs dirt
Race #7                                                            7 starters
CLF                                                   Age: 3+years, Male
```

```
------------------------------INPUT DATA------------------------------
                   #   #   #   #   $'S                              1st C  2nd C  Final
Horse name         ST  W   P   S   Earned  Date    Trk Dist. S     time   time   time
----------------------------------------------------------------------------------
Blue Eyed Danny    11  1   6   1   103560  9NOV91  BM  6.000 D     22.0   44.4   109.1
Past Prince        5   1   1   1   47285   9NOV91  SA  6.000 D     21.2   44.1   109.2
Sir Beaufort       9   2   1   4   85450   2NOV91  SA  6.000 D     21.4   44.3   108.3
Dominated Debut    8   2   0   0   50625   9NOV91  BM  6.000 D     22.1   44.3   109.0
```

```
                                 1st C   2nd C   Final
Horse name         Class Lvl     B.L.    B.L.    B.L.    SR    Var
--------------------------------------------------------------------
Blue Eyed Danny    CLF           0.00    0.00    1.00    89    19
Past Prince        CLF           1.00    1.50    4.00    85    11
Sir Beaufort       CLF           2.50    2.00    0.50    92    12
Dominated Debut    CLF           0.00    0.00    0.00    91    14
```

```
-----------------------------BETTING LINE-----------------------------
                   -------Rankings--------           Betting   Fair     Fair
Horse name         PEH  H-I  THAAI  P-H  ESP  Rating  Line    Place $  Show $
----------------------------------------------------------------------------
Dominated Debut    2    2    2      3    1    85.64   3-1
Sir Beaufort       3    1    1      2    3    85.41   3-1
Blue Eyed Danny    1    3    3      1    4  ' 84.65   7-2
Past Prince        4    4    4      4    2    70.91
```

```
-----------------------------EXACTA GRID-----------------------------
                  |Dominated Debut| Sir Beaufort  |Blue Eyed Danny|
------------------+---------------+---------------+---------------+
Dominated Debu    | . . . . . . . |   24    59     |   25    61     |
                  | . . . . . . . |               |               |
                  | . . . . . . . |               |               |
------------------+---------------+---------------+---------------+
Sir Beaufort      |   24    59     | . . . . . . . |   25    61     |
                  |               | . . . . . . . |               |
                  |               | . . . . . . . |               |
------------------+---------------+---------------+---------------+
Blue Eyed Dann    |   25    61     |   25    62     | . . . . . . . |
                  |               |               | . . . . . . . |
                  |               |               | . . . . . . . |
------------------+---------------+---------------+---------------+
```

```
-----------------------------SPEED/PACE SUMMARY-----------------------------
Race Profile:      22.69   45.68   115.57   Winners' Pace Profile: MID
Ability Par:       68.67                    Pace Contention Point:  4.24 lengths

Projected Times:                   Ability  Balance  Last   Proj  Con-
                   1st C  2nd C  Fin C   Time     Time    Frac   Pace  tender
---------------------------------------------------------------------------------
Dominated Debut    22.89  45.88  115.77  68.87    73.29   29.90  EARLY  Y
Sir Beaufort       23.75  46.64  115.47  69.53    73.21   28.83  LATE   Y
Blue Eyed Danny    22.63  45.86  115.66  69.09    73.18   29.81  FRONT  Y
Past Prince        23.07  46.15  116.94  69.24    74.26   30.79  EARLY  N
```

```
-----------------------------PACE GRAPH-----------------------------
      Profile:                  22.69              45.68              115.57
      Front Runner:             22.63              45.86              115.47
Horse name                      1C                 2C                 F
Dominated Debut    ----------------X+ ------------(----X ----------------X-+
Sir Beaufort       -----------X-----+ ------------(X---+ ----------------------X
Blue Eyed Danny    ----------------X ------------(----X ----------------------X+
Past Prince        ----------------X-+ ------------(---X+ -----------X------+
```

citizens love Sir Beaufort. Most of your fellow citizens are also losers. If you truly want to win, get in the habit now of loving bets. You'll suffer the agony of defeat in many races such as this, where your top-figure horse wins without you, but I guarantee you that in the long run you will fare much better than 98 percent of your fellow citizens.

SEVENTH RACE
Hollywood
DECEMBER 1, 1991

6 ½ FURLONGS. (1.14²) ALLOWANCE. Purse $50,000. 3-year-olds and upward which have not won $19,500 other than closed or claiming since June 25. Weights, 3-year-olds 119 lbs.; older, 121 lbs. Non-winners of $22,000 twice since April 25 allowed 3 lbs.; one such race since then, 5 lbs.; $19,500 twice since June 25, 7 lbs. (Claiming races not considered.)

Value of race $50,000; value to winner $27,500; second $10,000; third $7,500; fourth $3,750; fifth $1,250. Mutuel pool $316,657. Exacta pool $364,762.

Last Raced	Horse	M/Eqt.	A.	Wt	PP	St	¼	½	Str	Fin	Jockey	Odds $1
2Nov91 14SA6	Sir Beaufort	LB	4	118	5	4	4⁴	3³	3⁵	1¹½	McCarron C J	1.00
9Nov91 3SA9	Blue Eyed Danny	LBb	5	114	6	2	2⁵	1hd	1hd	2¹½	Pedroza M A	7.10
9Nov91 3SA3	Past Prince	LB	4	109	7	1	1hd	2²½	2½	3⁷	Torres H5	3.80
17Nov91 6Hol7	Profit Key	LB	4	114	4	5	5³	5¹½	5²½	4hd	Smith M E	19.50
6Jly91 3Hol5	Morlando	LBb	5	114	2	6	7	7	6²	5hd	Desormeaux K J	23.80
9Nov91 6BM6	Dominated Debut	Lb	5	109	3	3	3¹	4⁶	4³	6⁹	Martinez F F5	12.60
4May91 6CD8	Exemplary Leader	LB	5	116	1	7	6¹½	6hd	7	7	Delahoussaye E	3.70

OFF AT 3:48. Start good. Won driving. Time, :21³, :44², 1:08⁴, 1:15¹ Track fast.

$2 Mutuel Prices:

5-SIR BEAUFORT	4.00	3.00	2.40
6-BLUE EYED DANNY		5.20	3.20
7-PAST PRINCE			3.00

$2 EXACTA 5-6 PAID $18.60.

We lost $4 on this race, reducing our profits to $26.80.

8th Hollywood

1 ⅛ MILES. (Turf). (1.44⁴) 11th Running of THE MATRIARCH (Grade I). (Chute start). Purse $200,000. Fillies and mares. 3-year-olds and upward. By subscription of $200 each, which shall accompany the nomination, $2,000 additional to start, with $110,000 to the winner, $40,000 to second, $30,000 to third, $15,000 to fourth and $5,000 to fifth. Weights, 3-year-olds, 120 lbs.; older 123 lbs. Starters to be named through the entry box by closing time of entries. This race will not be divided. If the number of entries exceed the starting gate capacity, first preference will be given to graded or group stakes winners in 1991. Second preference will be given to those horses with the highest total earnings in 1991 and an also eligible list will be drawn. Failure to draw into this race at scratch time cancels all fees. Trophies will be presented to the winning owner, trainer and jockey. Closed Wednesday November 13 with 32 nominations.

Coupled—Sha Tha and Colour Chart.

Mutuel field— La Kaldoun-Fr, Free At Last-GB, Quilma-Ch.

LASIX—Elegance, Flawlessly, Kostroma-Ir, Countus In, La Kaldoun-Fr, Kikala-En, Reluctant Guest, Free At Last-Gb, Quilma-Ch.

Elegance — Gr. f. 4, by Providential—Carillon Special, by Hawkin's Special
ALVARADO F J — Br.—Bruce D (Ky) — 123
Own.—Steinmetz J — Tr.—Van Berg Jack C

Lifetime								
	1991	9	1	2	1	$77,516
24 6 5 5	1990	15	5	3	4	$88,310
$165,826	Turf	16	5	5	1	$150,816

21Nov91- 3Hol	fm	1	Ⓣ:48²	1:12¹	1:35²	3↑ⒻAlw 50000	2	7	7³½	6³½	4¹½	1²½	Delahoussaye E	LB	116	9.20	88-08	Elegance116²½ Silvered116no Flirty114¹½		7
21Nov91-Boxed in 1st turn, wide rally																				
2Nov91- 10CD	fm	1⅛	Ⓣ:48¹	1:12²	1:51	3↑ⒻCardinal H	7	7	7⁷	6⁵	6⁴½	6⁶	Stevens G L	LB	115	23.50	84-06	Christiecat118hdSuperFn115nkScreenProspect113³½	No factor	9
5Oct91- 6LaD	fm	1⅜	Ⓣ:49⁴	1:40²	2:17	3↑ⒻGldn Hvst H	6	3	3⁴	3½	1½	2½	Borel C H	L	113	4.90	86-12	Behaving Dancer113½Elegance113¹ExplosiveEle114¹¼	Gamely	7
5Oct91-Grade III																				
1Sep91- 10AP	fm	1	Ⓣ:49⁴	1:14²	1:37¹	3↑ⒻGold Flower	3	5	4²½	4²½	3¹½	3²	Desormeaux K J	L	117	7.00	88-07	Lady Shirl122² Indian Fashion117hd Elegance117½	Mild rally	6
22Aug91- 8AP	fm	*1	Ⓣ:46³	1:11¹	1:35¹	3↑ⒻAlw 32000	5	5	5⁸	4¹½	3³	2nk	Day P	L	116	1.80	101 —	ChrmingMolly119nkElgnc116²MysticlLss116²	4-wide into lane	6
10Aug91- 9AP	fm	1¹⁄₁₆	Ⓣ:49	1:13²	1:44	3↑ⒻBud BrdCpH	11	10	10⁵½	10⁶	8⁸	7⁷	Compton P	L	114	36.90	79-14	NiceServe112²DringDoone-En113nkScrtAdvic112hd	Wide turn	11
13Jly91- 9AP	fm	1	Ⓣ:46³	1:11¹	1:35²	3↑ⒻHanshin H	9	7	7⁹¼	6⁵	6³¼	5⁷¾	Silva C H	L	115	12.40	91-10	LadyShirl112²½TownsendLass111½FmilyHope115²	Even finish	12
10Feb91- 10GP	fm	1⅜	Ⓣ		2:15	3↑ⒻVery One H	2	5	5⁸	4³½	2³	4²¼	Fires E	L	116	21.20	— —	Rigamajig116² StarStanding114nkAhead-GB112no	Outfinished	11
26Jan91- 10FG	gd	*7½f	Ⓣ:25³	:50²	1:34⁴	ⒻSxty Sails H	1	3	5⁷	6⁴½	3²	4¹½	Walker B J Jr	L	118	*1.60	88-19	Chrnell'sDrem113¹PhoenixSunshin112noToughC:112nk	Evenly	10
15Dec90- 9FG	fm	*1	Ⓣ:47³	1:13²	1:39	ⒻP H Brds Cp	8	7	6⁵½	7⁴¼	4³	1nk	Walker B J Jr	L	118	2.50	99-06	Elegance118nk Play The Field-Ir113½ NurseDopey118¹	Got up	12

Speed Index: Last Race: -4.0 3-Race Avg.: -5.3 8-Race Avg.: -2.6 Overall Avg.: -2.4

Fire The Groom — Dk. b. or br. f. 4, by Blushing Groom—Prospector's Fire, by Mr Prospector
STEVENS G L — Br.—Calicchio & Seltzer (Ky) — 123
Own.—Allred-Hubbard-Sczesny — Tr.—Shoemaker Bill

Lifetime						
	1991	7	3	1	2	$594,343
15 8 1 2	1990	7	5	0	0	$151,368
$745,711	Turf	15	8	1	2	$745,711

10Nov91- 8SA	fm	1¼	Ⓣ:49²	1:37⁴	2:01	3↑ⒻYellow Rbn	12	6	9⁴¾	11⁷	10⁴¾	3²½	Stevens G L	B	123	3.50	80-17	Kostroma-Ir123²Flawlessly119½FireTheGroom123hd	Wide trip	13
10Nov91-Grade I																				
6Oct91 ♦6Longchamp(Fra)	yl	*1⅛			1:56¹	ⓉⒻPrix de l' Opera(Gr2)						4¹¼	Stevens G L		132	5.25	— —	Martessa126¾ ColourChrt128nk Polemic12⁴nk	Trailed, cl fast	14
31Aug91- 8AP	fm	1³⁄₁₆	Ⓣ:45⁴	1:09⁴	1:53²	3↑ⒻBeverly D	7	6	6⁶½	6⁵	4¹¼	1¹¾	Stevens G L		123	2.20	99-15	FirthGroom123¹¾ColourChrt123²½Mssuosn123¹½	Strong finish	7
31Aug91-Grade I																				

30Jun91- 8Hol fm 1⅛ (T):473 1:101 1:462 3+(F)Bvrly Hls H 7 5 55 55 44½ 21 Stevens G L B 120 *.90 97-03 Alcando-Ir1131 Fire The Groom120½ Countus In117no Rallied 8
30Jun91-Grade I
2Jun91- 8Hol fm 1⅛ (T):481 1:113 1:472 3+(F)Gamely H 10 10 107¾ 107½ 53½ 3½ Stevens G L B 120 *1.60 92-06 MssJosh118½IslndJmbor116noFrThGrm1201½ Off slowly, wide 11
2Jun91-Grade I
5May91- 8Hol fm 1 1/16 (T):47 1:103 1:40 3+(F)Wilshire H 5 5 57½ 56½ 44 1hd Stevens G L B 118 *.70 95-06 FireTheGroom118hdOdale-Ar1151Agirlfromrs1141 Strong kick 6
5May91-Grade II
14Apr91- 8SA fm 1 (T):45 1:084 1:332 3+(F)Bd Br Cp H 8 6 69 67 22½ 13 Stevens G L B 115 5.10 96-10 FrThGroom1153FlowrGrl-GB1162HrtOfJy119¾ 6-wide stretch 9
14Apr91-Grade III
3Nov90- 7Aqu fm 1 (T):454 1:104 1:351 3+(F)Bud BrdCpH 10 4 44 34 1hd 1¾ Dettori L F 114 6.90 113 — Fire TheGroom114¾SallyRous-Ir1141¾Christiecat1151½ Driving 12
12Oct90♦3Ascot(Eng) gd 1 1:42 (T)(F)Moss Bros October Stks 1¾ Dettori L 123 *1.60 — — Fire The Groom123¾ Samsova1261 PalaceStreet1252 Bid,drvg 10
28Sep90♦4Ascot(Eng) gd 1 1:414 (T)(F)TaylorWoodrowCharityH 14 Dettori L 132 11.00 — — FireTheGroom1324 LiffeyLc121¾ HomTruth130nk Led fnl fur 11

Speed Index: Last Race: -3.0 3-Race Avg.: +3.6 7-Race Avg.: +4.1 Overall Avg.: +4.1

LATEST WORKOUTS Nov 27 Hol (T) 5f fm 1:004 B (d) Nov 21 Hol (T) 5f fm 1:011 H (d) Nov 5 SA 5f fst 1:001 H Oct 29 SA 6f fst 1:141 H

Flawlessly

B. f. 3(Feb), by Affirmed—La Confidence, by Nijinsky II

MCCARRON C J Br.—Harbor View Farm (Ky) **120**

Own.—Harbor View Farm Tr.—Whittingham Charles

Lifetime 13 7 1 1 $530,836 | 1991 6 4 1 0 $342,550 | 1990 7 3 0 1 $188,286 | Turf 6 5 1 0 $417,550

10Nov91- 8SA fm 1¼ (T):492 1:374 2:01 3+(F)Yellow Rbn 6 3 32 31 42 22 McCarron C J LB 119 5.00 81-17 Kostrom-Ir1232Flwlessly119½FireTheGroom123hd Good effort 13
10Nov91-Grade I
5Oct91- 8SA fm 1 (T):454 1:102 1:332 (F)H C Rmsr H 10 7 73½ 2½ 2hd 1½ McCarron C J LB 123 *.70 96-09 Flawlessly123½Gravieres-Fr1174½ZmHummer1172 Game effort 10
25Aug91- 8Dmr fm 1⅛ (T):482 1:131 1:492 (F)Dmr Oaks 2 5 54 52 2hd 12 McCarron C J L 120 *.70 91-09 Flwlessly1202SettleSymphony120½Fowd1201½ Speed to spare 6
25Aug91-Grade III
10Aug91- 8Dmr fm 1 (T):463 1:102 1:344 (F)Sn Clmnt H 8 6 54 4¾ 1½ 11¾ McCarron C J L 120 *1.50 98-04 Flwlessly1201¾GoldFleece1142½MissHighBlde1172 Bumped 7/8 9
5Jly91- 7Hol fm 1 1/16 (T):482 1:124 1:422 (F)(S)St Dancer 4 3 32½ 31 2hd 11¾ McCarron C J L 118 *1.70 83-09 Flwlssly1181½Jol'sPrncss-GB114hdSprcory1142½ Strong effort 6
19Jan91- 7Aqu fst 1 70 [•]:472 1:111 1:414 (F)Busanda 7 3 44¾ — — — Krone J A 121 *1.40 — — I'mAThriller1124WinCraftyLdy1165I'mTickledPink112hd Bled 7
9Dec90- 8Aqu fst 1 1/16 [•]:494 1:134 1:463 (F)Tempted 4 6 51¾ 42 3nk 1hd Bailey J D 121 4.00 75-25 Flawlessly121hdDebutant'sHalo1211½SleptThrult1141½ Driving 12
9Dec90-Grade III
17Nov90- 8Aqu gd 1⅛ :50 1:153 1:534 (F)Demoiselle 6 1 1½ 1hd 2hd 44¾ Cordero A Jr 119 5.50 63-30 Debutnt'sHlo1162PrivteTresur121nkSlptThrult1122 Weakened 7
17Nov90-Grade II
27Oct90- 4Bel fst 1 1/16 :454 1:11 1:44 (F)Br Cp Juv F 5 12 1211 109½ 88½ 712¾ Pincay L Jr 119 46.20 69-15 MdowStr1195PrvtTrsr1191DncSmrtly119½ Improved position 13
27Oct90-Grade I
6Oct90- 7Bel fst 1 :461 1:11 1:352 (F)Frizette 1 3 2½ 21 26 314½ Bailey J D 119 5.20 70-11 MedowStr11914ChmpgneGlow119nkFlwlessly119½ Weakened 5
6Oct90-Grade I

Speed Index: Last Race: -2.0 3-Race Avg.: +1.0 5-Race Avg.: -0.6 Overall Avg.: -3.1

LATEST WORKOUTS Nov 27 Hol (T) 5f fm 1:014 B (d) ●Nov 22 Hol (T) 5f fm :592 H (d) ●Nov 17 Hol 3f fst :353 H Nov 8 SA 3f fst :361 B

Kostroma–Ir

B. m. 5, by Caerleon—Katie May, by Busted

DESORMEAUX K J Br.—Stack & Valerio Ltd (Ire) **123**

Own.—de Brgh–PrstwdFm–Seguter Tr.—Jones Gary

Lifetime 18 8 1 2 $480,965 | 1991 [illegible] | 1990 10 4 0 2 $182,277 | Turf 18 8 1 2 $480,965

10Nov91- 8SA fm 1¼ (T):492 1:374 2:01 3+(F)Yellow Rbn 1 5 42 42 31 12 Desormeaux K J LB 123 *3.10 83-17 Kostroma-Ir1232 Flawlessly119½ Fire The Groom123hd 13
10Nov91-Grade I; Rank early, lacked room into far turn, surged to front inside 1/8
28Oct91- 8SA fm 1⅛ (T):443 1:074 1:434 3+(F)Las Plmas H 6 2 2½ 11½ 12 1½ Desormeaux K J LB 117 *1.10 105 — Kostroma-Ir117½Kiki-En113½Cmpgnrde-Ar1181½ Held gamely 6
28Oct91-Grade II
7Sep91- 8Dmr fm 1 1/16 (T):463 1:104 1:411 3+(F)(S)Osunitas H 8 7 79 75¾ 21 12½ Desormeaux K J LB 118 2.50e 101 — Kostroma-Ir1182½ Re Toss-Ar117hd Agirlfromars118hd 8
7Sep91-5-wide into lane, ridden out
4Nov90- 8SA fm 1¼ (T):452 1:34 1:582 3+(F)Ylw Rbn Iv 13 3 31½ 21 43 87¾ Velasquez J B 123 28.00f 88-04 PlentyOfGrce1191PetitIl-Ir1231RoylTouch-Ir123¾ Rank early 13
4Nov90-Grade I
2Sep90♦4PhoenixPk(Ire) gd 1¼ 2:024 (T) PhnxChmpn(Gr1) 35½ Craine S 129 11.00 — — Elmaamul 1231½ Sikeston 1324 Kostroma 129½ Rallied 8
18Aug90♦3Curragh(Ire) gd 1 1:371 (T) Desmond Stakes(Gr3) 1nk Craine S 126 3.00 — — Kostroma 126nk Bold Russian 1281½ Thakib 1282 Led, held 6
6Aug90♦5Leopardst'n(Ire) gd 1 1:384 (T)(F)BrwnstwnStd 11½ Craine S 139 2.25 — — Kostroma1391½ Arpero1271 StrOfTheFuture1223 Bid, driving 6
28Jly90♦6Leopardst'n(Ire) gd 1⅛ 1:511 (T) Ballycuilen Stks 11½ Craine S 134 2.25 — — Kostroma1341½ Akamantis1165 NorthernPet1234 Bid, driving 9
15Jly90♦5Curragh(Ire) gd 1¼ 2:041 (T) TCBcntnryH 3nk Craine S 131 7.00 — — CrlssWrtng127nk Montfor124no Kostrm1316 Well up thruout 12
30Jun90♦4Curragh(Ire) gd 1¼ 2:064 (T)(F)PrtyPly(Gr2) 52½ Craine S 132 20.00 — — GamePln1181½ CerlessWriting132nk Briswick140½ Stride late 10

Speed Index: Last Race: 0.0 3-Race Avg.: +2.0 4-Race Avg.: -0.5 Overall Avg.: -0.5

LATEST WORKOUTS Nov 26 SA 6f fst 1:152 B Nov 21 SA 5f fst 1:012 H Nov 16 SA 3f fst :351 B ●Nov 5 SA 7f fst 1:251 H

Countus In

Ch. m. 6, by Dancing Count—Cloudy and Warm, by Cloudy Dawn

DAY P Br.—Middleton C G III (Ky) **123**

Own.—Middleton C G III Tr.—Rieser Steven M

Lifetime 29 11 6 1 $569,483 | 1991 8 2 3 1 $181,764 | 1990 6 4 1 0 $243,950 | Turf 21 8 5 1 $536,481

13Nov91- 8CD fm 1 1/16 (T):481 1:121 1:424 3+(F)Alw 37860 2 3 32 31 2hd 12½ Day P LB 116 *.90 99-01 CntsIn1162½SpnnkrsFlyng1173DncfrLcy1161 Brshed riden out 5
2Nov91-10CD fm 1⅛ (T):481 1:122 1:51 3+(F)Cardinal H 4 4 31½ 21½ 42 54¾ Krone J A LB 120 4.30 86-06 Christict110hdSuprFn115nkScrnProspct1133½ Bid inside, wknd 9
8Sep91- 9Pim fm 1⅛ (T):483 1:131 1:501 3+(F)Natl Ladies 4 2 2hd 1½ 13 13 Krone J A L 120 *.50 — — Countus in1203 Gaylord's Annie1203½ McKilts126nk Driving 6
17Aug91- 8Dmr fm 1⅛ (T):483 1:122 1:492 3+(F)Ramona H 6 1 11 1hd 1hd 64½ Nakatani C S LB 117 4.70 86-11 Cmpgnrde-Ar115noBqust1182½Somthingmrry118nk Weakened 10
17Aug91-Grade I
28Jly91- 8Dmr fm 1 1/16 (T):462 1:101 1:414 3+(F)Palomar H 6 2 24 21½ 21 2hd Nakatani C S LB 117 5.10 98-05 Somthngmrry117hdContsIn1171½SwtRbrt-Fr115½ Sharp effort 7
28Jly91-Grade II; Run in divisions
30Jun91- 8Hol fm 1⅛ (T):473 1:101 1:462 3+(F)Bvrly Hls H 5 2 2½ 2½ 22½ 31½ Santos J A LB 117 6.70 96-03 Alcando-Ir1131FireTheGroom120½CountusIn117no Rank early 8
30Jun91-Grade I
14Jun91- 7Hol fm 1 (T):47 1:103 1:34 3+(F)(S)Convenienc 2 4 43½ 42½ 33½ 23½ Stevens G L LB 116 3.50 91-09 HeartOfJoy1163½CountusIn116hdMySongForYou1142 2nd best 6
6Jan91- 8SA gd 1⅛ (T):462 1:102 1:474 (F)Sn Ggno H 4 2 24 22½ 2hd 2¾ Nakatani C S LB 119 7.90 84-15 RoyalTouch-Ir118¾CountusIn119¾Marsh'sDncer113¾ Good try 10
6Jan91-Grade II
2Dec90- 8Hol fm 1⅛ (T):454 1:092 1:461 3+(F)Matriarch 4 3 36 32½ 21½ 1nk Nakatani C S LB 123 13.20f 97-08 ContsIn123nkTfftAndTll123hdLttlBrnn1232 Broke out,bumped 14
2Dec90-Grade I
18Nov90- 8CD fm 1⅛ (T):471 1:12 1:512 3+(F)Cardinal H 7 4 44½ 44 56 57¾ Ramos W S LB 116 6.90 79-14 LdyinSilver1221½Coolwin1213½SplendidTry112¾ Flattened out 8
18Nov90-Run in divisions

Speed Index: Last Race: 0.0 3-Race Avg.: -3.6 9-Race Avg.: -1.3 Overall Avg.: -1.3

LATEST WORKOUTS Nov 23 CD 6f fst 1:16 B Oct 22 Lrl (T) 7f sf 1:33 B

Sha Tha

Dk. b. or br. f. 3(Mar), by Mr Prospector—Savannah Dancer, by Northern Dancer

SMITH M E Br.—Paulson A E (Ky) **120**

Own.—Darley Stud Farm Tr.—Drysdale Neil

Lifetime 10 3 3 2 $346,997 | 1991 6 2 2 0 $282,250 | 1990 4 1 1 2 $64,747 | Turf 10 3 3 2 $346,997

20Oct91-11Lrl sf 1⅛ (T):48 1:13 1:522 3+(F)All Along 1 1 12 12½ 11½ 1½ Smith M E 113 4.60 77-23 ShaTh113½JulieLRousse-Ir113nkOnceInMyLife-Ir114¾ Driving 11
20Oct91-Grade II
14Aug91♦5Deauville(Fra) gd*1 1:434 (T)(F)Prix de la Calonne 11½ Jarnet T 121 *.80 — — ShaTha1211½ Metamorphose1211 Srpos121½ Prom, led fnl fur 10
4Jly91♦4Evry(Fra) gd*1⅛ 1:541 (T)(F)Prix Chloe(Gr3) 21½ Cauthen S 121 *1.50 — — La Carene 1211½ Sha Tha 121nk Gravieres 123hd Led entr str 7
9Jun91♦3Chantilly(Fra) sf*1 5/16 2:102 (T)(F)Prix deDiane(Gr1) 63½ Cauthen S 128 11.00e — — Caerlin128¾ MgicNight128nk LouveRomine1281½ Well up, led 13
12May91♦5Longchamp(Fra) gd*1 1:383 (T)(F)PouleEssaiPoulches(Gr1) 22 Cauthen S 128 11.00 — — DanseuseduSoir1282 ShaTha128hd Caerlina128¾ Well up, led 9
21Apr91♦2Longchamp(Fra) gd*1 1:461 (T)(F)Prix de la Grotte(Gr3) 54½ Cauthen S 128 *1.25 — — DanseuseduSoir1282 LCrene1281½ Polemic128no Belated rally 8
7Oct90♦3Longchamp(Fra) gd*1 1:403 (T)(F)PrixMarcelBoussac(Gr1) 32 Asmussen C 121 5.50 — — Shadayid 1212 Caerlina 121no Sha Tha 1211 Closed well 9
11Sep90♦3Longchamp(Fra) gd*1 1:41 (T)(F)Prix d'Aumalc(Gr3) 2½ Asmussen C 121 *.80 — — Magic Night 121½ Sha Tha 121½ Caerlina 121½ Bid, led midstr 8
25Aug90♦2Deauville(Fra) gd*7½f 1:403 (T)(F)Prix Tanit(Mdn) 1¾ Asmussen C 123 *.60 — — Sha Tha 123¾ After the Sun 1232 Quilesse 1231½ Bid, driving 9
4Aug90♦6Deauville(fra) gd*6½f 1:223 (T)(F)Prix de Liseux(Mdn) 31 Asmussen C 123 *1.25 — — Polemic 123nk Danzante 123¾ Sabana 123¾ Finished well 10
4Aug90-Name changed from Sabana to Sha Tha after this race

Speed Index: Last Race: 0.0 1-Race Avg.: 0.0 1-Race Avg.: 0.0 Overall Avg.: 0.0

LATEST WORKOUTS Nov 26 Hol 6f fst 1:143 H Nov 20 Hol (T) 7f fm 1:314 H (d) Nov 14 Hol (T) 6f fm 1:144 H (d) Nov 9 Hol 4f fst :504 H

Colour Chart B. f. 4, by Mr Prospector—Rainbow Connection, by Halo — Lifetime 13 4 2 1 $339,995 — 1991 6 1 2 0 $184,811 — 1990 6 2 0 1 $143,249 — Turf 13 4 2 1 $339,995
NAKATANI C S — Br.—Hermitage Farm & Farish (Ky) — 123
Own.—Darley Stud Farm — Tr.—Whittingham Charles

10Nov91- 8SA fm 1¼ Ⓣ:492 1:374 2:01 3+ⒻYellow Rbn 3 8 63¼ 63¼ 63 63¼ Cauthen S B 123 7.00 80-17 Kostrom-Ir1232Flwlessly119½FirThGroom123hd Saved ground 13
10Nov91-Grade I
6Oct91♦6Longchamp(Fra) yl*1⅝ 1:561 ⓉⒻPrix de l' Opera(Gr2) 2¾ Cauthen S 128 2.25 — — Martessa 128¾ ColourChart128nk Polemic121nk Prom, driving 14
31Aug91- 8AP fm 1⅛ Ⓣ:454 1:094 1:532 3+ⒻBeverly D 1 5 54½ 53 51½ 21¾ Cauthen S 123 2.40 97-15 FiretheGroom1231¾ColourChrt1232½MissJosh1231½ Game 2nd 7
31Aug91-Grade I
3Aug91♦4Deauville(Fra) gd*1 1:371 ⓉⒻPrix d'Astarte(Gr2) 41½ Cauthen S 129 *2.00 — — Leariv1291 CrystlPth119nk OnceInMyLife122hd Prom thruout 12
2Jun91♦2Chantilly(Fra) gd*1⅛ 1:494 Ⓣ Prix d'Ispahan(Gr1) 76¼ Cauthen S 124 5.00 — — Sanglamore 128½ Priolo 128hd Zoman 128nk Prom to str 7
10May91♦4STCloud(Fra) yl*1 1:451 Ⓣ Prix du Muguet(Gr3) 1hd Cauthen S 124 9.00 — — ColourChart124hd Aldbourne1282 BoxingDy126nk Bid, up late 5
7Oct90♦6Longchamp(Fra) gd*1⅝ 1:543 ⓉⒻPrix de l'Opera(Gr2) 12 Asmussen C 123 *1.40e — — Colour Chart 1232 Lady Winner1301½ Tabdea121¾ Drew clear 14
2Sep90♦6Longchamp(Fra) yl*1¼ 2:064 ⓉⒻPxdlNntt(Gr3) 11½ Asmussen C 128 *.90 — — ColourChrt1281½ Spendomni1281 CruisingHeight128¾ Driving 8
24Jun90♦5Longchamp(Fra) yl*1¼ 2:072 Ⓣ GrPrdPrs(Gr1) 59 Asmussen C 124 4.50 — — Saumarez 1286 Priolo 1282 Tirol 1281 No threat 8
10Jun90♦4Chantilly(Fra) yl*1⅝ 2:113 ⓉⒻPrix de Diane(Gr1) 2½ Asmussen C 128 3.00[D] — — Rafha 128½ [D]Colour Chart 1282 Moon Cactus 128no Rallied 14
10Jun90-Disqualified and placed fourth for interference

Speed Index: Last Race: -3.0 2-Race Avg.: +4.5 2-Race Avg.: +4.5 Overall Avg.: +4.5
LATEST WORKOUTS Nov 27 Hol Ⓣ 4f fm :504 B (d) Nov 23 Hol Ⓣ 5f fm 1:021 H (d) Nov 18 Hol 3f fst :372 H

La Kaldoun–Fr Gr. f. 4, by Kaldoun—Solidarite, by Far North — Lifetime 24 11 6 1 $250,756 — 1991 7 0 2 1 $75,000 — 1990 11 8 1 0 $146,046 — Turf 23 11 6 1 $247,006
PEDROZA M A — Br.—Haras du Vieux Puits (Fra) — 123
Own.—Moreno R B & Lisa M — Tr.—Feld Jude T

26Oct91- 8SA fm 1¼ Ⓣ:464 1:353 2:002 3+[S]H P Russel H 6 2 31 31 32 32¾ Pedroza M A LB 113 10.20 83-14 Digression1142½EtonLad-En118nkLKldoun-Fr1131½ Inside bid 6
5Oct91- 7BM fm *1⅛ Ⓣ:471 1:111 1:464 3+ⒻCal J C H 4 3 32 42 32 21½ Pedroza M A LB 113 4.40 94-12 ApplingMissy1161½LKldoun-Fr113¾Kkl-En1152 Closed gamely 9
5Oct91-Grade III
31Aug91- 8AP fm 1⅛ Ⓣ:454 1:094 1:532 3+ⒻBeverly D 5 1 11 1½ 3nk 77½ Velasquez J L 123 27.70 92-15 Fire the Groom1231¾ Colour Chart1232½ MissJosh1231½ Tired 7
31Aug91-Grade I
28Jly91- 5Dmr fm 1⅛ Ⓣ:472 1:111 1:42 3+ⒻPalomar H 2 2 42 52½ 64½ 63¾ Pedroza M A LB 112 13.20 93-05 Guiza1141½ Agirlfromars114¾ Run To Jenny-Ir113½ Gave way 8
28Jly91-Grade II; Run in divisions
15Jun91- 8Hol fst 1⅛ :462 1:101 1:413 3+ⒻMilady H 7 7 79¼ 79 69½ 56 Pedroza M A LB 113 16.90 87-07 BroghtToMnd1104LnElgnt-Ar114¾VllVgn-Fr117hd No mishap 8
15Jun91-Grade I
2Jun91- 8Hol fm 1⅛ Ⓣ:481 1:113 1:472 3+ⒻGamely H 1 6 53½ 53 86 105¾ McCarron C J B 114 6.40e 87-06 MissJosh110½IslndJmboree116noFirThGroom1201½ Rank early 11
2Jun91-Grade I
28Apr91- 8GG fm 1⅛ Ⓣ:481 1:13 1:493 3+ⒻCnts Fagr H 4 2 22 21½ 21 22½ Patton D B 115 2.90 96-06 FrAtLst-GB1182½LKldn-Fr1152Smthnrr1151½ Carried out 1/4 6
28Apr91-Grade III
17Oct90♦1Marseille(Fra) gd*1⅛ :00 Ⓣ Prix du Roucas Blanc 14 Santos G 127 *.10 — — LKldoun1274 Vivennois1303 PinkHorizon130 Led throughout 3
17Oct90-No time taken
30Sep90♦6Toulouse(Fra) gd*1⅛ 00 Ⓣ Grand Prix Inter-Regional 11 Santos G 124 *1.30 — — La Kaldoun1241 Dounba1213 SuperHero1231 Well up, driving 12
30Sep90-No time taken

Speed Index: Last Race: -3.0 3-Race Avg.: +3.3 6-Race Avg.: +0.5 Overall Avg.: -0.4
LATEST WORKOUTS Nov 26 SA 5f fst 1:002 H ●Nov 21 SA 5f fst 1:00 H Nov 16 SA 4f fst :482 H Oct 21 SA 5f fst 1:00 H

Campagnarde–Ar B. f. 4, by Oak Dancer—Celina, by Lefty — Lifetime 11 5 1 3 $289,049 — 1991 4 2 0 1 $242,500 — 1990 7 3 1 2 $46,540 — Turf 5 2 0 2 $248,408
VALENZUELA P A — Br.—Haras Las Ortigas (Arg) — 123
Own.—Paulson A E — Tr.—Whittingham Charles

10Nov91- 8SA fm 1¼ Ⓣ:492 1:374 2:01 3+ⒻYellow Rbn 7 4 53 52½ 73½ 104¾ Valenzuela P A B 123 5.50 78-17 Kostroma-Ir1232Flwlessly119½FireTheGroom123hd Weakened 13
10Nov91-Grade I
20Oct91- 8SA fm 1⅛ Ⓣ:443 1:074 1:434 3+ⒻLas Plmas H 4 3 34½ 44½ 43½ 31 Stevens G L 118 2.60 104 — Kostroma-Ir117½Kikal-En113½Cmpgnrde-Ar118¾ Strong kick 6
20Oct91-Grade II
17Aug91- 8Dmr fm 1⅛ Ⓣ:483 1:122 1:492 3+ⒻRamona H 4 7 89 95¾ 62¾ 1no Garcia J A 115 12.70 91-11 Campagnarde-Ar115no Bequest118¾ Somethingmerry118nk 10
17Aug91-Grade I; Rank early, 5-wide stretch
31Jly91- 7Dmr fm 1 Ⓣ:47 1:111 1:36 3+ⒻAlw 50000 2 7 78½ 74 33 1no Stevens G L B 116 5.00 92-08 Cmpgnrd-Ar116noSeBrndy1162½Mmr-En116½ 5-wide stretch 7
8Dec90♦9SanIsidro(Arg) fm*1½ 2:012 ⓉⒻGrPrCopa dePlata(Gr1) 3nk Liceri E 119 5.40 — — Jewellery 119hd Fail 132nk Campagnarde 119nk Trailed early 12
14Oct90♦6Hipodromo(Arg) fst*1⅛ 2:022 ⒻGrnPremioSeleccion(Gr1) 11½ Liceri E 123 29.10 — — Campgnrde1231½ SilverBeuty1237 Psen123¾ Up final furlong 16
21Sep90♦5Hipodromo(Arg) fst*1⅛ 1:502 ⒻClasicoF JBeazley(Gr2) 37¼ Liceri E 123 *2.30 — — Pasena 1231½ Silver Beauty 1246 Campagnarde 123¾ Evenly 11
26Aug90♦6Hipodromo(Arg) fst*1 1:372 ⒻPolla dePotrancas(Gr1) 1010 Liceri E 123 2.50 — — Luna Rose 123¾ Totona 1231½ La Charlatana 1235 Tired 14
2Jly90♦5Hipodromo(Arg) hy*7f 1:272 ⒻClasico Bolivia 18 Liceri E 123 *.70 — — Campgnrde1238 MorMor1231 RoylGuin120hd Bid,led final fur 8
20May90♦5Hipodromo(Arg) fst*7½f 313 ⒻGarnPremioJorgAtch(Gr1) 25 Liceri E 121 2.00 — — Pulma 1215 Campagnarde 1211½ Totona121hd Rallied for 2nd 9

Speed Index: Last Race: -5.0 3-Race Avg.: +0.3 4-Race Avg.: +0.2 Overall Avg.: +0.2
LATEST WORKOUTS Nov 27 Hol Ⓣ 5f fm 1:01 H (d) Nov 22 Hol Ⓣ 5f fm 1:003 H (d) Nov 17 Hol 3f fst :363 H ●Nov 6 SA 5f fst :593 H

Kikala–En Gr. m. 5, by Kalaglow—Jhansi Ki Rani, by Far North — Lifetime 18 4 2 3 $118,842 — 1991 2 0 1 1 $85,080 — 1990 5 1 1 0 $33,760 — Turf 18 4 2 3 $118,842
SOLIS A — Br.—Whitsbury Manor Stud (Eng) — 123
Own.—Sharer-Stern-Vaughn — Tr.—Vienna Darrell

20Oct91- 8SA fm 1⅛ Ⓣ:443 1:074 1:434 3+ⒻLas Plmas H 5 4 44½ 32½ 22 2½ Solis A LB 113 21.60 104 — Kostroma-Ir117½Kikl-En113½Cmpgnrde-Ar118¾ Broke slowly 6
20Oct91-Grade II
5Oct91- 7BM fm *1⅛ Ⓣ:471 1:111 1:464 3+ⒻCal J C H 1 7 76¾ 74½ 44 32½ Baze R A LB 115 13.70 94-12 ApplingMissy1161½LKldoun-Fr113¾Kkl-En1152 Steadied early 9
5Oct91-Grade III
7Dec90- 8Hol fm 1⅛ Ⓣ:484 1:122 1:414 3+ⒻAlw 36000 1 4 42 52 64 62¾ McCarron C J LB 117 *1.60 83-14 Lyphrd'sMelody115nkTessl115nkTemptedQun115hd Rank early 7
14Nov90- 8Hol fm 1⅛ Ⓣ:474 1:12 1:413 3+ⒻAlw 34000 3 7 75 73½ 1hd 12¾ McCarron C J LB 115 *2.10 87-15 Kki-En1152¾Mrsh'sDncr1181½SplndorFrvr1154 4-wide stretch 7
20Oct90- 8SA fm 1 Ⓣ:464 1:101 1:341 3+ⒻL R Rwn H 7 10 62½ 4¾ 52½ 63¼ Meza R Q LB 113 7.10 89-08 Oeilldine-Fr115¾IslndJmboree113½PolrBird-Ir115nk Wide trip 10
8Sep90- 8Dmr fm 1⅛ Ⓣ:48 1:112 1:42 3+Ⓕ[S]Osunitas H 9 5 45 32 21½ 2¾ Meza R Q LB 113 50.90 96-06 Baldomero116¾ Kikala113nk Tessla118hd Good try 10
19Aug90- 3Dmr fm 1 Ⓣ:471 1:111 1:361 3+ⒻAlw 46000 7 1 11 87¾ 813 820¾ Pincay L Jr LB 117 *2.60 72-08 Decora116½ Flirty1182 Girl Of France1203 Lugged out 8
16Dec89- 7Hol fm 1⅛ Ⓣ:473 1:112 1:474 3+ⒻAlw 20000 10 6 41 31 12½ 13 Stevens G L 118 *1.90 89-14 Kikl1183RpAtTheDoor1185HilTheFoxybyb113no Wide 7/8 turn 10
1Aug89♦3Leicester(Eng) gd 1 1:382 Ⓣ Rutland H 41½ Cochrane R b 125 10.00 — — YouMssdM123½ StndngCount112¾ AnnbilRoyl105nk Bid, hung 10
23Jun89♦5Redcar(Eng) fm*1 1:382 Ⓣ DveMcHleAuctn 12 Perks S b 125 *.60 — — Kikala 1252 SimplyHenry 1282½ SmoothFlight 1284 Driving 4

Speed Index: Last Race: +4.0 3-Race Avg.: +2.3 8-Race Avg.: -1.1 Overall Avg.: -1.1
LATEST WORKOUTS Nov 24 Hol Ⓣ 7f fm 1:251 H Nov 19 SA tr.t 6f fst 1:142 H Nov 12 SA tr.t 6f fst 1:152 H Nov 6 SA Ⓣ 5f fm 1:01 H (d)

Reluctant Guest B. m. 5, by Hostage—Vaguely Royal, by Vaguely Noble — Lifetime 23 10 2 3 $782,225 — 1991 5 2 0 0 $87,625 — 1990 10 4 1 2 $574,400 — Turf 16 7 1 1 $697,225
PINCAY L JR — Br.—Hillstead Farm (Ky) — 123
Own.—Folsom R S — Tr.—Mandella Richard

3Nov91- 8SA fm 1 Ⓣ:462 1:101 1:33 3+ⒻL R Rowan H 1 7 85¾ 41½ 11½ 11¼ McCarron C J LB 119 5.30 98-02 RluctntGust1191¼IslndJmbor1171½Qunmr-Ir116nk Inside rally 9
28Jly91- 8Dmr fm 1⅛ Ⓣ:462 1:101 1:414 3+ⒻPalomar H 4 4 35½ 33 45 66 Valenzuela P A LB 117 7.90 92-05 Somthngmrry117hdContsIn1171½SwtRobrt-Fr115½ No mishap 7
28Jly91-Grade II; Run in divisions
30Jun91- 8Hol fm 1⅛ Ⓣ:473 1:101 1:462 3+ⒻBvrly Hls H 8 7 76½ 65½ 54½ 73½ McCarron C J LB 118 4.10 94-03 Alcando-Ir1131 Fire TheGroom120½CountusIn117no Wide trip 8
30Jun91-Grade I
30May91- 8Hol fm 1 Ⓣ:464 1:102 1:34 ⒻAlw 55000 2 3 33 21½ 1½ 12 McCarron C J LB 116 1.50 95-09 RluctntGust1162SlwOfPrls116¾Wychnor-NZ1141½ Ridden out 6
15May91- 8Hol fm 1 Ⓣ:451 1:09 1:331 ⒻAlw 55000 5 8 88½ 64½ 43 43½ McCarron C J LB 118 *.80 95-01 IslndJmbor1212¾TropclStphn114nkAlcnd-Ir116½ Bumped 7 1/2 9
4Nov90- 8SA fm 1¼ Ⓣ:452 1:34 1:582 3+ⒻYlw Rbn Iv 12 8 75¼ 94¾ 96½ 108¼ Davis R G LB 123 5.00 87-04 PlntyOfGrc1191PtitIl-Ir1231RoylTouch-Ir123¾ Impeded, wide 13
4Nov90-Grade I
14Oct90- 8SA fm 1⅛ Ⓣ:482 1:122 1:464 3+ⒻLs Plms H 4 5 56 53 53¼ 34 Davis R G LB 121 *1.70 87-09 LittleBrinne1154DoublWdg117noRluctntGust1211 Boxed in 1/4 5
14Oct90-Grade II
1Sep90- 8AP fm 1⅛ Ⓣ:461 1:101 1:531 3+ⒻBeverly D 11 11 106¼ 73¼ 61½ 1¾ Davis R G L 123 14.50 110 — RluctntGust123¾LdyWinnr1231½RoylTouch123hd Strong finish 12
18Aug90- 8Dmr fm 1⅛ Ⓣ:473 1:114 1:49 3+ⒻRamona H 2 3 32 31½ 1hd 2¾ Desormeaux K J LB 117 3.00 92-10 DoubleWedge114¾ReluctantGuest1173Nikishka116no 2nd best 8
18Aug90-Grade I
30Jun90- 8Hol fm 1⅛ Ⓣ:464 1:10 1:47 3+ⒻBv Hls H 2 6 63¼ 64 32½ 11¾ Davis R G 116A 3.30 93-07 [DH]BtflMld1151[DH]RlcttGst1161¾StlsStr1161¾ Closed strongly 6
30Jun90-Grade I; Dead heat

Speed Index: Last Race: 0.0 3–Race Avg.: –2.0 10–Race Avg.: –0.7 Overall Avg.: –0.7
LATEST WORKOUTS Nov 26 Hol 5f fst :593 H Nov 20 Hol 5f fst 1:023 B Oct 30 SA 5f fst :59 H ●Oct 25 SA 1 fst 1:39 H

Island Jamboree B. m. 5, by Explodent—Careless Virgin, by Wing Out
FLORES D R Br.—Penn S–O–J (Ky)
Own.—Proctor Mary Tr.—Proctor Willard L
123 Lifetime 35 10 11 1 $327,270 1991 9 2 3 0 $117,100 1990 11 1 4 1 $74,250 Turf 20 5 8 1 $221,000

3Nov91- 8SA fm 1 ①:462 1:101 1:33 3+ⒻL R Rowan H 2 9 96½ 94½ 53 21½ Stevens G L 117 4.50 97–02 ReluctntGust1191½IslndJmbor1171½Qunmr-Ir116nk Wide rally 9
30Oct91- 8SA fm 1 ①:471 1:101 1:332 3+ⒻAlw 55000 3 5 53½ 53½ 42½ 2¾ Stevens G L 119 6.00 95–04 Agirlfromars115¾ Island Jamboree119hd Bequest1192 Rallied 5
31Aug91- 7Dmr fm 1⅜ ①:48 1:381 2:162 3+ⒻHoney Fox H 6 7 79½ 65 64½ 77¾ Valenzuela P A 119 2.70 75–13 FryStrk-Ir115½MmmRst-Br115nkHlThFxybyb1091½ No mishap 9
30Jun91- 8Hol fm 1⅛ ①:473 1:101 1:462 3+ⒻBvrly Hls H 2 4 44½ 44½ 64¾ 83½ Delahoussaye E 116 8.50 94–03 Alcande-Ir1131FireTheGroom120½Countusln117no No mishap 8
30Jun91-Grade I
2Jun91- 8Hol fm 1⅛ ①:481 1:113 1:472 3+ⒻGamely H 7 9 96½ 84¾ 42 2½ Delahoussaye E 116 16.70 92–06 Miss Josh118½ Island Jamboree116no Fire The Groom1201½ 11
2Jun91-Grade I; Bumped early, wide backstretch and into stretch, closed strongly
15May91- 8Hol fm 1 ①:451 1:09 1:331 ⒻAlw 55000 4 6 66 32 11½ 12¾ Stevens G L 121 14.10 99–01 IslndJmbor1212¾TrpclStphn114nkAlcnd-Ir116½ Boxed 3/8–3/16 9
23Feb91- 8SA fm 1 ①:46 1:094 1:341 ⒻBna Vista H 9 8 810 89½ 89½ 79¾ Nakatani C S 112 16.90 82–08 TfftAndTull120hdBqust1172½Somthngmrry1141 Broke slowly 9
23Feb91-Grade III
20Jan91- 8SA fst 7f :221 :444 1:214 ⒻSta Mnca H 4 6 64½ 68½ 54½ 53¾ Nakatani C S 114 20.40 90–12 Dvl'sOrchd116½ClsscVl118¾StrmyBtVld1211½ 4-wide stretch 7
20Jan91-Grade I
1Jan91- 5SA fst 1 :471 1:114 1:364 ⒻⓈRunFrRoses 4 6 62½ 72¾ 41½ 1½ Stevens G L 114 *2.70 83–18 IslndJmbor114½Dcor1172Thisisyourluckydy1132½ Boxed in 1/4 11
17Nov90- 6Hol fm 1⅛ ①:474 1:112 1:412 3+ⒻDahlia H 1 4 42 1hd 2hd 3½ Nakatani C S 113 9.10 87–10 Petalia113hd Bequest117½ Island Jamboree1131½ Good try 6
17Nov90-Grade II; Run in divisions

Speed Index: Last Race: –1.0 3–Race Avg.: –4.6 8–Race Avg.: –4.0 Overall Avg.: –2.9
LATEST WORKOUTS Nov 26 Hol 5f fst 1:02 H Nov 20 Hol 5f fst 1:002 H Nov 13 SA 4f fst :48 B Oct 31 SA 5f fst 1:00 H

Susurration B. f. 4, by Erins Isle–Ir—Grease–Ir, by Filiberto
CARSON W Br.—Pin Oak Farm (Ky)
Own.—Pin Oak Stable Tr.—Gosden John H M
123 Lifetime 15 5 4 2 $114,128 1991 11 4 4 1 $98,764 1990 4 1 0 1 $15,364 Turf 15 5 4 2 $114,128

3Nov91♦5StCloud(Fra) sf*1 1:501 ① Prix Perth (Gr3) 15 Dettori L 122 3.30 – – Susurration 1225 Dolpour 1232 Hello Pink 123½ Prom, easily 8
19Oct91♦2Newmarket(Eng) gd 1⅛ 1:481 ① BaringIntern'lDarleyStks 13½ Carson W 121 *3.00 – – Susrrton1213½ HrtOfDrknss122¾ MltryFshon1261 Led thruout 10
4Oct91♦3Goodwood(Eng) gd 7f 1:281 ① Supreme Stks (Gr3) 2nk Ryan W 121 16.00 – – Osario124nk Susurration121no NortonChallenger1242 In close 13
14Sep91♦5Doncaster(Eng) gd 1 1:391 ①Ⓕ Sceptre Stks 64 Swinburn W R 122 2.00 – – You Know TheRules122no SilverBraid1171½ Souk1171½ Led 7f 7
6Sep91♦4Kempton(Eng) gd 1 1:362 ① MilcarsTempleFortuneStks 26 Swinburn W R 124 *5.00 – – Selkirk 1216 Susurration 1240 Zonda 1161½ Bid, led 14
27Jly91♦1Ascot(Eng) gd 1 1:431 ① Centenary Diamond Stks 13 Pearce L 137 *4.00 – – Susurration 1373 Sure Sharp 142hd Scatter 142no Led fnl 3f 14
27Jly91-Race for Lady riders
26Jun91♦4Kempton(Eng) sf 1⅛ 2:03 ① KemptonTrainers Challenge 10 Pearce L 142 1.75 – – Susurration 1420 Grammos 1363 Kausar 14712 Prom, easily 8
26Jun91-Race for Lady riders
12Jun91♦1Kempton(Eng) gd 1⅛ 1:562 ① AllyBrasseyStakes 21½ Pearce L 143 3.50 – – NorthernHl1481½ Susurrtion1431½ Scttr1481 Stumbled mdstr 16
12Jun91-Race for Lady riders
1Jun91♦5Lingfield(Eng) gd*7½f 1:33 ① Graduation Stks 33 Swinburn W R 132 2.00 – – Hail And Blest 1272 Greendale 1281 Susurration 1321 Led 6f 5

Speed Index: Last Race: (—) 3–Race Avg.: (—) 12–Race Avg.: (—) Overall Avg.: (—)

Free At Last–GB B. f. 4, by Shirley Heights—Brocade, by Habitat
DELAHOUSSAYE E Br.—Leigh G W (GB)
Own.—Leigh G W Tr.—Drysdale Neil
123 Lifetime 14 6 3 0 $299,994 1991 4 2 0 0 $156,625 1990 5 1 1 0 $103,950 Turf 14 6 3 0 $299,994

10Nov91- 8SA fm 1¼ ①:492 1:374 2:01 3+ⒻYellow Rbn 10 9 105½ 105½ 84½ 42½ Delahoussaye E LB 123b 27.00 80–17 Kostrom-Ir1232Flwissly119½FrThGroom123hd Steadied break 13
10Nov91-Grade I; Dead heat
20Oct91- 8SA fm 1⅛ ①:443 1:074 1:434 3+ⒻLas Pimas H 3 1 1½ 21½ 33½ 55 Delahoussaye E LB 118 3.80 100 – Kostroma-Ir117½Kikala-En113½Cmpgnrde-Ar1183½ Weakened 6
20Oct91-Grade II
11May91- 8GG fm 1⅜ ①:464 1:362 2:15 3+ⒻYrba Buena H 3 1 11 11 14 13 Hansen R D LB 120 *.80 97–08 FrAtLst-GB1203NoblAndNc117½LouvBlu1143 Steady handling 6
20Apr91- 8GG fm 1⅛ ①:481 1:13 1:493 3+ⒻCnts Fagr H 5 1 12 11½ 11 12½ Hansen R D LB 118 1.80 99–06 FrAtLst-GB1182½LKlda-Fr1157Smthrr1151½ Responded well 6
20Apr91-Grade III
24Nov90- 7BM fm *1⅛ ①:483 1:13 1:493 ⒻCarmel H 8 6 65 2hd 11½ 13 Dettori L F LB 117 *1.60 87–16 FreeAtLst-GB1173AnnulReunion1172MissJesy115½ Drew clear 8
27Oct90- 2Bel gd 1¼ Ⓣ:473 1:38 2:032 3+State Of N Y 11 6 54 31½ 23 2¾ Cochrane R 118 28.90 82–15 RelifPitchr-Ir126¾FrAtLst-GB1182PrudntMnnr-Ir121½ Rallied 13
18Aug90♦3Curragh(Ire) gd 1 1:371 ① Desmond Stakes(Gr3) 43¾ Clark A 117 3.50 – – Kostroma 126nk Bold Russian 1281½ Thakib 1282 Evenly 6
2Aug90♦3Deauville(Fra) yl*1 1:36 ①Ⓕ Pxd'Astrt(Gr2) 43½ Clark A 119 3.50 – – LadyWinner126¾ DaisyDnce1191 CtherinePrr1191½ Stride late 15
3May90♦4Newmarket(Eng) gd 1 1:38 ①Ⓕ 1000 Guineas(Gr1) 40¾ Clark A 126 16.00 – – Salsabil 126¾ Heart of Joy 1263 Negligent 1263 Evenly 10
6Oct89♦4Newmarket(Eng) gd 7f 1:283 ① Somerville Tattersall Stk 1nk Clark A 122 6.00 – – Free At Last122nk QuiDanzig1242½ CurraRegis1272 Led fnl 2f 7

Speed Index: Last Race: –3.0 3–Race Avg.: +0.6 6–Race Avg.: +1.1 Overall Avg.: +1.1
LATEST WORKOUTS Nov 21 Hol ① 7f fm 1:272 H (d) Nov 16 Hol 3f fst :36 H ●Nov 5 SA tr.t 6f fst 1:154 B Oct 31 SA ① 1 fm 1:411 H (d)

The feature race, the Grade 1 Matriarch at nine furlongs on the turf, is the winter calendar's premier grass stake for females. Of the 14 entrants, 10 have won a graded stakes and five have won a Grade 1 race. We're obviously dealing with the best female turf horses of their generation, so it looks as if "class will out."

Elegance Placing in a Grade 3 race is far from being a graded stakes winner. Repeated disappointments in unlisted stakes make her unlikely against this bunch. Throw out.

Fire The Groom Multiple graded stakes winner and Grade 1 heroine, she shows a relentless closing style that hasn't been winning on this surface. But the classiest horses find ways to win regardless of bias, and she's won over the Hollywood course. Rate her off that race.

Flawlessly She's a three-year-old in her second start against older rivals. We can forgive her for not winning a Grade 1 event because there just aren't any carded on the turf limited to three-year-old fillies. She certainly seems to be capable of competing against older, however, as her last running line shows. The profile also favors her early-stalking style. We can go two deep to her Oct. 5 paceline.

Kostroma That Oct. 20 race was a world-record-setting performance in the proper style necessary to win today's race. It bites us in the neck.

Countus In Popped up to win this race last year at 13-to-1, but hasn't done much lately. She has shown the class to win; unfortunately, her current form probably won't get the job done against these monsters. Non-contender.

Sha Tha Wire-to-wire winner of her first and only stateside start last time, a Grade 2 race. The great tendency of most foreign invaders is to win right off the plane and tail off thereafter. This could happen here. Leave her in, rating the lone American race, obviously.

Colour Chart Graded stakes winner in Europe finished within two lengths of Fire The Groom in her first race in the United States. Definite threat off that performance.

La Kaldoun Hasn't won a graded stakes and couldn't even beat restricted handicap runners last out. Elimination.

Campagnarde A Grade 1 winner earlier in the year, she's gone south since then. She won that Grade 1 at 12-to-1 against a less than stellar field, and when thrown in against legitimate Grade 1 rivals, got slaughtered. She's a late runner on a turf course that's been favoring early runners. Toss out.

Kikala That last race may signal improvement, as she closed to within a half-length of Kostroma at 21-to-1. Other than that, she shows no graded stakes victories and is inconsistent even against allowance foes. Non-contender.

Reluctant Guest Grade 1 winner last year; however, her last three attempts in graded stakes have been poor. Elimination.

Island Jamboree One good try in a Grade 1 race, but she's never won a graded stakes. Inconsistent performances against lesser stock recently make her a throw-out.

Susurration Never been tried higher than Grade 3, so we can forgive her lack of Grade 1 experience. She "could be any kind," especially after her last race, an easy win against Grade 3 opponents. Her morning line is 15-to-1. If the track odds-maker doesn't give her much of a chance, neither should we.

Free At Last Grade 3 winner whose two Grade 1 tries were uninspiring. Out.

As southern California track announcer Trevor Denman is fond of exclaiming, "Any one of six can win it." A healthy combination of Mark Cramer's "Stakes in the Action" and a wildly contentious field make legitimate favorites unlikely and a healthy win overlays the order of the day. We have a field full of proven graded stakes horses, some of which will have to go off at big odds. Here is ALL-IN-ONE's analysis of the race:

Kostroma	3-to-1
Fire The Groom	5-to-1
Flawlessly	5-to-1

In the turf chapter, Quinn said that late speed, or adjusted last fraction, is king (in this case, queen) on turf. Look at Flawlessly's last fraction. It towers over this field. She's got a decided edge in come-home time in this race. The public's odds are as follows:

Kostroma	1-to-1
Fire The Groom	7-to-2
Flawlessly	6-to-1

The only possible bet is Flawlessly.
Our profit on this race is $12.60. Our overall profit is $39.40.

```
1DEC91                             HOL                    9 furlongs turf
Race #8                                                        14 starters
STAKES                                                 Age: 3+years, Female
```

```
-----------------------------------INPUT DATA-------------------------------
```

Horse name	# ST	# W	# P	# S	$'S Earned	Date	Trk	Dist.	S	1st C time	2nd C time	Final time
Fire The Groom	7	3	1	2	594343	10NOV91	HOL	8.500	T	47.0	110.3	140.0
Flawlessly	6	4	1	0	342550	10NOV91	SA	8.000	T	45.4	110.2	133.2
Kostroma	13	7	0	2	471252	10NOV91	SA	9.000	T	45.4	107.4	143.4
Colour Chart	6	1	2	0	184011	10NOV91	AP	9.500	T	45.4	109.4	153.2
Free At Last	4	2	0	0	158625	10NOV91	GG	9.000	T	48.1	113.0	149.3
Sha Tha	6	2	2	0	282250	20OCT91	LRL	9.000	T	48.0	113.0	152.2

Horse name	Class Lvl	1st C B.L.	2nd C B.L.	Final B.L.	SR	Var
Fire The Groom	STAKES	7.50	6.50	0.00	95	6
Flawlessly	CLF	3.25	0.50	0.00	96	9
Kostroma	STAKES	0.50	0.00	0.00	105	1
Colour Chart	STAKES	4.50	3.00	1.75	97	15
Free At Last	STAKES	0.00	0.00	0.00	99	6
Sha Tha	STAKES	0.00	0.00	0.00	77	23

```
-----------------------------------BETTING LINE-----------------------------
```

Horse name	PEH	H-I	THAAI	P-H	ESP	Rating	Betting Line	Fair Place $	Fair Show $
Kostroma	1	1	1	3	1	88.65	3-1		
Fire The Groom	2	2	2	1	4	77.25	5-1		
Flawlessly	3	3	3	2	2	76.39	5-1		
Free At Last	4	4	4	4	3	71.93			
Colour Chart	5	5	5	5	5	67.01			
Sha Tha	6	6	6	6	6	60.00			

```
----------------------------------EXACTA GRID-------------------------------
```

	Kostroma	Fire The Groom	Flawlessly
Kostroma	. . . . / . . . . /	32 80	34 84
Fire The Groom	37 91	. . . . / . . . . /	63 158
Flawlessly	39 97	64 159	. . . . / . . . . / . . . .

```
--------------------------------SPEED/PACE SUMMARY--------------------------
```

```
Race Profile:    47.49  111.02  146.52    Winners' Pace Profile: EARLY
Ability Par:     82.99                     Pace Contention Point: 1.88 lengths
```

Projected Times:	1st C	2nd C	Fin C	Ability Time	Balance Time	Last Frac	Proj Pace	Con-tender
Kostroma	45.98	108.42	143.72	81.28	100.28	35.30	FRONT	Y
Fire The Groom	48.19	111.24*	145.84	82.79	102.19	34.60	REAR	N
Flawlessly	48.51	112.32*	146.32	82.51	102.83	34.00	REAR	N
Free At Last	47.69	111.42*	146.12	82.39	102.83	34.70	REAR	N
Colour Chart	46.73	109.19*	146.13	83.67	102.33	36.94	LATE	N
Sha Tha	49.49	113.53*	150.12	86.08	106.42	36.59	REAR	N

```
-----------------------------------PACE GRAPH-------------------------------
```

```
        Profile:            47.49            111.02              146.52
        Front Runner:       45.98            108.42              143.72
        Horse name            1C                2C                  F
Kostroma         ------------------X  ----------------(-X  -----------------X
Fire The Groom   -------X----------+  ----X-----------(-+  -------X----------+
Flawlessly       -----X------------+  ----------------(-+  ------X-----------+
Free At Last     ---------X--------+  ---X------------(-+  ------X-----------+
Colour Chart     -------------X---+   ---------------X-(-+ ------X-----------+
Sha Tha          X----------------+   ----------------(-+ ------------------+
```

EIGHTH RACE
Hollywood
DECEMBER 1, 1991

1 ⅛ MILES.(Turf). (1.44^{4}) 11th Running of THE MATRIARCH (Grade I). (Chute start). Purse $200,000. Fillies and mares. 3-year-olds and upward. By subscription of $200 each, which shall accompany the nomination, $2,000 additional to start, with $110,000 to the winner, $40,000 to second, $30,000 to third, $15,000 to fourth and $5,000 to fifth. Weights, 3-year-olds, 120 lbs.; older 123 lbs. Starters to be named through the entry box by closing time of entries. This race will not be divided. If the number of entries exceed the starting gate capacity, first preference will be given to graded or group stakes winners in 1991. Second preference will be given to those horses with the highest total earnings in 1991 and an also eligible list will be drawn. Failure to draw into this race at scratch time cancels all fees. Trophies will be presented to the winning owner, trainer and jockey. Closed Wednesday November 13 with 32 nominations.
Value of race $200,000; value to winner $110,000; second $40,000; third $30,000; fourth $15,000; fifth $5,000. Mutuel pool $446,490. Exacta pool $516,723.

Last Raced	Horse	M/Eqt.	A.	Wt	PP	St	¼	½	¾	Str	Fin	Jockey	Odds $1
10Nov91 ^{8}SA^{2}	Flawlessly	L	3	120	3	3	7^{1}	8½	$7^{1½}$	1^{hd}	$1^{1¾}$	McCarron C J	6.30
10Nov91 ^{8}SA^{3}	Fire The Groom	B	4	123	2	5	$4^{1½}$	4^{hd}	5½	5^{2}	2½	Stevens G L	3.60
10Nov91 ^{8}SA^{4}	Free At Last-GB	LB	4	123	14	12	13½	12½	12½	$7^{1½}$	3no	Delahoussaye E	f-16.60
20Oct91 ^{11}Lrl^{1}	Sha Tha	LB	3	120	6	8	8^{hd}	9½	8½	6½	$4^{1¾}$	Smith M E	a-10.20
10Nov91 ^{8}SA^{6}	Colour Chart	B	4	123	7	11	12^{hd}	14	14	11½	5no	Nakatani C S	a-10.20
10Nov91 ^{8}SA^{1}	Kostroma-Ir	LB	5	123	4	2	6^{1}	7^{1}	4^{1}	2½	6½	Desormeaux K J	1.00
21Nov91 ^{8}Hol^{1}	Elegance	LB	4	123	1	13	10^{hd}	11^{hd}	11^{1}	8^{hd}	7^{nk}	Alvarado F J	108.40
3Nov91 ^{8}SA^{2}	Island Jamboree	B	5	123	12	14	14	13^{1}	$13^{1½}$	12^{3}	8^{nk}	Flores D R	64.00
20Oct91 ^{8}SA^{2}	Kikala-En	LB	5	123	10	9	$9^{1½}$	5½	2^{hd}	3^{hd}	9^{hd}	Mena F	25.20
13Nov91 ^{8}CD^{1}	Countus In	LB	6	123	5	1	$2^{1½}$	2^{1}	3^{1}	4^{1}	10½	Day P	32.40
3Nov91 ^{8}SA^{1}	Reluctant Guest	L	5	123	11	10	$11^{1½}$	$10^{1½}$	9½	9½	11^{11}	Pincay L Jr	24.00
26Oct91 ^{8}SA^{3}	La Kaldoun-Fr	LB	4	123	8	4	3½	3^{1}	6^{hd}	14	$12^{5½}$	Pedroza M A	f-16.60
3Nov91 ^{5}Fra^{1}	Susurration	B	4	123	13	6	1^{1}	1^{1}	1^{hd}	13^{2}	13	Carson W	31.10
10Nov91 ^{8}SA^{10}	Campagnarde-Ar	B	4	123	9	7	5^{hd}	6^{hd}	10^{hd}	10½	—	Sorenson D	30.40

Campagnarde-Ar, Lost rider.
a-Coupled: Sha Tha and Colour Chart.
f—Mutuel field.

OFF AT 4:21. Start good. Won driving. Time, :23^{1}, :47^{1}, 1:10^{4}, 1:34^{4}, 1:46^{3} Course firm.

$2 Mutuel Prices:				
	4-FLAWLESSLY	14.60	6.00	4.60
	3-FIRE THE GROOM		4.60	3.40
	12-FREE AT LAST-GB (f-field)			6.60

$2 EXACTA 4-3 PAID $63.20.

Sun Streak Last won for a $50,000 tag, but is now dropping to the low-rent district. Last was an improvement, but why the raise back to $20,000, where his last two efforts have been dreadful? Also, he lays too close to the pace at a distance where mid-pack runners have been most successful. Out.

Explosive West Dropping to his lowest level ever, but not a drop that instills much confidence, as this guy lost as a short-priced favorite against slightly better last time. Can't really sprint, either. Easy toss-out.

Shakem Up Haughty After breaking his maiden in his debut, he's been toiling unsuccessfully against non-winners allowance company, finally coming back down to earth against this class his last two races. Slight improvement in last and his closing style has been advantaged here lately, but dropping beneath the price he was claimed for suggests damaged goods. Non-contender.

9th Hollywood

7 FURLONGS. (1.20⁴) **CLAIMING. Purse $14,000.** 3-year-olds and upward. Weights, 3-year-olds, 119 lbs.; older, 121 lbs. Non-winners of two races since October 6 allowed 3 lbs.; a race since them, 5 lbs. Claiming price $20,000; if for $18,000 allowed 2 lbs. (Races when entered for $16,000 or less not considered.)

LASIX—Sun Streak, Explosive West, Shakem Up Haughty, Zaleucus, Good Field No Hit, Fiesta Del Sol, Council Member, Power Base, Intercup, Gringo Greg.

Sun Streak
B. g. 5, by Sassafras (Fra)—Here's Sunshine, by Say Numero Uno
TORRES H $20,000   Br.—Seaman C O & Cole C (Ky)
Own.—Tons of Fun Stable   Tr.—Passey Blake
1115

Lifetime	1991 14 1 3 1	$41,570
37 2 10 7	1990 13 0 3 2	$31,290
$127,730	Turf 4 0 0 1	$7,650

Speed Index: Last Race: -3.0   3-Race Avg.: -3.6   9-Race Avg.: -1.1   Overall Avg.: -1.1
LATEST WORKOUTS   Nov 13 Hol 4f fst :47² H   Oct 27 Hol 5f fst 1:14¹ Hg   Oct 13 Hol 4f fst :50 H   Oct 6 Hol 4f fst :49² H

Explosive West
Dk. b. or br. g. 4, by Far Out East—Royal Explosion, by His Majesty
SORENSON D $18,000   Br.—Evans E P (Va)
Own.—Stephen & Summertime Stables   Tr.—Dollase Wallace
114

Lifetime	1991 5 1 1 0	$26,650
15 2 3 3	1990 9 1 2 3	$44,600
$71,730	Turf 4 0 0 1	$14,400

Speed Index: Last Race: (—)   3-Race Avg.: (—)   12-Race Avg.: (—)   Overall Avg.: (—)
LATEST WORKOUTS   Nov 27 Hol 4f fst :47³ Hg   Nov 7 SA 5f fst 1:00² Hg   Oct 31 SA 4f fst :48 Hg   Oct 25 SA 6f fst 1:14³ Hg

Shakem Up Haughty
Ro. g. 4, by Haughty But Nice—Shake'm all Up, by One for All
VALENZUELA P A $20,000   Br.—Daniels Mrs June L (Cal)
Own.—Cane P W   Tr.—Ellis Ronald W
116

Lifetime	1991 11 1 0 3	$33,960
11 1 0 3	1989 0 M 0 0	
$33,960		

180ct91-Placed fifth through disqualification

Speed Index: Last Race: +1.0   3-Race Avg.: -1.9   10-Race Avg.: -1.6   Overall Avg.: -1.5
LATEST WORKOUTS   Nov 26 SA 5f fst 1:03² Hg   Nov 5 SA 5f fst 1:01² Hg   Oct 28 SA 4f gd :58² H   Oct 18 SA 4f fst :47³ B

Zaleucus ✱
Ch. h. 6, by Wardlaw—Golden Fingers, by Precious Boy
STEVENS G L $20,000   Br.—Zellen L (Fla)
Own.—Cal Canadian Farms   Tr.—Vienna Darrell
116

Lifetime	1991 5 2 2 0	$24,450
36 10 7 2	1990 7 1 1 1	$41,550
$193,305	Turf 3 0 0 0	$3,150

180ct91-5-wide stretch, lugged in lane

Speed Index: Last Race: +2.0   3-Race Avg.: +1.3   3-Race Avg.: +1.3   Overall Avg.: -0.3
LATEST WORKOUTS   Nov 28 Hol 4f fst :49¹ H   Nov 14 Hol 5f fst 1:01² H   Nov 8 SA tr.t 4f fst :49² H   Nov 3 SA 5f fst 1:03¹ B

Good Field No Hit
Dk. b. or br. c. 4, by Diamond Prospect—Operette (Ger), by Sederini
FUENTES J A $20,000   Br.—Hunter Farm (Fla)
Own.—Cleveland Lila   Tr.—Cleveland Gene
1115

Lifetime	1991 3 1 0 0	$3,300
	1990 2 M 0 1	$5,175
$16,925		

280ct88-Dead heat

Speed Index: Last Race: -9.0   3-Race Avg.: -4.0   8-Race Avg.: -5.5   Overall Avg.: -5.8
LATEST WORKOUTS   Nov 23 SA 5f fst 1:01² H   Nov 16 SA 4f fst :49⁴ H   Nov 10 SA 4f fst :49⁴ H   Oct 28 BM 4f fst :50 H

Fiesta Del Sol *

B. g. 5, by Habitony—Princess Torsion, by Torsion
PEDROZA M A
$20,000 Br.—Malone Mr-Mrs J C (Cal)
Own.—Spinelli Gary Tr.—Spinelli Gary

116

Lifetime 1981 12 1 2 1 $21,945
35 8 6 5 1980 9 3 2 2 $61,274

Speed Index: Last Race: -2.0   3-Race Avg.: -0.6   10-Race Avg.: -3.1   Overall Avg.: -3.1
LATEST WORKOUTS Nov 27 SA 5f fst :511 H   Nov 14 SA 3f fst :37⅖ H   Oct 19 SA 5f fst 1:02⅖ H   Oct 14 SA 5f fst 1:01 H

Council Member

B. g. 3(Mar), by Rare Performer—Connemara Miss, by L'Enjoleur
ARGUELLO F
$20,000 Br.—Gens E (Ky)
Own.—H R S Inc Tr.—Smith Donald W

114

Lifetime 1981 15 2 2 2 $34,890
17 2 2 2 1980 2 M 0 0
$34,890 Turf 1 0 0 0

Speed Index: Last Race: -2.0   2-Race Avg.: 0.0   2-Race Avg.: 0.0   Overall Avg.: -8.1
LATEST WORKOUTS ●Nov 27 Fpx 4f fst :47⅗ Hg   ●Oct 16 Kee 4f fst :47⅖ H

Power Base

Ch. g. 4, by Woodland Lad—Pattilvr, by Preferred Position
DESORMEAUX K J
$20,000 Br.—Alvarez & Smith (Cal)
Own.—Alvarez & Smith Tr.—Sadler John W

116

Lifetime 1981 9 0 1 2 $13,800
34 3 2 5 1980 14 0 2 2 $61,605
$92,230 Turf 7 1 0 2

Speed Index: Last Race: (—)   3-Race Avg.: (—)   12-Race Avg.: (—)   Overall Avg.: -6.3
LATEST WORKOUTS Nov 21 Hol 6f fst 1:14⁴ H   Nov 4 SA 5f fst 1:00 H   Oct 13 SA 7f fst 1:26³ H   Oct 1 SA 6f fst 1:14 H

Smart Magician

Dk. b. or br. c. 4, by Clever Trick—Straight Edition, by Going Straight
ALVARADO F J
$20,000 Br.—Donamire Farm & Glencrest Farm (Ky)
Own.—Scott & Sullivan Tr.—Sullivan John

116

Lifetime 1981 10 1 2 0 $24,050
18 1 2 1 1980 4 0 0 0 $520
$24,970 Turf 11 0 0 1 $520

Speed Index: Last Race: -4.0   3-Race Avg.: -5.3   6-Race Avg.: -2.0   Overall Avg.: -4.3
LATEST WORKOUTS Nov 27 SA 4f fst 1:02¹ H   Nov 22 SA 4f fst :48³ H   Nov 17 SA 5f fst 1:01⁴ H   Nov 12 SA 7f fst 1:17¹ H

Intercup

Dk. b. or br. g. 5, by Interco—Coupling, by Dress Up
FLORES D R
$20,000 Br.—Neumann D O (Cal)
Own.—Mirage Stable Tr.—Truman Eddie

116

Lifetime 1981 21 2 3 3 $35,525
26 3 5 4 1980 9 1 1 1 $23,300
$66,000 Turf 1 0 0 0

Speed Index: Last Race: -6.0   3-Race Avg.: -1.3   10-Race Avg.: -1.4   Overall Avg.: -1.4
LATEST WORKOUTS Nov 27 SA 5f fst 1:00⁴ H   Nov 8 SA 4f fst :48³ H   Nov 2 SA 4f fst 1:02¹ H   Oct 26 SA 4f fst :47⅖ H

Gringo Greg

Ch. g. 4, by Lomax—Lynell, by Laomedonte
PINCAY L JR
$20,000 Br.—Fowler Joyce (Cal)
Own.—Isaacs S Tr.—Spawr Bill

116

Lifetime 1981 10 1 0 4 $33,100
19 1 0 4 1980 9 0 0 0 $27,095
$60,195 Turf 1 0 0 0

Speed Index: Last Race: +1.0   3-Race Avg.: -0.3   5-Race Avg.: -0.6   Overall Avg.: -3.1
LATEST WORKOUTS Nov 25 Hol 5f fst 1:02 H   Oct 29 SA 6f fst 1:15³ H   Oct 24 SA 5f fst 1:01⁴ H   Oct 17 SA 5f fst 1:01³ H

Zaleucus Not one of his last nine races has been disgraceful, and that's hard to say about most horses at this level. He also does whatever it takes to win, as indicated by his stellar record of 10 victories in 36 starts. Sprinting is no problem for him, either. Strong contender. The Oct. 6 race suggests itself as the proper paceline.

Fiesta Del Sol After a competitive race versus $25,000 claimers three lines back, he failed to repeat the effort against the same kind. The drop to $20,000 most recently may be a fire-sale class maneuver, but at least he stays above the level of his last win. Lukewarm contender rated off last line.

Council Member Forgive the last race—he's shown he can't compete in routes without folding up like cheap wallpaper—and you have a decent effort at Keeneland against horses similar to those in today's field. Since the public doesn't know how to handle shippers, we'll leave him in.

Power Base All his recent races have been dismal routes in which he's shown minimal speed. Out.

Smart Magician Broke his maiden here in wire-to-wire fashion and hasn't run loose on the lead since. It doesn't matter. The track is playing against front runners. Forget.

Intercup Three recent claims show he's a hot commodity. The rise is mandatory, and although he hasn't shown he can handle this level, his running style fits the track perfectly. Use the most recent race.

Gringo Greg Nice effort versus better last out, with prolonged involvement in the pace of the race. They may have finally dropped this guy into a winning spot. We'd like to use the most recent race, but the absence of a *Daily Racing Form* speed rating and track variant warns us off. Rate him off his Nov. 2 performance.

At first glance, this race seemed contentious. However, ALL-IN-ONE has narrowed it down to two horses: Zaleucus and Fiesta Del Sol. Zaleucus's very sharp current form and mid-pack running style give him a clear advantage over Fiesta Del Sol's pro-

```
1DEC91                              HOL                    7 furlongs dirt
Race #9                                                         10 starters
C20,000                                             Age: 3+years, Male
```

```
------------------------------------INPUT DATA------------------------------------
```

Horse name	# ST	# W	# P	# S	$'S Earned	Date	Trk	Dist.	S	1st C time	2nd C time	Final time
Zaleucus	5	2	2	0	24450	20NOV91	SA	6.500	D	21.3	44.1	116.1
Council Member	15	2	2	2	34000	16NOV91	KEE	7.000	D	23.2	46.3	125.1
Intercup	21	2	3	3	36525	10NOV91	SA	6.000	D	21.3	44.4	109.4
Gringo Greg	10	1	4	0	33100	15NOV91	SA	6.500	D	21.2	44.1	116.0
Fiesta Del Sol	12	1	2	1	21945	17NOV91	HOL	6.000	D	22.1	45.0	109.4

Horse name	Class Lvl	1st C B.L.	2nd C B.L.	Final B.L.	SR	Var
Zaleucus	C25,000	5.00	4.25	2.25	87	15
Council Member	C20,000	3.25	2.75	2.00	82	16
Intercup	C16,000	7.25	6.75	5.50	81	13
Gringo Greg	C20,000	10.00	10.00	3.25	87	14
Fiesta Del Sol	C20,000	2.25	2.75	4.75	86	12

```
------------------------------------BETTING LINE------------------------------------
```

Horse name	PEH	Rankings H-I THAAI	P-H	ESP	Rating	Betting Line	Fair Place $	Fair Show $
Zaleucus	1	1	1	1	1	90.82	5-2	3.80	3.00
Fiesta Del Sol	2	3	3	3	2	80.23	4-1		
Gringo Greg	3	2	2	2	4	69.10			
Council Member	4	5	5	5	3	63.86			
Intercup	5	4	4	4	5	60.90			

```
------------------------------------EXACTA GRID------------------------------------
```

	Zaleucus	Fiesta Del Sol
Zaleucus	. . . .	19 47
Fiesta Del Sol	22 54	. . . .

```
------------------------------------SPEED/PACE SUMMARY------------------------------------
```

```
Race Profile:      23.14   46.17   124.68   Winners' Pace Profile: MID
Ability Par:       69.20                     Pace Contention Point: 5.71 lengths
```

Projected Times:	1st C	2nd C	Fin C	Ability Time	Balance Time	Last Frac	Proj Pace	Con- tender
Zaleucus	23.86	46.10	124.53	68.34	80.86	38.43	EARLY	Y
Fiesta Del Sol	23.06	45.79	124.76	68.52	80.85	38.97	FRONT	Y
Gringo Greg	24.55	47.03*	124.51	69.50	81.38	37.48	REAR	N
Council Member	23.74	46.46	126.09	69.17	82.08	39.63	MID	N
Intercup	24.27	47.14*	125.36	70.01	81.99	38.22	REAR	N

```
------------------------------------PACE GRAPH------------------------------------
```

```
        Profile:                  23.14              46.17               124.68
        Front Runner:             23.06              45.79               124.51
    Horse name                     1C                 2C                     F
Zaleucus          ------------------X---+ -----------(---X-+ -------------------X
Fiesta Del Sol    ------------------X    -----------(-----X -------------------X+
Gringo Greg       ------------X-----+    -----------X----+  -------------------X
Council Member    --------------X--+     -----------(--X--+ -----------X-------+
Intercup          ------------X-----+    -----------X(-----+ --------------X---+
```

jected front-running style. We have no edge on Zaleucus, whose public odds match our betting-line odds. At nearly 12-to-1, Fiesta Del Sol is worth a win wager, the win profile notwithstanding.

NINTH RACE Hollywood DECEMBER 1, 1991 — **7 FURLONGS. (1:20⁴) CLAIMING. Purse $14,000. 3-year-olds and upward. Weights, 3-year-olds, 119 lbs.; older, 121 lbs. Non-winners of two races since October 6 allowed 3 lbs;. a race since then, 5 lbs. Claiming price $20,000; if for $18,000 allowed 2 lbs. (Races when entered for $16,000 or less not considered.)**

Value of race $14,000; value to winner $7,700; second $2,800; third $2,100; fourth $1,050; fifth $350. Mutuel pool $295,319. Exacta pool $370,072.

Last Raced	Horse	M/Eqt.A.Wt	PP	St	¼	½	Str	Fin	Jockey	Cl'g Pr	Odds $1
20Nov91 3Hol2	Zaleucus	LBb 6 116	4	9	7½	6½	1hd	1hd	Stevens G L	20000	2.80
29Aug91 5Dmr10	Smart Magician	B 4 116	8	4	3½	21	2hd	2½	Alvarado F J	20000	40.50
15Nov91 3Hol2	Gringo Greg	LBb 4 117	10	1	41½	4½	51½	32½	Pincay L Jr	20000	2.00
10Nov91 1SA3	Intercup	LBb 5 116	9	2	1hd	31½	3hd	41½	Flores D R	20000	7.30
17Nov91 2Hol5	Fiesta Del Sol	LBb 5 116	5	6	61	5hd	62½	51½	Pedroza M A	20000	11.90
23Nov91 2Hol2	Sun Streak	LBb 5 111	1	3	2hd	1hd	4½	61½	Torres H5	20000	13.70
15Nov91 3Hol7	Explosive West	LBb 4 114	2	10	10	10	81½	7nk	Mena F	18000	22.50
2Nov91 11SA3	Shakem Up Haughty	LBb 4 116	3	5	5½	72½	72	82½	Castanon J L	20000	6.70
9Nov91 2SA9	Power Base	LBb 4 116	7	7	8½	81½	92	93	Nakatani C S	20000	8.10
16Nov91 2Hol6	Council Member	LBb 3 114	6	8	96	95	10	10	Arguello F	20000	43.70

OFF AT 4:57. Start good. Won driving. Time, :22³, :45¹, 1:10 , 1:22³ Track fast.

$2 Mutuel Prices:		Win	Place	Show
	4–ZALEUCUS	7.60	4.20	2.80
	8–SMART MAGICIAN		24.20	10.20
	10–GRINGO GREG			3.20

$2 EXACTA 4–8 PAID $290.20.

We lost $2 in this race. Heading into the final race, we've amassed a profit of $37.40.

10th Hollywood

7 ½ FURLONGS. (1.27) CLAIMING. Purse $10,000. 3-year-olds and upward. Weights, 3-year-olds, 119 lbs.; older, 121 lbs. Non-winners of two races since October 6 allowed 3 lbs.; a race since then, 5 lbs. Claiming price $10,000.

LASIX—Telephone Canyon, Deferred, Za Loose Ski, Strogien, Clever Return, Radar Alert, Honest John, Secret Selection, Range Rider, Growler Sandue, Call the Tower, Secret Moves, Musique d'Enfer, Fools Hat-Br, Renne's Gold.

Telephone Canyon — Dk. b. or br. g. 7, by Assagai Jr—Determining, by Decidedly
DESORMEAUX K J — $10,000 — Br.—Van Berg J C (Ky) — 116
Own.—Fought & Tons of Fun Stable — Tr.—Passey Blake

Lifetime 64 10 14 6 $231,819 — 1991 15 1 4 2 $26,200 — 1990 8 2 1 0 $42,300 — Turf 16 3 2 2 $55,919

17Nov91- 4Hol	fst	1⅛	:472	1:12	1:51	3↑Clm 10000	3	8	55½	55½	42½	54¾	Nakatani C S	LBb	115	6.20	74-15	Waterzip1151¾ SirAlex-Ch118noFaixaOuro-Br1153	Even finish 10
10Oct91- 9SA	fst	1⅛	:471	1:112	1:491	3↑Clm 12500	6	5	53	54½	45	44¾	Nakatani C S	LBb	116	5.50	79-19	PortRainbow1172JazzIsland1131½IdeaQue1161½	4-wide stretch 11
30Sep91-10Fpx	fst	1 1/16	:47	1:12	1:441	3↑Clm 10000	4	5	53½	43	22	2½	Nakatani C S	LBb	119	6.80	86-20	Relnss122½TlphonCnyon1193Mdow'sIntrco116nk	Sharp effort 9
21Sep91-10Fpx	fst	1⅜	:483	1:391	2:181	3↑Hcp 12500s	3	9	109¾	99½	77	65½	Patton D B	LBb	113	11.70	81-16	Riflemaker116½Leasee1111Gibson'sChoice115nk	Wide in drive 11
12Sep91-13Fpx	fst	*1⅛	:483	1:142	1:531	3↑Alw 12500s	7	7	52¾	64¾	68½	613	Patton D B	LBb	113	5.50	63-27	Riflemaker113½ Desert Lover1161 Baffo1137	Wide final turn 12
13Aug91- 9LA	fst	1 1/16	:453	1:104	1:442	3↑Clm 10000	9	5	45½	45	22	1½	Patton D B	LBb	117	3.40	83-17	TlphonCnyon117½FnnclBoom117nkScrtSlctn1221	Perfect trip 9
31Jly91- 9LA	fst	1 1/16	:461	1:111	1:424	3↑Clm 10000	1	7	64½	56	44½	34¾	Corral J R	LBb	117	4.40	86-14	FerlessDys1173½ExoticEgle1141½TelephonCnyon1173¾	Evenly 8
2Jun91- 1Hol	fst	1⅛	:48	1:123	1:503	Clm 16000	8	6	86½	98½	99½	913	Solis A	LBb	115	18.10	68-19	Coronado Bay115hd Attesa1154½ Waterzip117no	Outrun 10
22May91- 5Hol	fst	1 1/16	:462	1:101	1:414	Clm 16000	2	7	88½	812	611	713½	Desormeaux KJ	LBb	115	11.00	78-13	RuleAll1165ThreeTimesOlder1152½ProvSpindid1174	No threat 9
4May91- 6Hol	fst	1 1/16	:461	1:11	1:442	Clm 16000	12	8	813	89¾	47	51¾	Parker S D5	LBb	110	12.80	77-22	Vote115½ Attesa110hd Gove115½	No rally 12

Speed Index: Last Race: (—) 3–Race Avg.: (—) 12–Race Avg.: (—) Overall Avg.: -4.3

LATEST WORKOUTS Nov 24 Hol 4f fst :48 H — Nov 13 Hol 4f fst :48 H — Nov 7 Hol 5f fst 1:022 H

Deferred — Ch. c. 4, by Affirmed—Seton's Encounter, by Spring Double
FLORES D R — $10,000 — Br.—Sagaponack II (Ky) — 116
Own.—Harbor View Farm — Tr.—Tinsley J E Jr

Lifetime 25 1 2 1 $41,020 — 1991 15 0 1 1 $21,000 — 1990 10 1 1 0 $20,020 — Turf 17 0 2 0 $24,225

17Nov91- 2Hol	fst	6f	:221	:45	1:094	3↑Clm 20000	1	9	83¾	94¾	97¼	78	Torres H5	LBb	111	25.20	83-12	BlindPlay116½LaurensQuest1161½SantaTecl-En116½	No threat 10
2Nov91-11SA	fst	6½f	:212	:441	1:16	3↑Clm 20000	7	6	55	43	3½	53½	Castanon A L	Lb	115	42.90	87-14	RnTnk1151½SntTci-En1101½ShkmUpHght115nk	Bid, weakened 11
24Oct91- 5SA	fst	1	:461	1:102	1:36	3↑Clm 32000	7	6	63½	64	66	67½	Torres H5	LBb	110	22.60	79-15	PrudntLdr115noSfToSy1152PorcupinRdg115½	Off slowly, rank 7
7Sep91- 5Dmr	fst	7f	:223	:454	1:23	3↑Clm 35000	4	8	63½	32½	44½	48¾	Lopez A D	LBb	114	24.50	77-15	His Legacy1171¾ Fancy Oats115no Conflictofinterest1156½	8
7Sep91-Bumped at start, boxed in 3/8-3/16																			
26Aug91- 3Dmr	fst	6½f	:22	:444	1:154	3↑Clm 32000	5	2	53½	53	57	35	Torres H5	LBb	110	28.90	84-14	Andimo115no Black Boots1155 Deferred1102	Wide trip 7
10Aug91- 9Dmr	fm	1 1/16 Ⓣ	:471	1:11	1:423	3↑Clm 55000	9	3	31½	52¾	1013	1012½	Martinez F F5	LBb	108	59.20	81-04	Preston-Fr116½Robinski-NZ118½GrnJudgement116nk	Faltered 10
25Jly91- 7Dmr	fm	1 1/16 Ⓣ	:482	1:114	1:422	3↑Alw 38000	4	6	43	42¾	54½	97¾	Solis A	Bb	122	31.30	87-07	PlosVrds-Ar119½BoldlyExcllnt1192¾TdyColony1161½	Gave way 10
19Jun91- 5GG	fm	1 1/16 Ⓣ	:472	1:121	1:444	+ 3↑Alw 24000	5	8	86½	73¾	55½	74¾	Miller D A Jr	LB	120	3.80	83-15	HndsomWd120hdBstnBold120hdTmonDncr1201½	Lacked room 11
6Jun91- 7Hol	fm	1 1/16 Ⓣ	:474	1:113	1:412	Clm 50000	2	6	74½	73	54	74	Berrio O A5	LB	111	31.60	84-12	OldExclusive111¾KohenWithK.116nkGreen'sLeder116½	Outrun 10
18May91- 9Hol	fm	1 1/16 Ⓣ	:47	1:104	1:412	Alw 35000	7	10	107½	95½	84	77	Desormeaux K J	B	120	24.20	81-10	Rudy's Fantasy120½ Majestic Moment1202Begar117nk	Outrun 12

Speed Index: Last Race: -5.0 3–Race Avg.: -4.0 4–Race Avg.: -3.5 Overall Avg.: -5.6

LATEST WORKOUTS Nov 24 SA 5f fst 1:01 H — Nov 10 SA 4f fst :481 H — Oct 19 SA 5f fst 1:024 H — Oct 12 SA 5f fst 1:024 H

Za Loose Ski
SORENSON D
Own.—Hoggard L

Dk. b. or br. g. 5, by Golden Reserve—Dogwood Poise, by Dogwood Passport
$10,000   Br.—Hoggard L (BC-C)
Tr.—Lausten Carl

Lifetime   1991 12 1 1 1 $8,708
42 6 3 3   1990 10 2 2 0 $15,793
116 $65,958

Speed Index: Last Race: -10.0   4-Race Avg.: -2.0   Overall Avg.: -1.8
LATEST WORKOUTS   Nov 21 Hol   5f fst 1:01¹ H   Nov 7 Hol   4f fst :50 H   ●Oct 8 EP   4f fst :47³ H

Strogien
NAKATANI C S
Own.—Garmon-McIver-Yanez

B. g. 5, by Sassafras (Fra)—Stone Cottage, by New Providence
$10,000   Br.—Pillar Stud Inc (Ky)
Tr.—Sadler John W

Lifetime   1991 9 0 0 1 $10,100
35 5 6 2   1980 11 1 2 1 $43,190
116 $125,972   Turf 24 5 6 1 $115,872

Speed Index: Last Race: -7.0   2-Race Avg.: -2.0   2-Race Avg.: -2.0   Overall Avg.: -6.1
LATEST WORKOUTS   Nov 28 Hol   7f fst 1:27¹ H   ●Nov 14 Hol   5f fst 1:00 H   Nov 7 SA   1 fst 1:43⁴ H   Nov 1 SA   6f fst 1:18¹ B

Clever Return
ORTEGA L E
Own.—Moran C V

Dk. b. or br. h. 5, by Clever Trick—Ferlis Key, by Ferli
$10,000   Br.—Kennelot Stable Ltd (Ky)
Tr.—Sweeney Brian

Lifetime   1991 9 1 1 0 $4,550
35 2 4 5   1980 17 1 2 0 $32,250
116 $88,185   Turf 9 1 3 0 $37,800

Speed Index: Last Race: -17.0   3-Race Avg.: -7.6   3-Race Avg.: -7.6   Overall Avg.: -6.6
LATEST WORKOUTS   Nov 21 SA   3f fst :37² B   ●Nov 11 SA   4f fst :46³ H   Oct 14 SA   3f fst :35 H

Radar Alert
PEDROZA M A
Own.—Trevino S G

Ch. g. 5, by Radar Ahead—Gold Martyr, by Gold Admiral II
$10,000   Br.—Vail S H (Cal)
Tr.—Trevino Stephen G

Lifetime   1991 11 1 1 3 $14,550
25 3 1 4   1980 5 0 1 0 $3,025
116 $67,900   Turf 1 0 0 0

Speed Index: Last Race: +1.0   3-Race Avg.: -2.0   3-Race Avg.: -2.0   Overall Avg.: -5.5
LATEST WORKOUTS   Oct 31 SA   5f fst 1:00 H   Oct 12 SA   3f fst :36² H

Honest John
MARTINEZ F F
Own.—Sawyer Carrie A

Dk. b. or br. g. 5, by John Casey—Kitchie's Girl, by Quandrangle
$10,000   Br.—Sanderson J (Wash)
Tr.—Harper David B

Lifetime   1991 15 0 1 2 $12,275
43 4 4 4   1980 14 1 4 1 $20,180
1115 $118,867   Turf 1 0 0 0

Speed Index: Last Race: (—)   3-Race Avg.: (—)   12-Race Avg.: (—)
LATEST WORKOUTS   Nov 15 Hol   4f fst :49¹ H   Nov 1 Hol   4f fst :49³ H   Oct 7 Hol   5f fst 1:03 H

Secret Selection
ALVARADO F J
Own.—Christine & Garcia

B. g. 7, by Convincingly—Proof Tested, by Olden Times
$10,000   Br.—Proctor J & W L (Tex)
Tr.—Garcia Victor

Lifetime   1991 10 1 2 3 $15,775
43 5 7 7   1980 10 1 2 3 $32,735
116 $113,700

Speed Index: Last Race: (—)   3-Race Avg.: (—)   12-Race Avg.: (—)
LATEST WORKOUTS   Nov 19 SA   5f fst 1:02¹ H   Nov 12 SA   5f fst 1:03 H   Nov 4 AC   5f fst :00⁴ H   Oct 29 AC   4f fst :52¹ B

Range Rider
BERRIO O A
Own.—Shields J J
$10,000
Br.—Proctor J & W L (Tex)
Tr.—Bernstein David
116

	Lifetime	1991	14	1	1	2	$12,230
	40 5 6	1990	18	3	4	3	$41,500
$69,105	Turf	1	0	0	0	

Speed Index: Last Race: -5.0   3-Race Avg.: -2.3   5-Race Avg.: -6.6   Overall Avg.: -5.2
LATEST WORKOUTS   Nov 23 SA   3f fst :36¹ H   Nov 18 SA   4f fst :48¹ H   Oct 26 Hol   3f fst 1:16² H   Oct 19 Hol   3f fst :38² H

Growler Sandue *
TORRES H
Own.—S S S Stables
$10,000
Br.—Benford R M (Cal)
Tr.—Chavez Tony
1115

	Lifetime	1991	16	3	1	1	$24,450
	69 15 5 7	1990	23	5	0	0	
$173,272							

Speed Index: Last Race: -16.0   2-Race Avg.: -11.5   2-Race Avg.: -11.5   Overall Avg.: -8.6
LATEST WORKOUTS   ●Nov 23 Fpx   4f fst :47² H

Call The Tower
CASTANON J L
Own.—Steinke A B
$10,000
Br.—James B C (Ky)
Tr.—Azcarate Dan
116

	Lifetime	1991	12	1	0	0	$9,000
	36 8 3 4	1990	11	1	2	3	$55,976
$197,326	Turf	2	0	0	0	$900

Speed Index: Last Race: -10.0   3-Race Avg.: -10.0   10-Race Avg.: -7.5   Overall Avg.: -7.5
LATEST WORKOUTS   Nov 25 Hol   4f fst :47⁴ H   Nov 9 Hol   3f fst :36¹ H   Nov 4 Hol   5f fst 1:00¹ H   Oct 13 Hol   4f fst :49 H

Secret Moves
STEINER J J
Own.—Perrin or Perrin & Toed
$10,000
Br.—Shemle E (Cal)
Tr.—Harlow Robert E
116

	Lifetime	1991	18	0	1	0	$825
	23 2 3 2	1990	7	1	0	0	$11,450
$35,830	Turf	0	0	0	0	

Speed Index: Last Race: -11.0   2-Race Avg.: -9.0   2-Race Avg.: -9.0   Overall Avg.: -7.3
LATEST WORKOUTS   ●Nov 25 SA   4f fst 1:00 H   Nov 5 SA   6f fst 1:13⁴ H   Oct 19 SA   3f fst :37⁴ H   Oct 12 SA   6f fst 1:14² H

Also Eligible (Not in Post Position Order):

Musique d'Enfer
ATKINSON S
Own.—Hop & Supich
$10,000
Br.—Whitney Mrs J H (Ky)
Tr.—Connor Kay
116

	Lifetime	1991	7	0	1	0	$4,215
	30 3 1 2	1990	14	1	0	1	$14,575
$44,495	Turf	1	0	0	0	

Speed Index: Last Race: -3.0   3-Race Avg.: -5.0   9-Race Avg.: -5.0   Overall Avg.: -6.7
LATEST WORKOUTS   ●Nov 23 Fpx   5f fst 1:03³ H   ●Oct 22 Fpx   4f fst :47⁴ H

Fools Hat-Br
FLORES D R
Own.—Quinlan-Shulmon-Sandspoint
$10,000
Br.—Haras San Francesco (Brz)
Tr.—Shulman Sanford
118

	Lifetime	1991	19	3	2	3	$35,195
	45 7 4 6	1990	14	3	2	2	$15,723
$52,907	Turf	14	3	2	2	$15,723

Speed Index: Last Race: -4.0   3-Race Avg.: -2.3   9-Race Avg.: -2.8   Overall Avg.: -2.3
LATEST WORKOUTS   Nov 17 Hol   5f fst 1:02³ H   Nov 12 Hol   3f fst :35² H   Oct 29 SA   4f fst :48⁴ H   Oct 16 SA   5f fst 1:00¹ H

Telephone Canyon No recent form in sprints. Elimination.

Deferred Zero for his last fifteen, and only one win in 25 career starts. Out.

Za Loose Ski First run in this country was dismal. Non-contender.

Strogien After being contentious for a $45,000 claiming price earlier in the year, this guy has been dropping steadily since—with no improvement. Toss out.

Clever Return Hit the bottom three races back, to no avail. Low-win trainer doesn't help. Forget.

Radar Alert Last two have been okay, and the drop to the basement seems appropriate, as he's not been disgraced there yet. Mild contender, although the profile has been favoring horses that possess sharp early speed. Use the Nov. 6 line.

Honest John Proven loser at this level. No recent sprint activity. Out.

Range Rider Although he's lost several times at this level, he's won on this track at almost this distance. His ability to be on or near the lead at the second call is in question, but at this class level and at this relative distance of seven to 7½ furlongs, he's been at his best. The last line can be used.

Growler Sandue The sharp route speed he flashed last out should put him in the pace profile in today's elongated sprint. Use the bottom Hollywood line.

Call The Tower Was unwisely claimed four back for $10,000 and never made the mandatory rise. Does show a win at a higher level. He stays in off his last line.

```
1DEC91                            HOL                      7.5 furlongs dirt
Race #10                                                          12 starters
C10,000                                                  Age: 3+years, Male
```

```
--------------------------------INPUT DATA-------------------------------
              #   #   #   #   $'S                            1st C  2nd C  Final
Horse name    ST  W   P   S   Earned  Date    Trk Dist. S    time   time   time
-------------------------------------------------------------------------
Radar Alert   11  0   1   3   14950   20NOV91 SA  7.000 D    22.0   45.1   124.2
Range Rider   14  1   1   2   12255   7NOV91  SA  8.000 D    46.2  111.1   137.2
Growler Sandue 16 3   1   1   24450   8NOV91  HOL 6.000 D    22.2   45.4   110.4
Call The Tower 12 1   0   0    9000   13NOV91 HOL 6.000 D    22.1   46.0   111.4
Fools Hat     19  3   2   3   35195   23NOV91 SA  7.000 D    22.1   45.0   123.3
```

```
                                 1st C   2nd C  Final
Horse name    Class Lvl          B.L.    B.L.   B.L.    SR    Var
-------------------------------------------------------------------------
Radar Alert   C12,500            11.00    9.25   0.20   81    20
Range Rider   C12,500             7.50    5.50   6.50   73    27
Growler Sandue C10,000            2.50    1.50   5.75   88    13
Call The Tower C10,000            8.50    7.25   4.75   76    14
Fools Hat     C12,500            11.00    4.75   0.00   85    14
```

```
-------------------------------BETTING LINE------------------------------
              -------Rankings--------        Betting   Fair    Fair
Horse name    PEH H-I THAAI P-H ESP  Rating   Line    Place $  Show $
-------------------------------------------------------------------------
Range Rider    3   3   3    3   1    85.35    5-2
Fools Hat      1   1   1    1   2    81.35    3-1
Growler Sandue 2   4   4    4   3    70.65
Radar Alert    4   2   2    2   4    70.61
Call The Tower 5   5   5    5   5    60.00
```

```
-------------------------------EXACTA GRID-------------------------------

            | Range Rider  |  Fools Hat   |
------------+--------------+--------------+
Range Rider | . . . . . . .|   19    47   |
            | . . . . . . .|              |
            | . . . . . . .|              |
------------+--------------+--------------+
Fools Hat   |    20    50   | . . . . . . .|
            |              | . . . . . . .|
            |              | . . . . . . .|
------------+--------------+--------------+
```

```
------------------------------SPEED/PACE SUMMARY-------------------------
Race Profile:    23.20   46.05  130.49   Winners' Pace Profile: FRONT
Ability Par:     68.91                   Pace Contention Point:  0.54 lengths

Projected Times:                      Ability Balance  Last  Proj  Con-
                 1st C   2nd C   Fin C   Time    Time   Frac  Pace  tender
-------------------------------------------------------------------------
Range Rider      23.52   45.37  129.96   67.22   85.56  44.59 FRONT   Y
Fools Hat        24.57   46.04* 129.49   67.50   85.78  43.45 MID     N
Growler Sandue   23.35   46.24* 131.16   69.13   86.91  44.92 LATE    N
Radar Alert      24.36   47.01* 130.32   69.66   86.97  43.32 REAR    N
Call The Tower   24.23   47.44* 131.96   70.64   88.21  44.52 REAR    N
```

```
--------------------------------PACE GRAPH-------------------------------
      Profile:                23.20              46.05            130.49
      Front Runner:           23.35              45.37            129.49
Horse name                    1C                 2C                    F
Range Rider    ----------------X+ ----------------(X ----------------X-+
Fools Hat      -----------X-----+ ---------------X-(+ ----------------X
Growler Sandue ----------------X ------------X--(+ ----------X------+
Radar Alert    -----------X---+ ----------X------(+ -------------X---+
Call The Tower -----------X---+ --------X--------(+ ------X----------+
```

Secret Moves Long ago he was good; now he's tragic. Dismiss.

Fools Hat All his starts at this lowest level have been very good, relatively speaking. The drop back there today should reawaken him, although his closing style is disadvantaged here. Use the Oct. 9 Santa Anita line.

These bottom-level claiming races are bonanzas for the handicapper/investor who loves to take a swing against the favorite. The public's top choice in these events, especially in full twelve-horse fields, as is the case today, typically goes off at about 7-to-2, and is rarely legitimate. Lacking strong favorites, these regrettable contests offer overlay players wonderful opportunities in both the straight and exotic pools. Today's race isn't contentious, but look where ALL-IN-ONE has ranked the betting favorite. What a lovely situation! Short prices absolutely cannot be tolerated in bottom-of-the-barrel races. Swinging for the fences is the order of the day. Thank goodness for the betting public. It's time to look to the heavens and bestow our gratitude upon the Great Handicapper. He's blessed us with the optimum scenario. The public has hammered down our third and fourth choices, but ignored our top two choices! What a thrill! We'll gratefully accept the generosity of our fellow citizens and sprint to the windows to take advantage of this wonderful opportunity.

TENTH RACE
Hollywood
DECEMBER 1, 1991

7 ½ FURLONGS. (1.27) CLAIMING. Purse $10,000. 3-year-olds and upward. Weights, 3-year-olds, 119 lbs.; older, 121 lbs. Non-winners of two races since October 6 allowed 3 lbs.; a race since then, 5 lbs. Claiming price $10,000.

Value of race $10,000; value to winner $5,500; second $2,000; third $1,500; fourth $750; fifth $250. Mutuel pool $236,671. Exacta pool $234,376. Trifecta pool $447,004.

Last Raced	Horse	M/Eqt.	A.	Wt	PP	St	¼	½	Str	Fin	Jockey	Cl'g Pr	Odds \$1
7Nov91 ^{5}SA^{3}	Range Rider	LB	5	116	8	7	$4^{1\frac{1}{2}}$	4^{3}	1^{2}	1^{3}	Berrio O A	10000	11.30
17Nov91 ^{2}Hol^{7}	Deferred	Lb	4	116	2	12	8^{1}	5^{hd}	2^{hd}	$2^{\frac{3}{4}}$	Alvarado F J	10000	5.10
17Nov91 ^{4}Hol^{5}	Telephone Canyon	LBb	7	116	1	10	10^{1}	$8^{\frac{1}{2}}$	6^{hd}	3^{2}	Ceballos O F	10000	13.70
2Nov91 ^{8}SA^{11}	Clever Return	LB	5	116	5	4	2^{hd}	3^{hd}	3^{1}	$4^{1\frac{3}{4}}$	Ortega L E	10000	53.40
8Nov91 ^{9}SA	Secret Moves	LB	7	116	11	1	$9^{1\frac{1}{2}}$	9^{1}	$10^{\frac{1}{2}}$	5^{hd}	Steiner J J	10000	94.20
13Nov91 ^{1}Hol^{4}	Call The Tower	LBb	5	116	10	8	$6^{\frac{1}{2}}$	$6^{1\frac{1}{2}}$	$7^{1\frac{1}{2}}$	$6^{\frac{3}{4}}$	Castanon J L	10000	31.10
21Aug91 ^{1}Dmr^{6}	Honest John	LBb	5	111	7	6	$5^{\frac{1}{2}}$	$7^{1\frac{1}{2}}$	$9^{1\frac{1}{2}}$	7^{nk}	Martinez F F^{5}	10000	30.90
20Nov91 ^{1}Hol^{4}	Radar Alert	LB	5	116	6	9	12	$11^{\frac{1}{2}}$	8^{hd}	8^{nk}	Pedroza M A	10000	4.30
23Nov91 ^{2}Hol^{4}	Fools Hat-Br	LB	7	118	12	2	$11^{\frac{1}{2}}$	$10^{\frac{1}{2}}$	$11^{3\frac{1}{2}}$	$9^{\frac{1}{2}}$	Flores D R	10000	5.30
8Nov91 ^{9}SA^{4}	Growler Sandue	LBb	8	111	9	3	$1^{1\frac{1}{2}}$	1^{hd}	5^{2}	10^{1}	Torres H^{5}	10000	3.60
4Oct91 ^{9}SA^{5}	Strogien	LB	5	116	4	5	$3^{\frac{1}{2}}$	$2^{\frac{1}{2}}$	4^{hd}	11^{5}	Nakatani C S	10000	4.00
14Nov91 ^{3}Hol^{6}	Za Loose Ski	LBb	5	116	3	11	$7^{1\frac{1}{2}}$	12	12	12	Arguello F	10000	54.40

OFF AT 5:31 Start good. Won driving Time, :22^{1}, :45^{2}, 1:10^{3}, 1:23^{3}, 1:30^{2} Track fast.

$2 Mutuel Prices:				
	8–RANGE RIDER	24.60	9.60	5.80
	2–DEFERRED		7.80	5.80
	1–TELEPHONE CANYON			7.60

$2 EXACTA 8–2 PAID $230.00. $2 TRIFECTA 8–2–1 PAID $2,524.60.

Races for bottom-of-the-barrel claimers are Kitts Anderson's specialty. If the field is full, as it was here, he automatically forsakes the public's top choice. Why? His research has concluded that this kind of favorite doesn't win its fair share of the races. He's then in the enviable position of correctly betting against a false favorite. In fact, Kitts is so convinced of his findings that he's promised to write a book on how to prosper from what many authors call these unpredictable, unbeatable, and unbettable contests.

Our profit on the final race is $20.60. Our profit for the day is $58.00. Let's recap our win betting for the day:

Race	Amt. Bet	Result	Race P/L	Daily P/L
1	$2.00	Won	+ $25.80	+ $25.80
2	2.00	Won	+ 5.80	+ 31.60
3	2.00	Lost	− 2.00	+ 29.60
4	4.00	Won	+ 7.20	+ 36.80
5	2.00	Lost	− 2.00	+ 34.80
6	4.00	Lost	− 4.00	+ 30.80
7	4.00	Lost	− 4.00	+ 26.80
8	2.00	Won	+ 12.60	+ 39.40
9	2.00	Lost	− 2.00	+ 37.40
10	4.00	Won	+ 20.60	+ 58.00

An outstanding day, needless to say. We played all ten races. We made fourteen bets for a total investment of $28. We cashed five winners for a total return of $86.00. Our profit was $58.00. Our ROI was 300 percent! I must warn you that this was a day for the ages. The natural order of things dictates that big days such as this will only come several times a year. The natural order of things is that only a handful of days will account for the bulk of your seasonal profits. Fortunately, today was one of them. You must take advantage of them when they are within your grasp. The truth of the matter is that on most days, "swing-for-the-fences" professionals trade money, either up or down slightly. As you can see, Christmas came early for Kitts this year. Good handicapping, good odds, and excellent results. Thorough preparation met wonderful opportunities, and good fortune resulted.

Many times, however, our best efforts in the win pools won't be rewarded as handsomely as they were today. Just ask Kitts

Anderson. Just ask Steve Unite. During Santa Anita's 1992 winter-spring meeting, they bet huge win overlays that were repeatedly finishing second by the slimmest of margins. A form of intelligent wagering kept them in the black. (Betting the longshot second in the exacta.) When the overlays just aren't winning, we must turn to additional sources of racetrack profits, lest our bankrolls and our psyches take too much of a prolonged beating. What are these sources? Place and show and the exacta. (Once you've mastered these bets.) The exacta is the most widely misunderstood and most abused form of parimutuel betting today. The public just doesn't know how to play it correctly. If you play exactas skillfully, the public will hand their money to you. And you don't even have to say thank you. This is to your mutuel advantage. Profits from public confusion, as I'm fond of saying.

We're getting down to the bottom. What remains is financial planning and execution.

Chapter 14

Financial Planning

You now have all the information you need in order to win consistently at thoroughbred handicapping. It's just a matter of taking these concepts and putting them into practice. This means that we have to practice with feedback. Remember, practice doesn't make perfect, practice makes permanent. You must make sure that you are practicing properly. The question becomes: How do I apply this in a systematic and orderly way so that I wind up at the *win window*?

Success is not a destination, it's a journey. Achievement is the destination, success is the process you used to get there. You have to understand that the price for success must be paid in full, no discounts, and all up front. You've got to put the wood into the fireplace to get heat. You can't say "First give me heat, then I'll give you wood." You don't become a winner overnight— you must pay your dues. Every winner, save one, that I have the good fortune to know, didn't start out that way. James Quinn is the exception. Quinn has never suffered the agony of defeat. But every other winner I know learned to win the hard way, and the hard way was by paying his dues. Usually the dues were small sums of money but lots of time. Then one day, all of a sudden, out of the clear blue it happened. They turned the corner and they never looked back. You have to realize that overnight success is a myth. Overnight success is preceded by lots of hours of dedication and hard work. The band Creedence Clearwater Revival became an overnight sensation in the sixties. Before they made their first album, they spent sixteen years doing one-night stands in bars and small nightclubs.

The first thing that you must understand is that if you handicap on paper, that is, if you pick up some old *Racing Forms*, go into your den, or sit at the kitchen table, or wherever you handicap—you'll win. It's practically absolutely guaranteed that you'll win. Let me share a metaphor with you. It's the one Ron Ambrose and I use in our seminars. I'll be lecturing and I'll turn to Ron and say, "Ron, did you bring the plank with you?" Ron will say, "Yes, it's upstairs." And then I'll tell the class, "We have a twenty-five-foot solid wood plank. This plank is twelve inches wide and two inches thick. We are going to tack a one-hundred-dollar bill at one end of the plank. We'll then ask you to very simply walk heel-to-toe, heel-to-toe, from one end of it to another. Very much like what you would be asked to do if you were stopped for drunk driving. If you can successfully complete the task of walking heel-to-toe, heel-to-toe, across the twenty-five-foot plank—when you get to the end, you simply bend over and pick up the one-hundred-dollar bill and put it in your pocket. It's yours and that's all there is to it." I ask the class, "Anybody interested in doing this—in trying this? And of course, if you fail and step off the plank before you reach the end, you don't get to keep the one hundred dollar bill." Just about every hand in the room goes up. And then I say, "Oh, by the way, there's one small thing that I've forgotten to tell you—I forgot to mention that the plank will be perched between the tops of two twenty-story buildings. Now how many of you will try it?" And, of course, I get no hands. And I ask, "Well, wait a minute, just a moment ago most of you were willing to do it, and now all of a sudden nobody wants to take me up on it." What happened? What dynamic was introduced? The answer is "fear of failure." When the plank was on the floor, what did you have to lose? Nothing. But once we put the plank between two twenty-story buildings, all of a sudden there is a new element introduced. Now there is a major consequence attached to failing.

When you handicap at home in the privacy of your den, and you're not risking real money, you're not around the same influences. It's not a true simulation of what happens at the racetrack. You don't have outside influences. Suppose you go to the window to make a bet and you meet a friend. Your friend asks, "Who do ya like?" You say, "The seven horse." He says, "Wait a minute, the four horse looks really hot. He looked good in the post parade and they're shooting with him today. His trainer is five out of his last six, plus he's going off at 8-to-1."

Now what do you do? At home, you don't have these distractions. You're able to maintain a very logical and rational approach to the game. The racetrack is anything but a logical and rational place. Emotions run rampant at the track. Handicapping in the privacy of your home doesn't properly simulate the environment that you'll have to succeed in. When you have nothing to lose, you tend to make bold, forceful decisions.

When you go up to the window and place a bet, and especially if it's a good-size bet, there is a certain amount of trepidation, a certain amount of fear that's present that's not there when you're at home. It can certainly cloud your judgment. You must test things with real money.

There's a truism in business: "What gets measured gets done." What you need to do is create a financial plan that can be measured. Actually, more than just a financial plan—a total approach. After you've mastered the material in this book and are feeling comfortable with it and have verified its truth at your racetrack, then you'll be ready to begin carrying out your plan. You'll be on the road to mastery.

There are going to be two phases. Imagine yourself as an artisan back in the Renaissance. You're training to be a sculptor and you're going to study under a master such as Michelangelo. Your education would consist of two phases: an apprentice phase and a mastery phase. You'll be doing the same thing, only updated to this century.

In the preparation phase (apprentice phase) you'll keep lots of records. You'll use the forms provided for each type of race. (See Appendix C.) You'll master them one at a time, beginning with maidens—they're the easiest. First you'll master each different kind of race, then you'll go on to master each different kind of bet. You'll first master win betting for maidens, then win betting for claimers, then win betting for non-claimers, and finally, win betting for turf races. Once you can demonstrate a 20 percent profit over a group of twenty races, and then repeat this five times in a row, you'll have passed your competency test. You'll first become competent with win betting, including the daily double and serial triple. Next, you'll master place and show betting. Then exacta and quinella wagering, and finally, the fancy exotics such as the trifecta and the Pick-6.

As you go up the ladder to mastery, you'll master one thing at a time. As you master each step and it becomes second nature, then you can add something new. What most handicappers do is scatter their interests as they try to master everything at once, and wind up mastering nothing. They're jacks-of-all-trades and masters of none. You want to do the very opposite. Remember: don't do what most other handicappers are doing, because what they're doing is losing. That's not only true at the track, it's true in life. Don't do what the majority are doing because they're invariably doing it wrong. They're following other people who are also doing it wrong. Don't do that—unless you want to get the same results.

We'll define the preparation phase as simply mastering the basic skills. Every profession or discipline has a certification procedure. For example, a lawyer has to pass a bar exam and a doctor has to pass the state board medical examinations. Our certification exams will consist of five groups of twenty races. You must be able to demonstrate a 20 percent or greater profit over the course of twenty races and repeat this performance five times in a row. If you have a losing sequence, you'll start over. The idea is to achieve five consecutive winning sequences of twenty races. In other words, one big group of a hundred races where you showed a steady and consistent profit. Once you can accomplish this level of mastery, you've certainly become a consistent winner as far as that type of race and that type of bet is concerned. You're now ready to move on to the next type of race and the next type of bet. As you can see, this process will take a long time. If you're a weekend player, it'll take at least six months just to finish mastery of win bets in maiden races. You can be practicing the other types of races during this time—you just can't bet a lot of money on them. Once you've mastered win betting for maidens, you then begin your mastery program for win betting on claimers, and at the same time you're ready for place and show mastery with maidens. Place and show betting has a goal of 10 percent ROI. Most professionals average between 8 and 20 percent on their place and show bets. Again, in the case of place and show betting, you want groups of twenty bets where you achieve a 10 percent profit. Your profit goal for place and show betting should be lower than win betting because you don't generate as big an edge. However, you do develop a much higher consistency. For example, in your twenty-race sequences of win bets, you may have only had five or six winning bets. Even with four wins or less, you may still manage to generate a profit on your win betting for the group of twenty races. In your place and show sequences you're going to have sixteen wins, seventeen wins—sometimes you'll win all twenty. Place and show betting is very safe. All other bets have a 20 percent ROI goal.

Most handicappers never master win betting to begin with, yet they're betting with both hands in the exacta pool. How silly. Suppose you wanted to become a commercial jet pilot. Would your instructor start you off behind the controls of a Boeing 747? Not in this life. How do you master any subject? You begin at the beginning. You master the fundamentals. As you become more and more adept at each fundamental, you become qualified to move on to the next challenge. This is the essence of mastery. You simply apply this success principle to thoroughbred handicapping.

Once you've mastered win betting in maiden races, you're ready to begin your mastery program for win betting in claiming races, followed by non-claimers and turf races. You'll follow this sequence to its logical conclusion for each category of bets: win bets, serial bets, place and show bets, exacta bets, and advanced exotics.

The hardest part of the preparation phase is that you're never, never going to bet on an underlay. In other words, you're gonna have to sit and watch horses win races that you know they dominate, and yet because they're going off at odds less than your betting line, you're not going to bet on them.

When you're finished with these one hundred races in each category, you then begin your execution phase for that type of race and that type of bet. Please understand that you're probably going to do each type of race a few times. Some of you may go right through the first five twenty-race sequences, get it right initially and then go on to your mastery phase, but it's rare. Most handicappers won't. You'll get one or two winning sequences and then you'll have a losing group and have to start over. Some of you will get three and four winning groups, then have a losing sequence and have to start over. It's frustrating, but hang in there. It's worth the pain. I guarantee it. After all, once you've completed your preparation phase, you'll have achieved financial security. You'll always be able to make a living, unless the government decides to outlaw gambling and close all the racetracks in this country. Highly unlikely. Even if this happens, you'll still have at least twenty-five countries to choose from, where parimutuel wagering is legal. Better yet, many of the same skills that allow you to excel in thoroughbred handicapping can be used successfully in the biggest casino of all, Wall Street.

While you are in your preparation phase, you should bet about half what you would normally bet. We've talked before about financial goals. Our goal is to earn so much per day on average. Let's say it's $100 per day and you know that you get an average of two to three playable races per day. Let's arbitrarily say three. In order for you to win $100 per day—assuming you have a 20 percent edge for win betting—you're gonna have to put $500 through the mutuel windows. That means that you're gonna have to be betting an average of $167 a race.

If $100 per day is going to be your ultimate goal, I recommend that during your preparation phase you use $50 per day as your daily goal.

Please view your preparation phase as on-the-job training. You are an apprentice at the craft of thoroughbred handicapping. After you can demonstrate mastery of your craft, you are then a journeyman. You still must continue to learn. The difference between a journeyman, which we'll call a professional, and an amateur, is smaller than you might imagine. This is a game of inches. It's similar to major league baseball hitters. The .250 hitter is paid a paltry $200,000 or so a year, while the .333 hitter earns multimillions of dollars a year. The difference is minuscule. It's about one hit every three games. A typical hitter bats about four times per game on average. A .250 hitter goes 3 for 12 while a .333 hitter goes 4 for 12. One hit more in three days makes the difference of as much as ten times the annual salary. This is true of handicappers, too. One more win every twelve races can make all the difference in the world with regard to profits.

Once you've passed the grueling tests of mastery for each type of race and each type of bet—you're ready for phase two. This is the execution phase. This is where your focus is on maximizing your income. At this point you've declared yourself a professional by virtue of passing your qualification exams.

I highly recommend that you keep a separate checking account for your "equine investments." It's an excellent idea to create a way to pay yourself. You should pay yourself on a regular basis, just as if you had a job. If your bankroll (hence this checking account) is getting bigger and bigger and you don't treat yourself and your loved ones—there's no tangible benefit to anyone and you'll soon lose your motivation. You definitely want to pay yourself on some regular schedule. I do it monthly and use my present bankroll size as the basis. We'll get back to this in a few moments.

Suppose your present bankroll is $2000, your maximum win bet is $100 (5 percent of it), and your maximum place and show bet is $200 (10 percent of it). As an aside, you should never make a win bet of more than 5 percent of your bankroll on any one event, or a place or show bet that exceeds 10 percent of your capital.

Your bankroll is growing at a minimum rate of 20 percent if you've achieved mastery at win betting. In theory, you are adding to your bankroll at a very nice pace—every time you bet $100 you are getting at least $120 back. Realize that this doesn't happen in an orderly way like compound interest on funds socked away in a bank account. What happens is that most days you are going to trade money. Most days you are going to be somewhere between minus three bets and plus six bets. If you're a $100 bettor, you'll be somewhere between minus $300 and plus $600 about 90 percent of the time. Every now and then you'll have those wonderful days that I call "Christmas." You'll win 20 to 30 units that day, sometimes more. It's the day you get to see the tax man. You'll hit a monster exacta, or you'll hit the Pick-6, or you'll hit some epic mutuel. A truly magnificent experience. It's a pity that these delirious days only happen two or three times a year. An infrequent, but horrible experience, is the opposite of this. It's the day when you don't cash a single ticket all day. The gods conspire and make sure that you lose every photo, hit every skip exacta (your choice comes in first and third), or you get two out of three winners in the serial triple that paid boxcars. Everything you try turns to do-do. Unfortunately, streaks, as opposed to a metered consistency, are the natural order of things for me. Because of my aggressive style of play, I have many more losing days than winning days. I'm from the Alexander the Great school of handicapping and betting strategy. "Conquer the world or forget about it." Attila the Hun was a sissy in my book—he lacked vision.

There are guys who are very consistent, like Tom Brohamer, Ron Ambrose, and Jim Quinn. They have more winning days than losing days. Ambrose is ridiculous. He wins almost every single day. I've never seen a handicapper who's more consistent. A losing day to him is a major disaster. Forget about two losing days in a row. He won't tolerate it. He's a very highly selective player, a very high-percentage player, and a very patient one, too.

It's never a good idea to commingle money. You should keep your equine investment fund separate from your regular day-today cash. Then figure out some rational way to pay yourself. One of the better ways is to keep an absolute minimum bankroll at the beginning of each month. I used to keep $2000 as a minimum balance in my equine investing checking account. At the end of every month I would pay myself whatever was in the account above $2000. Now the balance is much larger, but the principal remains the same. I would take the excess over $2000 and consider it as a paycheck. It was deposited into my safe until I was ready to spend it on my latest goal. I always have some goal in mind. I keep a picture of it on the wall in my office. For example, when it was a 486 Computer, I actually cut a picture of a full-blown 486 system from a computer magazine and I put it right in front of my desk. I wrote the price right on the picture. In this case, the price was $2300. When I had $3300 in my safe (I keep a $1000 cash reserve), I went out and bought this very 486 that I'm using to write this book. Lately, I've been taking trips all over the place. I took the family to Hawaii, to Disneyland, and to Disney World within the past six months.

My feeling is that you should have a goal that's not just money. It should be more concrete than that because you really don't want money—you want the things that money can buy. Maybe it's a car, maybe it's new furniture, maybe it's a new house, a vacation, whatever—put a picture of it where you'll see it every day just to remind yourself of your next major treat. Pay yourself accordingly. Put the money aside until you've saved enough to get your latest goodie. Then set a new goal. Start with small goals like having dinner with a friend or loved one at a very elegant restaurant. At the end of the month, if you have enough profit to afford the $200 to $300 bill (including a fine wine) that it costs to dine in a world-class restaurant—bon appétit. If not, save your profits until they accumulate to at least $200. Then bon appétit.

You should reward yourself, often. You really should. It's real important that these rewards be concrete, as opposed to just money, because most of us don't work just for money.

Once you've reached your execution phase, you can start betting the very limit of your comfort zone. Depending upon your goals, you'll have to start challenging your comfort zone. You do this a little at a time. My daily goal is $200. My maximum win bet is $500 and my maximum place and show bet is $1000. When my daily goal was $100, my maximum bets were $200 win and $500 place and show. There was a time when a $250 win bet caused me to have a violent visceral reaction. My pulse quickened, I could hear the blood pulsing in my temples, I felt that nervous jittery energy that made me pace up and down. Normally, I don't watch a race too intently, but when I make my maximum bet, I begin watching the warm-up with the intensity of watching a race. When the bell rings and the gate opens, I can tell you how many hairs the horse I bet has on its tail—I watch that closely.

Now, a $250 win bet is ho-hum. I hardly watch the race. It takes a $500 win bet to get me to react viscerally. This didn't happen overnight. It happened in $50 increments, and all with profits. When I increased my daily goal, I had to increase the bet size to correspond. My daily goals progressed from $100 per day to $200 in increments of $20. From $100 to $120, from $120 to $140, from $140 to $160, from $160 to $180, and finally from $180 to $200. At each increment my maximum win bet increased 20 percent, as did my place and show maximum. Each new level took me out of my comfort zone for a short period of time. It's amazing how quickly you adjust when your profits are growing. The problem comes when you hit a down cycle. The challenge is to be able to tell whether it's wise to persist or whether you should pull in your horns. When in doubt, pull in your horns. If you're not in touch with what's happening at your racetrack, it's best to take a break from betting and figure out what's happening.

If you honestly feel that completing the preparation phase sounds like the ordeal of Sisyphus or takes the discipline of a Tibetan Monk, then maybe there isn't a seat reserved for you in the professional section. Maybe you're meant to be a recreational player. If all this work takes the fun out of things and you really don't see handicapping as an investment, plus you don't want to go through all of the rigors of the preparation phase—I don't blame you. There's nothing wrong with making that decision. If you make the decision that says, "I don't want to go through all of this. I don't want to do this. I just want to go out and have some fun," that's perfect. That's a beautiful decision. Nobody said it's wrong not to make a commitment to become a professional. Just as it's perfectly okay not to make a commitment to become an actor, doctor, lawyer, or any other professional. It's perfectly okay to make any decision that you feel comfortable with. Just don't expect the same results as Quinn, Beyer, Ambrose, Cramer, and the thousands of other consistent winners.

Again, it's okay to make a decision that you're comfortable

with. But it's not okay to stay in your comfort zone. You must leave it if you wish to accomplish anything with your life. If you spend too much time in your comfort zone, you're destined for mediocrity. If you decide to be a professional handicapper and a consistent winner, you'll have to be willing to leave your comfort zone. You've got to pay the price. The price for success is always paid up front, no discounts, and that price is time and effort.

How long will it take? I haven't got a clue. In my case it took two years. Again, I don't know the answer for you. In Jim Quinn's case it started immediately. For some of us it'll take a few months, and for others it may take a few years. The major issue is whether to make the commitment or not. My vote is to make that commitment. Once you do, it's no longer a should, it becomes a must. (Most people "should all over themselves.") If your attitude is "I must do this" or, better yet, "I will do this or die"—your ship will come in a lot sooner. In fact, once you make this commitment—resources will appear out of nowhere. You'll have galvanized forces in this universe that will attract to you all the things that you need to realize and accomplish your purpose. (This is a universal law. It's called The Law of Purpose.)

You can make it happen within a year. Suppose it took two years? So what! Think about the end result. Here's another universal principle that you must understand—it's the principle of constant and never-ending improvement. Very small changes you'll make today will have a vast impact down the road. I don't know if this is apparent to you or not. If you were to simply increase your monthly income by two percent—each month you just made two percent more than you made the previous month—in less than three years you'd double your income. A very small change now produces dramatic results in the future. This is another universal principle of success: the principle of compound interest. When Einstein was asked, "What's the most amazing thing, the most wondrous thing that you've ever experienced?" His answer was, "Compound interest." What an answer!

Let's think about winning at the track in another way. Let's ask the question: Is it worth doing? The answer is a resounding **YES**. It satisfies all four of our basic needs, which are: physical, emotional, intellectual, and spiritual. It's a monumental achievement. Out of a thousand people who go to the racetrack, only a select few (between ten and twenty) can brag (truthfully) that they've mastered it. Here's an area of our life where 98 percent or more of the people fail, and you've mastered it. What a noble achievement.

Again, that's a nice psychic kind of a reward. But let's look at it from a monetary point of view. Consider for a second one of your children coming to you and saying, "Dad (or Mom), I want to be a schoolteacher and I want to go to a good school. I would like to go to a Big Ten school." They're willing to invest five years of their life and somewhere between $50,000 and $75,000 of your money. When they graduate they'll be qualified to earn somewhere between $100 and $200 per day.

Let's suppose your second child came to you and said, "Dad (or Mom), I want to become a professional handicapper." (In my case, I would do a dance. I would celebrate. I would embrace him, throw my arms around him and jump up and down and say "Whoopie! I'm a success as a parent." Society would surely not agree with me, but I personally think that would be a very noble goal for him to aspire to. If my son Sam, whom I love dearly, doesn't turn out to be a horseplayer, I think I'll have failed as a parent.) Anyway, I would be pretty excited about it. One of the reasons is economic efficiency. It's because I would save a lot of money and Sam would save a lot of time. We are talking about maybe $5,000 in materials, seminars, books, computer programs, and all the other necessary resources. I don't think you would be talking about any more than $5,000 invested in cash. The time investment would probably amount to one year full-time, certainly no more than two years. I would be saving $45,000 in four years, and Sam would be saving from three to four years of his time. In the end, he would certainly be qualified to earn at least $200 a day. In fact, he would be qualified to earn anything that he wanted to earn. Is it worthwhile? You "betcha sweet bippy" it is—it's more than worthwhile.

Once again, when you achieve mastery at handicapping, you'll have achieved financial security. Nobody can stop you from making a good living. Society won't crown your achievements by recognizing you as a "pillar of the community." On the contrary, you'll be considered the victim of a benign social disease. What society thinks, is wrong at least 80 percent of the time. Society thinks that a job is security. As usual, they're wrong. It's temporal. A company can lay you off tomorrow. Ask IBM. In 1991 IBM laid off 19,000 people. General Motors, in 1991, laid off more than 20,000 people. Here are two blue-chip companies, two of the most successful companies on earth, certainly in the top five of the Fortune 500, which failed to live up to the expectations of at least 39,000 people. We were sold a bill of goods. We were taught that going to work for a big company is security. It's a big lie. Look at the pain and anguish that this belief caused a large number of good people. Over 39,000 people had their aspirations and plans for financial security dashed on the rocks of false belief. Security isn't a job. It's a competence level. It's the confidence that no matter what happens in the economic and political world, "I will prevail." Handicapping can give this to you—IBM and General Motors can't.

When you achieve handicapping mastery, you'll have created a nice way to earn a second income, maybe a primary one. And that income will be dependent on nothing outside yourself. You won't be dependent on the government. You won't be dependent upon some huge monolithic company. You won't have to work to fulfill somebody else's goals—you'll be too busy fulfilling your own. Do you realize that your house could be confiscated tomorrow? Ask some of the residents of Kuwait. Did you realize that you could be thrown into prison tomorrow? Ask Nelson Mandela. Yes, these are remote possibilities; but they've happened to innocent people. All of your worldly possessions are temporal. Your only security lies in your abilities and your skills. Security is a feeling. It's the confidence in knowing that you'll prevail regardless of what happens in the economy or in the political world. By now you probably realize this is exactly what mastery of thoroughbred handicapping gives you.

People aren't going to change. You can set your watch by the fact that 96 percent of the people who go to the racetrack will behave in their usual indolent way. The overwhelming majority of them have never read a book on handicapping. Not a single book! Only 4 percent are even trying. Human nature being what it is, be assured that the same 96 percent are going to follow the members of the group that are probably following them. Conformity, rather than originality, is the order of the day. You don't have to worry about competition—most racegoers aren't willing to pay the price. I salute you for buying and reading this book. You've made a very definite statement. You won't settle for losing. You've set a much higher standard for yourself. Your destiny is the win window.

Please be grateful for all those players who refuse to learn what's necessary to win consistently. They'll continue to carry out their rituals of ignorance, superstition, and retribution. They'll try to find shortcuts. They'll listen to their buddies, who know less than they do. They'll ultimately pay the price for ignorance: losing.

Your choice is to do the work, pay the price, and earn financial security, or forever remain the victim of circumstances and slow horses. Sophie Tucker will love my next sentence: I've been both a winner and a loser; being a winner is better.

Chapter 15

The Short Line

I HAVE THE GOOD FORTUNE to personally know over two hundred successful handicappers. Each one is a consistent winner. That is, once they became winners, they kept repeating the experience year after year. Yes, they'll have losing weeks, losing months, and even losing meetings, but they'll still manage to come out ahead for the year—guys like Mark Cramer, Kitts Anderson, Steve Unite, and Gordon Pine. The guys I hang around with at the track are Lee Rousso, James Quinn, Tom Brohamer, and Ron Ambrose. These guys win year in, year out, and they all use different methods. How they won last year (the method they used) and how they did it this year may or may not have been the same. Chances are that it was somewhat different. In other words, they managed to grow. And managed to change with the changing times. You must understand that the winning selection ideas in this book, or any book for that matter, aren't immutable. They're not emblazoned on the wall of truth. They're not going to stand forever and ever and ever. They're simply methods that happen to show a profit in the recent short term. They may or may not persist. But the underlying or unifying principles will stand the test of time.

What I want to accomplish in this chapter is to share with you the unifying principles of winning, in such a way that you can take this information today, apply it, and win with it. Next year you'll change whatever you have to change to make it work for you. Once you learn how to win, you'll never look back. The really good news is, these principles work in every area of your life, not just handicapping.

This book is a road map for success in general and for success at thoroughbred wagering in particular. It's an overview of what it takes to be a consistent winner. There are a large number of individuals who are convinced that it's impossible to win at the races. For them, it is. If you listen to them, your only alternative is to abstain from the races. Why would you want to play the horses knowing that you can't win? If you listen to losers and believe what they say, you're destined to lose. Losing is like misery—it demands company. What's really astounding is that so many losers continue to go to the races, in spite of the fact that they have absolute faith in their inability to win. Avoid these players like the plague. It's impossible to learn how to win from losers.

If you'll do the very opposite, your chances of success will improve dramatically. Get around winners. One of the best-kept secrets in the science of success is the principle of "modeling." If you want to do, be, or have anything that's already been achieved in this world, simply "model" successful practitioners of what it is that you want. If you want to quit smoking, find an ex-smoker and have him or her tell you what they did to kick the habit. Do the same things. You'll get the same results. If you want to lose weight and keep it off, find an ex-fat person who has kept the weight off for at least two years, and have him or her explain exactly how they did it. Do the same things, you'll get the same results. To become a winning handicapper, find a winner and have him or her explain exactly what they do. Do the same things—you'll get the same results. If you think that winners won't share their methods, think again. Winners, by definition, are givers. My teachers were Mark Cramer, James Quinn, Steve Arthur, Ed Klauck, Howard Sartin, and Tom Brohamer. Each one answered every single question that I asked them without any hesitation. They kept no secrets. They were willing to give all they had. They still are. If somebody claims to be a winner and refuses to share his methods, you can bet that he's a loser. Steve Davidowitz said it best: "The more you share, the more you'll have to share." Every single winner that I know—and I have the good fortune to know hundreds of winners—will tell you anything that you want to know.

The second biggest-kept secret in achievement is one single word. This word has the power to turn darkness into light. This word has the power to get you anything in this life that you want or need. The word is: **ASK**. This secret is over two thousand years old. "Seek and ye shall find. Ask, and it shall be opened unto you." The trick is knowing whom to ask. Since you can only learn winning from winners, you now know whom to ask.

It's a very wise idea to spend time with consistent winners. You'll learn a lot. The easiest way to do this is to invite one of them out to dinner at an elegant restaurant. They'll be flattered that you asked and will bend over backward to help you. Most people can't resist the opportunity to help others. Contrary to the cynical notion that winners play things "close to the vest," the opposite is the case. Every winner whom I have the good fortune to know is more than willing to help anyone who asks. Hardly anyone asks!

It's possible to earn consistent profits at the track. If you'll abide by the principles set forth and get through the preparation phase, there's no question what the outcome will be: consistent profits. The problem is, it's not easy. Nothing of value is. It'll require a lot of work and study. In fact, it's damn near impossible for the average mortal to even keep records, much less do all that is required to complete the preparation phase. We all yearn for success, but very few of us are willing to pay the price, to do what's necessary to achieve it. Be the exception. Set a higher standard for yourself. Make a commitment to winning. Give yourself the gift of success. You deserve it.

The wherewithal needed for success is available to all of us and requires a much larger investment of our time than our money. You can't buy success—you must earn it. There are books, computer software programs, seminars, audiotapes, videotapes and a host of quality educational materials available at reasonable cost from ethical publishers. The way to tell the difference between an ethical publisher and a sleazebag scoundrel is to read the descriptive material. If it promises riches without any work, file it in the circular file—it's the same old trash that's been losing for years. Anytime you're promised something for nothing, don't just walk away, run, for as sure as day follows night, you're going to be separated from your cash. This piece of advice will save you a lot of money, grief, aggravation, and pain if you take it to heart.

Greed is your enemy. If you've ever been conned, it's because you've let your greed get in the way of your good judgment. Greed is a capital sin, and you don't have to wait until you die for punishment. You'll get it right here on earth. Whenever you enter any business deal or negotiation, don't ask "What's in it for me?" Ask, "What's in it for him?" Don't enter any deal where there aren't two winners. Enter all your deals with your opponent's satisfaction and benefit in mind. Always give more than the other person expects. If you don't believe me, try it. You won't make very many bad deals.

There are three components to winning: attitude, handicapping skills, and money management skills. If we change the words from handicapping skills to decision-making skills, and money management skills to financial-planning skills, we have the attributes of any successful business venture. Succeeding at the track takes the very same skills as succeeding at a business. All intelligent business ventures are guided by financial plans. We, as successful players, must make personal financial plans. The forward-looking business venture has a set of strategic plans. We must do the same. We'll choose a rational strategy (prudent selections) and validate it. All businesses take risks. They employ risk management techniques to prevent drastic losses that could endanger the survival of the company. We'll do the same. We'll choose the appropriate bankroll-to-bet ratio (prudent bet size) guided by the enlightened principles of mathematical expectation. We'll use a fraction of the optimum edge-to-odds ratio. When you think about it, we're just like a commercial business venture, a profit-making entity. Why shouldn't we use the same techniques as professional business people?

The reason so few horseplayers succeed is because so few are trying. Again, over 90 percent of the people who attend thoroughbred races have never read a single book on handicapping. Imagine risking your hard-earned money on a game far more difficult than chess or bridge and being that unprepared. Most of the people at a racetrack on a given day are there for recreational purposes. Sure, they want to win, but they'll do very little about it. Have you noticed how few of them have copies of the *Daily Racing Form*? My own estimates range from 25 percent at tracks such as Oaklawn Park and the Fairgrounds, to 40 percent at the New York and southern California tracks. Imagine, at least sixty percent of the spectators don't have the most basic and essential information needed for intelligent decision-making. They're betting on a hunch, the advice of their friends, or a tout. That's not your main competition. Your competition is the informed minority. The balance of your opposition is to be taken very seriously. Unfortunately, a good portion of the money put through the mutuels represents informed opinions. In a study done on New York racetrack wagering patterns, it turned out that

3 percent of the bettors accounted for over 30 percent of the handle. It also concluded that the opinions this money represented were "well-informed." Your job is to stay well ahead of the public and at least keep up with the informed minority. This is accomplished by research, study, and most of all, practice.

The secret of thoroughbred handicapping is, *there is no secret.* There's no one method that'll explain all the races. The best any method can do is to achieve a statistical validity. Even then, if too many handicappers use it, the odds will drop and its ability to generate profits may be history. This happened with speed handicapping. Your job isn't to select winners exclusive of odds, it's to select winners at bargain prices. In fact, your job is to select appropriate wagers, not horses. Your focus is to select wagers that offer the best financial opportunity. In other words, don't fall in love with horses—fall in love with bets. You must acquire the skills to be able to accurately estimate the chances (probability) of success of a particular wager and assure yourself that you have an edge. You should be decision-oriented, not selection-oriented.

I was amazed at a recent seminar when I asked the rhetorical question, "What percentage of this game is represented by betting skills?" I was trying to elicit the answer of 50 percent. No one volunteered, so I turned to the other two presenters—Ron Ambrose and Mark Cramer. Their answers were both the same: 70 percent. Wow! To these two consistent winners, making the proper bet is much more important than selecting the winner. I hope that this dramatizes the importance of acquiring betting skills.

If your financial goals are modest, between $75 and $150 per day, they can be accomplished in far less time than it takes to become a nurse or a teacher who'll earn approximately the same amount of money. You'll be paid very generously for your time and effort once you've mastered the skills of thoroughbred handicapping. Please don't delude yourself into thinking that a horse-race investing career is a "made in the shade" occupation. It's anything but easy. You're committing yourself to at least sixty hours a week of hard work. The races themselves require at least forty hours, including travel time. Handicapping is another two hours or more per day. The additional hours must include research, record-keeping, note-taking, and a host of additional tasks that voraciously consume time. The pay is your profits. No guarantee. No pension plan. You'll have to get used to living with uncertainty. You'll experience very wide swings in size of bank-roll. You'll also experience very wide emotional swings. One day you're "King of the World," and a few days later you won't be able to believe how stupid you've become. Professionals have to be very careful not to let things get to the burn-out stage. It's very wise to target specific times for intensive investing and other times for casual investing. If you go at things full throttle all the time, you'll burn out. If you think air traffic controllers live in a pressure cooker, talk to some of the professionals around your local track.

Horse racing offers a wonderful and profitable vocation or avocation—it depends upon you. When you master the skills of thoroughbred handicapping, you'll have achieved financial security. It's very comforting to know that you'll never have to stop earning money. The track has no compulsory retirement age. It doesn't discriminate by sex, race, creed, national origin, or any other characterization. It only discriminates by winning tickets and losing ones. It pays on the former and commiserates with holders of the latter. It's very democratic.

The way to succeed at the track is identical to the way to succeed in any endeavor. It all starts with desire. You have to want it. It has to be a worthy goal or ideal. You must banish the demons that whisper "gambling is evil"; "you can't win at the races"; or, "it's not respectable to play the horses." The insidious part of being possessed by these demons is that it's mostly manifested on an unconscious level. You aren't even aware that your subconscious mind has been given the instruction, "Find a way to lose." When the conscious battles with the subconscious, the subconscious always wins. Hence it's best to assume that you're possessed by these demons. The best way to exorcise them is to use a technique called "visualization." Imagine yourself at your local racetrack, sitting in your usual spot. A race has just ended and you're jumping up and down. Your pocket contains several winning tickets. You wait until the race is declared official. You then leave your seat and head to the win window. Get all your senses involved in this visualization. If you pass a popcorn stand, smell the popcorn. Hear the sounds of the moaning and groaning of the losing bettors. Listen for "the jockey stiffed the horse," "it was a boat race," and all the usual attributions. See all the sights from your seat to the win window. Feel the tickets. Hand them to the clerk. Watch him put them into the scanner. Watch his eyes bulge a little bit when he sees the total. Watch him reach for the money. Watch him count a large pile of bills. After he hands them to you, you count them. Then stuff them into your pockets or purse. See your pockets or purse overflowing with cash. Walk back to your seat and experience all the sights and sounds of the track. Notice the envy on your neighbors' faces. Feel the pride when they ask you, "Who do ya like?" End visualization. What you have just done is to program the most powerful computer on earth. You've given your subconscious the instruction, "Find me a way to collect a lot of money at the track." There's only one legal way to accomplish this. In order to remove the old programming and substitute it with success conditioning, perform this visualization at least three times a day for the next twenty-one days. It's fun and you have nothing to lose but losing by doing it. It works. I know. Ever since I started to do this, I have been winning.

You must believe in yourself and your ability to be a consistent winner. Here again is where positive affirmations play a vital role. One of the best-kept secrets in the universe is, "We become what we think about." Think about being a professional. Tell yourself often, "I'm a winning player. I'm a winning player. I'm a winning player."

Another secret is the fact that just as thoughts influence behavior, behavior influences thoughts. Act like the person you want to become and you'll think like him. If you think like him, you'll become him.

Study the subject of success. Read the books and listen to the audiotapes. If you'll get in the habit of reading for only thirty minutes per day on the subject of success, you'll receive so many beneficial ideas that it'll be like digging in a vein of pure gold. The time you spend in your car can be put to good use listening to audiotapes. Listen to handicapping tapes, success tapes, and self-improvement tapes. Why not make your car a "university on wheels"? The drive to and from the track and the time spent in the parking lot waiting to enter and exit can be used very productively—take advantage of it. It's also very wise to schedule reading time for the subject of handicapping. If you read for one hour per day on any subject, in five years' time you'll be considered an authority on that subject.

If you study and understand the principles of success, achieving success at the racetrack is just a matter of the applying these principles to horse racing. The basis of all success is belief. Your mental picture of yourself must be the picture of a successful player. In order to activate your success mechanism, you must have specific goals and a plan to achieve them. This means writing a success plan. Write your goals down and read them every day. Put a copy in a place where you can't help but see it daily. A shaving or makeup mirror is an excellent place. The first part of our success plan is actually covered by the preparation phase. We've agreed to achieve a specific minimum performance and repeat this performance for five consecutive twenty-race groups. When we complete our preparation phase, we're ready to execute the balance of our plan. Our plan is quite simple: We'll earn so much per day, which will translate into so much per week and so much per month, and finally, to an annual goal.

Thoroughbred handicapping is the ability to make decisions under conditions of uncertainty. It's a skill. Any skill can be improved with practice. The more races that you handicap, the more you'll notice patterns. Races will become more and more predictable. You'll learn the most from those playable races on which you bet and lost. A losing day will no longer be a dreadful situation; it'll be an opportunity to learn something new. You don't learn from your winning tickets. You get paid for your knowledge, as it should be. In this game, you can only learn from your mistakes. Make sure that you're able to isolate the thing that beat you when you lose a race. There'll be races that'll be complete mysteries. They'll have no rational explanation. As long as this group doesn't exceed 20 percent of the races that you've lost, all is fine. It's my estimate that from 15 to 20 percent of the playable races are very tough to explain. When you leave the track after a losing day, be grateful—you'll be getting some excellent lessons. The racetrack is your personal bank. Think of the money you lost as a temporary loan you made to your bank—you'll be back to collect both principal and interest.

The quintessential skill in thoroughbred handicapping is the ability to make a betting line. John Templeton, one of the most successful investors in history, says, "Never buy an investment unless you know how to value it." This is an absolute, fundamental principle of wealth. You apply this unifying principle to handicapping by learning to make a betting line. Always, always, always make a line on every race that you consider playable. When you can't make a line on a race because of chaos or because of too many unknowns—the race is absolutely unplayable with respect to regular win betting. (The way you define a playable race is by the fact you can make a line on that race. It's a race that contains at least one contender that can run to the pars and profiles.)

At the end of the hundred races, go back and look at all the horses you put at 2-to-1. Did they win 33 percent of the time? For all the horses you put at 3-to-1, did they win 25 percent of the time? And so on. Your ability to make accurate lines will tell on the bottom line. Your profits will skyrocket as your skills improve.

Remember, a small positive change can cause your results to improve dramatically. Consider the 30 percent handicapper who has an average mutuel of $7; he has a 5 percent edge on the game. If he wins just three more races in a hundred, his edge is now greater than 15 percent. In other words, a 10 percent increase in skills earned him 300 percent more money! He won three more races per hundred and tripled his income.

To affect a small change in your betting strategy skills, ask yourself the question: Are my lines accurate? In other words, did your own betting lines match reality? It's okay if your 2-to-1 shots hit 31 out of 100. That's fine—you're in the ballpark. You can expect a variance of about 10 percent on either side due to the small sample size. In other words, you're in the ballpark with your 4-to-1 shots if you get between 18 percent and 22 percent of these to win. If you're in that range, you're fine. If you're outside that range, you're in trouble. If you're higher, then you're underestimating. If you're lower, you're overestimating. (Imagine if you were precisely right on—exactly 33 percent winners on your 2-to-1 shots. And your 3-to-1 shots hit exactly 25 percent of the time—wow! This would be a good reason for celebration. This would be better than an Olympic gold medal. Yes, our ideal is perfection—but we'll settle for 90 percent. The closer you get, the larger your bankroll will become.)

You have to be able to validate that your lines are empirically correct—at least empirically correct within an acceptable statistical range. Unfortunately, they're not going to be as exact as you like. But the good news is, they'll get better and better with practice.

Again, the hardest part is going to be playing "watch 'em win." Watching horses win when you haven't got a nickel on them and you knew damn well that they dominated.

In my last book, *Winning Thoroughbred Strategies,* I recommended that you simply don't make a win bet on any horse less than 5-to-2. That was good advice for the strategy of betting two horses per race. I no longer advise players to always bet two horses per race in their preparation phase. I now highly recommend that you bite the bullet and learn to make a betting line. Betting skills are critical to winning at the races. In fact, they're more important than selection skills.

I admit that you can win with selectivity, it's just harder on your patience. In other words, you can be selection-oriented and still win, providing you have a lot of forbearance. If you're a 25 percent handicapper and are willing to sit there and wait for your top choices to be going off at 7-to-2 or greater, you'll win in the long run. If you're a 25 percent handicapper, you have to have averaged at least 3-to-1 just to break even. So you must demand average odds greater than or equal to 7-to-2 on your top choice. My solution is to forget about your top choice and bet the overlays on your betting line. You'll get many more plays, hence the opportunity to make more money in less time. In other words, if you make a line on every playable race, you'll have a lot more opportunities, you'll participate more, you'll have more fun, and you'll win more money.

Needless to say, I'm not denying the existence of selection-oriented winners. But the fact remains that decision orientation is by far the most efficient way to play this game.

In *Winning Thoroughbred Strategies* I shared a study asking handicappers to compare three methods of betting on twenty-race groups using some professional computer software. I asked them to, first, use the computer's betting line and bet all the overlays. Second, to bet the program's top two choices regardless of odds; and third, to bet the two longest-odds horses of the computer's top three choices. All three betting methods were profitable because the software was excellent. Betting the overlays outperformed betting the top two choices by a factor of 300 percent! In fact, betting the two longest of the top three, outperformed selection orientation by over 68 percent! Unless you've taken vows of poverty, betting on your top two horses isn't nearly as effective as simply betting the top two longest-odds horses among your top three. Try it. Prove it to yourself. (This is a challenge to all Sartin Methodology users. Simply go over your last ten twenty-race groups and test which method would have won the most.) The real skill of handicapping is the assignment of fair odds to a contender. This is the key to it all. The more accurately you can estimate the chances of horses winning a race, the larger your rate of return will be.

You must remember that selection skills are based on statistical realities, not absolute realities. Our goal is to be right a certain percentage of the time. The most important consideration is our edge. This is the basis of what we do. We'll never make a wager unless we have at least a 20 percent edge. Our bet size will be a function of our edge and average odds.

We'll always stay in touch with the three R's of winning. Our methods will be **reality** based. We'll take full **responsibility** for what happens to us. We'll keep accurate **records** and always know where we stand in relation to our goals.

We'll learn the rules and principles of intelligent wagering. We'll practice good money management. Whenever we make a wager, it'll be the best value obtainable from the situation. We'll use larger bankrolls for our more successful portfolio entries. If we're earning a greater ROI on exacta wagering than any other type of wager, then we'll allocate the largest bankroll to exacta wagering. Funds will be distributed proportionally to the success we're having with each different type of wager.

We'll concentrate our energies on improving our performance in the areas that need it, but will invest the most money in the most productive areas. Each month we'll do a review of our portfolio and adjust the bankrolls accordingly.

My opinion is that the personal computer is civilization's gift to the horse-race investor. It's an indispensable tool for both record-keeping and research. The pocket computer is absolutely necessary to affect place and show and exotic strategies. If you're unfamiliar with computers, it would be very wise to take an introductory course at a local college or computer store.

All the really exciting developments in modern handicapping are the result of using technology. The fact that we now can get the *Daily Racing Form* electronically, plus have access to a huge data base of information at the touch of a finger, is exciting. The recent developments in observational skills such as trip handicapping and equine body language can be exploited by using video technology. Off-track wagering sites are proliferating, making it much more convenient to make judicious equine investments. The future is bright.

I want to share a quote with you from Peter Lynch's outstanding book, *One Up on Wall Street*. Lynch is the most successful mutual fund manager in the history of Wall Street.

Once the unsettling fact of the risk in money is accepted, we can begin to separate gambling from investing not by the type of activity (buying bonds, buying stocks, betting on horses, etc.) but by the skill, dedication and enterprise of the participant. To a veteran handicapper with the discipline to stick to a system, betting on horses offers a relatively secure long-term return, which to him has been as reliable as owning a mutual fund or shares in General Electric. Meanwhile, to the rash and impetuous stockpicker who chases hot tips and rushes in and out of his equities, an "investment" in stocks is no more reliable than throwing away paychecks on the horse with the prettiest mane, or the jockey with the purple silks.

Here's the most successful fund manager in the world telling his readers that thoroughbred handicapping offers "a relatively secure long-term return." He's absolutely right. It's not the activity, it's the participant's character. Those willing to pay the price will prevail, those unwilling will lose. It's as simple as that.

Human nature being what it is guarantees that we'll continue to be able to make nice profits. Most of our competition want something for nothing. They'll refuse to do the necessary work. They'll continue to purchase junk systems from unethical scumbags who prey upon their greed. They'll listen to the guy next to them, who knows less than they do. Best of all, they'll spread the gospel of ignorance and superstition. Bless them. May their numbers increase.

It's my fond hope that this book will help you accomplish your goals. Thank you for letting me share these ideas with you. My wish for you is peace, love, joy, harmony, abundance, mastery, and fulfillment. See you on the short line.

Appendix A

Handicapper's Resources

Bloodstock Research of Lexington, Kentucky, supplies the *Daily Racing Form* electronically. You must have a computer and modem to avail yourself of most of their services. In addition, they have a Handicapper's Data Base which includes Beyer speed figures, trip notes, trainer and jockey information, and much more. They also publish a number of reports such as trainer statistics and pedigree data.

Handicapper's Report, published biweekly by Jeff Siegel and Bob Selvin in Los Angeles. Covers the southern California racing scene. Is a very comprehensive summary of previous races. They develop good pace and speed figures. They also emphasize workout data. They have hired their own staff clocker and he points out hot first-timers, layoff horses coming back, and improving horses.

Today's Racing Digest, published daily by William Archer and associates in San Diego. It's a great publication and each issue is a handicapping lesson. They publish great statistical summaries. They publish trainer stats, jockey stats, track bias stats, how often the favorite wins for every class of race, and loads of information not found in the *Daily Racing Form*.

The Cramer-Olmsted Report is a monthly newsletter published in Annapolis, Maryland, by Mark Cramer and Bill Olmsted. It contains articles by some of the most competent thoroughbred writers in the country. It's jammed full of good handicapping tips and research. They even give a profitable system or method in each issue. It's great. It's also underpriced at $89 per year. Write to: TBS, P.O. Box 6283, Annapolis MD 21401.

The Northern California Track Record is a weekly publication that covers Golden Gate and Bay Meadows. It's very similar to *Handicapper's Report*, mentioned above. Its author is Ron Cox of Pleasanton.

The Northwest Track Review, published weekly by Paul Braseth of Seattle. This is very similar to *The Northern California Track Record*, but especially outstanding on trainer performance data.

The Inside Edge, published weekly in Omaha by Dave Maycock. Provides speed, trip, and bias information for Ak-Sar-Ben racegoers. He also publishes speed figures for about twenty other racetracks.

O. Henry West, the publishing company in Beaumont, California, writes and distributes all the Sartin Methodology books, tapes, and computer programs. Its head is Dr. Howard Sartin.

Lawlor Enterprises, a quality company, publishes and distributes excellent instructional videotapes. In addition, Greg Lawlor, of San Diego, compiles elaborate trainer statistics.

Sports Institute, in Las Vegas, Nevada, offers personalized instruction by one of the top professionals in the country—Ron Ambrose. They also publish high-quality, hard-to-get information such as pace profiles for all the major tracks, sires of maiden winners, horses-for-courses, trainer statistics, and a host of other quality information. Call or write: Sports Institute, 1055 E. Tropicana Suite 400, Las Vegas, NV 89119, (702) 798-7262.

Cynthia Publishing, in Studio City, California, publishes and distributes books, instructional videotapes, computer programs, and handheld computers. They publish an extensive catalogue of thoroughbred handicapping resources, which includes Gordon Pine's *Par Times*, Dick Mitchell's *Insider Newsletter*, plus handicapping courses and seminars. Write or call for a free catalogue: CPC, 11390 Ventura Blvd. #5, Studio City, CA 91604, (818) 509-0165.

Phillips Racing Newsletter, published by Russ & Alan Dietrich in Auburn, California, is the Consumers Union of thoroughbred handicapping products. They review books, videotapes, computer programs, systems, and methods. If you're a consumer of these kinds of products, they can save you a lot time and money by warning you against the charlatans. Write for a sample back issue. PRN, Box 5817, Auburn, CA 95604-5817.

Gambler's Book Club is the best source for books on the subject of gambling. If there's any obscure book or reference you are trying to find—chances are they have it in stock. Their staff is very knowledgeable. Write or call for a free catalogue. GBC, 630 S. 11th St., Las Vegas, NV 89101 (800) 634-6243.

Pegasos Press is a mail-order source of books and videos on horses, including a good selection of handicapping books. Call or write: Pegasos Press, 535 Cordova Road #163, P.O. Box 30001, Santa Fe, NM 87502 (800) 537-8558.

TR Publishing publishes and distributes books, instructional video-tapes, and handicapping resources. For California players, they publish *Barry Meadow's Master Class Ratings.* This is a comprehensive rating based upon speed, pace, and bias. Every horse that has run in California gets a rating. For information write: TR Publishing, 527 S. Sonya, Anaheim, CA 92802.

Quirin's Grass Stallion Statistics

	(first and second grass starts only, through 1991)					
Name of Stallion	Starts	Wins	W.Pct.	In Money	M.Pct.	$ Net
Ack Ack	149	14	9.4%	52	34.9%	$ 1.39
Acaroid $	52	11	**21.2%**	26	50.0%	**$ 5.92**
Affirmed	104	21	20.2%	38	36.5%	$ 2.42
Air Forbes Won	52	8	15.4%	23	44.2%	$ 1.73
Alleged	117	19	16.2%	50	42.7%	$ 2.19
Apalachee $	108	11	10.2%	43	39.8%	$ 1.92
Assert $	57	13	22.8%	27	47.4%	$ 2.35
At The Threshold	17	3	17.6%	6	35.3%	**$ 4.72**
Bailjumper	49	9	18.4%	21	42.9%	**$ 3.99**
Believe It	67	6	9.0%	21	31.3%	$ 1.99
Ben Fab	22	3	13.6%	8	36.4%	$ 1.50
Big Spruce $	157	22	14.0%	46	29.3%	$ 2.48
Blue Ensign $	17	4	23.5%	7	41.2%	$ 2.55
Blushing Groom	95	11	11.6%	34	35.8%	$ 0.99
Cannonade	54	8	14.8%	16	29.6%	**$ 3.29**
Caro	111	23	20.7%	45	40.5%	$ 2.50
Caucasus	86	11	12.8%	27	31.4%	$ 2.37
Caveat $	50	16	**32.0%**	31	62.0%	**$ 6.00**
Chief's Crown	13	2	15.4%	7	53.8%	$ 1.23
Coastal	71	13	18.3%	28	39.4%	**$ 3.07**
Conquistador Cielo	55	5	9.1%	19	34.5%	$ 1.11
Court Trial $	12	5	**41.7%**	6	50.0%	**$10.17**
Cozzene	30	6	20.0%	15	50.0%	$ 1.32
Current Hope	17	3	17.6%	11	64.7%	$ 2.88
Czaravitch	52	5	9.6%	15	28.8%	$ 2.16
Dance Bid $	34	7	**20.6%**	14	41.2%	**$12.38**
Danzig $	120	23	19.2%	52	43.3%	$ 2.34
Darby Creek Road	107	24	22.4%	49	45.8%	$ 2.90

| | | | (first and second grass starts only, through 1991) | | | |
Name Of Stallion	Starts	Wins	W.Pct.	In Money	M.Pct.	$ Net
Devil's Bag	33	9	**27.3%**	16	48.5%	**$ 4.55**
Diesis $	26	9	**34.6%**	17	65.4%	**$ 6.63**
Dixieland Band $	33	8	24.2%	16	48.5%	$ 2.04
Exceller $	88	10	11.4%	25	28.4%	$ 2.10
Exclusive Era	19	2	10.5%	10	52.6%	$ 1.17
Explodent $	191	34	17.8%	85	44.5%	$ 2.59
Explosive Bid	50	11	**22.0%**	20	40.0%	**$ 4.01**
Fappiano	87	16	18.4%	32	36.8%	$ 1.90
Far North	116	11	9.5%	33	28.4%	$ 0.80
Fifth Marine	55	7	12.7%	17	30.9%	$ 2.99
Fire Dancer	117	8	6.8%	27	23.1%	$ 1.91
Five Star Flight	25	5	20.0%	7	28.0%	$ 1.78
Florescent Light	88	8	9.1%	22	25.0%	$ 2.21
Forever Sparkle	33	6	18.2%	13	39.4%	$ 3.24
Forli	155	21	13.5%	51	32.9%	$ 2.04
General Assembly	23	1	4.3%	11	47.8%	$ 0.41
Give Me Strength $	43	3	7.0%	12	27.9%	$ 2.64
Great Above	95	15	15.8%	35	36.8%	$ 3.36
Great Neck	43	7	16.3%	17	39.5%	**$ 9.70**
Green Dancer $	101	20	19.8%	44	43.6%	$ 3.98
Green Forest $	16	5	**31.3%**	8	50.0%	$ 3.39
Grey Dawn	380	47	12.4%	113	29.7%	$ 2.14
Halo	170	27	15.9%	70	41.2%	$ 1.87
Hawaii $	200	25	12.5%	61	30.5%	$ 1.95
Hero's Honor	34	7	20.6%	15	44.1%	$ 2.62
Highland Blade	54	3	5.6%	15	27.8%	$ 0.98
His Majesty $	132	22	16.7%	46	34.8%	$ 2.82
Hostage	43	4	9.3%	13	30.2%	$ 0.89
Icecapade $	216	28	13.0%	67	31.0%	$ 2.12
In Reality	180	22	12.2%	66	36.7%	$ 1.23
Irish River $	51	13	**25.5%**	26	51.0%	**$ 4.69**
J.O. Tobin $	58	10	17.2%	25	43.1%	$ 3.39
Key To The Mint	154	15	9.7%	46	29.9%	$ 0.77
Kris S.	58	9	15.5%	25	43.1%	**$ 4.18**
L'Enjoleur	135	16	11.9%	42	31.1%	$ 1.60
Linkage $	27	5	18.5%	9	33.3%	$ 2.64
Little Current $	158	32	**20.3%**	81	51.3%	**$ 4.37**
London Company	101	10	9.9%	34	33.7%	$ 2.10
Lyphard	97	16	16.5%	35	36.1%	$ 1.50
Lyphard's Wish	79	9	11.4%	39	49.4%	$ 2.77
Lypheor $	13	2	15.4%	7	53.8%	$ 2.90
Majestic Light	219	38	17.4%	94	42.9%	$ 3.24
Mr. Justice	55	6	10.9%	22	40.0%	$ 3.12
Mr. Leader	331	39	11.8%	117	35.3%	$ 2.45
Naked Sky $	18	5	**27.8%**	8	44.4%	**$ 5.88**
Naskra $	301	32	10.6%	96	31.9%	$ 1.48

	(first and second grass starts only, through 1991)					
Name Of Stallion	Starts	Wins	W.Pct.	In Money	M.Pct.	$ Net
Native Royalty	113	12	10.6%	38	33.6%	$ 1.85
Nijinsky	310	67	21.6%	155	50.0%	$ 1.58
Nijinsky's Secret $	18	3	16.7%	5	27.8%	**$ 7.90**
Nodouble	335	54	16.1%	117	34.9%	$ 2.68
Northern Baby	43	8	18.6%	19	44.2%	**$ 4.04**
Northern Fling	82	7	8.5%	30	36.6%	$ 1.45
Northern Jove $	138	11	8.0%	47	34.1%	$ 1.27
Northrop $	23	8	**34.8%**	13	56.5%	**$ 9.38**
Oh Say	46	6	13.0%	15	32.6%	$ 2.40
One For All	210	29	13.8%	86	41.0%	$ 2.80
Our Native $	103	12	11.7%	37	35.9%	$ 2.76
Overskate $	103	12	11.7%	36	35.0%	$ 1.55
Perrault	21	1	4.8%	6	28.6%	$ 0.18
Pleasant Colony $	123	10	8.1%	40	32.5%	$ 0.83
Proud Birdie	98	7	7.1%	26	26.5%	$ 1.69
Quack	122	14	11.5%	39	32.0%	$ 2.51
Qui Native $	38	7	18.4%	17	44.7%	$ 2.14
Relaunch	26	3	11.5%	11	42.3%	$ 1.28
Rich Cream $	54	5	9.3%	19	35.2%	$ 1.04
Riverman $	69	15	**21.7%**	30	43.5%	$ 3.63
Roberto $	244	52	21.3%	126	51.6%	$ 2.45
Rock Talk $	186	23	12.4%	63	33.9%	$ 2.37
Runaway Groom	37	6	16.2%	10	27.0%	**$ 4.73**
Run The Gantlet $	74	5	6.8%	25	33.8%	$ 0.85
Seattle Slew	102	15	14.7%	36	35.3%	$ 1.60
Secretariat $	179	23	12.8%	64	35.8%	$ 1.39
Secreto $	23	4	17.4%	10	43.5%	$ 3.58
Sharpen Up	79	9	11.4%	32	40.5%	$ 2.77
Silver Hawk $	32	15	**46.9%**	25	78.1%	**$ 7.63**
Sir Ivor	231	26	11.3%	86	37.2%	$ 1.03
Slew O'Gold $	26	4	15.4%	10	38.5%	$ 1.70
Slewpy	28	3	10.7%	12	42.9%	$ 3.17
Sovereign Dancer $	86	17	19.8%	42	48.8%	**$ 5.79**
Spectacular Bid	83	13	15.7%	34	41.0%	$ 1.96
Sportin Life $	41	6	14.6%	18	43.9%	$ 3.39
Stage Door Johnny $	281	72	25.6%	129	45.9%	$ 2.73
Stalwart $	49	8	16.3%	23	46.9%	$ 3.62
Stay The Course	10	2	20.0%	3	30.0%	$ 1.40
Stop The Music	116	8	6.9%	32	27.6%	$ 0.90
Storm Bird	45	5	11.1%	17	37.8%	$ 0.84
Stutz Blackhawk	47	5	10.6%	14	29.8%	**$ 4.74**
Summing $	55	8	14.5%	20	36.4%	$ 1.89
Sunny's Halo	21	4	19.0%	7	33.3%	$ 1.50
Superbity	45	10	**22.2%**	24	53.3%	**$ 6.18**
Temperance Hill	71	4	5.6%	22	31.0%	$ 0.57
The Bart	29	5	17.2%	14	48.3%	**$ 5.84**

Name Of Stallion	Starts	Wins	W.Pct.	In Money	M.Pct.	$ Net
(first and second grass starts only, through 1991)						
The Minstrel	93	8	8.6%	35	37.6%	$ 1.30
Told	21	1	4.8%	6	28.6%	$ 0.89
Tom Rolfe $	339	42	12.4%	117	34.5%	$ 1.35
Top Command	40	6	15.0%	16	40.0%	**$ 4.52**
Topsider $	100	7	7.0%	26	26.0%	$ 1.95
Transworld	68	10	14.7%	23	33.8%	**$ 4.08**
Tri Jet $	55	9	16.4%	25	45.5%	$ 2.25
True Colors	35	8	**22.9%**	17	48.6%	**$ 9.71**
Tsunami Slew $	48	7	14.6%	17	35.4%	$ 2.95
Tunerup	30	6	**20.0%**	13	43.3%	**$12.37**
T.V. Commercial	247	26	10.5%	91	36.8%	$ 1.58
Upper Case	73	7	9.6%	23	31.5%	**$ 4.56**
Vaguely Noble	79	7	8.9%	22	27.8%	$ 1.34
Verbatim $	217	33	15.2%	85	39.2%	$ 2.93
Vigors	119	17	14.3%	41	34.5%	$ 2.09
Wavering Monarch $	40	11	**27.5%**	17	42.5%	**$ 6.93**
Wild Again	18	3	16.7%	8	44.4%	$ 1.92
$ means profitable for 1991						
1991 Totals (All Sires)	1127	186	16.5%	462	41.0%	$ 2.69
1991 Top 10	77	21	27.3%	36	46.8%	$ 2.53
1991 Young Turfs	67	15	22.4%	33	49.3%	$ 2.68

Top 10 For 1991: Acaroid, Caveat, Dance Bid, Great Neck, Runaway Groom, Silver Hawk, Sovereign Dancer, Superbity, True Colors, Wavering Monarch

Young Turfs For 1991: Blue Ensign, Court Trial, Current Hope, Diesis, Green Forest, Lypheor, Naked Sky, Nijinsky's Secret, Northrop, Secreto

Suspects (less than 10 starts): Dahar, Dauphin Fabuleux, Herat, Saratoga Six, Time To Explode, Time For A Change, Beaudelaire, Loose Cannon, Minshaanshu Amad, Morning Bob, Parfaitment, Shananie

Please note the sires that are in boldface type. They are particularly productive and deserve our attention. It would be a good idea to commit these to memory. Sires not on the list are either very recent or unproductive. This list is updated annually.

Boldface type should get your attention. When the W.Pct. (win percentage) is 20 percent or greater, the figure is boldface. Same with $ Net (money net on $2 bet). When this figure exceeds $4, the figure is boldface. These boldface statistics are extremely positive.

Blank Handicapping Forms

MAIDENFORM

Date _____   Distance _____   Win Pars This Type Race:
Race # _____   Class   _____   _____ _____ _____

Ability Time Par _____

PP	Name	# Races	Class Last Race	Days Since Last	Ability Time	Fur. Per Day	6F Works	Tr.	Jock	Sire FTS Index	L	B	G
1													
2													
3													
4													
5													
6													
7													
8													
9													
10													
11													
12													
13													
14													
15													
16													

Claiming Form

Date _____   Distance _____   **Win Pars This Type Race:**

Race # _____   Class   _____

_____   _____   _____

Turn Time Par   _____

PP	Name of Horse	Jockey Status	Age	# Races Since Layoff	Surface Distance Suitable S D		Win Ratio Wins/Races	Recency Works Form Cycle R W F		
1										
2										
3										
4										
5										
6										
7										
8										
9										
10										
11										
12										
13										
14										
15										
16										

TT = Turn time ?

Please note: Ability Time is different for turf.

Dirt Ability Time = TT + 2F
Turf Ability Time = FF + 3F

bility Time Par _____

Class	Pace Fractions			TT	Ability Time	SR + TV	Odds Last Race	Morn Line Odds	L	B	G
	1st Call	2nd Call	Final								

Allowance & Stakes Form

Date _____   Distance _____   Win Pars This **Type Race:**

Race # _____   Class _____   _____ _____ _____

Conditions _____   Purse _____   Ability Time Par _____

PP	Name of Horse	Jockey Status	A g e	# R S L	Surface Distance Suitable S D	W %	Recency Works Form Cycle R W FC	G S W	C R W	Class
1										
2										
3										
4										
5										
6										
7										
8										
9										
10										
11										
12										
13										
14										
15										
16										

Please note: Ability Time is different
for turf.

Dirt Ability Time = TT + 2F
Turf Ability Time = 1F + 3F

Last Fraction Par _____

Pace Fractions			TT	Ability Time	SR + TV	Adj LF	O L R	M L O	L	B	G
1st Call	2nd Call	Final									

Turf Form

Date _____   Distance _____   Win Pars This Type Race:

Race # _____   Class _____

Conditions _____   Purse _____   Ability Time Par _____   _____   _____

PP	Name of Horse	Jockey Status	A g e	# R S L	Breeding vs exper #T QROI	W %	Recency Works Form Cycle R W FC			G S W	P T W	Class
1												
2												
3												
4												
5												
6												
7												
8												
9												
10												
11												
12												
13												
14												
15												
16												

Please note: **Ability Time is different for turf.**

Dirt Ability Time = TT + 2F
Turf Ability Time = FF + 3F

Last Fraction Par _____

Pace Fractions			TT	Ability Time	SR + TV	Adj LF	O L R	M L O	L	B	G
1st Call	2nd Call	Final									

Bibliography

BEYER, ANDREW. *Picking Winners.* Houghton Mifflin, 1975

BEYER, ANDREW. *My $50,000 Year at the Races.* Harcourt, Brace, Jovanovich, 1978

BEYER, ANDREW. *The Winning Horseplayer.* Houghton Mifflin, 1983

BROHAMER, TOM. *Modern Pace Handicapping.* William Morrow & Company, 1991

CRAMER, MARK. *Fast Track to Thoroughbred Profits.* Gambling Times Incorporated, 1984

CRAMER, MARK. *The Odds on Your Side.* Cynthia Publishing Company, 1987

CRAMER, MARK. *Ten Winning Exacta Situations.* Cynthia Publishing Company, 1989

CRAMER, MARK. *Thoroughbred Cycles.* William Morrow & Company, 1990

DAVIDOWITZ, STEVEN. *Betting Thoroughbred.* E. P. Dutton, 1977

DAVIS, FREDERICK. *Thoroughbred Racing: Percentages and Probabilities.* Milwood Pubs, 1974

FABRICAND, BURTON P. *The Science of Winning.* Whitlock Press, 1979

HAMBLETON, TOM. *Pace Makes the Race.* O. Henry House Publishing, 1991

HELLER, BILL. *Overlay, Overlay.* Bonus Books, 1990

HILL, NAPOLEON. *Think and Grow Rich.* Fawcett Crest, 1960

LYNCH, PETER. *One Up on Wall Street.* Simon & Schuster, 1989

MEADOW, BARRY. *Money Secrets at the Racetrack.* TR Publishing, 1988

MITCHELL, DICK. *Winning Thoroughbred Strategies.* William Morrow & Company, 1989

MITCHELL, DICK. *A Winning Turf Strategy.* Cynthia Publishing, 1991

MITCHELL, DICK. *A Winning Speed Handicapping Strategy.* Cynthia Publishing, 1991

QUINN, JAMES. *The Handicapper's Condition Book.* William Morrow & Company, 1987

QUINN, JAMES. *The Best of Thoroughbred Handicapping.* William Morrow & Company, 1987

QUINN, JAMES. *ABCs of Thoroughbred Handicapping.* William Morrow & Company, 1988

QUINN, JAMES. *Recreational Handicapping.* William Morrow & Company, 1990

QUIRIN, WILLIAM L. *Winning at the Races.* William Morrow & Company, 1979

QUIRIN, WILLIAM L. *Thoroughbred Handicapping State of the Art.* William Morrow & Company, 1984

ROBBINS, ANTHONY. *Awaken the Giant Within.* Summit Books, 1991

SARTIN, HOWARD. *55% Solution—Finding the Place Horse.* O. Henry House Publishing, 1987

ZIEMBA, BILL, and DON HAUSCH. *Beat the Racetrack.* William Morrow & Company, 1987

Index